D0849567

The Economics of Nature and the Nature of Economics

ADVANCES IN ECOLOGICAL ECONOMICS

General Editor: Robert Costanza, *Director, University of Maryland Institute for Ecological Economics and Professor, Center for Environmental Science and Biology Department, USA*

This important series makes a significant contribution to the development of the principles and practices of ecological economics, a field which has expanded dramatically in recent years. The series provides an invaluable forum for the publication of high quality work and shows how ecological economic analysis can make a contribution to understanding and resolving important problems.

The main emphasis of the series is on the development and application of new original ideas in ecological economics. International in its approach, it includes some of the best theoretical and empirical work in the field with contributions to fundamental principles, rigorous evaluations of existing concepts, historical surveys and future visions. It seeks to address some of the most important theoretical questions and gives policy solutions for the ecological problems confronting the global village as we move into the twenty-first century.

Titles in the series include:

Sustainability and Firms
Technological Change and the Changing Regulatory Environment
Sylvie Faucheux, John Gowdy and Isabelle Nicolaï

Valuation and the Environment
Theory, Method and Practice
Edited by Martin O'Connor and Clive Spash

Sustainability in Question
The Search for a Conceptual Framework
Jörg Köhn, John Gowdy, Friedrich Hinterbergr and Jan van der Straaten

Capital and Time in Ecological Economics
Neo-Austrian Modelling
Malte Faber, John Proops and Stefan Speck with Frank Jöst

The Economics of Nature and the Nature of Economics
Edited by Cutler J. Cleveland, David I. Stern and Robert Costanza

A Theory of the Environment and Economic Systems
A Unified Framework for Ecological Economic Analysis and Decision Support
Reinout Heijungs

The Economics of Nature and the Nature of Economics

Edited by

Cutler J. Cleveland

Center for Energy and Environmental Studies, Boston University, USA

David I. Stern

Centre for Resource and Environmental Studies, Australian National University, Australia

Robert Costanza

Center for Environmental Science and Biology Department and University of Maryland Institute for Ecological Economics, USA

In association with the International Society for Ecological Economics

ADVANCES IN ECOLOGICAL ECONOMICS

Edward Elgar

Cheltenham, UK • Northampton, MA, USA

Published by
Edward Elgar Publishing Limited
Glensanda House
Montpellier Parade
Cheltenham
Glos GL50 1UA
UK

Edward Elgar Publishing, Inc.
136 West Street
Suite 202
Northampton
Massachusetts 01060
USA

A catalogue record for this book is available from the British Library

Library of Congress Cataloging in Publication Data
The economics of nature and the nature of economics / edited by Cutler J. Cleveland, David I. Stern, Robert Costanza.
    p. cm. — (Advances in ecological economics)
    1. Sustainable development. 2. Ecology—Economic aspects. I. Cleveland, Cutler J. II. Stern, David I., 1964– III. Costanza, Robert. IV. Series.

    338.927—dc21

                              00–024326

ISBN 1 85898 980 9
Printed and bound in Great Britain by MPG Books Ltd, Bodmin, Cornwall

Contents

Figures

Tables

Contributors

Robert U. Ayres, Sandoz Professor of Environment & Management, Center for the Management of Environmental Resources, INSEAD, Fontainebleau, France.

Daniel W. Bromley, Anderson-Bascom Professor of Applied Economics, University of Wisconsin, Madison, Wisconsin, USA.

Beatriz Castaneda, ecological economist, Buenos Aires, Argentina.

Paul P. Christensen, Department of Economics and Geography, Hofstra University, Hempstead, New York, USA.

Cutler J. Cleveland, Director, Center for Energy and Environmental Studies, Boston University, Boston, Massachusetts, USA.

Robert Costanza, Professor, Center for Environmental Sciences and Biology Department, Director, University of Maryland Institute for Ecological Economics, College Park, Maryland, USA.

Richard W. England, Professor, Center for Business and Economic Research, Whittemore School of Business and Economics, University of New Hampshire, Durham, New Hampshire, USA.

Steve Farber, Professor, Graduate School of Public and International Affairs, University of Pittsburgh, Pittsburgh, Pennsylvania, USA.

Monica Grasso, graduate research assistant, Institute for Ecological Economics, University of Maryland, College Park, Maryland, USA.

Joan Martinez-Alier, Professor, Department of Economics and Economic History, Universitat Autonoma de Barcelona, Barcelona, Spain.

Mohan Munasinghe, Chairman, Munasinghe Institute for Development (MIND), Colombo, Sri Lanka and Vice Chair, Bureau of the Intergovernmental Panel on Climate Change (IPCC), Geneva, Switzerland.

Giuseppe Munda, Professor, Department of Economics and Economic History, Universitat Autonoma de Barcelona, Barcelona, Spain.

Richard B. Norgaard, Professor of Energy and Resources and of Agricultural and Resource Economics, University of California at Berkeley, Berkeley, California, USA.

Sabine U. O'Hara, Provost and Professor of Economics, Green Mountain College, Poultney, Vermont, USA.

John O'Neill, Professor, Department of Philosophy, University of Lancaster, Bailrigg, Lancaster, UK.

David I. Stern, Research Fellow, Centre for Resource and Environmental Studies, Australian National University, Canberra, Australia.

Introduction: the changing nature of economics – towards an ecological economics

Cutler J. Cleveland, Robert Costanza and David I. Stern

Like any field of scientific inquiry, ecological economics has evolved along several different fronts. One important element is an understanding of the history of the field, which is characterized by interwoven strands from ecology, physics, the physiocratic and classical schools of economics, and other fields in the social and natural social sciences. Another important area is the relation of neoclassical economics to ecological economics. Part of the impetus behind the creation of the International Society for Ecological Economics was the growing recognition that, by itself, neoclassical economics could not fully explain the sources of depletion and degradation, nor could it provide a reliable compass for future development. A third broad strand of work is the empirical analysis of energy and material flows within and between economic and environmental systems. This work ranges widely, from the construction of sustainability indicators to land use models.

This book covers some of the important recent developments in the theory, concepts and empirical applications of ecological economics and sustainable development. It contains contributions from some of the leading scholars in the field of ecological economics. The book is divided into two parts. Part I, The Nature of Economics, includes chapters on the contribution of classical economics to ecological economics, valuation in ecological economics, the role of communication in the discourse on sustainable development, and a classification system for theories and methods in ecological economics. Part II, The Economics of Nature, includes chapters on alternatives to the growth paradigm, case studies of sustainable development and critical reviews of the environmental Kuznets curve, green national accounting, indicators of natural resource scarcity, and alternatives to gross domestic product.

THE NATURE OF ECONOMICS

The history of the evolution of ecological economics provides insight into the current state of the field. Part of this history is the continuing tension between the neoclassical approach and alternative economic paradigms within ecological economics. In his chapter, Paul Christensen points out that the relationship between ecological economics and neoclassical economic theory continues to be problematic. Many ecological economists argue that standard market theory, when corrected for externalities or extended to include environmental accounting, provides a satisfactory framework for analysing economic processes and environmental problems.

Christensen argues that the mechanistic individualism of modern (neoclassical) economic theory is inconsistent with the materials, energetic and organismic interdependence that structures ecological systems. Most working economists admit that the assumptions of neoclassical theory are excessively abstract and unrealistic and argue that the theory has to be extended. But what is not sufficiently understood is that this extension cannot take place without a fundamental recasting of basic assumptions.

Christensen traces the very different way in which physiocratic and classical economics evolved relative to the later neoclassical theory. The former emerged as part of the early evolution of the natural sciences, moral philosophy and a naturalistic psychology. Early economic theories of production were developed from contemporary ideas of active matter employed in chemical and physiological theories of the way nature reproduced itself through time. The result is a body of theory that provides a framework for an explicit account of the interdependence between materials and energy and the technologies of material and energy conversion. It is a framework, moreover, that is connected to psychological models concerned with the interdependence between emotion and reason and with learning through time.

Neoclassical theory, by contrast, took its concepts and mathematical structure from the maximization framework of analytical mechanics and field theory. The result is a treatment of economic agents as charged particles at equilibrium in a field of forces. Precisely because it is structured by the field model of a conserved gradient of potential energy, the neoclassical model of production (and utility) lacks a physically realistic treatment of materials and energy or the technologies by which materials, energy and information are transformed in economic activity.

Christensen describes the steps in the development of an ecological approach to economics. The first is a scientifically informed characterization of production inputs and processes. This would be based on an ecological characterization of flows of materials, energy and information, and the technologies, organization and learned skills that transform and convert materials, energy and information. A second and related step is an accurate representation of the distinct differences, constraints and productive potential of the biological and ecologically based 'sectors' of nature's economy versus the technologically constructed sectors of human industrial activity which are currently dependent on the entropic use of vast supplies of inorganic minerals and fossil fuels.

Joan Martinez-Alier and his colleagues provide a useful classification of concepts, theories and methods in ecological economics. The classification is made according to the criterion of comparability of values, emphasizing weak comparability as the foundation of ecological economics. The economy is embedded not only in the social perception of energy and material flows (which is historically changing), but is also in social institutions, such as the distribution of property rights, the distribution of power and the distribution of income. While conventional environmental and resource economics rests on principles of compensation and substitution, which sometimes might be operative, ecological economics emphasizes the difficulties in substituting for the loss of environmental goods such as biodiversity (which is not even inventoried), or in compensating future generations for the uncertain, irreversible negative externalities we cause today. As a consequence, theories and methods such as reflexive complexity, biophysical indicators and non-compensatory multicriteria evaluation become useful.

Martinez-Alier *et al.* note that ecological economists understand and sometimes share the conventional economists' attempts to 'internalize' externalities into the price system. But they emphasize the uncertainties and complexities which make it difficult to obtain physical measures of external impacts, let alone economic measures of externalities. Attempts at internalization are likely to be successful in some specific cases only. Instead, ecological economists often sympathize with the less ambitious 'cost-effectiveness' approach where standards are devised by methods from outside conventional economics but conventional economic instruments may be used to realize those standards. Martinez-Alier *et al.* emphasize how economic values depend on the intergenerational and intragenerational inequalities in the distribution of the burdens of pollution and in the access to natural resources. They argue that ecological economics must explicitly refuse the complete commensurability paradigm and recognize the existence of *incommensurability* of values. This is mainly because the environment is a site of conflict among competing values and interests and among different groups and communities that hold them.

Martinez-Alier *et al.* conclude that policy recommendations should be defensible to the technical expert, but also to politicians, the media and the various stakeholders. This does not imply that a consensus will be reached. Indeed, the possibility of irreconcilable differences is recognized and allowed for by promoting a plurality of approaches. Since multicriteria evaluation techniques are based on a 'constructive' rationality and allow one to take into account conflictual, multidimensional, incommensurable and uncertain effects of decisions, they appear to be a promising assessment framework for (micro and macro) environmental policy. Multicriteria evaluation techniques cannot solve all conflicts, but they can help to provide more insight into the nature of conflicts and into ways to arrive at political compromises in case of divergent preferences, thereby increasing the transparency of the choice process.

In Chapter 3, Richard Norgaard emphasizes the importance of understanding and communication to achieving sustainability. While ecology and economics share many conceptual roots, the modern orchestration between the disciplines proved dysfunctional, the cacophony ringing out in raucous political debate, during the second half of the twentieth century. Norgaard identifies some clear differences between the now fading modern orchestration and the emerging improvisation. First, ecological economists are actively engaged in encouraging a paradigm shift. We are very aware that modern Western and Westernized societies have been constructed around fundamental beliefs in material progress driven by science dedicated to controlling a malleable natural system without resource limits. We believe that these beliefs are not only fundamentally in error but also the cause of environmental as well as social problems. Ecological economics exists in part to actively challenge scientists and policy makers to make the necessary changes in their thinking on these matters.

Second, the 'social scientists' among ecological economists are keenly interested in biophysical measures of human resource use. Third, ecological economics pays as much attention to scale and equity as to efficiency. A fair system of access to resources is critically important to the way people interact with the environment. As important as the mechanics of the market can be, we do not stress efficiency alone. We know that prices are not only a function of whether the market is working efficiently but also a matter of how rights to resources are distributed among people within nations, between nations and over generations.

Fourth, ecological economists realize that understanding problems and finding and implementing solutions requires the contextual, experiential and, in some cases, traditional or indigenous knowledge of local people and practitioners. Accuracy to two significant figures in the aggregate does not imply that good solutions will be achieved across a diversity of ecological, technological, social and cultural contexts. Participatory research conducted in a partnership between scientists and those who will actually implement a solution is frequently the only way to reach workable answers and effective solutions. Finally, ecological economists are historically and philosophically conscious of the interplay between assumptions, models and the types of answers they can generate. We know that the viability of answers depends on the broader social structure in which such answers may be effective. We are wary of the ideology supporting existing approaches to economic research, with their feigned objectivity. We are concerned that these approaches were largely designed to replace democratic decision making and the broad empowerment that makes implementation of solutions possible. We do not have workable solutions within the historic orchestration and in the transition to new improvisations we find ourselves in awkward contradictions. We are open to what we do not know, aware that learning more also entails learning more about what we do not know, and find adaptive environmental management a suitable approach for these reasons.

According to Daniel Bromley, sustainability is at once a fine idea and a hopeless concept. It is good because it reminds us of the fate of future persons; it is hopeless because it begs for operational content. The better part of wisdom suggests that we should take it on its own terms – but not ask too much of it. As a metaphor to guide action, it is probably quite adequate. But we must move to another epistemological programme to ascertain what we should do about the future. That alternative programme is not the Smithian machine and its providential spontaneous order. It is, instead, the Kantian imperative of Pure Reason applied to future persons. From this comes the demand for a constructed order that will ensure particular settings and circumstances for future persons.

Bromley observes that traditional approaches to sustainability rely on models that depend upon judgments of welfare across future generations, 'right prices' and some sense as to what future persons will find giving of utility. These models both accept the spontaneous order of market processes and rely on that order to derive optimal consumption paths into the future. However, sustainability is not a problem of divining optimal paths predicated upon right prices. Rather, sustainability, to be operational, requires the idea of a constructed order predicated upon rights for future persons. It also implies duties for those now living who sit in a position of dictator over the settings and circumstances that will be passed on to future persons. Rights-based approaches to sustainability do not rely upon unknowable preferences of future persons, but rather upon an environmental regency in which those now living agree to preserve *settings and circumstances* for the future. This reminds us that the central issue in sustainability concerns not how much to preserve but rather what to preserve.

The issue of valuation is central to economics. Its pursuit has been cast in questions of what constitutes value, how value is created and how value is expressed in economic activity and economic institutions. In Chapter 5, Sabine O'Hara shows that, while the interest in value and value creation is equally pertinent to ecological economics, ecological economists have framed valuation questions differently from their mainstream colleagues. Ecological economists generally view with scepticism the reliance on prices as the primary expression of value. The reason for this is that ecological economics has added considerable complexity to the model of market exchange advanced in mainline economics. Ecological economics views economic activity as taking place within a larger context of material flows which originate in the environment, are processed in economic activity and released back into the environment as high entropy waste. Further complexity is added by those who contend that material flows are not simply an expression of 'natural processes' linking human economic activity to its biophysical context, but reflect the social and cultural context of human activity as well

O'Hara calls for a methodology that allows the complexities of all systems to be explicitly admitted to the valuation process, rather than being implicitly considered in 'corrected' market prices. One such method is the open and uncoerced discourse of individuals in a process of mutual acceptance and respect. Such discourse can be viewed as a decentralized coordination mechanism, which gives expression to the life world with all its material constraints, social relationships and valuation patterns. For ecological economics such discourse-based valuation is of particular importance for two reasons: (1) discourse can link all systems levels and thus provides the basis for expanding familiar disciplinary valuation methods to an expressly multidisciplinary process; (2) discourse invites participation from affected stakeholders and thus questions the institutionalized segregation of 'expert' judges and 'non-expert' victims.

THE ECONOMICS OF NATURE

The second part of the book turns to more specific analyses of the economics of energy, natural resources and the environment. Robert Ayres' chapter provokes questions such as whether the need for a new paradigm means that an old one must be discarded. What does 'growth paradigm' mean? Is the chapter about the end of growth? Is it about 'limits to growth' in the sense of the 1970s debate? Or is it, perhaps, about the nature of a hypothetical 'no growth' or 'steady state' society, and some of the implications of such a society? The answer to all of these questions is no. Rather than writing just another neo-Malthusian anti-growth tract, Ayres argues that economic growth is both possible and essential for social and political reasons. But the economic growth engine, as it operates today, is running amok. Economic growth in most of the world is so inequitable that by far the largest share of the benefits is being appropriated by a tiny group of those who were already rich or well connected. The so-called 'Asian Miracle' was touted as growth with equity, but its collapse has revealed a very different reality. Worse, globalization led by the multinational corporations leaves an increasing part of the population – and *most* of the population in many parts of the world – with little prospect of benefit, either now or in the foreseeable future. Growth as measured by gross domestic product (GDP), even where it is more than keeping up with population, is not producing comparable increases in real social welfare. In short, the present pattern of growth is socially unsustainable.

Ayres argues that the present pattern of economic growth, which is based on increasing labour productivity by substituting physical capital based on fossil resources for human workers, is also ecologically and environmentally unsustainable. The most binding limits are of so-called renewable and environmental resources. The two most immediate problems are water and wood. A third, and arguably more serious, problem is that the toxic waste assimilative capacity of the earth is declining – as a consequence of the degradation and loss of topsoil, deforestation and loss of biodiversity – while the demand for this service of nature is rising. A fourth problem, much more widely known, albeit still difficult to evaluate quantitatively, is climate change and its associated dangers.

Ayres points out that economic growth in the future must provide the resources to compensate for these problems, while not being short-circuited by them. Clearly, it must be technology driven. But the technologies that are needed will have to substitute solar energy and non-material resources – especially information – for material resources. Of course, the ultimate resource is trained human intelligence, which is the main source of our hopes for long-term survival as a species. Unfortunately, politicians in all the countries of the West, but especially in continental Europe, have unwittingly compromised this one essential resource. They have sharply limited the possibility of investment in the needed education and scientific research by committing future 'growth dividends' to current consumption by and subsidies to all sorts of politically well connected groups. The research and development (R&D) and investment deficit is slowing growth when and where it is most needed. A day of reckoning is fast approaching.

Mohan Munasinghe sets out a practical framework to better integrate economic, social and environmental components of sustainability based on ecological economics. The approach seeks to make development more sustainable by eliminating unsustainable activities, which is more practical than to define the ideal state of sustainable development. The use of this framework is described at various hierarchic levels of decision making – project/local, sectoral/subnational, economywide/national and global/transnational. Concepts and techniques for valuation of environmental impacts of projects and policies are presented that enable such environmental considerations to be explicitly considered in the conventional cost–benefit calculus used in economic decision making. The process of internalizing these environmental externalities may be facilitated by extending the techniques of conventional economic theory, with particular reliance on willingness-to-pay as a measure of value. Problems caused by discounting, risk and uncertainty are discussed. When economic valuation of environmental impacts is difficult, reliance may have to be placed on multi-criteria methods. Economywide policies (both sectoral and macroeconomic) often have significant environmental effects. The solution is not necessarily to modify the original broader policies (which have conventional economic or poverty-related goals), but rather to design more specific and complementary environmental measures that would address the particular policy, market or institutional imperfection and thereby help mitigate negative effects or enhance positive impacts of the original policies on the environment.

Munasinghe presents a series of case studies that span the hierarchic levels of decision making: rainforest management in Madagascar, improving energy sector decision making in Sri Lanka, and several case studies of the environmental and social impacts of countrywide policies such as structural adjustment programmes. Overall, the case studies suggest that economic techniques exist – and, for most countries, so does natural resource information – to improve the way environmental issues are addressed at the project, sector and macro levels. While significant data problems remain, the studies illustrate the feasibility of making rough assessments, not simply of environmental impacts of projects, but also of economic policies (and in particular economywide policies), thereby hastening the integration of the environment into the mainstream of economic decision making.

David Stern reviews the theory and applications of the environmental Kuznets curve (EKC), a hypothesis that proposes an inverted U-shape relation between various indicators of environmental degradation and income per capita. This has been taken to imply that economic growth will eventually redress the environmental impacts of the early stages of economic development and that growth will lead to further environmental improvements in the developed countries. Far from being a threat to the environment in the long term, as argued in *The Limits to Growth* (1972) Universe Books, New York, and *Beyond the Limits* (1992) Earthscan, London, among others, economic growth is seen as necessary in order for environmental quality to be maintained or improved. This is an essential part of the sustainable development argument as put forward in *Our Common Future* (1987), Oxford University Press.

Proponents of the EKC hypothesis argue that, at very low levels of economic activity, environmental impacts are generally low but as development proceeds the rates of land clearance, resource use and waste generation per capita increase rapidly. However, at higher levels of development, structural change towards information-intensive industries and services, coupled with increased environmental awareness, enforcement of environmental regulations, better technology and higher environmental expenditures, result in levelling off and gradual decline of environmental degradation. Thus there are both proximate causes of the EKC relationship – changes in economic structure or product mix, changes in technology and changes in input mix – and underlying causes such as environmental regulation, awareness and education. These effects act to counteract or exaggerate the gross impact of economic growth or the scale effect.

Stern reviews the four main types of contributions to the literature: estimation of 'basic' EKCs, studies of the theoretical determinants of the EKC, studies of the empirical determinants of the EKC and critiques of EKCs. Stern concludes that there has been progress on understanding the EKC in the last few years and some progress in methods of investigation. Evidence continues to accumulate that the inverted U shape relation only applies to a subset of impacts and that overall impact, perhaps approximately indicated by per capita energy use, rises throughout the relevant income range.

Stern describes advances in our understanding of the determinants of the EKC. It is clear that structural change and technological progress are of importance. Democracy, a variable that is also a correlate of development, is also associated with lower emissions. There is, however, increasing evidence that the EKC is partly determined by trade relations. If this is so, the poorest countries of today will find it more difficult than today's developed countries to reduce environmental impact as income rises. Some studies present more disaggregated evidence that is of interest in evaluating the performance of individual countries and the influence of particular events. Change may occur quite rapidly in crisis periods such as those of the oil price shocks of the 1970s or the CFC negotiations of the 1980s. Some of the empirical relationships that have been uncovered may not be robust, though this is not yet known: the issue of omitted variables bias has not been adequately investigated.

In Chapter 9, Richard England summarizes the many continuing efforts to develop alternatives to gross domestic product. Efforts to measure a nation's aggregate income date back to the seventeenth century when Sir William Petty devised one of the first national income estimates. It is widely recognized, however, that the economic crisis of the Great Depression, the political and military conflict of the Second World War and the emergence of Keynesian macroeconomic theory prompted the creation of modern national income accounting. National income statistics have found a variety of practical uses. For instance, they help to inform the design of government fiscal and monetary policies, influence corporate investment plans and are commonly used to assess economic development strategies in less developed nations. From their inception, however, the national income and product accounts have also been used to make international comparisons of wellbeing and to track changes in a country's level of welfare.

During the past quarter century, national income, GDP and allied accounting concepts have been sharply criticized by a wide array of commentators. Many of those critics have questioned whether national income data adequately measure the level of, or changes in, economic wellbeing. England notes that a typical defence of GDP has been to simply deny that they serve as measures of economic welfare. Yet leading economic historians and macroeconomists readily cite data on real per capita GDP as though they can provide insights into standards of living and economic progress. England goes on to identify the major issues involved in the development of complements to, or substitutes for, GDP. These include the need to properly specify the distinction between intermediate and gross final output, the need to account for asset depreciation in a comprehensive manner, the need to divide net final output between consumption and capital accumulation on a reasonable basis, and the need to take account of the welfare implications of various forms of social inequality.

Cutler Cleveland and David Stern review the different methods used to analyse resource scarcity, including their underlying theories, methodologies and principal empirical results. In general terms, an increase in scarcity is defined by a reduction in economic wellbeing due to a decline in the quality, availability or productivity of natural resources and vice versa. A major issue in the literature on the measurement of natural resource scarcity is which of the alternative indicators of scarcity, such as unit costs, prices, rents, elasticities of substitution and energy costs, is superior. Most neoclassical economists argue that, in theory, price is the ideal measure of scarcity. The unit cost indicator is derived from the classical school of economics. Some ecological economists favour a biophysical model of scarcity and derive energy-based indicators. A central issue is under what economic, technological, institutional and environmental conditions each indicator provides clear or ambiguous signals of scarcity.

Cleveland and Stern propose the terms *use scarcity* and *exchange scarcity* to distinguish between two broad approaches to measuring scarcity. These terms relate to the classical concepts of use and exchange value. Definitions of use and exchange value have varied among the different economic paradigms. Broadly speaking, use value is the value derived from consumption of a good, while exchange value is the value of goods or money that can be obtained in exchange for the good in an actual or potential market. Use scarcity refers to the ability of natural resources to generate use value and is typically measured in terms of the balance between the productivity and availability of the resource base and the level of technology. Exchange scarcity is commonly measured by price or rent, depending on whether the scarcity of in situ natural resources or of resource commodities is being measured.

Cleveland and Stern argue that a research programme aimed at modelling resource supply that takes into account both physical and economic factors would perhaps be more useful than the simple calculation of scarcity indicators. Rather than just observing the trend in costs or prices and assuming that this will continue into the future, this approach seeks to differentiate between the various causes of change in scarcity. This would give us a better picture of the limits to improvements in the future. Together with information on the possibilities for future technical change and natural processes, such models could be used to produce scenarios about possible future scarcity trends that could inform debate and policy making.

Finally, Costanza *et al.* review the goals and methods of green national accounting. They argue that a clear understanding of the different goals being served by different accounting frameworks is a prerequisite for their effective interpretation and use. They describe the range of goals for green accounting and the corresponding frameworks and methods which are most appropriate for each goal. The goals are divided into three broad categories, measuring economic income, economic welfare and human welfare. Most conventional national accounting measures, such as gross national product and net national product (GNP, NNP), limit themselves to measuring economic income, which is admitted to have no direct relationship to welfare. Despite this admitted lack of connection to welfare, economic income measures are routinely used as welfare surrogates, on the assumption that more income means more welfare. Within this category of income measures one can distinguish marketed, weakly sustainable and strongly sustainable versions, depending on how the depletion of capital and the substitutability between natural and human-made capital is dealt with.

But increases in economic *income* may not correlate with increases in economic *welfare*, especially if the income measures do not adequately distinguish 'costs' from 'benefits'. For example, an oil spill can increase GNP because more activity and income are generated, but it does not increase welfare since this activity is a cost to be avoided. The goal of measuring economic welfare requires adjusting income to better reflect which items in the income measures are costs and benefits and subtracting the costs (such as natural capital depletion and pollution), imputing values to missing services (such as household labour) and adjusting for income distribution effects using indices of income distribution. The Index of Sustainable Economic Welfare (ISEW) is one such economic welfare measure.

But economic welfare measured as the production of net benefits may still not correlate with overall human welfare, since many human needs are not related to consumption of economic products or services. The goal of measuring overall human welfare requires directly assessing the degree to which human needs are actually being met, the economic production involved being only one of many possible means to these ends. Costanza *et al.* further elaborate these distinctions and the specifics of measuring economic income, economic welfare and human welfare to produce a much needed clarification of these increasingly important issues.

PART I

The Nature of Economics

1. Early links between sciences of nature and economics: historical perspectives for ecological and social economics

Paul P. Christensen

INTRODUCTION

The relationship between ecological economics and neoclassical economic theory continues to be problematic. Many ecological economists argue that standard market theory when corrected for externalities or extended to include environmental accounting provides a satisfactory framework for analysing economic processes and environmental problems. Daly and Cobb (1989), for example, 'affirm the value and validity of marginal analysis' (p. 85) and accept (with corrections to the model of homo economicus) the basic framework of microeconomics (ibid., pp. 145, 164). In a paper intended to introduce the economics profession at large to the concepts and methods of ecological economics, Perrings *et al.* (1995) define ecological economics as the joint dynamics of economic and ecological systems (p. 3). A central concern of their paper is the need for 'the development of a coherent theory of the dynamical behaviour of ecological–economic systems based on an axiomatic structure that respects the properties of ecological and economic systems' (ibid., p. 35).

But what properties of economic systems are to be respected? It is readily apparent that the mechanistic individualism of modern (neoclassical) economic theory is inconsistent with the materials, energetic and organismic interdependence that structures ecological systems. Indeed, a similar interdependence necessarily characterizes the resource, technological and organizational structures of human production systems. Given the joint interdependence of human and environmental production, we cannot avoid a confrontation with the marginalist and equilibrium conceptions of neoclassical theory which explicitly posit a radical Cartesian individualism inconsistent with the physical, biological, psychological and social properties of economic systems. Most working economists admit that the assumptions of neoclassical theory are excessively abstract and unrealistic and argue that the theory has to be extended.

What is not sufficiently understood is that this extension cannot take place without a fundamental recasting of basic assumptions (see Clower, 1975).

The problematic nature of neoclassical assumptions was revealed in the course of the axiomatization programme of neo-Walrasian theory and has been considerably clarified in recent discussions (see Kirman, 1989; Ingrao and Israel, 1990). The discovery, known as the Sonnenschein–Mantel–Debreu result, is that the Arrow–Debreu model cannot provide a workable theory of the operations of a market economy. A theory composed of individualistic maximizers who act independently cannot, under any reasonable assumptions, be used to construct aggregate excess demand functions and thus establish the out-of-equilibrium behaviour (uniqueness and stability) necessary to supply and demand theory. High theory has been thrown into a state of deep crisis. The aggregation difficulties are so severe, Kirman (1989) argues, that neo-classical general equilibrium theory is '*intrinsically* incapable of generating verifiable propositions'. Since the general equilibrium model provides 'the fundamental underpinnings of most modern economic work and indeed quantitative work in economics', the conclusion is that neoclassical theory is incapable of providing microfoundations for empirical and policy work (ibid., pp. 127, 137).

It is now admitted that the attempts to establish a grand unifying theory of economics on 'equilibrium models analogous to mechanics' have failed (Arrow, 1995, p. 1618). Marshall's suggestion that biology 'is a more appropriate paradigm for economics' is increasingly invoked (see Hahn, 1991; Ingrao and Israel, 1990). The high priests of the profession recognize that the game of doing mathematical economics from neoclassical microfoundations is over. A new conceptual approach and theory must be found.

At least one theorist (Hildebrand) has suggested that perhaps a consideration of production theory might provide a way forward since it is widely recognized that neo-Walrasian production theory is little more than an extension of the economic allocation of scarce resources.[1] A biophysical and ecological approach to economics suggests that a first task of economic theory should be the development of the production foundations of economic activity. Neoclassical theory cannot provide these foundations. In the first place, it lacks any realistic treatment of production processes. The more serious problem, however, is the inconsistency between the neoclassical principle of marginal productivity of individual inputs and the biophysical principles governing real-world production activities, in particular the first and second laws of thermodynamics. It would be inappropriate to base production theory and environmental economics on concepts which are incompatible with the operations of the physical and biological world.

The problems with neoclassical production theory cannot be corrected by simply adding the missing variables (material and energy flows) to existing production functions. The difficulty is that the neoclassical formulation of diminishing returns in terms of the positive marginal products of individual inputs violates physical principles. Marginal productivity theory states that an increase in an individual factor of production will yield an increase in output when all other inputs are held constant. But this assumption violates the first law of thermodynamics which dictates that a change in physical output requires (1) corresponding flows of the materials which will be embodied in output and (2) the free energy required to do the work of production. It is an unavoidable consequence of the principles of matter and energy conservation and the entropy law that positive marginal products do not and cannot exist in the real world.[2]

The neglect of material and energy flows in production activity goes back to Walras (1874) who declared that 'machines, instruments, tools ... engender incomes in the same way' that a field grows a crop year after year (1954 edn, p. 213). But Walras neglects the fact that a field grows a crop in conjunction with flows of sunlight, water and nutrients. If any of these essential requirements are not available, output is nil according to Liebig's law of the minimum. Machines and industrial processes can only produce physical output in conjunction with available material and energy flows. Adam Smith's fixed and circulating capital are required together. They are complementary and not substitutable inputs. Although Walras recognizes that materials are produced on the land, he does not see that production from the land depends on material and energetic flows through the land. Thus his step of vertically aggregating agricultural and manufacturing production into a one-stage sequence of producing final output from appropriate quantities or 'primary' factors of land, labour and capital effectively eliminates materials (and energy) from theoretical consideration (ibid., pp. 237, 241). Production functions were subsequently written without any specification of materials or the energy required to do work. Each primary factor was assumed to produce output in the same way and it was a short step to assuming the existence of positive marginal products from changes in single inputs.[3]

The importance of marginal productivity theory to neoclassical theory is emphasized by Brue (1993):

> Without this law [the law of diminishing returns], economists lack satisfactory explanations of short-run marginal cost curves, short-run product supply curves, and short-run factor demand curves, *as they relate to individual competitive enterprises.* And without strong short-run theories of individual enterprises, we have neither contemporary microeconomics nor modern macroeconomics. (Ibid., p. 191)

The assumptions and methods on which neoclassical theory is based were borrowed from nineteenth-century mechanics and field theory (Mirowski, 1989; Foster, 1993). They were an inherent feature of the mathematical framework of mid-nineteenth-century physics. An individual, Foster (1993) notes, is treated as a particle of mass at equilibrium in a field of forces. Changes in input use are treated as changes in location in a pre-existing energy field. It is thus assumed that any input can substitute for any other input (this is just a change in spatial dimension and the strength of the field remains unchanged). Changes in technology are in turn treated as exogenous changes in the strength of the field; that is, all the isoquants shift inward. The relation between input productivity and energy flow (the strength of the field) remains entirely outside the analysis and, more troubling, entirely invisible.

There is also the critical assumption of path independence or reversibility. The firm can go anywhere in input space and produce output with any combination of inputs without causing any change in the underlying structure of production and productivity. There is no dissipation of resources and no learning. Productivity is perennial and undisturbed by the activity of production. It should be apparent that not only are neoclassical assumptions of input substitution woefully inadequate but their extension to environmental economics in the form of statements about the substitutability of human capital for environmental capital are deeply problematic. Neoclassical economists are working from a pre-written script generated by equilibrium energy mechanics.

An ecological or biophysical and organizational approach to production challenges the central foundation of neoclassical theory. The convexity assumptions of neoclassical production theory and the theory of market demand and supply rest on marginal productivity and substitutability assumptions inconsistent with the physical, biological and psychological connectivity which characterize the natural, technological and social domains. Marginal products of individual inputs do not exist. Taking the Cartesian road, neoclassicals assume the individuals are prior to the society and economy. Individuals are, moreover, assumed to act independently of other individuals. Individual resources are likewise assumed to act independently of other resources. The hyperindividualism and atomism of neoclassical production and consumption theory are inappropriate for the complex and interactive connections and dynamics that characterize economic systems and human behaviour. Adopting an ecological and evolutionary perspective entails an ecological, evolutionary and social epistemology and ontology for economics.

The necessary reconstruction of economics will obviously require insights from many scientific disciplines and schools of economic thought. In particular, a synthesis of biophysical, ecological, organizational and evolutionary approaches is required. But an interdisciplinary approach still requires a theoretical framework. How can ecological economics build an interdisciplinary approach which incorporates both natural and social sciences? A possible model is provided by early physiocratic and classical economics which drew on a succession of physical, chemical, physiological and natural history models to construct a production approach to economics by analogy with the producing capabilities of nature's realm. Although based on outdated scientific concepts, this approach shows the rich possibilities offered by developing a closer relationship between economics and the other sciences.

THE CLASSICAL PRODUCTION ALTERNATIVE TO EXCHANGE ECONOMICS

On the basis of a detailed investigation of the scientific roots of early economic ideas (Christensen, n.d.), I divide early theory into four periods according to the scientific models taken up by economic writers. An important feature of this work is the central role played by contemporary ideas in physiology, chemistry and natural history which provide the basic framework for understanding material transformations and sources of motion in organisms, nature and human economy. These sciences also provide ideas about regulatory mechanisms and feedback. The specific theories change as the scientific currents shift and evolve, but throughout there is a clear understanding that an economic system, like a living body, depends on material and energetic substances drawn from the earth and transformed into the forms appropriate for constructing and powering processes of life and work.

Era 1

The first period of theory development employs a mix of the new science of mechanics pioneered by Kepler and Galileo and new physiological theories of Harvey. A common thread in both was the Aristotelian idea of a self-producing nature (Mittelstrass, 1988, pp. 28–9). In contrast to Aristotle, who confined mechanics to the study of 'unnatural' motions, a central idea of the new physics was its treatment of mechanics as a general theory of the motion of bodies under the influence of physical forces. The philosopher Thomas Hobbes (1651) used Galileo's new science of mechanics to construct his philosophy of bodies and motion in general. It has escaped notice how he used Harvey's physiological theories of circulation, nutrition and generation to recast and extend Aristotle's materials-provisioning approach to economics (Christensen, 1989). The land and the sea, the two breasts of our common mother, Hobbes writes, provide the matter (animal, vegetable and mineral) which is carried in the economic circulation and which labour transforms into necessities and the surplus products of trade. A central feature of Hobbes' approach is the unification of agriculture and manufacturing in the same framework of materials extraction, productive transformation and distributive circulation, thus overcoming Aristotle's

dichotomy between the 'natural' activities of agriculture and domestic provisioning and the 'unnatural' activities of trade and manufacturing.

William Petty is justly regarded as the originator of the classical surplus
model but it is clear that his theory builds on Hobbes' suggestive ideas about
materials production and circulation. Petty's (1662) contribution is to recast
these ideas into a simple multi-sector theory of net product and 'intrinsic' or
production prices. Trained as a geographer, mathematician, mechanist and
medical doctor (who spent nine months with Hobbes in Paris), Petty constructs
a simple model of the ratio between net output (total product minus costs) over
costs. This ratio is equalized between sectors by the flow of labour in response
to prices. Informed by the Epicurean ideas about active matter of Gassendi and
Hobbes and the energetic mechanics of Galileo, Petty reduces production costs
(via heroic abstraction) to the organic energy required in production. Thus Petty
alternatively relates prices to labour, land or food, since men and beasts must
'eat, so as to live, labor and generate' (1691).

Era 2

The second phase of theory development drew on the rapid development of
natural history and especially botany in the second half of the seventeenth
century. The complexity of animal tissues under the microscope led Malphigi
and other investigators to study the simpler structures of plants. Efforts to
understand the structures and functions of plants and the revelation of the
repetitive nature of nature's designs led to an overall picture of the circulation
and multiple transformations of materials and energetic substance in nature's
larger 'oeconomy'. Boisguilbert (1695–1707), a second cousin of Fontenelle,
was an early beneficiary of the new conception of nature developed by the
Academy of Sciences in Paris. He applies, for example, a theory of the circulation of sap in vegetables to a conception of parallel circuits of materials,
products and money in human production and trade. In the first phase of the
material circuit, food and other materials produced on the land flow to the professions and the state. In the second phase, the products of artisans and the
professions flow to farmers and other consumers. His concern is the consequence of a disruption or crisis which impoverishes all the sectors given the
dual dependence of an economy on food and materials and on the payments
flowing from the purchases of the other sectors. The primary cause of the
monetary disruptions was the heavy exactions and interference of the French
state. Here Boisguilbert drew on the revival of Stoic ideas of nature and Hip-
pocratic medical theory to emphasize the self-healing and regulative powers of
nature. The wise physician assists but lets nature take its course (laissez-faire).

Cantillon (1755 [circa 1730]) is the other great figure in this period of theory
development. He knows his Petty and his emphasis on materials transformation

in production suggests he was familiar with the work of Boisguilbert. He was friends with Montesquieu, who began his career as a natural and economic historian and with Bolingbrooke and the French Newtonians. He also knew Newton, whose methodological principles of reasoned theory construction and induction (as developed in the *Optics*) he clearly adopts. Cantillon's great achievement is the construction of a general model of food and materials extraction and production, distribution between classes and a materials–labour theory of production prices.[4] Brilliant in its own right, this is clearly the launching platform for Quesnay's *Tableau économique*.

Era 3

The next period of theory development, encompassing Quesnay, Smith and Ricardo, is distinguished on the history of science side by its close connection to the emergence of a new chemistry which replaces the early attempts to construct a physical chemistry on Newtonian mechanics with an energetic model of chemical production. Chemistry was defined by Stahl in Germany, Rouelle in France and Cullen in Scotland as an autonomous science based on laws of selective affinity. The energetic foundation of nature's operations was provided by various theories of fire which were conceptualized in terms of subtle and very active ethers, caloric fluids or phlogiston theory. The source of this elemental fire was the light of the sun which circulated between the plant, animal and mineral kingdoms providing the energetic potential for the ever-continuous cycles of molecular decompositions, and syntheses which kept the channels and warehouses of nature's vast systems of production stocked and operating. Enlightenment chemistry was the fundamental science of material transformations and circulations in nature's system and provided an account of nature's productive powers as manifest in the laboratory and the economy of nature and harnessed by humans in the agricultural and industrial economy.

Before turning to economics, François Quesnay wrote extensively on medicine, physiology and chemistry. Two of the three volumes of his *Physical Essay on the Animal Oeconomy* (1747) are devoted to chemistry and the organic molecules composing the body. Underlying the composition and decomposition of these highly transitory compounds are the subtle operations which variously fix this elemental fire in chemical reactions. This protoenergetic theory of chemical production informs his theory of production and consumption in the human economy (Christensen, 1994). Economic activity first generates and then consumes and degrades the organic molecules which carry this subtle and active substance. Plants (agriculture) are the original producer of this energetic substance. Since Quesnay does not consider any non-agricultural source of energy, only agriculture allied to the chemical reconstitutions in the soil is productive in the sense that it regenerates these motion substances. Trade and manufacturing only consume energetic and prime materials.

Three of Adam Smith's closest associates (William Cullen, Joseph Black and James Hutton) were leading advocates of the new 'philosophical' chemistry which provided naturalistic (and materialistic) explanations of nature's mechanisms via the transformations of solar fire in the hidden operations of heat in chemistry, physiology and geology. Smith's 'Essay on Ancient Physics' (1795) reveals a keen understanding of the close connections between the ancient materialism and the still dangerous chemical philosophy of his friends. Psychological theories of sentiment of Hume and Smith were linked to physiological theories about the communication of sympathy in the body advanced by Scottish physicians including Cullen and Hutton. Chemistry, physiology and psychology were distinct but interdependent sciences. Unfortunately, Smith's application of these ideas in explaining economic productivity in terms of the powers of nature and labour was rather weak.

Robert Malthus, like Petty and Quesnay, was trained as a natural scientist. He gained a degree in mathematics (applied mechanics) at Cambridge, but he was also a student of biology. It appears he turned to economics to apply his training in natural philosophy. The evolutionary theodicy he presents in his *Essay on Population* (1798) is obviously based on the radical materialist ideas of the psychologist David Hartley, the chemist and theologian Joseph Priestley, and the physician Erasmus Darwin, grandfather of Charles Darwin. The early Darwin employs the self-organizing active matter ideas of Hume, Maupertuis, and Buffon to construct a theory of the gradual evolution of plants and animals and the formation of mind in the context of the struggle of organisms for scarce resources (made scarce by the high rates of reproduction of most species). Malthus, in turn, uses biology and mechanics to formulate the principles of food and population growth and requisite regulatory mechanisms governing population (and market prices). Malthus' subsequent economics writing presents an unfinished synthesis emphasizing the importance of food and resource availability and the destabilizing effects of rapid technological change on macrodynamics. But despite acute observations on differences between returns and costs in agriculture versus industry, Malthus fails to develop any theory of industrial process and an underlying biophysical treatment of material and energy flows between nature and economic sectors of production. He confines his theory to value and distribution categories and neglects production theory, apart from his treatment of diminishing returns in agriculture.

Ricardo begins to apply the energetic (phlogiston) ideas of Priestley (a co-discoverer of photosynthesis) and Hutton (1947, 1957) to the human economy. Production in the agricultural sector, as in Malthus, is limited by diminishing returns to the application of labour and implements but the industrial side of the economy, where raw materials such as cotton, silk, and iron ore are more easily made available by production, is characterized by constant returns to the employment of additional workers, capital (corn and implements), and raw materials. For Ricardo, the essential constraint on the growth of the economy is the availability of corn (American wheat) which feeds the animals and workers employed in the sectors of the economy (I am making a 'rational reconstruction' of Ricardo's insistence on the key role of corn and corn prices in the functioning of the economy from his knowledge of the chemistry of Priestley and Hutton). Ricardo also gives more attention to industrial production than Malthus. He is obviously familiar with Hutton's theory of geology where the powers of heat and pressure in the earth transform sedimentary into igneous rock and the sun's phlogiston powers plant and animal production. Ricardo recognizes that the human economy, using powers of wind and water and the heat from coal to run engines, is also dependent on nature's natural powers and he uses these ideas to refute Smith's notion that nature does nothing in manufacturing. Unfortunately, he does not go very far in the application of these ideas to industrial productivity and technical change. We can see, however, how the availability and quality of energy resources in the economy (confined to wheat) are the physical foundation for his theory of value and profits. We can also see that diminishing returns in agriculture is due to the limited availability in the soil of the essential nutrients necessary for plant production (the requirements for these resources will not be understood by agricultural chemists for several decades). We cannot legitimately criticize Malthus and Ricardo for the attention they gave to the constraints they saw on future agricultural production.

Era 4

The fourth phase of the development of classical theory in the nineteenth century was based on the application of the late eighteenth-century engineering mechanics of Coulomb and Lazare Carnot comparing the work of machines, labour and animals. This suggests the basis for a general theory of economic production based on the work of land, capital and labour for three French writers (Canard, Garnier and J.-B. Say). Say (1803) takes up Verri's ([1773] 1800) critique of the physiocrats which points out that all production, agriculture and manufacturing involves the transformation of materials from one form into another. Say extends use of the principle of the conservation of matter to argue that all production requires materials, forces of nature and the action of labour and implements. While the full implications of Say's treatment of production were obscured by a diffuse presentation and an apparent divorce of value from production, his work had some influence on the production theories of Malthus and Ricardo.

British classical economists began to consider the role of inanimate power in industrial production in the 1830s, under the influence of Smeaton, Babbage and Ure, who recognized the importance of power and prime movers in Britain's industrial ascendancy. In reviews of Babbage and Ure, McCulloch (1833) connects the industrial prosperity of the British nation to its exploitation of coal and coal-using technologies. The rapid increase in the quantity and quality of coal-made iron, for example, lowered the costs of machinery (including steam engines) which produced more output at a lower cost, increasing the demand for and production of coal, iron and machines (initiating a positive feedback loop of demand and innovation).

While McCulloch confined himself to emphasizing the importance of coal in economic growth, Nassau Senior (1836) attempted to incorporate the new prime movers and inanimate sources of power into a theory of physical production. He sets out a tripartite physical classification of production agents: labour and skills, natural agents, and abstinence (the source of capital). Capital is divided into fixed and 'circulating' components in order to distinguish tools and instruments from the materials which will be embodied in production. Unfortunately, he includes food, coal and other powers with fixed capital on the grounds that these are not embodied in output. Following Babbage's (1832) study of technologies and machines, he divides implements into two classes: those which produce power (steam engines, water wheels and so on) and those which transmit and apply power. He also recognizes the application of the conservation of matter to manufacturing production. In sum, he provides most of the essential elements for a physical theory of production.

J.S. Mill (1848) also notes the importance of motive powers in production. He follows Senior in classifying production inputs under the headings of labour, natural agents and capital. Nature provides the materials and the powers which cooperate with and substitute for labour. But he fails to maintain Senior's distinction between materials and motive powers, subsuming the latter – coals for engines and food for workers – under the class of materials 'to avoid a multiplication of classes of no scientific importance'. When Senior (1848) objects to treating fuel as a material, Mill replies that although his terminology is not in accord with the physical meaning of material, the distinction between materials and fuels is of 'almost no importance to political economy' (Mill [1848], 1871, pp. 34–5). Mill's lack of concern with accurate scientific terminology informed by physical principles was unfortunately followed by Marshall, who adopted a 'commercial' rather than a scientific or technical language. Classical theory seemed to run out of steam following Mill's important but flawed synthesis which bungled the physical production framework pioneered by Say and Senior.[5]

For two centuries, early economic theorists employed a mix of physiological and machine analogies to establish a physically informed production theory. All economic activity, it was obvious, required materials and natural powers drawn from nature, the skills and work of human labour, and the tools, machinery and physical structures specific to field, workshop and factory. The explanation of economic production clearly required information and models taken from other sciences. Economics was a mixed science dependent for its physical understanding of production on the physical and natural sciences (including natural history). On the social–organizational side, there was also an early link to the social sciences and psychology. Hobbes' project of grounding a materialist psychology on physiology and the natural sciences was continued in the eighteenth century by Hume and Diderot.[6] In the next section we offer a closer examination of the connections between late eighteenth-century sciences of nature and society and the development of economics in this period.

A CLOSER LOOK AT ENLIGHTENMENT SCIENCE AND ECONOMICS

In this section we look more closely at the eighteenth-century scientific ideas which were used by economic theorists for the construction of social and economic theory. Our purpose is to explore one important way in which economics was linked to the natural and social sciences. While there is a considerable amount of reductionism involved in the work we will examine, this is not the lesson we want to take away. It is rather the idea that economic theory, if it is to help us understand the connections and interactions between the natural environment, the economy and the social sphere, needs to be much better informed by the attitudes, methods and conceptual understandings of the natural and human sciences. The strength of eighteenth and early nineteenth-century economics comes from the fact that it took the scientific attitude seriously and attempted to develop a moral philosophy and economic theory of production from the sciences of its time. A new economics, to which ecological economics has much to contribute, must similarly absorb some basic lessons from physics, biology, environmental science, and psychology.

A first component of the new eighteenth-century sciences of the Enlightenment was its naturalistic epistemology. This derived mainly from Locke and Hume, especially Hume's devastating attack on seventeenth-century rationalism and theological metaphysics. Locke writes as a physician influenced by the Epicurean physiology of Thomas Willis, and by Sydenham, who incorporates the ideas of Glissen's theories of organic sensitivity and nature's healing powers into his revival of the observational methods of Hippocrates' study of disease. Hume, a close student of the natural sciences and the great sceptic Pierre Bayle, attempts to found a new science of human nature by linking an experiential and observational psychology to contemporary developments in physiology. What Hume meant by observation, Moore (1994) points out, was 'perception' as it was understood by physiology and developed within early physiological theories of instinct. For Hume, 'natural instinct supersedes the conceptual analysis of impressions and ideas' as events composed of discrete parts.[7] By contrast, 'it makes us suppose a continuity in the objects themselves [and] to allow for the possibility of real forces in nature (Wright, 1983, p. 160). Since knowledge of causes is based on generalization from experience and scientific reasoning about connections between events, it cannot provide absolute or total knowledge but only answers justified by probability.

A basic ingredient of mid-eighteenth-century thinking was a belief in a natural order and system that is produced, not by a creator God, but by the inherent productive powers of nature. Nature constituted a self-producing, self-organizing system operating on principles of natural design and inherent sources of motion (energy) and possessing intrinsic capacities for judgment, discrimination and regulation (although these were not without limits). The generative sciences for these ideas were chemistry and matter theory, physiology and natural history. There were, of course, different ideas about the source of this order. Hume (possibly influenced by the physical and biological papers of Maupertuis) proposes an evolutionary theory. He 'revive[s] the old EPICUREAN hypothesis' that matter is endowed with motion without any first mover, that it continually produces by its 'perpetual agitation' new forms and combinations, and that some of these forms will be capable of supporting and reproducing themselves. Those which bear sufficient connection with other forms can survive and prosper. The result is 'a system, an order, an economy of things' in which each part is adapted to the whole as the whole is adapted to the part. These adaptations are selected by the elimination of the unfit and are not the result of providential action. Nature thus produces 'all the art and contrivance which we observe at present' (Hume, 1779, pt. 8, pp. 143–4; written in the very early 1750s). Smith likewise favours an explanation of nature's system that sees the powers of motion and design as immanent in nature. He explains nature's production capacities as elaborations from principles elaborated in other parts of nature. While he adopts an evolutionary approach in explaining human behaviour and the economic stages of society, he is careful not to commit himself in print to dangerous principles of biological evolution (which were also advanced by Hutton).

The foundational science of mid-eighteenth-century science is chemistry. In contrast to the mechanistic chemistry of Boyle and Newton's immediate followers, Scottish chemists and their French counterparts develop chemistry as an autonomous science, not directly reducible to mechanics, whose concern is the composition and decomposition of compound substances (molecules). According to Cullen, founder of the Scottish school and a close friend of Smith at Glasgow and later in Edinburgh, the primary cause of the changes in matter studied by chemistry was the principle of fire, which he also treated as a subtle aether. The source of this active substance was the light from the sun which, as experiments showed, takes different forms in nature (heat, electricity, an aetherial fluid in the body, and so on). It is this 'very same aether acting by different circumstances,' Cullen proposes, 'that is the cause of the phenomena we observe in nature' (Christie, 1981, p. 93). Smith indicates his familiarity with this 'philosophical chemistry' in his essays on ancient science which were published posthumously by his friends Joseph Black and William Hutton (both chemists). He notes how it provides the connecting principles 'between seemingly disjointed objects' such as acids and bases and the principle explaining the 'common fire' used to prepare daily necessities and the fire which is required for 'the continual support of the vital principle which actuates both plants and animals' (Smith, (1795), p. 107).

A fourth element of this scientific and philosophical programme was the distinctive system of physiology and medicine taught in the Edinburgh medical school by Robert Whytt and by Cullen with its emphasis on the organic sensibility manifested in the body. This was explained by Whytt (1751) in terms of an immaterial 'sentient principle' which was present throughout the body which could feel stimuli and respond purposefully. Cullen, by contrast, based his theory of the 'nervous power' on the operations of a highly refined form of aetherial fluid transmitted by the nerves to the muscles. This repository of sensibility, according to Cullen, is the 'vital principle' (Cullen, 1789, I, p. 59). Building on new studies of tissue sensitivity, the response of the body to chemicals and disease, the functioning of the internal organs and glands and studies of learning in humans and animals, the Edinburgh professors developed a broad vision of the physiological communication of sensibility (which they also termed 'sympathy') through the system of nerves to all parts of the body. They also drew parallels between the sentient principles operating in physiology and the operations of moral sense. Indeed, three of Smith's closest friends, Hume, Cullen and Hutton, developed ideas about moral philosophy, natural sociability and learning grounded in physiology.

The most well-known feature of the thought of Smith's circle is psychology and moral philosophy. What is distinctive in this work is the primacy given to emotions and feelings in psychology and moral philosophy. This emphasis has been almost singularly attributed to Francis Hutcheson, Smith's teacher of moral philosophy at Glasgow. But the attack on reason as the guiding principle of action and moral behaviour had a physiological base. Hutcheson built on the ideas of Shaftesbury, who held that feelings, natural instincts and developed habits provide better explanations of man's sociability than reason. A neglected influence on Shaftesbury was the theory of sensitivity and natural perception in physiology of Francis Glissen, a physician (as was Locke) to Shaftesbury's family. Hume, it is also now understood, was less influenced by Hutcheson than by Hobbes, Bayle and Mandeville, from whom he took his model of human nature (Connon, 1977) and by his early study of physiology and natural history (Moore, 1994). As we have indicated above, the psychology and moral philosophy were central topics in mid-eighteenth-century physiology and medical theory. Smith's important contribution to moral philosophy in his *Theory of Moral Sentiments* builds on Hume, but goes beyond him in providing a more extended treatment of the principle of sympathy and its evolutionary development (apparently building on Rousseau's (1755) evolutionary model). Smith also disagrees with Hume, who based sympathy on utility or self-interest. Smith's account is more naturalistic than Hume's, stressing, for example, the deep instinctual nature of feelings of justice. It is unfortunate that Smith then constructs his *Wealth of Nations* on a psychology of self-interest and separates the domain of economic behaviour from the concerns of moral philosophy. The result has favoured a treatment of economic philosophy which neglects psychology and moral philosophy in economic teaching and understanding.

An integration of the greater naturalism of Smith's account of moral philosophy and Hume's emphasis on the 'artificial' or constructed nature of morals may be helpful here. Smith's moral spectator obviously assumes a psychologically healthy individual. The wide differences in the personal and cultural histories which mould personality and temperament may be interpreted in a Humean framework allowing more scope to history, culture and individuality. Similarly, an integration of the central roles of self-interest and moral concerns in the economic domain is critical. Smith's strategy of separately constructing social theory on sentiment and economics on self-interest is obviously unacceptable. Moral concerns have to be built into the metaphysical foundations of economics just as self-interest and concern for others are each essential to individual development and social processes. Smith's optimism and belief in natural checks and balances is vastly overdone and applies the idea of a self-correcting (self-healing) economic system far beyond its range of application.

We have earlier noted the failure of Quesnay, Smith and Malthus to develop a general theory of physical productivity which applies both to land and to industrial activities. A Ricardo–Senior model extended to include an explicit distinction between materials and energy resources provides a framework for reconstructing a production theory consistent with physical principles. Senior's quandary about where to include books and seed corn raises the critical role of information and knowledge in an economic system. Obviously, each production activity involves a complementary combination of flows of materials, energy and information, and the technologies, organization and skills that transform or convert material, energy and information flows. A useful heuristic for developing the classical approach to production is m–e–i–t–o–s, that is, materials, energy and information plus technologies, organizations and skills. Ecological economics provides the biophysical (and moral) foundations which have been missing from modern economics, including the recent turn to an evolutionary and organizational economics (Nelson and Winter, 1982).

Modern economics fails to make an essential differentiation between different kinds of markets. Marshall and Walras each based their theory of market operation on the stock market where demand and supply enter simultaneously into the determination of prices (although these forces are neither stable nor independent). But this 'one version fits all markets' notion which dominates current teaching fails to understand the important role which production, costs and time play in market operation and price determination, especially in industrial markets. Classical economics (apart from J.B. Say) emphasized production prices and gave a much less central role to day-to-day market prices. What is needed now is the recognition that different markets operate under different conditions and are subject to substantially different forces. Malthus was correct to criticize Ricardo's neglect of demand in prices, but he was quite wrong to argue (as does Marshall) that cost factors can be collapsed into the supply curve. Production conditions, cost structures and demand are each important in price determination. In conditions where products can be produced from extracted flows of materials and energy and where information and technology are produced from information and technology (and the requisite materials and energy), firms face downward-sloping or flat cost curves (which are being continually shifted downwards by technological and organizational change). Given that products are carriers of information and distinguishable by quality, then demand, supply and cost-of-production are all interdependent, not autonomously given forces which determine equilibrium prices. The demand faced by a firm determines how much the firm can successfully supply and sell over time. Technology, costs and quality influence the demand for a firm's products. The physical interdependence of a production system is paralleled by interdependence within and between markets.

CONCLUSION

Physiocratic and classical theory emerged as part of the early evolution of the natural sciences, moral philosophy and a naturalistic psychology. Early economic theories of production were developed from contemporary ideas of active matter employed in chemical and physiological theories of the way nature produced itself through time. The result is a body of theory that provides a framework for an explicit development of the interdependence between materials and energy and the technologies of material and energy conversion. It is a framework, moreover, that is connected to psychological models concerned with the interdependence between emotion and reason and with learning through time.

Neoclassical theory, by contrast, took its concepts and mathematical structure from the maximization framework of analytical mechanics and field theory. The result is a treatment of economic agents as charged particles at equilibrium in a field of forces (Foster, 1993). Precisely because it is structured by the field model of a conserved gradient of potential energy, the neoclassical model of production (and utility) lacks any treatment of materials and energy or the technologies by which materials, energy and information are transformed in economic activity. Inputs or factors of production in this model are simply represented as dimensions in space over which the production gradient is defined. A technique of production is simply a point in multidimensional space representing amounts of various inputs. Any point may be chosen for production and there is neither learning nor entropic dissipation of resources. Not only is the energetic potential of the production function not eroded by the production process, it is subject to a magical process of global intensification via the neoclassical theory of technological change which defines technical progress as a global shift of the production function (that is, energetic potential). The hollowness of the neoclassical theory of factor substitution and the more astounding claim of the ability to substitute human-produced capital for natural capital is apparent.

A first step in the development of an ecological approach to economics is a scientifically informed characterization of production inputs and processes. Boulding (1978) suggested that the basic factors of production are materials, energy and know-how. This needs to be broadened to an ecological characterization of flows of materials, energy and information and the technologies, organization and learned skills that transform and convert materials, energy and information. The dependence of modern industrial systems on vast but depletable supplies of inorganic material and energy resources and on biological systems of considerable vulnerability must be built into the structure of economic theory. Technological change not only discovers new resources, products and processes, it also increases the scale of use of resources relative to existing ecosystems and the biosphere.

A second and related step is an accurate representation of the distinct differences, constraints and productive potential of the biological and ecologically based 'sectors' of nature's economy versus the technologically constructed sectors of human industrial activity which are currently dependent on the entropic use of vast supplies of inorganic minerals and fossil fuels. Neoclassical theory is constructed on a mistaken generalization of a 'Ricardian model of land' (positive and diminishing marginal productivity) to every factor and every sector of production. Classical theory, by contrast, noted important differences in the diminishing returns conditions attributed to agricultural and primary sector production and the increasing returns characteristic of manufacturing and industrial activities which operated under significantly different conditions of input availability, technology and, thus, cost conditions. The material–energy–technology characterization of production implicit in the classical approach must be extended and developed and integrated with new approaches in organizational and evolutionary economics. This will provide a new theoretical framework integrating the critical interactions between the quite different conditions and requirements of the earth's biological production systems and the rapidly evolving industrial systems of the human economy. An economy fed from vast stocks of high-quality material and energy reserves and replicated by accelerating technological change is not well characterized by the generalized diminishing returns model of neoclassical theory. An ecological and organizational approach to economics is needed. This must be informed by contemporary natural and social sciences, but a theory of economy is required. Early physiological and classical economics has an important contribution to make to this enterprise.

NOTES

1. Kirman (1989) thinks that production will raise more difficulties for neo-Walrasian theory than it solves.
2. See Ayres (1978, ch. 3) for a critique of aggregate production functions as inconsistent with the principles governing material and energy use. The impossibility of marginal products of individual capital goods is noted in Christensen (1987). See also Daly and Cobb (1989, pp. 112–13).
3. A belief in the existence of 'the marginal productivity of individual capital goods' was reaffirmed by neoclassical theorists during the Cambridge controversies in capital theory (Brown, 1980).
4. Historians of theory ignore the food/materials components of Cantillon's theory of manufacturing prices in order to interpret him in Walrasian terms.
5. The failure of economic writers to take up the energy ideas of the new thermodynamics is perhaps the most puzzling issue. On the attempts by scientifically informed writers to interest economists in the energetic underpinnings of production, see Martinez-Alier (1987).
6. On Hume's links to Hobbes, see Emerson (1990); on the connections of Diderot to Hobbes, see Barnouw (1978).
7. This idea may have been developed from Boerhaave's medical lectures.

BIBLIOGRAPHY

Arrow, K.J. (1995), 'Viewpoint: the future', *Science*, 267, 17 March, 1617.
Arrow, K. J. and F. Hahn (1972), *General Competitive Analysis*, San Francisco: Holden-Day.
Ayres, R.U. (1978), *Resources, Environment and Economics: Applications of the Materials Balance Principle*, New York: John Wiley.
Babbage, C. (1832), *On the Economy of Machinery and Manufactures*, London.
Barnouw, J. (1978), 'Materialism and freedom: commentary', *Studies in Eighteenth Century Culture*, 7, 194–212.

32 *The nature of economics*

Boisguilbert, P. (1966), Pierre de Bosguilbert ou la Naissance de l'économie politique, Paris, Institut National d'Etudes Démographics, 2 vols.

Boulding, K. (1978), *Ecodynamics*, Beverly Hills: Sage Publications.

Brown, M. (1980), 'The measurement of capital aggregates: a postreswitching problem,' in D. Usher (ed.), *The Measurement of Capital*, Chicago: University of Chicago Press.

Brue, S. L. (1993), 'The law of diminishing returns', *Journal of Economic Perspectives*, 7, 185–92.

Cantillon, R. (1755), *Essay sur la Nature du Comerce en General*, in H. Higgs (ed. and trans.) (1965), New York: A.M. Kelley.

Christensen, P. (1987), 'Classical roots for a modern materials–energy analysis', *Ecological Modelling*, 38, 75–89.

Christensen, P. (1989), 'Hobbes and the physiological origins of economic science', *History of Political Economy*, 21 (4), 689–709.

Christensen, P. (1994), 'Fire, motion and productivity: the proto-energetics of nature and economy in François Quesnay', in P. Mirowski (ed.), *Natural Images in Economic Thought*, Cambridge: Cambridge University Press.

Christensen, P. (forthcoming), *Materials, Natural Powers, and Machines: the Natural Science Origins Economic Theory, Hobbes to Mill*.

Christie, J.R.R. (1981), 'Ether and the science of chemistry: 1740–1790', in G.N. Cantor and M.J.S. Hodge (eds), *Conceptions of Ether: Studies in the History of Ether Theories, 1740–1900*, Cambridge and New York: Cambridge University Press.

Clower, R. (1975), 'Reflections on the Keynesian perplex', *Zeitschrift für Nationalökonomie*, 35, July, 1–24, reprinted in R. Clower (1984), *Money and Markets: Essays by Robert W. Clower*, Cambridge: Cambridge University Press.

Connon, R.W. (1977), 'Hume's MS alterations to the Treatise III', in B.P. Morice (ed.), *David Hume: Bicentenary Papers*, Edinburgh: Edinburgh University Press.

Daly, H. and J. Cobb (1989), *For the Common Good*, Boston: Beacon Press.

Emerson, R.L. (1990), 'Science and moral philosophy in the Scottish Enlightenment', in M.A. Stewart (ed.), *Studies in the Philosophy of the Scottish Enlightenment*, Oxford: Oxford University Press.

Foster, J. (1993), 'Economics and the Self-Organization Approach: Alfred Marshall Revisited', *The Economic Journal*, 103, pp. 975–90.

Frank, R.G. (1980), *Harvey and the Oxford Physiologists*, Berkeley: University of California Press.

Georgescu-Roegen, N. (1971), *The Entropy Law and the Economic Process*, Cambridge, Mass.: Harvard University Press.

Hahn, F.H. (1991), 'The next hundred years', *Economic Journal*, 101 (1), 47–50.

Hobbes, T. (1651) *Leviathan*, reprinted in C.B. Macpherson (ed.) (1968), New York: Penguin.

Hume, D. (1779), *Dialogues Concerning Natural Religion*; reprinted in S. Tweyman (ed.) (1991), London: Routledge.

Hutton, J. (1794), *Dissertation upon the Philosophy of Light, Heat, and Fire*, Edinburgh.

Hutton, J. (1795), *Theory of the Earth with Proofs and Illustrations*, 2 vols, Edinburgh: William Creech.

Ingrao, B. and G. Israel (1990), *The Invisible Hand: Economic Equilibrium in the History of Science*, Cambridge, Mass.: MIT Press.

Kirman, A. (1989), 'The intrinsic limits of modern economic theory', *Economic Journal*, 99 (Conference), 126–39.

McCulloch, J.R. (1833), 'Babbage on machinery and manufactures', *Edinburgh Review*, 59 (January), 313–30.

Malthus, T.R., (1798), *An Essay on the Principle of Population*, London: J. Johnson.

Martinez-Alier, J. (1987), *Ecological Economics: Economics, Environment and Society*, Oxford and New York: Basil Blackwell.

Mill, J.S. (1848), *Principles of Political Economy*, 7th edn (1871), London: Longmans, Green & Co.

Mirowski, P. (1989), *More Heat than Light: Economics as Social Physics*, Cambridge: Cambridge University Press.

Mittelstrass, J. (1988), 'Nature and science in the Renaissance', in R.S. Woolhouse (ed.), *Metaphysics and Philosophy of Science in the 17th and 18th Centuries*, Boston: Kluwer.

Moore, J. (1994), 'Hume and Hutcheson', in M.A. Stewart and J.P. Wright (eds), *Hume and Hume's Connections*, Edinburgh: Edinburgh University Press.

Nelson, R. and S. Winter (1982), *An Evolutionary Theory of Economic Change*, Cambridge, Mass.: Harvard University Press.

Perrings, C., K. Turner and C. Folke (1995), 'Ecological economics: the study of interdependent economic and ecological systems', University of York: Department of Environmental Economic and Environmental Management, January.

Petty, W. (1662), *Treatise of Taxes*; reprinted in Petty (1899).

Petty, W. (1691), *Political Anatomy of Ireland*; reprinted in Petty (1899).

Petty, W. (1899), *Economic Writings of William Petty*, I, ed. W. Hull Cambridge: Cambridge University Press.

Quesnay, F. (1747), *Essai physique sur l'oeconomie animale*, 3 vols, 2 edn, Paris: G. Cavelier.

Rousseau, J.-J. (1755), *Discours sur l'origine et les fondements de l'inégalité*, Amsterdam; reprinted in V. Gourevitch (ed. and trans.), J.-J. Rousseau, *The First and Second Discourses*, New York: Harper & Row.

Say, J.-B. (1803), *Traité d'économie politique*, Paris: Crapelet.

Senior, N. (1836), *An Outline of the Science of Political Economy*, reprinted 1965, New York: Augustus M. Kelley.

Senior, N. (1848), 'J.S. Mill on political economy', *Edinburgh Review*, 88, pp. 297–325.

Smith, A. (1795), *Essays on Philosophical Subjects*, ed. J. Black and J. Hutton; reprinted in W.P.D. Wightman and J.C. Bryce (eds) (1980), *Works and Correspondence of Adam Smith*, Oxford: Clarendon Press.

Veblen, T. (1898), 'Why is economics not an evolutionary science?', *Quarterly Journal of Economics*, 12.

Verri, P. (1773), *Meditazioni sulla economia politica*, Milan; French trans. (An. VIII, 1800), *Economie Politique du Comte Verri*, Paris: Chez Ducauroy.

Walras, L. (1874), *Elements of Pure Economics*, reprinted in W. Jaffe (ed. and trans.) (1954), London: Allen & Unwin.

Whytt, R. (1751), *An Essay on the Vital and Involuntary Motions of Animals*, Edinburgh.

Wright, J. (1983), *The Sceptical Realism of David Hume*, Manchester: Manchester University Press.

2. Theories and methods in ecological economics: a tentative classification

Joan Martinez-Alier, Giuseppe Munda and John O'Neill

ECOLOGICAL ECONOMICS: THE STUDY AND ASSESSMENT OF (UN)SUSTAINABILITY

Ecological economics has been defined as 'the science and management of sustainability' (Costanza, 1991). More modestly, we define ecological economics as 'the study and assessment of (un)sustainability'. Ecological economics does not resort to a unique type of value expressed in a single numeraire. On the contrary, in our view, ecological economics encompasses neoclassical environmental and resource economics, but it also goes beyond it, by including the physical appraisal of the environmental impacts of the human economy.

Ecological economists have often argued in favour of 'methodological pluralism' (Norgaard, 1989). In the tradition of analytical philosophy, Otto Neurath may be seen as an ecological economist both for his part in the discussion in the 1920s on the economics of socialism, where he pointed to uncertain future externalities as one reason for his defence of physical indicators, against commensurability of economic values, and also for his work on the unity of the sciences (O'Neill, 1995). Neurath, though a logical positivist, already advocated a pluralism of methods (Neurath, 1946, p. 232). True, Neurath mistakenly thought that all sciences would advance towards a physicalist language, and this we oppose. We concur with him, however, in his vision of the 'orchestration of the sciences', an encyclopaedia in which the findings of the different sciences would be coordinated, and the contradictions and incompatibilities would be addressed, instead of being dismembered into the departments of the universities and the journals of the different disciplines. Thus, for instance, following Neurath, the explanation of the 'demographic transition', or the judgment on the techniques of agrochemistry or biotechnology, or the views on whether the world economy may still grow tenfold (as recommended by the Brundtland Report), require knowledge of different sciences, and contradictions might arise. A macroeconomic growth model following the Solow–Hartwick rule and a modelling exercise from Meadows *et al.* are different not only in their language and methodology, but also in their predictions (and in their historical explanations, if applied to the past). Ecological economics must address the incompatibilities between them. *This is a most practical task, which should rest on a sound theoretical base.*

The project of ecological economics as an 'orchestration of the sciences' for the study of (un)sustainability fits well with the idea of 'reflexive' or 'self-aware' complex systems. To see ecosystems in terms of 'reflexive complex systems' (O'Connor *et al.*, 1996) implies the study of the human dimensions of ecological change and of the transformations of human environmental perceptions; that is, the introduction of historical human agency and human interpretation in ecology. The metaphor of the 'orchestration of the sciences' also fits well with the idea of 'post-normal science' and 'extended peer review' put forward by Funtowicz and Ravetz (1990, 1991, 1994b). Such democratization of discourse arises from the nature of the problems at hand, from their urgency, their interdisciplinarity, their uncertainty and their irreversibility.

WEAK COMPARABILITY OF VALUES AS A FOUNDATION FOR ECOLOGICAL ECONOMICS

The environment is a site of conflict between competing values and interests and different groups and communities that represent them. How are such conflicts to be resolved? Conventional economics assumes the existence of value commensurability. Is that assumption justified? In the following we argue that it is not.

From a philosophical perspective, it is possible to distinguish between the concepts of *strong comparability* (there exists a single comparative term by which all different actions can be ranked) and *weak comparability* (irreducible value conflict is unavoidable but compatible with rational choice employing practical judgment). Within strong comparability, we distinguish between *strong commensurability* (cardinal scale of measurement) and *weak commensurability* (ordinal scale of measurement) (O'Neill, 1993).

We say that there is strong comparability of values when it is possible to arrange objects or situations to be valued, according to a single type of value. For instance, students in a class may be ordered according to how well they have performed in an exam. The ordering might be as follows, 'first', 'second', 'third'... (weak commensurability), or there might be a cardinal scale of measurement (strong commensurability), by which a student gets '10', another one gets '8.5', the next one gets '7', and so on. A student might be the best student in her class, but from the fact that all students are persons, we may not infer that she is the best person in her class. If someone is 'good' or if something is 'valuable', we must ask on which type of value the judgment is based. There is weak comparability of values (or perhaps incomparability of values) when there are different types of value. Thus, in project evaluation, there would be strong comparability of values in cost–benefit analysis, when the situations to be valued are all valued in the same numeraire (present value in money terms of costs and benefits, including of course externalities). Thus in cost–benefit analysis there is usually strong commensurability, beyond an ordinal ranking of alternatives (Munda, 1996). In contrast, in some forms of multi-criteria evaluation, there is irreducibility among the different types of value. At most, there is only weak comparability. In our view, ecological economics rests on a foundation of weak comparability of values, but it also includes (in appropriate cases) other approaches (contingent valuation, or energy analysis, or 'ecological footprint' analysis in terms of land requirement), which, taken one by one imply strong comparability and even strong commensurability (Martinez-Alier *et al.*, 1998).

A simplified scheme of the possible scientific approaches to environment–economy interactions can be found in Figure 2.1. The left half concerns those approaches using simultaneously several evaluation criteria for analysing

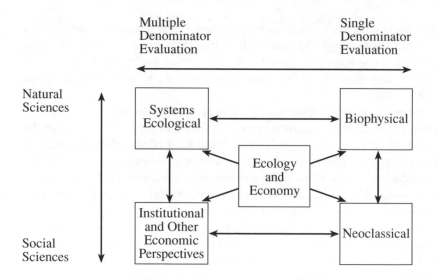

Source: Folke and Kaberger, 1991, p. 275.

Figure 2.1   A simplified conceptual model of ecological and economic perspectives and approaches to environmental issues

the interactions between ecological and economic systems, and the right half those using a single currency for this evaluation, such as money or energy. Ecological economics explicitly refuses the complete commensurability paradigm and recognizes the existence of *incommensurability* of values.

Systemic approaches to environmental issues consider the relationships between three systems: the economic system, the human system and the natural system (Passet, 1996). The economic system includes the economic activities of humans, such as production, exchange and consumption. Given the scarcity phenomenon, such a system is efficiency-oriented. The human system comprises all activities of human beings on our planet. It includes the spheres of biological human elements, of inspiration, of aesthetics, of social conflict and of morality which constitute the frame of human life. Since it is clear that the economic system does not constitute the entire human system, one may assume that the economic system is a subsystem of the human system. Finally, the natural system includes both the human system and the economic system (Nijkamp and Bithas, 1995).

The economy is embedded not only in the social perception of energy and material flows (which is historically changing), but also in social institutions, as shown in Figure 2.2; that is, in the distribution of property rights, the distribution of power and the distribution of income.

Ecological economists understand and even share the conventional economists' valiant attempts to 'internalize' externalities into the price system, and we sympathize with the more realistic 'cost-effectiveness' approach; but we emphasize the uncertainties and complexities which make it difficult to give physical measures of externalities (let alone economic measures) and we

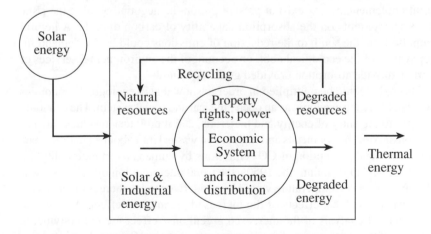

Figure 2.2   The economy embedded in social institutions and in the ecosystem

emphasize also how economic values depend on the intergenerational and intragenerational inequalities in the distribution of the burdens of pollution and in
the access to natural resources. Thus a pioneer ecological economist such as
Kapp saw externalities as 'cost-shifting'. Externalities may be understood as
'ecological distribution conflicts' (Martinez-Alier, 1991; Martinez-Alier and
O'Connor, 1996).

There appear to be cases in some southern countries in which poor children's
sexual services (over which they themselves presumably have property rights)
are sold cheaply to northern tourists; and there are plausible rumours that body
parts are carved up and exported cheaply for transplanting, which might be
deemed an efficient allocation of such 'fictitious commodities' given the
existing distribution of income. ('Fictitious commodities' was Karl Polanyi's
term for land and labour in *The Great Transformation*.)

One good example to show how the economy is embedded in physical
realities and social institutions is the enhanced greenhouse effect. Approximately one-half of the carbon dioxide produced by humans by burning fossil
fuels does not accumulate in the atmosphere, but is placed gratis in the 'natural'
sinks. The rich act therefore as if they were owners of a disproportionate part
of the carbon dioxide absorption capability provided by the new vegetation and
the oceans. The remaining carbon dioxide they dump into the atmosphere, as
if they were also its owners. In this sense, 'joint implementation', that is
exporting carbon dioxide to outside sinks, beyond one's own environmental
space, has been going on for many decades. What is now being proposed is
that, in specific cases, amounting to a minute amount of the excessive emissions
of carbon dioxide, a payment will be made for the use of one of the 'natural'
sinks, new vegetation (Kuik *et al.*, 1994). Therefore such explicit proposals for
joint implementation as exist at present put on the negotiating table the issue
of property rights on the absorption capability of carbon dioxide. A helpful
impulse from the south to the reduction of emissions could be the demand for
repayment of the ecological debt, on account of the environmental services of
carbon dioxide absorption provided gratis up to now.

Examples could be multiplied in order to show that in ecological economics
we should see the economy as an open physical and social system. The economy
is open to the entry of energy and materials, and it produces residues, such as
carbon dioxide, heavy metals and radioactive waste. Until about a hundred years
ago, the social perception of CO_2 emissions by humans as an externality did
not exist, and in fact, until the 1950s, the usual interpretation by scientists was
that an increase in temperature would be good. Even today there is much uncertainty as to the local effects of the increased greenhouse effect. Attempts at
cost–benefit analysis of the increased greenhouse effect are not convincing
because of the arbitrariness of the discount rate (Azar and Sterner, 1996) and also
because many items are not easily measured in physical terms, much less easily

valued in money terms (Funtowicz and Ravetz, 1994b). Moreover, both property values and the economic values of human lives depend on social institutions.

From an ecological perspective, the expansion of the economic subsystem is limited by the size of the overall finite global ecosystem, by its dependence on the life support sustained by intricate ecological connections which are more easily disrupted as the scale of the economic subsystem grows relative to the overall system. Since human expansion, with the associated exploitation and disposal of waste and pollutants, not only affects the natural environment as such but also the level and composition of environmentally produced goods and services required to sustain society, the economic subsystem will be limited by the impacts of its own actions on the environment (Folke, 1991). A central issue, then, is: does any *'optimal' scale* exist for the economy? This point has been tackled especially by Daly.

The term 'scale' is shorthand for 'the physical scale or size of the human presence in the ecosystem, as measured by population times per capita resource use' (Daly, 1991, p. 35). The standard economics point of view about economic growth seems quite optimistic, but as an economy grows, it increases in scale. Scale has a maximum limit defined by either the *regenerative or the absorptive capacity of the ecosystem*; therefore, 'until the surface of the earth begins to grow at a rate equal to the rate of interest' (ibid., p. 40), one should not take this optimistic attitude too seriously. Thus the concept of strong sustainability is needed. Such a definition is based on the assumption that certain sorts of natural capital are deemed critical, and not readily substitutable by man-made capital (Barbier and Markandya, 1990). In particular, the characterization of sustainability in terms of the 'strong' criterion of non-negative change over time in stocks of specified natural capital provides a strong justification for development of non-monetary indicators of ecological sustainability based on *direct physical measurement* of important stocks and flows (Faucheux and O'Connor, 1998; Munda, 1997).

The operationalization of strong sustainability requires biophysical indicators, or 'satellite accounts' of variations in natural patrimony, not integrated in money terms within national income accounting. However, behind a list of indicators there would always be a history of scientific research and political controversy. Moreover, one should note that a list of indicators is far from being a list of targets or limits for those indicators. Also a question arises: how could such indicators be aggregated? Often some indicators improve while others deteriorate. It has to be noted that this is the classical conflictual situation studied in multi-criteria evaluation theory (Munda, 1995); in particular, non-compensatory methods are quite relevant, since compensability implies substitutability between different types of capital (Martinez-Alier *et al.*, 1998).

In the next sections, we discuss the relevance of the incommensurability principle at both the micro and the macro level of analysis. Table 2.1 presents

Table 2.1 *Theories and methods in ecological economics: a proposal for discussion*

Comparability of Values	Macroeconomics	Microeconomics and Environmental Policy	Project Evaluation
Strong comparability *Strong commensurability of values*	'Weak' sustainability Solow–Hartwick rule Pearce–Turner 'constant capital stock' and 'constant natural capital stock' Green GNP (El Serafy's correction) Green GNP (Repetto's correction) Biological and physical indicators of sustainability (e.g. HANPP, MIPS, ecospace, energy cost of energy, etc.).	Internalization of externalities at 'optimum' social level (Turvey's diagram, 1963) Coasian bargaining and fusions Hotelling's rule (1931) Renewable resource management (Gordon-Scott, etc.) Cobb–Douglas, CES and other standard production functions Contingent valuation and similar methods Conventional utility theory, use value, existence value	Cost–benefit analysis (including Krutilla's modification of discount rates applied to 'commodities' and 'amenities')
Weak commensurability of values	Green GNP (Hueting's correction) ISEW (Daly & Cobb)	Cost-effectiveness analysis (and related instruments: markets in emission permits, etc.) Lexicographic ordering of consumer's preferences Industrial ecology and industrial metabolism (Ayres, Ruth, etc.) Biophysical production functions	Cost–benefit analysis (with ordinal rankings only) Cost-effectiveness analysis Compensatory multi-criteria evaluation based on utility functions Discrepancies between WTP and WTA

Weak comparability Incommensurability of values	'Strong' sustainability (in physical accounts), 'satellite' accounts	Social evaluation of environmental limits or standards	Non-compensatory multi-criteria decision aid
	Simultaneous use of monetary and non-monetary indicators by means of reflexive complexity and macroeconomic multi-criteria evaluation	Integrated assessment of sectoral indicators of sustainability (in physical accounts) for urban planning, agriculture, water management, etc.	Environmental impact assessment techniques
	Coevolution	Precautionary principle, liability rule, environmental bonds, and other methods for dealing with uncertainty and 'surprises'	Sagoff's 'consumers' versus 'citizens'
		Eco-auditing, product life cycle analysis and other methods of physical environmental accounting at firm's level	

a tentative classification of theories and methods of ecological economics. The upper part of the table includes environmental and resource economics and the lower part includes ecological economics. While conventional environmental and resource economics rests on principles of compensation and substitution which sometimes might be operative , ecological economics emphasizes the difficulties in substituting for the loss of environmental goods such as biodiversity (which is not even inventoried) or in compensating future generations for the uncertain, irreversible negative externalities we are causing today. There are allocations without any possibility of transactions in actual or fictitious markets. Traditional monetary evaluation methods such as cost–benefit analysis are based on phenomena such as consumer's surpluses, market failures and demand curves which are just a partial point of view, since connected with one institution only: markets. From an ecological economics point of view, issues connected with actions outside of markets and behaviour of people different from the class of consumers should also be taken into account (Duchin and Lange, 1994). As a consequence, theories and methods such as reflexive complexity, biophysical indicators and non-compensatory multi-criteria evaluation become essential.

CHOICE OF INDICATORS, TARGET SETTING AND COST-EFFECTIVENESS

This section deals with the setting of environmental standards and their implementation through green taxes or marketable permits or other instruments. In microeconomics, there is strong commensurability when externalities are internalized into the price system. Thus the definition of a Pigouvian tax as the value of the externality at optimum pollution level implies strong commensurability and also a belief in substantive rationality. 'Cost-effectiveness' (the analysis of which would be the cheapest instrument, in money terms, in order to achieve tolerable levels of pollution, which are themselves socially negotiated) implies, in our view, weak commensurability only, but this is a point which needs more discussion.

In conventional environmental economics, 'external' effects are given present money values. For instance, if a power station produces SO_2, NO_x and CO_2 as by-products, then such externalities are measured in money terms. The external costs, which will depend on the amount of electricity produced, are then compared (in the same numeraire: money) to the profits obtained by producing and selling electricity, attempting to reach the 'optimum' amount of pollution by such a comparison. This is a starting point for many textbooks in environmental economics (for example, Pearce and Turner, 1990). The analysis requires counting the value of the damages, or of remediation work, or of preventive measures. For instance, if the power station works with nuclear energy, we would have to give money values to radioactive waste. Is plutonium a positive or a negative externality? At which rate of discount should future negative (or positive) impacts be discounted, in order to obtain present values? The valuation of future, uncertain, irreversible externalities is not always convincing. This is certainly not a new point in the discussion.

Turvey's diagram (Turvey, 1963) which compares marginal private profits and marginal external costs, in order to determine the 'optimum' amount of pollution, is called in economics a 'partial' equilibrium analysis. It is based on strong commensurability. One critique, from inside economic analysis, is that the modification of prices in one branch or in one firm of the economy (that is, the 'internalization' of externalities into the cost structure) will modify to some extent the pattern of prices in the whole economy. Therefore what is required (always inside the strong commensurability straitjacket) is a 'general' equilibrium analysis. Another critique, which economists such as Baumol and Oates put forward, is that in some cases it is just too difficult to assign money values to 'external' effects, and that economists should settle for something more modest than an 'optimum' amount of pollution. The chosen approach is called 'cost-effectiveness'.

Thus 'critical loads' measure whether discharges are harmful, and they are similar to limits on fishing quotas, or to limits on water extraction, or to standards of air quality, in that such norms are not set by the calculus of marginal costs and marginal benefits but from *outside* the economy. Then the economists come back into the scene to discuss the policy instruments which could be used in order to adjust the economy to such environmental norms. Instruments could be charges or taxes, marketable permits or voluntary agreements, for instance. The cheapest instrument is called the most 'cost-effective' instrument. Let us see one concrete example. A 'critical load' approach to the amounts of SO_2 and NO_x emitted by power stations works as in the European RAINS model, which divides Europe into a grid of squares, and then determines how much acidifying load each square can take without damage, and how much it is actually taking (and where it is coming from). The model is based on the maximum amount of acidifying substances which can be received without damage (the 'critical load'). Such critical loads are different in different parts of Europe, depending for instance on whether the soils are more or less calcareous. How to reduce emissions so that critical loads are not exceeded, and how to achieve such reductions in the cheapest, most 'cost-effective' way? In reality, in the early 1990s, it was decided to close only one part of the gap between the present situation and the desired situation of strict compliance with the 'critical load' norms, so that negotiations were on the 'gap closure' percentage, and on which policy instruments to choose in order to achieve this new norm (Castells and Munda, 1999).

Therefore, even when 'critical loads' exist, the norm accepted may be less ambitious than full compliance. Moreover, critical loads can be contested. Ecological economists are interested not only in the economics of policy instruments but also in researching how such norms are set. The notions of 'postnormal' science and 'extended peer reviews' will again apply. Thus, changing the example, to accept a 'safe' limit of CO_2 concentration in the atmosphere of 300 ppm (which is already exceeded), 400 ppm, 500 ppm or 600 ppm (or any number in between), is largely a matter of political choice. Here it is obvious that there are *several* environmental norms possible. This is explictly acknowledged in many instances, such as water quality standards negotiated quite legally among stakeholders. So the idea of a norm, limit or standard or 'critical load' established from outside the economy by scientific experts (such as the Intergovernmental Panel on Climate Change – IPCC), beyond which the environment is endangered and below which everything remains green, must regrettably be abandoned in practice.

If there were an indisputable norm, we would discuss whether, in money terms (in a single scale of value, and with cardinal measurements), compliance with such a norm could be achieved by a 'cost-effective' instrument A (marketable permits, for instance, with associated monetary costs of $100), or by instrument B (say, taxes, or fines, with associated monetary costs of $200). The context would be strong commensurability despite the fact that the costs of compliance and the benefits of compliance are not compared in the same numeraire. However, if the extended expert and stakeholder 'review process' is allowed for, what we have in practice is a combination of several different physical norms possible, where X is less strict than Y, and Y less strict than Z, and different policy instruments (see Table 2.2).

Table 2.2   Cost of compliance (in money terms) with different physical norms: an imaginary example

	Physical norm X	Physical norm Y	Physical norm Z
Instrument A	$100	$150	$200
Instrument B	$200	$300	$400

One possible ranking of acceptable situations could be:

situation	physical norm	cost
(1)	Z	$200
(2)	Y	$150
(3)	X	$100

Could the three situations be compared in terms of strong commensurability? They could not, for the costs of attaining the norms are expressed in money values, but the norms themselves are in physical terms (for instance, CO_2 emissions). Z is better than Y and Y is better than X in their own physical ranking, but Z is more expensive than Y and Y more expensive than X in money terms.

Which is better: (Z, \$200), (Y, \$150) or (X, \$100)? Perhaps a discussion would lead to a judgment that the improvement of Z over Y is really worth the extra economic cost, and also that Y is 'better' than X, at the extra economic cost. Or perhaps the judgment could be that, given the costs of compliance, Y is better than X and X is better than Z. In both cases we would have an ordinal ranking of alternatives; that is, weak commensurability. Perhaps, however, a consistent ranking of the three alternatives proves impossible to achieve. Then, in this case, 'cost-effectiveness' could not make it even to the weak commensurability grade, and it would 'fall down' into weak comparability only, that is incommensurability operationalized by means of multi-criteria evaluation. Clearly, however, the analysis of 'cost-effectiveness' requires further work, which should no longer be focused mainly on instruments but on the social evaluation processes and reflexive practices which lead to the choice of concrete indicators and target setting. In the next section we will extend the discussion to macroeconomics.

GREEN NATIONAL ACCOUNTING AND PHYSICAL INDICES OF (UN)SUSTAINABILITY

The purpose of 'green accounting' is to provide information on the ecological (un)sustainability of the economy, but there is no settled doctrine on how to combine different and sometimes contradictory indices in a way immediately useful for policy (in the sense that GNP or other macroeconomic statistics have been useful for policy). How to count depletion of resources, when they are not inventoried, or when no property rights exist? How to monetize non-market impacts (because of trade or because of international externalities such as carbon dioxide 'exports') outside, for example, the European borders? Leaving money values aside, how to integrate the physical indicators themselves? Different physical indicators will sometimes show contradictory trends, and then 'aggregation' of indicators (in order to be able to rank situations) becomes difficult.

The aim of this section is to dispel confusion in the assessment of (un)sustainability, by carefully classifying and discussing, in practical terms, the proposals for green accounting and for physical indices of (un)sustainability.

Our objective is to help create a consensus on the respective place of, and the relations among, the tools for assessing (un)sustainability.

Does the expression 'taking nature into account' imply money valuation, or rather appraisal through physical indices (which themselves might show contradictory trends)? Are countries, regions, cities moving towards sustainability or away from sustainability? Which is (are) the 'measuring rod(s)' to be employed? For instance, statistics are available which show that the Netherlands is sustainable (in the 'weak' sense of the word), while other statistics (on environmental space) show the Netherlands occupying 15 times their own territory, that is, appropriating the 'carrying capacity' of a much larger territory than their own. Such incongruences (if such they are) also apply to Japan, for instance.

Some believe that computation of 'weak sustainability' in money terms (equivalent to 'net capital accumulation' or to the 'genuine savings' published by the World Bank) is easily achievable, even including trade flows, once some technical difficulties are solved, but many believe that there is no methodology for assigning monetary values to future, uncertain, irreversible environmental damages. Also in macroeconomics, the proposals to correct GNP measures in a 'green' direction, as introduced by El Serafy (Yusuf *et al.*, 1989), the results of which in actual practice will depend more than anything else on a rate of discount or interest chosen arbitrarily, do not go beyond strong commensurability in money terms. Not all receipts from the sale of exhaustible resources should be included in GNP. Only one part should be included – 'true' income – and the rest is counted as 'decapitalization' or the 'user cost' of such 'natural capital' which should be invested at compound interest over the period until the resource is exhausted, so as to allow the country to live at the same standard of living even when running out of the resource. This is an interesting proposal for correcting the macroeconomic accounts. It is based on a notion of 'weak sustainability' only. But other criteria are available in order to judge whether the economy moves towards sustainability.

A number of indicators and indices have been proposed in order to judge the overall impact of the human economy on the environment. We shall leave aside monetary indicators which correct GNP. These would include Cobb and Daly's Index of Sustainable Economic Welfare. Calculating ISEW involves qualitative assessments (for instance, which expenditures to include as 'defensive expenditures', which algorithms to use in order to evaluate inequality in the distribution of income) (Daly and Cobb, 1989) and, in this sense, the strong comparability of the ISEW, a monetary indicator, calculated for different countries and periods, is not so straightforward as it would appear. This is why, in Table 2.1, ISEW is classified under 'weak commensurability'. In this section, we take knowledge of 'green' corrections to GNP for granted (and the related discussion on 'weak' and 'strong' sustainability; see also Cabeza Gutes, 1996,

O'Connor *et al.*, 1996, Gowdy,1996, Munda, 1997) and go on to provide a short list of some physical synthetic indicators and indices.

1. HANPP (human appropriation of net primary production) was proposed by Vitousek *et al.* (1986). The NPP is the amount of energy that primary producers, the plants, make available for the rest of living species, the heterotrophs. Of this NPP, humankind 'coopts' about 40 per cent in terrestrial ecosystems, according to Vitousek *et al.*'s calculations. The higher HANPP is, the less biomass is available for 'wild' biodiversity.

The proportion of NPP appropriated by humans is increasing because of population growth, and also because of increasing demands on land per person, for urbanization, for growing feedstuffs, for growing timber ('plantations are not forests' is a slogan of environmental activists in the Tropics).

This indicator should be regionalized, in the world and inside Europe. Thus, in Latin America as a whole, the part of NPP 'coopted' by the local population is still much lower than in Europe or in Southeast Asia. However, pressure on NPP comes not only from population density in the region itself, but also from pressure of exports. Therefore HANPP and 'environmental space' (or 'ecological footprint') are related measures.

2. MIPS is an indicator, developed at the Wuppertal Institute (Schmidt-Bleek, 1994), which adds up all the materials used for production directly and also indirectly (the 'ecological rucksack'). The materials include mineral ores, the energy carriers such as coal or oil, and all biomass, including the whole product 'life cycle', that is, the disposal or recycling phases. This is the material input which is *measured in tons*. It then compares the material input with the services provided, sector by sector (and, in principle, for the whole economy). For instance, in order to provide the service of travel of one passenger one kilometre, or in order to provide the service of living space of so many square metres, which is the amount of materials involved, comparing different regions in the world, or historically? Comparisons over time of the material requirements of the economy (direct and indirect) will show whether there is really a trend towards *dematerialization* of the economy. It may of course be objected that tons of materials say nothing about the toxicity of the materials used or of their residues. MIPS is a synthetic indicator, but again not the only one.

3. The material intensity of consumption. When MIPS are calculated there are difficulties in determining the services provided. For instance, one passenger kilometre might be considered a clear unit of service, but perhaps travelling by car (higher MIPS) or travelling by train (lower MIPS) should be considered different life experiences. Needs and tastes are so complex that one may understand the conventional economist's temptation to consider only preferences revealed in actual or fictitious markets, through willingness to pay. In contrast to conventional economics, ecological economics adopts the principle of irreducibility of needs.[1] There is no general principle of substitution amongst

goods and services; rather, some goods and services are more important, and cannot be replaced by other goods and services. There is a connection between Georgescu-Roegen's early work in the 1930s on utility theory (and on what was later called 'lexicographic ordering of preferences') and the physical view of the economy which he developed in the 1960s and which culminated in *The Entropy Law and the Economic Process* (1971) (cf. Gowdy, 1992). Thus, for instance, the minimum amount of endosomatic energy necessary for human life cannot be replaced or compensated by anything else. However, this does not mean that ecological economics adopts a biological, reductionist view of human needs. On the contrary, ecological economists adopt Lotka's distinction between endosomatic consumption and exosomatic use of energy (also of materials) and we point out that the human species has no genetic instructions as regards exosomatic use. There are enormous intraspecific differences.

To call the endosomatic consumption of food energy (of 1500 or 2000 kcal per person/day) a 'revealed preference' would be to betray the economist's metaphysical viewpoint. But to call either the endosomatic consumption of 1500 or 2000 kcal, or the exosomatic use of 100 000 kcal or 200 000 kcal per person/day, a 'socially constructed need or want', and to go no further, as those with an institutional approach to economics would perhaps do, would be to leave aside the ecological explanations and/or ecological implications of such use of energy.

4.   There is another approach, which is currently becoming an important element in the study of (un)sustainability. It builds upon Maslow's work on needs from social psychology, on Georgescu-Roegen's 'principle of irreducibility' of needs, and on the 'basic needs' approach in development economics. This novel approach analyses the 'satisfactors' employed to satisfy needs. According to Max-Neef (Max-Neef *et al.*, 1995) all humans have the same needs, described as 'subsistence', 'affection', 'knowledge' and so on, and there is no generalized principle of substitution among them. Such needs can be satisfied by a variety of 'satisfactors'. For instance, 'subsistence' implies, at one level, endosomatic energy intake, and in this sense there is only one possible 'satisfactor', kcal or joules, but food may come in many different forms. There might be vegetarians by tradition, choice or income level, but also there might be a Veblenian conspicuous consumption of meat, as in Spain or Italy in the last 30 years. The 'satisfactors' of other types of needs are still more varied. Research by Jackson and Marks (1999) has asked the following question: 'How material and energy-intensive are the "satisfactors" of non-material needs?'

Instead of taking economic services as given, as in MIPS (passenger kilometres, square metres of living space) and then computing the material inputs throughout the whole product life cycle to provide such services, Jackson and Marks (building on Max-Neef) discuss the services themselves: for instance, why is there so much travel; why is there so much new building (instead of restoration); which are the needs which are being satisfied in such a material and energy-intensive manner? Taking the British standard of life around 1950 as a standard of life which satisfied material needs, their research considers that there is a trend to use 'satisfactors' which are themselves very intensive in energy and materials in order to satisfy predominantly 'non–material' needs. Duchin's research on household lifestyles through input–output analysis (Duchin, 1996) attempts to show the material and energy requirements in order to provide for alternative patterns of consumption.

5. EROI. This acronym, coined by Charles Hall, stands for energy return on (energy) input, and it was the first physical indicator widely employed in ecological economics in the 1970s, mainly by direct or indirect disciples of Howard Odum. In fact, the idea of looking at the basic economics of human society, and particularly of agriculture, as a flow of energy, goes back to the 1880s, through Podolinsky's work, if not earlier (Martinez-Alier, 1987). Clearly, for an economy to be sustainable, the energy productivity of human labour (that is, how much energy is made available per day, by one day of human work) must be higher (or equal, if everybody is working) than the efficiency of the transformation of energy intake into human work. This is a minimum condition for sustainability. However, as Podolinsky himself wrote, the economies of hunter gatherers and of agriculturalists were different from industrial economies. The energy productivity of a coal miner was much larger than that which a primitive agriculturalist could obtain, but this energy surplus from fossil fuels was transitory: it was not sustainable because coal reserves were limited.[2] We may ask: is there a trend towards an increasing energy cost of obtaining energy? (See Cleveland, 1991.)

In the 1970s there were a number of studies on energy flow in agriculture, of which the best known were those of Pimentel (Pimentel *et al.*, 1973) showing the decreasing energy efficiency in maize cultivation in the United States. The human labour input had become very small, but energy inputs in the form of fuel for machinery, pesticides and fertilizers increased in proportion more than the energy in the crop. Perhaps in Europe the trend towards decreasing energy efficiency in agriculture was halted in the 1970s because of the increase in oil prices (Bonny and Dauce, 1989, cited by Passet, 1996, p. 179). In any case, a fruitful new field of research was opened by such studies (historic and cross-section) on the efficiency of the use of energy in different sectors of the economy, including the energy sector itself.

Naturally, although all kinds of energy can be counted in the same units, not all sources of energy have the same meaning from other points of view. In use, some forms of energy are more versatile than others. In origin, some arise from non-renewable resources and/or in their use they have more negative impacts than other sources. There have been attempts at giving equivalencies between types of energy (aside from their energy contents) but the ratios for transforming the values of different types of energy seem to be based (in our view) on ad hoc decisions.

The analysis of energy flow which has been a constant feature of ecological economics since its beginnings over one hundred years ago does not imply the 'energy dogmas' denounced by Nicholas Georgescu-Roegen. It is true that in the 1970s there was a strong belief that economic and social policy advice could be based on the study of energy efficiencies (Odum, 1971, Slesser, 1979), coming close to a revival of the 'social energetics' of 1900. Figures of use of energy (mainly EROI) are one more indicator (macroeconomic or sectoral), which does not supersede other indicators, such as *material* balances in 'industrial ecology' or in the study of 'industrial metabolism' (Ayres, 1989; Ayres *et al.*, 1994). Such interesting contradictions among the trends of physical indicators and indices are grist for the mills of multi-criteria evaluation.

It is relatively easy to reach consensual figures on energy efficiency, but the economic meaning of such figures is a different question. Max Weber, in 1909, wrote that Wilhelm Ostwald's discussion of economic history in terms of (a) an increased use of energy and (b) *also*, an increased efficiency in the use of energy, was irrelevant, because the adoption of new industrial processes or new products had little to do with energy efficiency; it had to do with price relations. Nowadays we interpret Ostwald's propositions in the sense that energy relations sometimes point in a contrary direction to price relations because energy is 'too' cheap as a result of the discrepancy between biogeochemical time and economic time. The economy discounts the future.

6.   The concepts of ecospace and ecological footprint, with similar contents, address the following issue: which is the demand for natural resources which an economy makes, expressing this demand in terms of space?

The authors who have developed the ideas on environmental space, ecospace or the ecological footprint (Opschoor, 1995; Rees, 1996) would concur on the crucial importance of time in ecological economics. However, for practical purposes, they chose to give a spatial representation of the environmental load of the economy. Rather than asking what population a particular region or country can support sustainably, which would depend not only on its geography and resources but also on its average level of exosomatic consumption of energy and materials, on the material and energy intensity of the technologies employed and on the ecological terms of trade (that is, whether the region is a victim of, or profits from, ecologically unequal exchange), the question of carrying capacity becomes: how large an area of productive land is needed in order to sustain a given population indefinitely, at its current standard of living, and with current technologies? (See Rees, 1996, p. 203.)

In German, the discussion on ecospace makes use of the word *Umweltraum*, which philologically is similar to the word *Lebensraum* that came from scientific ecology and then was taken over by the Nazis. Although *Umweltraum* as used today does not refer to a space to which a people claims a 'natural' right, still it reminds us that someone has appropriated a carrying capacity which in principle belongs to somebody else. Environmental space (see, for example, Buitenkamp *et al.*, 1993) is a notion related to the ecological footprint, or appropriated carrying capacity, and also to the notion of Dasman, applied to India by Gadgil and Guha (1995), of 'ecosystem people' versus 'ecological trespassers': the contrast between people living on their own resources and people living on the resources of other territories and peoples.

The main categories of land use for the calculation of the ecological footprint would be as follows:

- crop and grazing land required to produce the current diet (the sea area could also be included);
- land for wood plantations for timber and paper;
- land occupied or degraded or built over, as urban land;
- land needed to absorb CO_2 emissions through photosynthesis, or alternatively land required to produce the ethanol equivalent to current fossil energy consumption.

In Rees' home town of Vancouver, the respective figures for these four items, per person, would be 1 hectare, 0.6 ha., 0.2 ha. and 2.3 ha. (of middle-aged Northern temperate forest): that is, over 4 hectares per person. Notice that only CO_2 is translated into a land requirement, and not other wastes, such as domestic waste, or other greenhouse gases, or radioactive waste – not for any reason of principle, but because of difficulty of computation. Notice also that the water catchment area and the waste water disposal area are not included. (For more details, see Wackernagel and Rees, 1995).

Similar computations, not for cities or metropolitan regions (whose 'ecological footprint' is hundreds of times larger than their own territories) but for whole countries, show that some densely populated European countries (assuming per capita ecofootprints of only 3 ha.) or Japan or Korea (with per capita ecofootprints of only 2 ha.) occupy ecospaces 10 times larger (for the Netherlands, 15 times larger) than their own territories.

7. Why so many different indicators – it may be asked – when there could be a unique physical indicator of whether human impact on the environment is excessive, simply by using the concept of carrying capacity, as defined in ecology: the maximum population of a given species (frogs in a lake, for instance) that can be supported sustainably in that given territory, without spoiling its resource base? Authors who come from a background in biology and from an emphasis on population growth, such as Paul Ehrlich and his collaborators, have, over the years, become aware of the shortcomings of the notion of carrying capacity applied to humans. This is why they proposed the

formulation I = PAT, where I is the human impact on the environment, P is human population, A is affluence and T is technology. Compared to the physical indicators previously described, all of which may be calculated with a reasonable amount of consensus on computation, the formula I = PAT has been up to now a teaching metaphor, a symbolic device (Duchin, 1996, p. 289). T stands for the effects of technology on the environment per unit of affluence, but how is it to be operationalized? In terms of material intensity? in terms of energy intensity? in terms of impact on biodiversity? This will be a growing field of research in the coming years.

The definition of carrying capacity is irrelevant for humans, for several reasons. First, the human ability to establish large differences in exosomatic use of energy and materials means that the first question should be, maximum population at which level of consumption? Second, human technologies change at a much quicker pace than in other species; thus an early objection to the use of carrying capacity was Boserup's thesis, according to which changes in agricultural systems defined as shortening of rotation period were seen as responses to increases in population density, turning the tables on the Malthusian argument. Boserup's thesis of endogenous technical change is relevant for the development of agriculture until the change in techniques around 1840 in industrial countries, when outside inputs into agriculture became the defining trait of the technology based on the new knowledge of agricultural chemistry. Third, the territories occupied by humans are not given. We compete with other species, which are pushed into corners, as shown by the Vitousek *et al.*'s (1986) indicator of Human Appropriation of the Net Primary Production of Biomass. Also, inside the human species, territoriality is socially and politically constructed. This is why migration from Sweden to Spain, or vice versa, is nowadays free inside the European Union, while many people die at sea every year trying to cross illegally, but not unnaturally, from Morocco into Spain.

There is still another reason why the notion of carrying capacity is not directly applicable to humans, in any particular territory. This is international trade. Trade may be seen, indeed, as the appropriation of the carrying capacity of other territories, as we have seen in the discussion on the ecological footprint and ecospace. Between the two extremes of globalization of production based on the growth of trade, and no trade at all, there is room for an ecologically sensible middle position. Even from a strict bioregional point of view, it might be argued (Pfaundler, 1902) that if one territory lacks one very necessary item which is abundantly present in another territory, then Liebig's 'law of the minimum' would recommend exchange. Therefore the joint carrying capacity of all territories would be larger than the sum of the carrying capacity of all such autarchic territories. This point of view links up with recent proposals for fair and ecological trade, coming from non-governmental organizations.

CONCLUSIONS

Ecological economics includes the attempts to construct a 'green' GNP (by means of appropriate corrections, such as those proposed by Hueting, El Serafy, Repetto, Leipert and so on), and it includes the construction of alternative indices such as ISEW (measured also on the single dimension of money). Ecological economics goes beyond one single dimension of value, and resorts to monetary and non-monetary indicators and indices, such as those we have described, in order to assess (un)sustainability. So far, the elementary question of whether a given country's economy is moving towards sustainability or away from sustainability cannot be answered with consensus on the 'measuring rod(s)' to be employed. Moreover, a further question arises: how could such indicators be aggregated? Often some indicators improve while others deteriorate. For instance, when incomes grow, SO_2 might go down while CO_2 increases, or, at a different level of aggregation, MIPS might improve while HANPP deteriorates. It must be noted that this is the classical conflictual situation studied in multi-criteria evaluation theory.

In microeconomics, ecological economists understand the conventional economists' attempts to 'internalize' externalities into the price system. Such attempts are successful in some specific cases only. We emphasize also how economic values depend on the intergenerational and intragenerational inequalities in the distribution of the burdens of pollution and in the access to natural resources. We emphasize the uncertainties and complexities which make it difficult to give physical measures of externalities (let alone economic measures). We think that ecological economics must explicitly refuse the complete commensurability paradigm and recognize the existence of *incommensurability* of values, mainly because the environment is a site of conflict among competing values and interests and among different groups and communities that represent them.

In a postnormal science framework, any recommendations which emerge should be defensible to the technical expert, but also to politicians, the media and the various stakeholders. This does not imply that a consensus will be reached. Indeed, the possibility of irreconcilable differences is recognized and catered for by promoting a plurality of approaches.

Since multi-criteria evaluation techniques are based on a 'constructive' rationality and allow one to take into account conflictual, multidimensional, incommensurable and uncertain effects of decisions, they look like a promising assessment framework for (micro and macro) environmental policy. Multi-criteria evaluation techniques cannot solve all conflicts, but they can help to provide more insight into the nature of conflicts and into ways to arrive at political compromises in case of divergent preferences, and values, so increasing the transparency of the choice process.

ACKNOWLEDGMENTS

Comments by Charles Hall, Jae-Youg Ko, M. Ruth and an anonymous referee are gratefully acknowledged.

NOTES

1. Nicholas Georgescu-Roegen, 'Utility', in *Encyclopedia of Social Sciences*.
2. Podolinsky wrote also that, at the meeting of the British Society for the Advancement of Science in the autumn of 1878, Sterry Hunt had proposed a theory of climatic change in geological periods according to carbon dioxide contents in the atmosphere. This was some years before Arrhenius established the theory of the greenhouse effect.

REFERENCES

Ayres, R.U. (1989), 'Industrial metabolism', in J. Ausubel (ed.), *Technology and Environment*, Washington, DC: National Academy Press.
Ayres, R.U., W.H. Schlesinger and R.H. Socolow (1994), 'Human impacts on the carbon and nitrogen cycles', in R. Socolow, C. Andrews, F. Berkhout and V. Thomas (eds), *Industrial Ecology and Global Change*, New York: Cambridge University Press.
Azar, C. and T. Sterner (1996), 'Discounting and distributional considerations in the context of global warming', *Ecological Economics*, 19(2), 169–84.
Barbier, E.B. and A. Markandya (1990), 'The conditions for achieving environmentally sustainable growth', *European Economic Review*, 34, 659–69.
Buitenkamp, M. *et al.* (eds) (1993), *Action Plan Sustainable Netherlands*, Amsterdam: Friends of the Earth.
Cabeza Gutes, M. (1996), 'The concept of weak sustainability', *Ecological Economics*, 17(3), 147–56.
Castells N. and G. Munda (1996), 'International environmental issues: towards a new integrated assessment approach', in M. O'Connor and C. Spash (eds), *Valuation and Environment*, E. Elgar, Cheltenham: 309–27.
Cleveland, C. (1991), 'Natural resource scarcity and economic growth revisited: economic and biophysical perspectives', in R. Costanza (ed.), *Ecological Economics: the science and management of sustainability*, New York: Columbia University Press.
Costanza R. (ed.) (1991), *Ecological Economics: the science and management of sustainability*, New York: Columbia University Press.
Daly H.E. (1991), 'Elements of environmental macroeconomics', in R. Costanza (ed.), *Ecological Economics: the science and management of sustainability*, New York: Columbia University Press.
Daly H.E. and J.J. Cobb (1989), *For the Common Good: redirecting the economy toward community, the environment and a sustainable future*, Boston: Beacon Press.
Duchin, F. (1996), 'Ecological Economics: the second stage', in R. Costanza, O. Segura and J. Martinez-Alier (eds), *Getting Down to Earth: practical applications of ecological economics*, Washington, DC: Island Press/ISEE.
Duchin F. and G.M. Lange (1994), *The Future of the Environment*, Oxford: Oxford University Press.

Faucheux S. and M. O'Connor (1998), 'Weak and strong sustainability', in S. Faucheux and M. O'Connor (eds), *Valuation for Sustainable Development: Methods and policy indicators*, Cheltenham, UK and Lyme, US: Edward Elgar.

Folke C. (1991), 'Socio-economic dependence on the life-supporting environment', in C. Folke and T. Kaberger (eds), *Linking the Natural Environment and the Economy: Essays from the Eco-Eco Group*, Dordrecht: Kluwer.

Folke C. and T. Kaberger (1991), 'Recent trends in linking the natural environment and the economy', in C. Folke and T. Kaberger (eds), *Linking the Natural Environment and the Economy: Essays from the Eco-Eco Group*, Dordrecht: Kluwer.

Funtowicz, S.O. and J.R. Ravetz (1990), *Uncertainty and Quality in Science for Policy*, Dordrecht: Kluwer Academic Publishers.

Funtowicz, S.O. and J.R. Ravetz (1991), A new scientific methodology for global environmental issues, in R. Costanza (ed.), *Ecological Economics: the science and management of sustainability*, New York: Columbia University Press.

Funtowicz, S.O. and J.R. Ravetz (1994a), 'Emergent complex systems', *Futures*, 26(6), 568–82.

Funtowicz, S.O. and J.R. Ravetz (1994b), 'The worth of a songbird: ecological economics as a post-normal science', *Ecological Economics*, 10, 197–207.

Gadgil M. and R. Guha (1995), *Ecology and Equity. The use and abuse of nature in contemporary India*, London and New York: Routledge.

Georgescu-Roegen, N. (1971), *The Entropy Law and the Economic Process*, Cambridge, Mass.: Harvard University Press.

Gowdy, J. (1992), 'Georgescu Roegen's Utility theory applied to environmental economics', in J.C. Dragan, M. Demetrescu and E. Seifert (eds), *Entropy and Bioeconomics*, Milan: Nagard Publishers.

Gowdy, J. (1996), 'Sustainability as a concept of social science: Economic concepts of sustainability', paper presented in UNESCO-MOST project 'Sustainability as a concept of social sciences', Frankfurt.

Hueting, R. (1992), 'Calculating a sustainable national income: A practical solution for a theoretical dilemma', in M.C. Demetrescu, J.C. Dragan and E.K. Seifert (eds), *Entropy and Bioeconomics*, Milan: Nagard Publishers.

Jackson, T. and N. Marks (1999), 'Consumption, sustainable welfare and human needs: with reference to UK expenditure patterns between 1954 and 1994', *Ecological Economics*, 28, 421–41.

Kuik, O., P. Peters and N. Schrijver (1994), *Joint implementation to curb climate change*, Dordrecht: Kluwer.

Martinez-Alier J. (1987), *Ecological Economics*, Oxford: Basil Blackwell.

Martinez-Alier, J. (1991), 'Environmental policy and distributional conflicts', in R. Costanza (ed.), *Ecological Economics: the science and management of sustainability*, New York: Columbia University Press.

Martinez-Alier J. and M. O'Connor (1996), 'Ecological and economic distribution conflicts', in R. Costanza, O. Segura and J. Martinez-Alier (eds), *Getting Down to Earth: practical applications of ecological economics*, Washington, DC: Island Press/ISEE.

Martinez-Alier J., G. Munda and J. O'Neill (1998), 'Weak comparability of values as a foundation for ecological economics', *Ecological Economics*, 26, 277–86.

Max-Neef, M., A. Elizalde and M. Hopenhayn (1995), *Desarrollo a escala humana*, Barcelona: Icaria.

Munda, G. (1995), *Multicriteria Evaluation in a Fuzzy Environment. Theory and applications in ecological economics*, Heidelberg: Physica-Verlag.

Munda, G. (1996), 'Cost–benefit analysis in integrated environmental assessment: some methodological issues', in *Ecological Economics*, 19 (2), 157–68.

Munda, G. (1997), 'Environmental economics, ecological economics and the concept of sustainable development', *Environmental Values*, 6 (2), 213–33.

Neurath, O. (1946), 'The orchestration of the sciences by the encyclopedism of logical empiricism', reprinted in R.S. Cohen and M. Neurath (eds) (1983), *Philosophical Papers 1913–1946*, Dordrecht: Reidel.

Nijkamp P. and K. Bithas (1995), 'Scenarios for sustainable cultural heritage planning: a case study of Olympia', in H. Coccossis and P. Nijkamp (eds), *Planning for our Cultural Heritage*, Aldershot: Avebury.

Norgaard, R.B. (1989), 'The case for methodological pluralism', *Ecological Economics*, 1, 37–57.

O'Connor M., S. Faucheux, G. Froger, S.O. Funtowicz and G. Munda (1996), 'Emergent complexity and procedural rationality: post-normal science for sustainability', in R. Costanza, O. Segura and J. Martinez-Alier (eds), *Getting Down to Earth: practical applications of ecological economics*, Washington, DC: Island Press/ISEE.

Odum, H.T. (1971), *Environment, Power and Society*, New York: John Wiley.

O'Neill, J. (1993), *Ecology, Policy and Politics*, London: Routledge.

O'Neill, J. (1995), 'In partial praise of a positivist', *Radical Philosophy*, 74, 29–38.

Opschoor, J.B. (1995), 'Ecospace and the fall and rise of throughput intensity', *Ecological Economics*, 15(2), 137–40.

Passet R. (1996), *L'économique et le vivant*, 2nd edn, Paris: Payot.

Pearce, D.W. and R.K. Turner (1990), *Economics of Natural Resources and the Environment*, Baltimore: Johns Hopkins University Press.

Pfaundler, L. (1902), 'Die Weltwirtschaft im Lichte der Physik', *Deutsche Revue*, 22.

Pimentel, D. *et al.* (1973), Food production and the energy crisis', *Science*, 182, 443–4.

Rees, W.E. (1996), 'Revisiting carrying capacity: Area based indicators of sustainability', *Population and Environment: A Journal of Interdisciplinary Studies*, 17(39), January .

Ruth M. (1995), 'Thermodynamic constraints on optimal depletion of copper and aluminium in the United States: a dynamic model of substitution and technical change', *Ecological Economics*, 15, 197–213.

Schmidt-Bleek, F. (1994), *Wieviel umwelt braucht der mensch? MIPS Das Mass für ökologisches wirtschaften*, Berlin: Birkhäuser.

Slesser, M. (1979), *Energy in the economy*, London: Macmillan.

Turvey, R. (1963), 'On divergences between social cost and private cost', *Economica*, August.

Vitousek, Peter, Paul Ehrlich, Anne Ehrlich and Pamela Matson (1986), 'Human appropriation of the products of photosynthesis', *Bioscience*, 34(6), 368–73.

Wackernagel, M. and W.E. Rees (1995), *Our Ecological Footprint: Reducing human impact on the earth*, Gabriola Island, BC and Philadelphia: New Society Publishers.

Yusuf, J.A., S. El Serafy and E. Lutz (1989), 'Environmental accounting for sustainable development', a UNEP World Bank Symposium, Washington, DC.

3. The improvisation of discordant knowledges

Richard B. Norgaard

Many are frustrated by our inability to come to a shared understanding of the meaning of sustainability. How can we work together to achieve a common goal when the term elicits widely divergent reactions from ecologists, economists and entrepreneurs, to say nothing of the dissonance in the responses of Eskimo and Ecuadoreans. Ecologists emphasize the excessive human pressure put on ecosystems, while economists see a multitude of externalities that need to be internalized. It would be easier if each of us held the same understanding. On deeper reflection, we realize that it would be even better, however, if our different understandings complemented each other in a rich, harmonious whole reflecting the complexity of the problems we face. Holding the same understanding would be comparable to each of us playing a single instrument and hitting the same notes together. Holding complementary understandings would be comparable to having each of us playing the different instruments of an orchestra or a large band. To play together takes a more elaborate score and considerable practice, but an ensemble of instruments provides richer, more varied sounds and is far more interesting. The global discourse on sustainability, however, sounds like musicians who have just brought their instruments in from the blustery February streets of New York and are just beginning to warm them up on the stage of Carnegie Hall. Even the biennial conferences of the like-minded members of our International Society for Ecological Economics remind me of young musicians from several dozen high schools converging on Saturday morning on the local college campus for 'band day'. How might our raucous efforts lead to sustainability?

Globally, a multitude of different voices further contribute to the cacophony. Many scientific disciplines are involved, all speaking in their special tongues. Business interests are raging about the difficulties of regulation, while advertising in our newspapers about all of their wonderful environmental achievements. Labourers, mothers and a multitude of others with critical experiential knowledge are trying to be heard. Talk-show hosts declare that no one knows how many species there are anyway and that climate has changed naturally before. The international development community is arguing that free trade will solve everything. Those still waiting for the development that was supposed to come their way are loudly complaining. And the voices of indigenous peoples are in the distant corner. Getting such discordant voices together is surely hopeless. And yet hope springs eternal and many of us work furtively towards a new convergence of understanding.

I emphasize in this chapter the importance of understanding to achieving sustainability. I am not arguing that other factors are less important. I am not forgetting the tremendous importance of corporate power, individual greed, unequal wealth, short-sightedness, and other social ills and human frailties. Let me be specific.

When I gave the paper on which this chapter is based as a keynote address in Boston, I acknowledged at the beginning of my talk that the orchestra metaphor had a very serious problem. A percussion section is critical to provide and change the beat, introduce and close movements, build tension and complement dramatic passages, but, while the rest of the instrumentalists are just warming up, the percussion section is in full swing. In tantalizing, inane synchrony, the triangles are dinging, *consume, consume, consume*; the cymbals are clashing, *grow, grow, grow*; the snare drum is snarling *work, work, work, compete, compete, compete*; the tympani, with their multiple, variable and mellow tones, have assumed the more complex and socially awkward message of *take-over–lay-off, take-over–lay-off*; while the bass drum is deeply booming, *globalize, globalize, globalize*. With such a percussion section, the possible scores are limited to brain-deadening titles like 'March to the Market'. Clearly, if we are going to orchestrate sustainability, something has to be done with the drums.

Towards the end of my talk in Boston, I came to the awkward realization that the metaphor of an orchestra has yet another major failing. Musicians rarely get to choose the scores they play together or even choose their own conductor. Today our problem is that the musicians have been practising different scores and no conductor is in sight. Only the inane percussion section is together. And yet, even though the metaphor of orchestrating knowledges does not seem appropriate today, it can help us understand the recent past, our expectations for the present, and the appropriateness of a new metaphor, that of improvisation, for the future.

I develop the following arguments. First, differences in understanding are especially noticeable today; second, the modern orchestration of knowledge was initially soothing; but third, modern premises about the nature of knowledge also helped produce today's dissonance in our knowledges; and fourth, a new improvisation is arising that could prove to be quite revolutionary.

DISCORDANT KNOWLEDGES

Let me first summarize the nature of the cacophony we hear while trying to modify the old development 'score' to make it more environmentally sustainable. It is important to keep in mind that sustainability is not the only problem. Those addressing the problems of equity, health, drugs, crime, refugees, peace and a host of other social issues also find they are dealing with discordant knowledges. I argue in the next section that the dissonance is a part of the transition from modernity to another phase of human history and that this transition is being experienced by all.

Environmental problems seem to arise where scientists disagree most, in the gaps between our disciplines. As we look at the disciplinary organization of knowledge, we see separate cultures of like-minded people working together on separate problems, as if they were on separate islands. On each island, scientists share what they have been learning together, developing their own language in the process. When trying to bridge their knowledge in a fuller picture of the complexities of the larger whole, the inhabitants of each island invoke common assumptions and evolve a shared set of myths about the world beyond their island that they do not study. And with repeated invocation and sharing, the assumptions and myths become ever more tightly bound up with the inhabitants' understanding of their island itself (Norgaard, 1992). Unfortunately, environmental problems are complex and tend to drape themselves over numerous islands in a most unstructured way, forcing scientists with different cultures from different islands to actually try to combine their understandings in order to comprehend the problem. But after decades of effort encouraging interdisciplinary scientific ventures, sharing knowledge across the disciplines continues to be hampered by the differences in the languages, knowledges, assumptions and myths associated with the scientific cultures and disciplinary islands created through the social organization of science.

Some scientists have looser ties to the island that honoured them with a PhD and communicate and work out problems together a little better. Interdisciplinary teams are beginning to make music together. But their orchestrations are typically touted as unscientific by the keepers of the truth, of cultural purity and tonal monotony, from each of the individual islands. Surely, this continued social distance, discordance in science and distrust of learning each other's cultures does not bode well for orchestrating sustainability as a whole.

Environmental problems are also well known to occur between and across the boundaries of governmental agencies. Many agencies are organized along disciplinary lines paralleling those of academia. Economists dominate one agency, biologists the next, and engineers others. Agencies taking a more inter-disciplinary approach, such as the US Forest Service, have strong academic ties with professional schools such as forestry in universities. Here professional cultures emerge for the same reasons that disciplinary cultures do so within departments of universities. These linkages or tonal similarities between agencies and academia have been dubbed 'epistemic communities' because members in each share a similar way of knowing particular things and they communicate within a set of shared assumptions and myths (Haas, 1990). And, of course, they communicate their knowledge poorly beyond their own community. Again, with environmental problems inevitably overlapping the agencies and their respective epistemic communities, even agreeing upon the nature of, let alone resolving, environmental problems which overlap agencies is difficult.

Environmental problems also seem to arise among the differences between the scientific knowledges of academics and technocrats and the experiential knowledges of those people who are closest to particular social and ecological systems. The mothers of Love Canal, New York, had great difficulty convincing physicians and public health experts that something really was environmentally awry. The practices of indigenous and traditional agriculturists are frequently misunderstood by Western scientists (Altieri, 1995, Lélé and Norgaard, 1996). Everyone in society has some knowledge special to the varied and particular contexts in which they work and inevitably learn, and sometimes this particular knowledge can be extremely important. Like the scientists in the separate disciplines, people supplement their experiential, or practical, knowledge with a combination of simple assumptions and more complex myths to form a whole world view. And these world views which give wholeness and continuity to any particular group's understanding create divisions and discontinuities between us.

Most importantly, environmental problems arise in the clash between the understandings held by scientists and the community at large and those held, or at least those propagated, by the 'business community'. Capitalists and their industrial managers significantly affect how the economy interacts with ecosystems. Like other people around the world, entrepreneurs have also accumulated considerable working knowledge within that subsystem of the larger world in which they operate. And like others, they combine this knowledge with simple assumptions and more elaborate myths about the rest of the system. Their knowledge will certainly be critical to an orchestration of sustainability. Yet, at the same time, many understandings of environmental problems are typically of little use to the music they want to play, the messages they want others to hear. For businesspeople, indeed, some scientific understandings of environmental issues are a problem, something that must be respun with a different tinge of green in newspaper advertising and television commercials. This group of people is especially important, not because their knowledge is more important, but because they are in a position of power to see that their understanding is disseminated widely, to criticize views they oppose, and to see that those who do not conform to their views are marginalized economically. Conversely, should this group 'get it right' – this percussion section develop a more open, flexible, complementary line – they could play a critical role in effecting the orchestration (Hawken, 1993).

Thus we live in a world wherein each of us has some special knowledge to offer, a special instrument we play, though some are certainly louder than others. It is possible that these special knowledges could be relatively harmonious and that we simply need to find the appropriate score. In the conventional wisdom of modernity, whatever we really know mirrors reality and by definition must be harmonious with what other people really knew. Perhaps this is in fact the case, but the problem is also with what each of us does not know but presumes to be true. The assumptions and myths of the specialized communities of similar-minded people in which each of us lives are dramatically different. These are clearly the source of many of our difficulties in our performing together. Moreover, few of us, perhaps especially those of us with PhDs, can distinguish the boundaries between our knowledge, our assumptions and our myths. While we may be able to see these boundaries in the arguments of others, each of us is confident that our own knowledge component is far bigger than it is, the importance of assumption and myth much less significant. Development at home and abroad has been slowed and distorted towards environmental and social destruction because we do not have a 'score' which unites our understanding of the whole.

THE MODERN ORCHESTRATION

One of the reasons current times seem so cacophonous is that our discordant knowledges seemed pretty well orchestrated, at least to dominant modernists, in the recent past. Indeed, until relatively recently, it was widely thought that humanity was merging into one harmonious whole, the clamour of past cultural clashes replaced through progress by a shared, correct, scientific understanding of the reality around us. To the extent that dissonance could still be heard, it was merely evidence that we had not arrived yet at this oneness of understanding. Science not only distinguished modern peoples from their ancestors and other contemporaries but also drove modern history. The modern orchestration became increasingly embedded in our social organization during the nineteenth century with the establishment of 'progressive' agencies staffed by scientists and engineers and the adoption of administrative procedures which mirrored aspects of what was thought to be the scientific method. The legitimacy of these institutions and procedures brought divergent voices together for much of the twentieth century.

I have argued that modernity can be characterized by the ascendance of several key cosmological and epistemological beliefs (Norgaard, 1994). These are atomism, mechanism, universalism, monism and objectivism. Atomism is the belief that the world consists of separate parts that can be understood apart from each other. Atomism justifies the division of science into multiple, separate disciplines and problem solving into separate government bureaucracies. Mechanism is the belief that the parts behave systematically in predictable ways like Newton's motions of the planets. Mechanism has led to the idea that science is about prediction and that scientific arguments are proven when predictions prove true. Universalism is the belief that there are a relatively small number of relationships which in combination explain how everything in the universe works. This belief encourages scientists in Boston and Berkeley, as well as experts in business, bureaucracies and the World Bank, to issue proclamations in which all are supposed to believe regardless of the social and ecological contexts in which they live. Monism is the belief that all of our separate knowledges will ultimately come together in one coherent whole, that one truth will win out. The choice of word here deliberately suggests the parallel to monism in Judaeo-Christian theology and the unity some expect with the second coming of Christ. Objectivism, of course, is the belief that facts and values can be kept separate. Objectivism was critical to the belief that church, science and state could be separated, beginning some four centuries ago. The myth of scientific objectivity has obscured how scientists have made value judgments on behalf of society while working in government over the last century.

Widespread adherence to these beliefs kept many people thinking in relative harmony until recently. Western scientists believed that differences between the way scientists in the different disciplines thought would eventually go away. Besides, few problems were being addressed wherein these differences were confronted. Similarly, if one did not investigate too deeply, it appeared that science was relatively value-free. The dominance of these beliefs, or at least the economic, political and military dominance of those who believed in them, also marginalized and muffled dissonant voices with experiential or traditional knowledge, the vast majority of people on earth.

During the last quarter-century, the modern orchestration has broken down. In the process of addressing environmental problems increasingly comprehensively, we discovered that economic and ecological models inherently value different things by emphasizing some factors and leaving others out. We have observed confrontations between ecologists employed by corporations and those hired by environmental organizations over the scientific quality of each other's arguments, with both groups arguing with ecologists employed by governmental agencies. Furthermore, we became aware that neither evolving nor chaotic systems are predictable. Our mechanical characterization of phenomena such as global climate change are known actually to be more complex and to have irreversible properties and long time lags. Modern beliefs about prediction, experiment and truth are still being invoked in corporate advertisements critiquing the science of climate change and by congressmen who want to slow the implementation of environmental management programmes. Not infrequently, scientists themselves criticize each other on these old standards, hampering the effective use of the knowledge generated by the way science actually works. Both scientific communities and the international agencies still issue universal proclamations, but now we are much more aware of how they clash with experiential knowledge garnered in diverse socioeconomic and ecological systems around the world. Much of this discordance in understanding has developed because of modern beliefs about science. Acting on our belief in atomism, for example, we generated more and more disciplines of separate, like-minded communities with every greater differences between them. Acting on our belief in objectivity, we have developed the conditions which have generated distrust of government and experts.

One modern belief about science is particularly important to both the generation and the mediation of dissonance. Progress is believed to be a process in which scientific truth becomes ever more clear and ever more widely shared. Much as monism in Western science is attributed to monotheism in Western religion, the idea that science becomes ever more clear over time parallels the Christian belief that God reveals himself ever more fully and to more and more people over time. Until recently, and to some even today, this belief meant that scientific understanding should and would increasingly replace experiential knowledge until only scientific knowledge would be used. Acting on this belief, scientists and technical experts have been arrogant when working with people with less scientific training and closed-minded about experiential knowledge, both accentuating the cacophony between knowledges and increasing the volume.

This belief in the way science progresses, however, also means that, when scientists disagree, we only need to try harder and wait till the truth reveals itself. This has been used as a mediating mechanism, albeit not an entirely satisfactory one in the face of current problems. When the powers that influence legislators disagree with new developments in science, the most often invoked approach to mediation is to renew the scientists' budgets and tell them to go meditate another year. Corporations seem to lead the public on with the same belief, arguing that environmental regulatory decisions should not be made until truth is reached. Belief in how science progresses also leads scientists to pile theoretical arguments and empirical findings higher and higher, hoping the base of knowledge will somehow spread over a wider and wider populace. Frequently, however, the problem is that questions posed from different disciplinary islands simply never merge, leading to modern 'information' wars between different epistemic communities.

Tolerance, however, has also been held up as a critical component of both liberal and scientific thought, themselves hallmarks of modernity. Tolerance can play a critical role in mediating knowledge differences. After 30 years of religious war in Europe at the beginning of the seventeenth century, tolerance, also one of Christ's key messages, was recognized as sorely needed. By the end of that century, tolerance was becoming a central tenet of modern liberal political philosophy and a foundation to democratic governance. Clearly, the search for and practice of truth entails the elimination of incorrect understandings through critical analysis, but it also entails tolerance in the form of keeping a mind open to new understandings that might prove correct. Since proof may take some time, tolerance of a diversity of views becomes a characteristic of being a good scientist. Philosophers of science well into the twentieth century argued that, because scientists were both open and critical, good scientists would also be good citizens; indeed, the teaching of science, or at least the methods of science, would improve citizenship (see, for example, Dewey, 1916).

Tolerance between scientists who keep themselves separate in different disciplines, until the day that they merge into one coherent truth in the distant future, is especially easy. But scientists with conflicting, or simply alternate, theories working in the same field fight with a vengeance. And interdisciplinary practitioners, who necessarily intrude in the territories of multiple disciplines, have become well aware of the limits of scientific tolerance.

We can also query whether practical knowledge is merging or not. Certainly, our dominant perception of economic modernization is that the world's economies are becoming more and more alike. Within this systemic merging, we see more and more of the world's population fitting into modern categories. Industrial workers, farmers, managers, bankers and so on now perform work which is increasingly similar around the globe. This being the case, differences in our experiential knowledge ought to be declining rapidly. Another process, however, is also taking place. Historically, the vast majority of the world's people shared roughly similar experiences, a multitude of diverse farming tasks. Economic development has increased the number of tasks and they are now undertaken by separate workers. The economic arguments of comparative advantage and the gains from specialization have meant that each worker engages in an increasingly specialized task. So now we have specialized types of labourers, managers and even capitalists. Farmers have become managers, who hire special firms to prepare the soil and plant the crop, soil specialists to advise them on fertilization, insect management specialists and a special firm to harvest the crop. The practical knowledge one gains as an operator in the control room of a nuclear power plant bears little relation to the knowledge one gains as a grammar school teacher. In this sense, modernity has generated diversity and dissonance of experiential knowledge as a part of the process of development. And, of course, since there is more disparity between developed and less developed countries than two hundred years ago, it seems safe to argue that total dissonance in experiential knowledge has increased.

Again, let me emphasize that the modern beliefs that have determined the diversity of instruments and the nature of the score of scientific institutions and economic organization are not our sole problem in orchestrating sustainability. Since the early 1980s, we have experienced quite blatantly how power can dominate knowledge. The reduction of the national science budget in the United States and its redirection away from research on environmentally friendly technologies, for example, is not the consequence of the return on investments in publicly funded science or environmental technologies having diminished. On the contrary, this political decision seems to be clearly motivated by the increase in the dissonance between the understandings of scientists and the interests and understandings of economically and politically powerful sectors. But it is also important to realize that such exercises of power are frequently rationalized to the public in terms of various long-standing, that is modern, beliefs about how science is supposed to work.

Modern beliefs about science are neither holding us together as well as they did nor as useful for muting other voices. Indeed, by helping escalate the dissonance, modern beliefs have provided the conditions for their replacement. Top-down, science-will-win-out strategies have created environmental, as well as social, problems that are necessarily being worked on in new ways. But we are in an awkward period of history, a transition labelled 'postmodern' by some until a definitive new label is clear to all.

TOWARDS IMPROVISATION

During the past quarter-century we have been improvising a vast number of experiments in bringing dissonant knowledges together, improvisations which are not consistent with the dominant premises of modern science. No doubt such improvisations have earlier precedents, but it is equally sure that the rate of improvisation has increased. Let us consider some obvious examples in roughly historical order from a US perspective.

Interdisciplinary Environmental Studies

It is important to consider the continuing saga of interdisciplinary environmental studies programmes within our colleges and universities. Discussion of the need to have people who can work across disciplines to understand and resolve environmental programmes arose during the 1960s and the initiation of environmental programmes flourished during the 1970s. Today, we marvel at the way the scientists in the disciplines continue to denigrate environmental programmes for being too political and too practical and thereby keep these programmes marginalized in the educational structure. But it is important to keep in mind that what are now recognized as disciplines barely existed a century ago, when the curriculum debate was over whether students could learn all that was important by studying the pure examples of human dilemmas presented in the Greek and Roman classics, with perhaps a few key works from the Renaissance, or whether they should actually be allowed to study the mundane material discovered by scientists during the nineteenth century. A century ago, the sciences, as well as everything else that was current, were denigrated as mundane, and marginalized accordingly. Practical considerations nevertheless forced universities to allow science courses as electives. And after the turn of the century, students were even allowed to select separate majors after studying the core material offered by the classics. On this schedule, the slow progress of interdisciplinary environmental studies in higher education, though still very irritating, is at least understandable (Levine, 1996).

Inter-agency Task Forces

Over the past quarter-century, it has become standard practice to cross agency cultural barriers through the formation of inter-agency task forces to work out complex environmental and social problems. Within government, it is now well recognized that the sciences pursued separately are not merging and that the agency parallels to the sciences cannot manage joint problems separately.

Public Comment on the Adequacy and Completeness of Science

We need to keep in mind that the National Environmental Policy Act passed in the US in 1969 mandated public hearings on the adequacy and completeness of environmental assessments. While this clause in the act may have been inserted to see that the public was informed, it has proved a forum for citizens to introduce new information and ask critical questions missed by those who undertook the assessment. It has also served as a forum for scientists to contest the conclusions and wholeness of work undertaken by other scientists. The assessment of risk has proved to be the most contentious part of environmental assessment, pitting cold, calculating, impartial analysts against the culturally embedded concerns of the people who have little choice but to live with the threats imposed upon them. After two decades of contention and multiple assessments of the problem by scientists assembled under the umbrella of the National Research Council, the most recent report recommends striving for risk 'characterization' through a participatory reiterative process of presentations, critiques and consensus building between experts and those who actually live with the dangers (National Research Council, 1996).

Participatory Research

In the wake of 'green revolution' approaches to modernizing agriculture, agro-ecology and participatory research techniques have been developed. Rather than providing traditional farmers with advanced inputs and information which may not be appropriate to the farmers, their community or the ecosystem, agro-ecologists learn with traditional farmers, sharing what they know in a mutually designed and implemented research and demonstration projects. Their discordant knowledges become the basis for developing new understandings combining traditional and modern inputs with scientific and experiential ways of learning. Scientists who are participating in these approaches are scoffed at by 'real' scientists, but interacting with and helping real people on real problems has its rewards.

Non Governmental Organizations

In spite of the advantages of being a 'free rider', people are organizing themselves into a plethora of interest groups whose staff gather data, share in collective learning processes, disseminate information, coordinate with each other and participate in political arenas far more effectively than can people acting individually. Though NGOs have been around for a long time, they have only proliferated dramatically and become critical to social learning and governance during the past two decades. The larger, better funded NGOs in the developed countries hire staff with PhDs who typically work along task, not disciplinary, lines. Smaller organizations serve the grass roots, including the poor and people of colour, providing them with new sources of information and avenues of empowerment. Many governmental agencies, especially those in developing countries, are unable to function without the participation of NGOs. While many of us are actively engaged in NGOs and take them for granted, it is important to remember that this additional element of our social organization is so new and beyond our modern understandings of governance that they are elaborated upon in only a few political science and sociology textbooks.

Intergovernmental Panel on Climate Change

The IPCC is an exciting example of a new approach to building scientific knowledge. Scientists from multiple disciplines are thinking interactively through numerous exchanges at workshops and other processes, collectively building knowledge of the causes, consequences and methods of mitigating climate change. They have also drawn in scientists from around the world and interacted intensively with policy makers, special interests and non-governmental organizations as well. The collective, discursive process has been slow and extremely awkward, but it seems to be the only way to link the disparate knowledges of the sciences and get scientists to orient their research activities towards understanding a complex problem together. The outreach to policy makers and interest groups has also been unusually interactive. Among participants within the process, an ever larger majority agrees that significant steps should be taken earlier rather than later. The dissenters are largely outside the process, arguing that the scientific interactions have led to a false consensus, that the process itself is bad science. The process certainly does not fit modern understandings of the way science is supposed to work. The critics do not understand how the procedures of modern science created the problems we are trying to overcome.

Other Experiments

Other improvisations include the use of conflict mediation techniques to bring discordant scientific positions together (Ozawa, 1991), the use of science shops in Europe to provide citizens' groups with technical assistance (Irwin, 1996; Sclove, 1995) and the use of science juries to query scientists from multiple perspectives and build public understanding (Sclove, 1995). In Sweden, 50 scientists jointly crafted a statement on the underlying processes of environmental degradation that was distributed to every household in Sweden. From this emerged 'The Natural Step' programme with four principles for transforming the way in which businesses evaluate their long-term strategy (Holmberg *et al.*, 1996). Paralleling these innovations, those concerned with democracy itself have moved towards deliberative opinion polls and are experimenting with political caucuses made up of randomly selected people identifying through a discursive process the issues they really want politicians to address (Fishkin, 1991). Some of these new improvisations may evolve to become dominant forms of joining discordant understandings in the future.

The important point is that none of these improvisations fits the modern orchestration. They have been experiments motivated by 'common sense' that have succeeded because they work. The dominant premises of modernity do not rationalize these governance structures: quite the contrary, these improvisations are responses to the discordance between the modern orchestration of knowing and need for effective public knowledge to respond to the environmental and social problems that arose under this orchestration. In social theory, there is a parallel development. The idea that effective governance requires communities in which people can share values and understanding is gaining credence in social theory (Dryzek, 1990; Bellah *et al.*, 1991; Putnam *et al.*, 1993; Sandel, 1996). Democracy is about shared learning, vote counting is a last resort.

At the same time, these improvisations raise serious questions. For example, the discourse among scientists and policy makers facilitated by the IPCC is an ideal but limited model, and it is at the limits that problems arise. Who is to be inside these processes, how can anyone justifiably be excluded, how can they work at a broader level and how can economic power be kept from directing and distorting the answers to these questions, so that these processes of sharing knowledge do not mimic the current 'misrepresentativeness' of representative democracy? Furthermore, these improvisations require serious commitments of time. Acknowledging that all cannot be full participants all of the time raises the issue of how we can make the burden of citizenship equitable. Participation currently entails considerable material sacrifice. This sacrifice can be spread more broadly, obligations to serve can be distributed like notices to serve on juries, but five dollars a day compensation, a typical reimbursement for jurors in the United States, is inadequate. In the longer run, however, members constituting a substantial portion of the demos could establish their identities through shared learning in diverse communities rather than material consumption. The time spent learning together could reduce material demands, a key driving force of the problems we are trying to solve.

ECOLOGICAL ECONOMICS WITHIN THE EVOLVING IMPROVISATION

Ecological economists are setting their course amidst this transition in the way we have historically orchestrated and are currently increasingly improvising individual learning, public understanding and collective implementation. While ecology and economics share many conceptual roots, the modern orchestration between our disciplines proved dysfunctional, the cacophony ringing out in raucous political debate, during the second half of the twentieth century. Ecologists and economists got together to form the International Society for Ecological Economics (ISEE) in 1987 to initiate a new improvisation incorporating scientists, practitioners and interpreters of, and occasionally participants in, the political debate. Having participated in the founding of the Association of Environmental and Resource Economists some 15 years before we founded the International Society for Ecological Economics, I can identify some clear differences between the now fading modern orchestration and the arising improvisation.

First, ecological economists are actively engaged in encouraging a paradigm shift. We are very aware that modern Western and Westernized societies have been constructed around fundamental beliefs in material progress driven by science dedicated to controlling a malleable natural system without resource limits. We believe that these beliefs are not only fundamentally in error but also the cause of environmental as well as social problems. From a physical perspective, stocks and flows are limited and substitution between types of energy and materials is also limited. From an ecological perspective, the world does not simply consists of parts for us to rearrange and toss out as we wish. The parts dynamically interact as systems and are dependent on each other and the structure at any given time. From a coevolutionary perspective, systems evolve over time, human culture including science evolves within this process, and every decision we make has ramifications for the future. We are conscious of how our own successes and failures affect the social and ecological systems we are trying to know. The physical, ecological and coevolutionary perspectives indicate critical aspects that economic thinking needs to address even while they highlight some incongruences in our understanding of a complex world. We accept these incongruences as indicative of our limited ability to understand the whole from any particular perspective and are methodological pluralists for this reason. We realize that truly different ways of knowing do not merge to a single answer, that atonality is inherent in different ways of knowing. The dissonance of Bartok played well is part of the message that is lost when Bartok is played poorly. ISEE exists in part to actively challenge scientists and policy makers to make these physical, ecological and coevolutionary paradigm shifts (Arrow *et al.*, 1995; Daly, 1973; Georgescu-Roegen, 1972; Norgaard, 1994).

Second, the 'social scientists' among ecological economists are keenly interested in biophysical measures of human resource use, for we realize that the aggregate values of economic measures are affected by price changes and other aggregate changes. The declining share of agriculture in the total product of developing and developed nations, for example, does not make food any less significant or the environmental impacts of farming any less important. How we interact with our environment and use resources must be tracked in real terms as well as in monetary terms (Hall *et al.*, 1986; Martinez-Alier, 1996).

Third, our improvisation pays as much attention to equity as to efficiency. A fair system of access to resources is critically important to the way people interact with the environment. As important as the mechanics of the market can be, we do not stress efficiency prices alone. We know that prices are not only a function of whether the market is working efficiently but also a matter of how rights to resources are distributed among people within nations, between nations and over generations (Howarth and Norgaard, 1995). The modern orchestration of environmental economics has functioned under the myth that growth will take care of equity problems through a process of 'trickle down'. Such a musical score simplified achieving harmony and allowed economists to feign objectivity as econocrats and present one right solution. But there is neither a theory as to how 'trickle down' might reduce economic disparities nor empirical evidence for the vast majority of countries or the world as a whole. Ecological economists realize that they must interact with and participate in the moral discourse and politics of economic justice (Martinez-Alier, 1996; Martinez-Alier and O'Connor, 1996).

Fourth, we realize that understanding problems and finding and implementing solutions requires the contextual, experiential and, in some cases, traditional or indigenous knowledge of local people and practitioners. Accuracy to two significant figures in the aggregate can result in totally wrong solutions across a diversity of ecological, technological, social and cultural contexts. Participatory research conducted in a partnership between scientists and those who will actually implement a solution is frequently the only way to reach workable answers and effective solutions (Norgaard and Sikor, 1995; Altieri *et al.*, 1996).

Fifth, we are historically and philosophically conscious of the interplay between assumptions, models and the types of answers they can generate. We know that the viability of answers depends on the broader social structure in which such answers may be effective. We are wary of the ideology supporting existing approaches to economic research, with their feigned objectivity. We are concerned that these approaches were largely designed to replace democratic decision making and the broad empowerment that makes implementation of solutions possible. We do not have workable solutions within the historic orchestration and in the transition to new improvisations we find ourselves in awkward contradictions. We are open to what we do not know, aware that learning more also entails learning more about what we do not know, and find adaptive environmental management a suitable approach for these reasons (Walters, 1986; Funtowicz and Ravetz, 1994; Norgaard, 1994; O'Connor *et al.*, 1996; Faber *et al.*, 1996).

I am excited by the improvisations of discordant knowledges now under way and the role being played by ecological economists in the larger effort. I am concerned, however, by the dominance of the percussion section, the way its simple rhythm all by itself attracts so many, and the tendency of others to let this simple beat guide our otherwise diverse improvisations. The role the percussion section is now playing, however, reflects the power and short-run interests of the capitalists it represents, combined with the voices of 'free' market ideologues. Our improvisation needs the wisdom of capitalists. Ideologues of every stripe are poor improvisers and should be left on the sidelines.

BIBLIOGRAPHY

Altieri, Miguel A. (1995), *Agroecology: The Science of Sustainable Agriculture*, Boulder, Col.: Westview Press.
Altieri, Miguel A., Andres Yurjevic, Jean Marc Von der Weid and Juan Sanchez (1996), 'Applying Agroecology to Improve Peasant Farming Systems in Latin America: An

Impact Assessment of NGO Strategies', in Robert Costanza, Olman Segura and Joan Martinez-Alier (eds), *Getting Down to Earth: practical applications of ecological economics*, Washington, DC: Island Press.

Arrow, Kenneth *et al.* (1995) 'Economic Growth, Carrying Capacity and the Environment', *Science*, 268, 520–21.

Bellah, Robert N., Richard Madsen, William M. Sullivan, Ann Swidler and Steven M. Tipton (1991), *The Good Society*. New York: Alfred A. Knopf.

Daly, Herman E. (1973), 'The Steady-State Economy: Toward a Political Economy of Biophysical Equilibrium and Moral Growth', in Herman E. Daly (ed.), *Toward a Steady-State Economy*, San Francisco: W.H. Freeman.

Dewey, John (1916), *Democracy and Education: An Introduction to the Philosophy of Education*, New York: Macmillan.

Dryzek, John S. (1990), *Discursive Democracy: Politics, Policy and Political Science*, Cambridge: Cambridge University Press.

Faber, Malte, Reiner Manstetten and John Proops (1996), *Ecological Economics: Concepts and Methods*, Cheltenham, UK and Brookfield, US: Edward Elgar.

Fishkin, James S. (1991), *Democracy and Deliberation: New Directions for Democratic Reform*, New Haven: Yale University Press.

Funtowicz, Silvio and Jerome R. Ravetz (1994), 'The Worth of a Songbird: Ecological Economics as a Post-Normal Science', *Ecological Economics*, 10, 197–207.

Georgescu-Roegen, Nicholas (1972), *The Entropy Law and the Economic Process*, Cambridge, Mass.: Harvard University Press.

Haas, Ernst B. (1990), *When Knowledge is Power: Three Models of Change in International Organizations*, Berkeley: University of California Press.

Hall, Charles A.S., Cutler J. Cleveland and Robert Kaufman (1986), *Energy and Resource Quality: The Ecology of the Economic Process*, New York: John Wiley.

Hawken, Paul (1993), *The Ecology of Commerce: A Declaration of Sustainability*, New York: Harper Business.

Holmberg, John, Karl-Henrik Robert and Karl-Erik Eriksson (1996), 'Socio-Ecological Principles for a Sustainable Society', in Robert Costanza, Olman Segura and Joan Martinez-Alier (eds), *Getting Down to Earth: practical applications of ecological economics*, Washington, DC: Island Press.

Howarth, Richard B. and Richard B. Norgaard (1995), 'Intergenerational Choices Under Global Environmental Change', in Daniel W. Bromley (ed.), *Handbook of Environmental Economics*, Oxford: Basil Blackwell.

Irwin, Alan (1996), *Citizen Science: A Study of People, Expertise and Sustainable Development*, London and New York: Routledge.

Jasanoff, Sheila (1990), *The Fifth Branch: Science Advisors as Policy Makers*, Cambridge, Mass.: Harvard University Press.

LaPorte, Todd (ed.) (1975), *Organized Social Complexity: Challenge to Politics and Policy*, Princeton: Princeton University Press.

Lélé, Sharachchandra and Richard B. Norgaard (1996), 'Sustainability and the Scientist's Burden', *Conservation Biology*, 10, 354–65.

Levine, Lawrence W. (1996), *The Opening of the American Mind: Canons, Culture and History*, Boston: Beacon Press.

Martinez-Alier, Joan (1996), 'Ecological Economies as Human Ecology: Sustainability as a Concept in the Social Sciences', manuscript prepared for MOST-UNESCO project, Department d'Economia i História Economica, Universitat Autonóma de Barcelona.

Martinez-Alier, Joan and Martin O'Connor (1996), 'Ecological and Economic Distribution Conflicts', in Robert Costanza, Olman Segura and Joan Martinez-Alier (eds), *Getting Down to Earth: practical applications of ecological economics*, Washington, DC: Island Press.

National Research Council (1996), *Understanding Risk: Informing Decisions in a Democratic Society*, Washington, DC: National Academy Press.

Norgaard, Richard B. (1992), 'Environmental Science as a Social Process', *Environmental Monitoring and Assessment*, 20, 95–110.

Norgaard, Richard B. (1994), *Development Betrayed: The End of Progress and a Coevolutionary Revisioning of the Future*, London and New York: Routledge.

Norgaard, Richard B. and Thomas Sikor (1995), 'The Methodology and Practice of Agroecology', in Miguel A. Altieri (ed.), *Agroecology: The Science of Sustainable Agriculture*, Boulder, Col.: Westview Press.

O'Connor, Martin, Sylvie Faucheux, Geraldine Froger, Silvio Funtowicz and Giuseppe Munda (1996), 'Emergent Complexity and Procedural Rationality: Post-Normal Science for Sustainability', in Robert Costanza, Olman Segura and Joan Martinez-Alier (eds), *Getting Down to Earth: practical applications of ecological economics*, Washington, DC: Island Press.

Ozawa, Connie P. (1991), *Recasting Science: Consensual Procedures in Public Policy Making*, Boulder, Col.: Westview Press.

Putnam, Robert D., Robert Leonardi and Raffaela Nanetti (1993), *Making Democracy Work: Civic Traditions in Italy*, Princeton: Princeton University Press.

Sandel, Michael J. (1996), *Democracy's Discontent: America in Search of a Public Philosophy*, Cambridge, Mass.: Harvard University Press.

Sclove, Richard E. (1995), *Democracy and Technology*, New York: The Guilford Press.

Walters, Carl (1986), *Adaptive Management of Renewable Resources*, New York: Macmillan.

4. Searching for sustainability: the poverty of spontaneous order

Daniel W. Bromley

Economists became interested in the idea of sustainability as a theoretical offshoot of early work in growth theory. From the original concern for the causes and consequences of economic growth, the gradual shift in emphasis began to concern how one might model economic growth so that the future would not be impoverished. Because economic growth is usually consumptive of natural resources, it is logical to ask how much growth can be accommodated in the present without leaving future generations with a depleted or degraded stock of natural resources. This problem has been addressed by a number of theorists (Dasgupta and Heal, 1974, 1979; Dasgupta and Mäler, 1995; Hartwick, 1977; Howarth, 1995, 1997; Howarth and Norgaard, 1990, 1995; Krautkraemer, 1985; Mäler, 1974; Page, 1977; Pearce, 1988; Solow, 1974, 1992). Solow and Hartwick, among others, adopted intergenerational equity as their guiding principle. Solow approaches sustainability as a problem of ensuring that the capital stock, whether natural or constructed, is adequate to provide a level of consumption for each future generation that is not less than that enjoyed by the current generation. This position is similar to that adopted by Pearce and Atkinson (1993). Pezzey (1989, 1992) sees the problem as one of ensuring that aggregate welfare is non-declining over time. Howarth (1995) takes a similar tack on the premise that this is the Kantian imperative. Bishop (1978) suggests a safe minimum standard of conservation, an idea originally propounded by Ciriacy-Wantrup (1968).[1]

The traditional economic approach to sustainability starts from utilitarianism. Central to these models of sustainability are concepts of capital, commodities, utility, consumption, savings and investment, income and aggregate welfare over time. Finally, there is a reliance on 'right prices'. This approach has added much-needed clarity to a difficult conceptual problem. And yet that clarity seems to offer us little in terms of operational coherence. The essential problem for operationality centres on the key role in these models of two elusive ideas in economics: commodities and utility. For example, Dasgupta and Mäler (1995) claim that much sustainability policy would have certain natural resources preserved despite an efficiency loss because greater benefits could be obtained by substituting constructed capital for, perhaps, old-growth forests. But this indictment of strong sustainability presumes precisely that which is unknown about the future: namely, how can we possibly know how future persons will value the allocational decisions made today on the basis of current relative prices? In the absence of that knowledge, we cannot label as *inefficient* particular sustainability policies and practices (Bromley, 1990). The opprobrium of inefficiency requires clarity about the commodities under consideration, and the value that future persons will place on those commodities. For us to place our values (current prices) on them is to substitute our realm of reason for the realm of reason of future persons. To do so is to step outside economics and to engage in something akin to ethical pre-emption. Sustainability deserves to be approached on more solid ground.

ON THE FICTIONS OF COMMODITIES AND UTILITY

Modern economics regards the natural environment as a commodity in two respects. First, the natural environment is considered a capital asset (itself a commodity) which gives rise to goods and services that also are regarded as commodities. The idea that the natural environment has been commoditized is underlined by the widespread programme of research by economists to assign monetary values to both of these classes of commodities.[2]

Karl Polanyi (1957) was an early commentator on the *commodity fiction*. John R. Commons had earlier argued that commoditization was the logical prerequisite of the economic approach worked out by Adam Smith. The Smithian system operates on the *principle of mechanism*. To Commons, the economy of Adam Smith, defined by the centrality of divisible commodities delivering utility to those who consume them, is simply a machine. The Smithian machine is informed by Newtonian mechanics (Mirowski, 1987).

As for the idea of utility, once the principles of the machine were worked out by Smith and his followers, economics moved on to a preoccupation with feeling (utility). The centrality of scarcity gave rise to the notion of hedonism through maximization in the face of scarcity. Then the switch from Pareto's notion of ophelimity (satisfaction) to the idea of utility – where utility was itself transformed from the Paretian (and everyday) idea of 'useful' into something denoting happiness or satisfaction – set welfare theory on a tangent from which it has yet to recover (Cooter and Rappoport, 1984). Utility was transformed from an idea connoting usefulness into the realm of feeling, thus displacing the more awkward term 'ophelimity'. And now there is no longer a place in economic discourse for the concept of usefulness. In consequence, the province of sustainability, if it is to remain true to the reigning canon, must concern not usefulness to future generations, but the level of welfare to be experienced by those yet unborn. In blunt terms, the atmosphere must be kept fit for breathing, not because it would be useful for future generations to be able to breathe, but because future generations will otherwise suffer a loss in utility and that might signal some putative efficiency loss.

This is not a minor point. Utility perceived by the autonomous consumer of commodities is the conceptual core of contemporary economics. We see this enshrined in the two *Paretian value judgments*: that only individuals count, and that, if one person can be made better off under a new social arrangement, and no one is thereby made worse off, then the new situation is judged to be a social improvement. Mishan (1980) offered a fundamental critique of this approach for evaluating public policy. He notes that in the absence of an ethical consensus – a virtual constitution – concerning the Paretian value judgments, they remain just that (value judgments). While economists imagine that these value judgments command universal assent, there is no proof to support that contention (Bromley, 1990).

Indeed, the centrality of commodities and feelings, in the hands of Adam Smith and his successors, has led us to imagine an economy that is dominated by the principles of individualism, self-interest, divisibility and exchange. The logical outgrowth of a preoccupation with commodities and feelings is the idea that, out of the wonders of the Smithian machine, divine providence will lead individuals, through self-interest, to benefit others without intending to do so. That is, material provisioning (production and consumption) by individuals is alleged to solve automatically and effortlessly the problem of social order. Under this happy result, there is nothing for any collective to do but sit back and let the economy run itself. On this view the economy is a machine, fuelled by individual acquisitiveness. But how is this acquisitiveness by those of us now living in the long-run interest of those yet unborn? If it is not, then the presumptiveness beneficence of the Smithian machine is suspect.

The Smithian Machine and Sustainability

The conventional economic approach to sustainability is concerned with finding the maximum (or optimal) path of present valued utility (or of consumption), subject to a production function that converts both constructed capital and natural capital into goods and services. In other words, the logic of provisioning is, in simple terms, a *machine problem* in which inputs are efficiently converted into consumption goods that yield utility. In the hands of the economic theorist concerned with sustainability, this machine represents a continuous-time, deterministic, representative–agent economy. The essence of this machine is the existence of a consumption path – and a vector of the path of all capital (both constructed and natural) – that, over time, maximizes the present value of utility from that consumption path. The machine incorporates technical progress as it runs through time. While the assumptions of this machine formulation are no more severe than those found in much of economics, certain inconveniences do arise.

For instance, since the Smithian machine is concerned to maximize the utility from consumption across infinitely many time periods into the future, it would seem important to have some idea about what those living in the future might find giving of utility. That is, how do we know what those living in the future will value or prefer? Since we cannot know what they will value, the essential idea of 'right prices' fails to take us very far. Moreover, we cannot know what will be regarded as capital in the future and so how can one model a path of capital into the future? Indeed, we cannot even know what will be a commodity in the future and so net national product and its income equivalent as a measure of wellbeing of those in the future becomes problematical. We cannot know future tastes and preferences and so we see that consumption and its utility are curious concepts on which the machine must run. The enduring fictions of commodities and feeling (utility) plague the serious analyst searching for sustainability.

In short, the logic of provisioning inherent in the conventional machine problem of sustainability is a scientific fiction. As fiction, does it still provide a useful heuristic? Is it useful to think of the future in this way? Does it make sense to conjure present valued utility for all individuals in the world over infinite time?

The time machine certainly tells us that we must leave something for the future. But does it tell us how much is enough? Can we determine the optimal level of carbon dioxide emissions that will be consistent with maximizing intertemporal utility? Can we tell if one should increase the land area devoted to national parks, wildlife reserves and wilderness areas? More fundamentally, do we need the time machine to tell us to leave something for the future? In other words, is the time machine necessary?

The problem of sustainability has little to do with optimal utility levels over time. Rather, the essential problem of sustainability arises from the absence of knowledge about what those in the future would wish for us to do. Note that this is not a mere problem of uncertainty or of risk. This is a problem of ignorance.

Sustainability is a serious problem for economists, not because of the provisioning machines we build to try to understand the sustainable path, but because of information problems that preclude us from knowing what we should ask the time machine to do for us and for those who will follow in the future. Those of us living today stand as dictators over the future and our analytical problem is that we are seeking to solve a provisioning problem for infinitely many individuals in the future whose desires are totally unknown – and unknowable – to us. We cannot optimally model future provisioning for the simple reason that we can never know how to provision the future. Because agents from the future are not present to discuss their provisioning with us, we have no basis for arranging their provisioning, for contracting with them over that provisioning plan, or for addressing the compliance problems associated with any particular provisioning plan (Bromley, 1989b).

In short, conventional approaches to the problem of sustainability are treated as *machine problems*; we have attempted to solve the sustainability problem in terms of some optimal path of provisioning. By conjuring an economy of autonomous Benthamite maximizers, by then allowing for the autonomous evolutionary innovation of incentive-compatible working rules, and by keeping so-called 'government interference' to a minimum, agents could get on with the happy business of maximizing to solve ever-present scarcity problems. But these efficient solutions are not necessarily compatible with sustainability (Woodward and Bishop, 1995). And so we come to the inconvenient fact that the machine cannot assure the future. But does not the legacy of Smith, at least in the hands of the more fervent, promise otherwise?

THE MACHINE AND SPONTANEOUS ORDER

Recall that out of scarcity comes conflict, but out of scarcity comes also dependence. And from the conjunction of conflict and dependence comes order. Smith managed to finesse the problem of order by arguing that it was the logical outcome of the age-old problem of provisioning. Political conservatives, libertarians – and not a few anarchists – have taken great comfort from this idea. And a fine idea it is. How wonderful to avoid the difficult business of having to agree upon mechanisms for achieving, and the rules for evaluating, that order. Much better to let it emerge, spontaneously, from the material acquisitiveness of all. This is what Hayek called *spontaneous order* (Hayek, 1960).

Notice that the social order to emerge from this process of autonomous maximizing is presumptively good. That is, if it is possible to obtain agreement on the first principles of the process of provisioning, then the outcome of that process commands immediate and widespread assent. When a machine is allowed to run under these precepts, then its outcomes are deemed socially preferred. Arrow's results on the ultimate futility of social choice buttressed the idea that no self-conscious human effort at social design could hope to do as well as the market – and the machine.

This is a story of spontaneous order arising from the process of provisioning. To Hayek and others opposed to governments, this was the indispensable conjuring that could guarantee individual freedom by keeping coercion at bay. But it took a definitional trick to make it appear legitimate (Bromley, 1989a).

Hayek grounded his alleged freedom to arise from markets on the absence of will and intent. Specifically, he argued that coercion was present when an individual was restrained from acting as a result of the will of others. When individuals were restrained by physical circumstances then this was not coercion as far as Hayek was concerned. Jacob Viner, in commenting on Hayek's artful approach, was quick to notice that 'Freedom is thus defined as freedom *from* subjection to the will of others, and not as freedom *to do* anything in particular, or for that matter to do anything at all, in the sense of power or ability or opportunity to do it' (Viner, 1961, p. 231).

The Smith–Hayek vision is that markets produce a form of double dividend: commodities as well as spontaneous order. The Friedman–Hayek elaboration is that markets also produce, or result in, freedom. Friedman justifies this claim for freedom by noting that markets permit individuals to enter into whichever transaction they desire. However, C.B. Macpherson (1973) challenges Friedman's exuberance by insisting that real freedom implies that individuals need not engage *in any transaction at all*. That is, as long as individuals must sell (or rent) their labour power in order to eat, they are not free. We see, therefore, that the presumed wonders of the Smithian machine – individual freedom and the existence of a socially optimal spontaneous order – are illusory.

This alleged linkage between markets and freedom is a venerable one in economics and thus, if sustainability must be achieved through means other than spontaneous order arising from provisioning, we must first confront the fear that this will result in a loss of freedom for some individuals. That is, if sustainability must somehow be self-consciously constructed rather than arising gratuitously from autonomous maximizing through market processes, we must first come to grips with the belief that markets guarantee freedom. If we are to consider an argument for sustainability based on a prior *constructed* order rather than on a consequentialist spontaneous order, we must first address the claims for freedom made by those who imagine that market-driven provisioning is somehow consistent with individual sovereignty.

Amartya Sen (1993) suggests that the idea of markets and freedom cannot be understood without recognizing three constituents of freedom: autonomy, opportunity and immunity. Autonomy concerns the freedom to choose; opportunity concerns the freedom to achieve; immunity concerns the freedom from encroachment by others. Those who believe that markets guarantee freedom stress autonomy (choice) and a limited version of immunity. The limited interest in immunity shows up in a deep aversion to encroachment by governments (say in the form of regulation), but ambivalence about market-sanctioned encroachment. We see this in the aversion to regulations (a form of constructed order) that redefine working conditions in factories and other private firms.

Interestingly, those who celebrate markets see regulations as an encroachment on owners of firms, but they fail to see the absence of those regulations as an encroachment on workers.

The third dimension of freedom, opportunity, is even more troublesome for those who claim that markets guarantee freedom. For instance, civil rights laws that prohibit firms denying service to members of certain groups are sometimes seen as an intervention in the market. But, of course, opportunity for the owner of the firm clashes with opportunity for the individual who is turned away.

Looked at through the eyes of future individuals, our destruction of unique habitats and ecological capabilities constitutes a violation of all three constituents of freedom; we compromise their autonomy, their opportunity and their immunity. The constructed order necessary for a logically coherent view of sustainability cannot claim to leave future persons exactly the physical environment and domain of choice they would select for themselves. But neither does it hide behind the obvious deception of the presumptively beneficent spontaneous order emanating from the Smithian machine.

BEYOND THE MACHINE

The enigma of sustainability poses a threat to the presumptive beneficence of Smith's spontaneous order. Indeed, the very need to ponder sustainability is evidence of the poverty of models of provisioning and the spontaneous order arising therefrom. Sustainability can only be addressed from outside the logic of provisioning.

In other words, locating the optimal sustainable path for an economy is logically impossible because of the presence of information costs, contracting costs and enforcement costs. Information costs arise because we cannot know what will be preferred – let alone optimal – in the future. Contracting costs are pertinent because we cannot possibly negotiate with the unborn about what sort of future they might like. Enforcement costs are high because there is no way for subsequent generations to bind each other into some optimal bargain. These transaction costs stand between our investment and consumption choices and the circumstances of those who will come after us. Given these transaction costs, the concept of sustainability is necessarily devoid of any positive analytical content for the economist. Rather, the problem of sustainability becomes simply a normative judgment about the ability of autonomous maximizing agents to establish and sustain mutually beneficial patterns of consumption and investment over time. But how will we ever know if we have achieved even this weaker condition of 'mutually beneficial' consumption and investment over time?

TOWARDS A CONSTRUCTED ORDER

The interest in, and the popularity of, the idea of sustainability arises from the very real concern that the process of current provisioning may threaten future provisioning. Of course that very concern undermines the universal providence claimed for the spontaneous order that emanates from unfettered market processes. The analytical solution to emerge from orthodox modelling efforts is of the form that the utility of future generations should not be allowed to decline from that level of utility enjoyed by those currently living. While a useful finding in its own right, this result lacks operational content. What, exactly, must we do today to ensure that those living, say 100 years (or even 25 years) from now experience a level of welfare that is not less than that level of aggregate utility we now enjoy? Indeed, what is the level of welfare enjoyed by those of us currently living? Equally problematical, we are told that society's stock of capital should not be allowed to diminish over time. But what, after all, is capital?

The tradition in economics is to treat natural capital and constructed capital as fungible (Norton, 1995). This approach allows for the replacement of degraded or destroyed natural capital with constructed capital. While Saudi Arabia may well convert its petroleum reserves into constructed capital – universities, research institutes, factories – one must wonder if future persons would evince contentment upon learning that the majestic California redwoods had been destroyed so that the derived income could be used to create yet another campus of the University of California system. Since the income from destroying the redwoods would be most unlikely to end up other than in private hands, the value of this trade-off falls under a yet more serious cloud. Not only are we unsure what constitutes capital, we are often quite certain that one form of capital is no substitute for another form of capital.

ON INTERTEMPORAL CONTRACTING: THE REGENCY

Sustainability is not about autonomous provisioning giving rise to spontaneous order. Nor is sustainability rendered operational by models of optimal consumption into the future. Rather, sustainability can only be operationalized by the recognition that we must discuss a prior *constructed order* that defines a socially acceptable provisioning programme now and into the future. It is impossible to rely on models of provisioning, and the spontaneous order said to emanate therefrom, to tell us what to do about securing the future. The problem of sustainability must be approached as one of intertemporal contracting, and this approach is a problem of constructed order motivated and informed by regard for the circumstances of the future (Bromley, 1989b).

At the most fundamental level, the current social concern for intertemporal provisioning and sustainability is a clear denial of the automatic beneficence of spontaneous order. Not only does that delegitimation pertain to the intertemporal problem, it pertains to contemporary resource allocation as well. Once this is recognized, there is nothing to justify the provisioning programme under way in the present, let alone that programme as it pertains to the future.

But what sort of prior constructed order is called for? It cannot be a constructed order predicated on intertemporal welfare considerations. Nor can it be a constructed order predicated on preserving constructed plus natural capital. But what grounds might provide this basis? In traditional provisioning, transactional insecurity and possessional insecurity are dealt with by contracts and sundry property regimes (Bromley, 1991). In intertemporal provisioning there are no contracts because there is no way to negotiate a contract with future persons. One escape from this dilemma is to construct an *environmental regency* in which the present generation controls provisioning until the next generation is able to assume that control. In the machine problem of sustainability we call this an overlapping-generations model. We might also think of it as the rolling-horizon approach. But this contract is in a state of nature where there is no enforcement mechanism across generations. The only feasible solution is for those in the present, acting as regents, to pledge collateral against the possibility that we may, in a moment of weakness, violate the interests of the future. We can do this by setting aside natural and constructed assets for future persons.

To collateralize the future it is probably best to avoid endangered-species thinking. The problem with species fetishism is that it denies the reality of nature and of evolution. What must be conserved for the future is not species per se, but the conditions for the maintenance of ecosystems. We might think of the ecosystem as part of the globe's social infrastructure, and therefore sustainability should be concerned with the maintenance of this infrastructure.

The constructed order we require for sustainability consists in the conditions that ensure the viability of certain essential ecological processes and circumstances. Operational coherence in environmental policy requires that we must adopt the idea of *essential settings and circumstances* as guides to what must be set aside for future persons. Not only does this supplant species fetishism, it permits the consideration of constructed assets on the same plane as natural assets. And it forces us to get on with the important task of discussing and demarcating such settings and circumstances.

The logical flaw in the traditional economic approach to sustainability is that it invites, through its manifestations in the Smithian machine, consideration of minimalist actions by those now living. By minimalist I mean that such models invite those of us now living to consume and squander environmental resources up to a level just necessary to ensure that all future generations will be no worse off than we are now. While some may consider this behaviour as showing regard for the future, others may consider it as selfish and intent on making sure that those who will follow are no better off than we are. If this machine version of sustainability were to inform the conversation between parents and children, the latter might be understandably perplexed to learn that their parents were aggressively intent on ensuring that the wealth position of the children could never exceed their own.

Or, put another way, the prevailing economic idea of sustainability suggests that those of us now alive can never be better off than any representative future generation. This view places the present generation in a situation of guilt and insecurity.

ON SOCIAL AND PRIVATE BEQUESTS

By moving beyond the machine approach to sustainability we are able to imagine new metaphors for the problem. One possibility is *regard for the future* operationalized through the idea of *social bequests*. This approach liberates us from a zero-sum game in which our gain is an automatic loss for future generations. Regard for the future through social bequests shifts the analytical problem to a discussion about deciding what, rather than how much, to leave for those who will follow. This moves the discourse to a level that each family undertakes as it reaches advanced age. The issue is not really how much to pass on to one's children. Rather, the question becomes one of what to pass on: A few things will be sold off, a few things will be given to dear friends, and a few things to highly regarded charities.

Then one comes to the core, our legacy to our heirs. These artifacts represent our essential values, objects we hope they will value as we valued them. We acquire our concerns for the future from our knowledge of the past. And it is this knowledge of the past that comprises the essence of what shall be left to the future. This value is manifest through our acquisition of these objects, through their maintenance, and now through their transmission to the future.

The traditional approach suggests that sustainability criteria can be imposed as a constraint on the maximization of social preferences concerning the welfare between present and future generations. This is operationalized by arguing that each successive generation has a duty to ensure that the expected welfare of its offspring is no less than its own perceived wellbeing. But this approach is to view sustainability as a problem of *substantive rationality*. Rather, the future must be provided for through social bequests informed by the logic of *procedural rationality* (Simon, 1987). Procedural rationality calls for a variety of processes whereby choices about what shall be left for the future will occur.

These processes will not be informed by maximization algorithms concerning future capital, or future levels of welfare. They will, instead, be informed by a consideration of the various kinds of artifacts, both natural and constructed, that our descendants might value. The procedurally rational approach seeks to consider the social bequest problem in much the same way that good parents (or regents) seek to shape those who will follow. This is a process of imposed values, indeed of imposed tastes and preferences. Pushpin is not the same as Pushkin, any more than tall redwoods are the same as paved parking lots.

Of course there will be disagreements about what will be *useful* and *essential* to the future. Similarly, families worry about that which will be both useful and essential to their offspring. But is the problem of social bequests of a different order than that within the family? While more involved, it is fundamentally identical: we do not leave the values of our children to chance and there seems scant reason to suppose that we should do so with respect to future generations. We do not want our children, or future persons for that matter, to grow to like plastic trees.

Economists can contribute to this discourse in a way that will enhance its procedural rationality. We can warn about unnecessary costs to achieve certain outcomes. We can inform the process by alerting decision makers to the idea of opportunity costs, marginal costs and benefits, uniqueness and irreversibilities. The twin concepts of uniqueness and irreversibility are central to informed choices about bequests for the future.

The present generation stands in the unique position of influencing all of those aspects of our descendants. We do not shrink from it in the private economics of our own household and, as the early Greeks knew so well, the economy of the earth is but a logical extension of one's home. But how does one approach the problem of constructed order?

PROPERTY REGIMES AND SUSTAINABILITY

I have stressed the importance of the idea of constructed order as an essential approach to sustainability. This idea is advanced as the antithesis of the spontaneous order to arise from market processes. The contrast concerns the presumptions that underlie the two approaches. If one starts from the perspective of intertemporal modelling then sustainability must be introduced as a constraint on optimal behaviour over time (Howarth, 1997). On this approach, the spontaneous order to arise from market processes is judged to be inadequate and that order – and the associated outcomes – must be modified (constrained) in line with some analytical judgment about intertemporal efficiency and equity. Once the new 'optimal path' is determined, predicated on the relevant sustainability constraints, some would be inclined to speak of the 'economic costs' of abiding by the sustainability constraints.

However, such calculations of unconstrained optimality, and the alleged costs of meeting the sustainability constraint, are without logical support since we have no basis for conjuring either the optimal path unconstrained by concern for sustainability, or the constrained path. With this difficulty in mind, we can approach sustainability in a more intellectually honest fashion. The idea of a constructed order captures this approach. On this tack, there is conscious discussion and negotiation both within individual nation-states and in the international community. Decisions will be reached concerning what will be conserved for future persons. As indicated above, these discussions will concern essential settings and circumstances. Of course attention will need to be devoted to the apparent costs of particular choices, but we should not suppose that these calculations represent anything other than rough first approximations to the problem at hand. No one should ever assume that efficiency or optimality is served (or violated) by the choices made. But the challenge is not to let the best become the enemy of the better. We need not be assured of all-around efficiency before we act. Those who have come before us, and who were responsible for the creation of Yellowstone National Park, for preserving the Grand Canyon and for striving to clean up our air and water resources, were certainly not impeded by the lack of insight concerning the efficiency properties of the chosen policies (Vatn and Bromley, 1994).

On this tack, one approaches sustainability by focusing attention on which settings and circumstances will be set aside and protected for future persons. To do so is to bind those of us living in the present with legal duties. It is only through such *duties* on present persons that we can bestow *rights* on future persons. Nature does not, despite popular thought, have rights; only persons have rights. And those rights are secured through duties on other persons who would otherwise contravene the interests of the right holder, in this case future persons (Bromley, 1991). The duties on those of us living today represent the mechanism whereby social bequests are made in the interest of the future.

This approach may seem threatening to landowners who imagine that their ownership bestows full control of land use without regard for the implications of that use for future persons. Owners of forest lands, however, are not free to disregard the interests of future persons with respect to, for example, spotted owls or red cockaded woodpeckers. Urban landowners have long been cognizant of the larger social interest in the land use decisions of private landowners; urban zoning is addressed to precisely that end. Rural landowners are now confronted with that same imperative; they are increasingly bound by duties over draining wetlands or destroying habitats essential to the survival of certain species. The recent Supreme Court decision in *Babbitt* v. *Sweet Home Chapter of Communities for a Greater Oregon* [115 S. Ct. 2407 (1995)] was a stark reminder to landowners that the content and meaning of property rights in land are *discovered* as courts seek to reconcile the varied and conflicting interests in natural habitats (Bromley, 1993, 1997). Environmental sustainability means maintaining choices for future persons which, inevitably, means restricting choices for present persons. This is what I mean by a constructed order.

Sustainability is at once a fine idea and a hopeless concept. It is good because it reminds us of the fate of future persons; it is hopeless because it begs for operational content. The better part of wisdom suggests that we should take it on its own terms, but not ask too much of it. As a metaphor to guide some action it is probably quite adequate. But we must move to another epistemological programme to ascertain what we should do about the future. That alternative programme is not the Smithian machine and its providential spontaneous order. It is, instead, the Kantian imperative of Pure Reason applied to future persons. From this comes the demand for a constructed order that will ensure particular settings and circumstances for future persons.

NOTES

1. I should call attention here to a special issue of *Land Economics* on Sustainability (73(4), November 1997) under the editorship of Richard Howarth. This issue contains 10 excellent articles on sustainability.
2. For a comment on that research programme, see Vatn and Bromley (1994).

REFERENCES

Bishop, Richard C. (1978), 'Endangered species and uncertainty: the economics of a safe minimum standard', *American Journal of Agricultural Economics*, 57, 10–18.
Bromley, Daniel W. (1989a), *Economic Interests and Institutions: The Conceptual Foundations of Public Policy*, Oxford: Blackwell.
Bromley, Daniel W. (1989b), 'Entitlements, missing markets and environmental uncertainty', *Journal of Environmental Economics and Management*, 17, 181–94.
Bromley, Daniel W. (1990), 'The ideology of efficiency: searching for a theory of policy analysis', *Journal of Environmental Economics and Management*, 19, 86–107.
Bromley, Daniel W. (1991), *Environment and Economy: Property Rights and Public Policy*, Oxford: Blackwell.
Bromley, Daniel W. (1993), 'Regulatory takings: coherent concept or logical contradiction?', *Vermont Law Review*, 17(3), 647–82.
Bromley, Daniel W. (1997), 'Constitutional political economy: property claims in a dynamic world', *Contemporary Economic Policy*, 15(4), 43–54.
Ciriacy-Wantrup, S.V. (1968), *Resource Conservation: Economics and Politics*, Berkeley: University of California Press.
Commons, John R. (1990), *Institutional Economics*, New Brunswick, NJ: Transaction Publishers.

Cooter, Robert and Peter Rappoport (1984), 'Were the ordinalists wrong about welfare economics?', *Journal of Economic Literature*, 22, 507–30.

Dasgupta, Partha and Geoffrey Heal (1974), 'The optimal depletion of exhaustible resources', *Review of Economic Studies*, 41, 3–28.

Dasgupta, Partha and Geoffrey Heal (1979), *Economic Theory and Exhaustible Resources*, Cambridge: Cambridge University Press.

Dasgupta, Partha and Karl-Goran Mäler (1995), 'Poverty, institutions and the environmental resource base', in J. Behrman and T.N. Srinivasan (eds), *Handbook of Development Economics*, Amsterdam: North-Holland.

Hartwick, John M. (1977), 'Intergenerational equity and the investing of rents from exhaustible resources', *American Economic Review*, 67, 972–4.

Hayek, F. (1960), *The Constitution of Liberty*, London: Routledge & Kegan Paul.

Howarth, Richard B. (1995), 'Sustainability under uncertainty: a deontological approach', *Land Economics*, 71(4), 417–27.

Howarth, Richard B. (1997), 'Sustainability as opportunity', *Land Economics*, 73(4), 569–79.

Howarth, Richard B. and Richard B. Norgaard (1990), 'Intergenerational resource rights, efficiency and social optimality', *Land Economics*, 66, 1–11.

Howarth, Richard B. and Richard B. Norgaard (1995), 'Intergenerational choices under global environmental change', in D.W. Bromley (ed.), *Handbook of Environmental Economics*, Oxford: Blackwell.

Krautkraemer, Jeffrey A. (1985), 'Optimal growth, resource amenities and the preservation of natural environments', *Review of Economic Studies*, 52, 153–70.

Macpherson, C.B. (1973), *Democratic Theory*, Oxford: Clarendon Press.

Mäler, Karl-Goran (1974), *Environmental Economics: A Theoretical Enquiry*, Baltimore: Johns Hopkins University Press.

Mirowski, Philip (1987), 'The philosophical bases of institutional economics', *Journal of Economic Issues*, 21, 1001–38.

Mishan, E.J. (1980), 'How valid are economic evaluations of allocative changes?', *Journal of Economic Issues*, 14, 143–61.

Norton, Bryan G. (1995), 'Evaluating ecosystem states: two competing paradigms', *Ecological Economics*, 14(2), 113–28.

Page, Talbot (1977), *Conservation and Economic Efficiency*, Baltimore: Johns Hopkins University Press.

Pearce, David W. (1988), 'Economics, equity and sustainable development', *Futures*, 21, 598–605.

Pearce, David W. and Giles D. Atkinson (1993), 'Capital theory and the measurement of sustainable development: an indicator of "weak" sustainability', *Ecological Economics*, 8, 103–8.

Pezzey, John (1989), 'Economic Analysis of Sustainable Growth and Sustainable Development', World Bank, Environment Department Working Paper No. 15, Washington, DC.

Pezzey, John (1992), 'Sustainability: an interdisciplinary guide', *Environmental Values*, 1, 321–62.

Polanyi, Karl (1957), *The Great Transformation*, Boston: Beacon Press.

Sen, Amartya (1993), 'Markets and freedoms: achievements and limitations of the market mechanism in promoting individual freedoms', *Oxford Economic Papers*, 45, 519–41.

Simon, Herbert (1987), 'Rationality in psychology and economics', in R. Hogarth and M.W. Reder (eds), *Rational Choice*, Chicago: University of Chicago Press.

Solow, Robert M. (1974), 'Intergenerational equity and exhaustible resources', *Review of Economic Studies*, 41, 29–45.

Solow, Robert M. (1992), *An Almost Practical Step Toward Sustainability*, Washington, DC: Resources for the Future.

Vatn, Arild and Daniel W. Bromley (1994), 'Choices without prices without apologies', *Journal of Environmental Economics and Management*, 26, 129–48.

Viner, Jacob (1961), 'Hayek on freedom and coercion', *Southern Economics Journal*, 27, 230–36.

Woodward, Richard T. and Richard C. Bishop (1995), 'Efficiency, sustainability and global warming', *Ecological Economics*, 14(2), 101–12.

5. The challenges of valuation: ecological economics between matter and meaning

Sabine U. O'Hara

INTRODUCTION

The issue of valuation is central to the discipline of economics. Its pursuit has been cast in questions of what constitutes value, how value is created and how value is expressed in economic activity and economic institutions. While the interest in value and value creation is equally pertinent to ecological economics, ecological economists have framed valuation questions differently than their mainstream colleagues. For today's economic mainstream, prices are fundamental to the expression of value. Prices state the revealed preferences of consumers and the profit-seeking behaviour of firms. They are thus a 'democratic' expression of the self-interested behaviour of consumers and producers as well as a reflection of the organization and coordination of consumers' and producers' competing human needs and wants in decentralized markets. In fact, it is not the individual expression of utility or profit maximization per se but this process of coordinating and negotiating competing interests that ultimately assigns value.

Ecological economists generally view the reliance on prices as primary expression of value with scepticism. The reason for this ambiguity is that ecological economics has added considerable complexity to the model of market exchange advanced in mainline economics. Ecological economics views economic activity as taking place within a larger context of material flows which originate in the environment, are processed in economic activity and released back into the environment as high entropy waste (Boulding, 1993; Georgescu-Roegen, 1971; Daly, 1991). Further complexity is added by those who contend that material flows are not simply an expression of 'natural processes' linking human economic activity to its biophysical context, but reflect the social and cultural context of human activity as well (Martinez-Alier and Schluepmann, 1987; Norgaard, 1994; Gowdy and O'Hara, 1995). For ecological economists, economic activity is therefore more accurately described as a complex system of four interrelated spheres: (1) *market exchange*, described by the familiar models of neoclassical economics; (2) *unaccounted-for economic activity*, described by the numerous 'informal' economic contributions of households, communities and the reciprocal systems of subsistence economies; (3) *human activity*, described as social interactions, participation and personal identity associated with institutions and culture; and (4) *biological, ecological and physical processes*, commonly labelled 'the environment'.[1]

Borrowing from physics and biology, this contextual view of market economics presents economics as a subsystem of nested economic, human social and non-human biophysical systems organized in a complex hierarchy. While each subsystem is characterized by distinct time frames, spatial configurations, behaviours and rules, all subsystems are interconnected, overlapping and coequal. Prices are, at best, a reflection of one subsystem's rules and behaviour, namely the allocative and distributive activity of an economy relying on monetary value as the expression of individual market participants' interests and desires. An unfettered price mechanism, however, is unable to express the time frames, spatial characteristics or relational links relevant to the social or environmental systems within which monetary market exchange takes place. Unless deliberate efforts are made to 'internalize' neglected social and environmental considerations, prices fail to register such essential processes and attributes as the value of lost ecosystems functions, lost biodiversity, lost security, lost care or lost knowledge resulting from increasingly homogeneous social structures.

Internalizing such essential social and ecological functions, however, is not a one-way street. It is not enough to ask how social and environmental functions can best be assigned monetary value so as to 'correct' prices. What is needed instead is an understanding of the complex social, cultural, physical, biological and ecological systems themselves. Such reversed thinking is a challenge for economists. It demands nothing less than relinquishing the centrality of the subsystem 'monetary market exchange' and internalizing economics into the material and non-material context of human lives and the environment (O'Hara, 1998). This view of internalization requires alternative assessment methods which do not rely on one subsystem's (the market's) measure of evaluating all others. Instead, it requires a methodology that allows the complexities of all systems to become explicitly admitted to the valuation process rather than being implicitly considered in 'corrected' market prices.

One such method is the open and uncoerced discourse of individuals in a process of mutual acceptance and respect. Such discourse can be viewed as a decentralized coordination mechanism which gives expression to the life world (Habermas' term, *Lebenswelt*) with all its material constraints, social relationships and valuation patterns. For ecological economics such discourse-based valuation is of particular importance for two reasons: (1) discourse can link all systems levels and thus provides the basis for expanding familiar disciplinary valuation methods to an expressly multidisciplinary process; (2) discourse invites participation from affected stakeholders and thus questions the institutionalized segregation of 'expert' judges and 'non-expert' victims.

The following discussion of discourse-based valuation addresses three specific aspects: first, a theoretical discussion of discourse versus price-based valuation outlines differences and necessary extensions of a context-based understanding of valuation; secondly, a brief description of empirical examples of discourse-based valuation serves to identify conditions of ethical rather than manipulative discourse; and thirdly, critical issues of perceptive biases are identified. It is argued that addressing such biases is essential both to a successful discourse-based valuation process and to a more mature understanding of ecological economics itself.

MATERIAL FLOWS AND BEYOND

Placing economic activity within its larger context of interrelated social and environmental systems has not been the standard economic approach to confronting the problem of neglected negative externalities. A review of the literature on valuation shows the reverse strategy. Rather than internalizing economics, economists have devised a variety of valuation techniques (for example, hedonic pricing, travel costs assessment and various types of survey-based contingent valuation) to internalize unaccounted-for environmental services into economic valuation categories of use value, option value or existence value. Critics of this approach argue that even expanded economic valuation methods remain firmly embedded in the very conceptual framework which causes the inadequate representation of ecosystems qualities and functions in the first place. This does not simply refer to the fact that economic valuation seeks to assign monetary value to the environment's assimilative, recreative, restorative and spiritual functions.[2] It also addresses broader valuation biases of economic abstraction and its insistence on individualistically defined rational choice as the relevant valuation framework. The political scientist Dryzek, for example, argues that the utilitarian discourse reflected in economists' approach to valuation is merely one along a spectrum of environmental values from 'market rationalism and faith in growth' to 'survivalism' and 'green romanticism' (Dryzek, 1987, 1997).

There are exceptions within the economics profession as well. Some have advocated leaving the framework of economics and defining ecosystems-based limits to economic activity such as safe minimum standards or standards based on the precautionary principle instead (Bishop 1978; Krutilla 1967). Proponents of material flows and structural analysis also step outside a purely economic

valuation framework. This school of thought views the analysis of measures
of energy, material flows or land – including the network connections between
various types of economic activity – as a more appropriate basis for evaluating
impacts of economic activity (Ayres and Kneese, 1969; Duchin and Lange,
1994; Reeves and Wackernagl, 1994). As biophysical systems provide natural
resources and receive emissions and wastes, the direct and indirect impacts of
alternative production and consumption activities on resource use, waste,
toxicity or entropy generation are by no means self-evident but require careful
analysis.

An analysis of material and energy flow often pays less attention to social and
cultural factors that influence physical flows and the valuation of trade-offs
between various valuation categories. Cultural preferences for green New
England lawns, for example, affect the irrigation demand in the arid and semi-
arid climates of New Mexico or Southern California. Social and cultural
perceptions also influence the relative value of jobs versus environmental
protection, of store-bought goods and service (provided in markets) versus
home-made ones, and of the value assigned to various types of material impacts
such as the loss of rain forests, the extinction of whales or the extinction of
plankton (Kellert, 1993; Cobb, 1992). Such valuation differences often have
little to do with the actual seriousness of material impacts. And social/cultural
biases have an impact even on the observation of material or energy flows
themselves. Inuit, for example, have many different expressions for our word
'snow', indicating a much more detailed awareness of qualitative differences
between various kinds of precipitation than is common for other ethnic groups
whose perceptions are shaped by different environmental contexts (Whorf,
1963). Freeman describes similar examples of the Inuit's awareness of 'material'
connections based on 'essentially esoteric knowledge' that escapes the perspective of Western science (Freeman, 1986). He recounts, for example, that
wildlife biologists instructed Inuit in Arctic Canada to hunt only a few large
male caribou from each herd. The Inuit argued that, according to their traditional hunting practices, older animals are spared since they play an important
stabilizing role in the herd. Hunting the old males would therefore have a
different effect than hunting other caribou and lead to a collapse of the caribou
population. The Inuit were correct. Despite lower hunting quotas, formerly
abundant caribou populations dropped sharply.[3] These examples illustrate that
measurable, quantifiable observations are not simply value-neutral. They are
shaped by cultural perception and cognition.

This then raises the question whether quantitative analysis alone provides
an adequate basis for a context-conscious approach to valuation in which
multiple systems hierarchies and linkages can be expressed. Georgescu-Roegen
reviews the rationale for a departure from quantitative valuation. He writes:

To use words, instead of numbers, for truly qualitative changes cannot be represented by an arithmomorphic model. Qualities are not pre-ordered, as numbers are, by their own special nature. The most relevant part of history is a story told in words, even when it is accompanied by some time series that mark the passage of time. (Georgescu-Roegen, 1979, p. 325)

Discrete information about systems linkages, changes and overlaps in complex systems and subsystems can best be expressed through 'dialectical approaches'. Monetary as well as non-monetary quantitative valuation seeks to assign distinctly discrete, numerical value to qualitative differences. Qualitative evolutionary change introduces novelty that is unique and unpredictable. Its qualities overlap and are not distinctly discrete. Information contained in a new product embodies previous information. Information about the impact of this new product on workers, workers' families, their communities, the communities' water supply or species within the regional watershed cannot simply be logically deduced from the characteristics of the product itself, its input demands, or even its emission and waste stream. Attempts to compress the infinite properties and endless possibilities of complex human and environmental systems into numerical value invariably result in significant loss of differentiated information.

Discourse, as a 'dialectical alternative', offers a verbally based, qualitative approach to valuation. Analogous to the price mechanism as 'democratic' expression of individual participants' interests, discourse reflects the organizational task of coordinating competing human needs and wants in decentralized markets.[4] Analogous to the price mechanism, discourse-based coordination assigns value ultimately through the negotiation task itself and not through the preassigned, predetermined value brought forth by any one individual. Given its relational nature, discourse attempts to recover what the economist Biesecker calls 'the market as a realm of social interaction', not coordinated by money and power but by discursive reciprocity (Biesecker, 1994). Discourse does not rely on one system's success measure alone but admits complex and multiple valuation criteria like the biophysical world's assimilative capacity, a society's distinct ways of organizing social institutions, or participants' value systems and attitudes towards the valuation process. Value, therefore, is not simply assigned through monetary power (the central measure of market economics) but through measures associated with other life world contexts like health, social participation, satisfaction, or responsibility to future generations.

To view discourse as an alternative to monetary valuation is not as radical a proposition as it might seem at first glance. Markets as institutional mechanisms were and still are, in many parts of the world, places of communicative interaction where a wide variety of rules, behaviours and attitudes are expressed. The farmers' market in the small town in southwestern German where I grew up is still a place for communicative interaction, as are local markets all over the world. Communicative interaction here means buying things from people one knows and trusts (especially in times of beef scares, milk hormones and pesticide-sprayed apples), exchanging information, meeting neighbours and strangers, and even being recognized as an individual with one's own personal idiosyncracies. My frugal grandmother, for example, always went to the market just before 1:00 p.m. since by that time eggs were cheaper than early in the morning when the market first opened. Yet I am sure that the farmer my grand-mother went to week after week had had the small brown paper bag with eggs waiting under the counter since early in the morning.

Discourse can preserve the decentralized institutional character of markets while at the same time recovering their forgotten dimension as places of social interaction that communicate much more than what is captured in market prices. By including the life world context in the valuation process, discourse-based valuation points not only to the limitation of monetary or, more generally, quan-titative valuation; it also points to the limits of a rational choice framework which is rooted in individualistically based notions of reason. Thus discursive reason is inseparably linked to and informed by human experience of a social, cultural and environmental context that shapes and informs individual lives. Table 5.1 summarizes five characteristics that distinguish discourse from familiar market valuation through prices (see also Biesecker, 1996).

First, discourse allows the life world, that is the larger social and environ-mental context of peoples' lives, to become visible. Context is not simply reduced to information hidden or contained in price signals, but is given explicit expression.

Secondly, discourse views individual actors not in isolation but as acting within a network of social relationships and contexts. The philosopher Apel (1973) refers to the 'discursive person' and the sociologist Habermas (1982, 1984) to the 'person in communicative interaction'. As behavioural research shows, such discursive interaction changes decision outcomes. Dawes *et al.* (1990), for example, conducted a number of 'public goods' experiments where small groups of randomly chosen subjects were asked to make a monetary con-tribution for the benefit of all. Some participant groups were given the opportunity to meet and talk for 10 minutes prior to the start of the experiment, while others were kept in isolation. The results were striking. Given the same information at the outset of the game, groups who had met prior to the start of the game were far more likely to contribute to the 'common good' (75–85 per cent of participants) than groups whose members had not interacted (30–45 per cent). Caporael *et al.* report similar differences between individual decisions made in isolation and decisions made in interaction (Caporael *et al.*, 1989; see also Bohnet and Frey, 1995).[5]

Table 5.1   Comparison of price- and discourse-based assessment

Coordination through market prices	Coordination through discourse
Price mechanism	Discourse process
Individual in isolation	Individual in life world
Seeking success (maximize self-interest)	Seeking understanding (communicative reciprocity)
Instrumental reason (goal-oriented)	Communicative reason (multifaceted orientation)
Utilitarian ethic	Discursive ethic

Thirdly, discourse defines rationality more broadly than the instrumental rationality of the individual interest-maximizing 'homo economicus' of economic theory. Discursive reason does not simply presume to reflect predetermined individual interests or existing preferences but instead seeks to increase understanding of complex processes. Understanding change in a life world characterized by uncertainty and evolutionary change becomes the essential basis for valuation, and not reductionist notions of value summarized in the form of costs and benefits.[6]

Fourth, discourse allows for an integrated valuation process instead of a compartmentalized one. People express their preferences not only as consumers, but also as citizens, not only as producers but also as family members and neighbours. Sagoff uses the term 'citizen preferences' to refer to the multiple facets of human decision making which are far more than conduits of consumer preferences (Sagoff, 1990, 1998). To express their multiple moral, spiritual, social, economic and aesthetic values people do not simply rely on one uniformly applicable measure of value but consider multiple, complex, and partially overlapping ones. This may lead to quite unexpected results in the overall valuation process. At the very least it illustrates that valuation far exceeds the simple rational choice framework of mainline economics.

And finally, the discursive ethic of the discourse process is distinctly different from the utilitarian ethic underlying the market pursuits of self-interest-maximizing individuals. Ethical discourse insists that discourse participants do not simply pursue a pre-established ethical norm, but instead allow norms to be questioned and redefined by the discourse process itself. All five areas point to numerous applications of discourse-based valuation, particularly in a field like ecological economics with its multidisciplinary and empirical orientation.

NAVIGATING BETWEEN MANIPULATION AND ETHICAL DISCOURSE

Since discourse is based on communicative interaction between competent individuals, a discursive valuation cannot be theorized or contemplated in the abstract. It needs to be practised. Empirical examples of discursive interaction include mediation in environmental policy or land use conflicts (Cormik, 1987; Pruitt and Kressel, 1985), cooperative approaches to land use and resources management (Renn and Webler, 1994; IREE, 1996), corporate discourse between producers and users on product quality, product safety and price (Biesecker, 1996), and vertical discourse between intermediate producers, contractors, marketing and retail on who carries the costs of policy changes affecting production processes and methods.

Three types of discourse are particularly relevant for ecological economics. First, discourse can facilitate an increased understanding of disciplinary valuation criteria as well as disciplinary assumptions and value judgments which shape definitions of rationality and scientific inquiry. Such 'internal' discourse is essential to a multidisciplinary field like ecological economics and to the public policy debate it informs. Yet simply exchanging disciplinary information is not sufficient to increase understanding. Geisler *et al.* observe that, in the multidisciplinary discourse involving participants in engineering design teams, 'mutual knowledge is neither necessary nor sufficient for the public discourse required of multi-disciplinary work ... public discourse depends upon efforts to create and maintain intersubjective understanding' (Geisler *et al.*, 1996 p. 4). Successful discourse thus needs to acknowledge that intradisciplinary and interdisciplinary debates about acceptable versus unacceptable criteria and methodologies, or about the relative and absolute importance of selected measures, carry the normative presuppositions of our respective disciplines. Such disciplinary thinking is exacerbated by institutionalized scientific thinking which functions as gatekeeper to disciplinary knowledge and is more intent on advancing established disciplinary styles than on increasing understanding. In contrast, open discourse requires that participants view their differences with mutual acceptance and acknowledge all contributions as essential to a common goal of increasing understanding of complex systems and systems interactions.

Secondly, discourse can bridge the gap between practitioners and academicians, local knowledge and scientific information, those affected by and those affecting decisions. This kind of participatory discourse breaks through the insulation of scientific knowledge from its surrounding culture. As Mary Douglas argues, it is the insulation of science from culture which allows it to preserve its paradigms of value neutrality and objectivity despite its undeniable marks of cultural subjectivity. Douglas (1986, p. 56) writes:

Scientific theory is the result of a struggle between the classifications being developed for professional purposes by a group of scientists and the classifications being operated in a wider social environment.... Both kinds of classification depend on social interaction. One (that of the scientists) makes determined efforts to specialize and refine its concepts so as to make them fit for use in a discourse that differs from though it is contained within the entrenched ideas of the larger, encompassing social group.

Information and perception contributed by practitioners rather than distanced experts may well shed new light on the physical, social or ecosystems functions people view as essential to their own health and wellbeing or to that of future generations (Tisdell, 1995). To accept such experiential knowledge, however, experts must give up the pretence of a scientific knowledge that insists on being objective and unaffected by social and cultural values. At the same time, it cannot be the aim of a culturally aware discourse to establish a set of culturally aware universally applicable value measures much like attempts to establish social indicators or indicators of ecosystems health. Instead, the discursive ethic formed in the discourse process itself must focus its attention on the process of valuation. Inviting participation, local control and access to decision making, and questioning established value categories in the process, is a vital quality of discourse-based valuation. Ulrich writes:

It cannot be the purpose of an ecological ethic to conclusively define environmental quality based on content criteria as systems of social indicators attempt to do, but instead it should work toward an institutional and methodological opening of processes which form ecological policy decisions.... Viewed in this way the ecological crisis points ultimately to the functional weaknesses of existing democratic decision-making processes. There is a deep connection between our political culture and the way we deal with nature. Ecological questions have in essence to do with our overcoming technocratic models of environmental policy which reduce them to technical control systems of environmental processes, and with showing instead more courage for ecological democracy. (Ulrich, 1989, p. 135; translated by the author)

Third, discourse provides a process for developing scenarios of utopianism (Wallerstein, 1996). Such scenarios cannot simply be derived from established 'expert' knowledge or technical capabilities but must come from a shared vision of the future beyond standard conceptions of technical or economic competence. They articulate instead a vision of long-term sustainable human–human and human–environment relationships. Standard formats of relating the effects of policy, management or lifestyle alternatives in disciplinary jargon and abstract impact assessments are not likely to invite innovative visions of a sustainable future. Stories of people's lives, hopes and aspirations do. An example of a story-based scenario is a report prepared by the Governor's Commission for a Sustainable South Florida (1995; see also Correia, 1995). It presents a narrative vision of sustainable land use and lifestyle practices in the Florida Everglades and Kissimmee River system. The story takes place in the year 2015 and describes life in the twenty-first century, as well as the steps taken in the late 1990s to restore the unique South Florida ecosystem.

Yet discourse around sustainable scenarios is not necessarily comfortable. It questions accepted 'given' consumer preferences, established definitions of welfare and the accepted certainties of certain scientific knowledge and opens them up for scrutiny. Confronting these certitudes, however, may well be the prerequisite for developing a vision of the future that recognizes people's varied material and social needs without jeopardizing the health of ecosystems. The capacity to change does not increase with our insistence on knowing but with our willingness to acknowledge our uncertainty and unknowing. As Robert Ayres has argued: 'It is the great defect of price theory of economic value ... that price makes economic value seem very much more definite and quantitative than it is.'

Discourse-based valuation, however, also has its dangers. Since access to the discourse table shapes the discourse process itself, discourse can, at its best, make hidden normative assumptions, behaviours and motivations visible. At its worst, it simply reinforces established institutionalized thought and knowledge patterns. Seven conditions distinguish a static and manipulative discourse process from open, ethical discourse:[7]

1. inclusion – all potentially affected parties must be given access to the discourse table;
2. mutual acceptance – participants must be willing, and held accountable, to accept all discourse participants and their contributions;
3. equal rights – all participants' contributions must be given equal weight in the discourse process and every participant must have the opportunity to influence the whole;
4. equal access to information — participants must have equal access to information and be willing to share information;
5. procedural flexibility – all participants must have the opportunity to revise their positions, preliminary results and procedural rules of the discourse process;
6. openness – process results must be open to all parties;
7. absence of power – formal equality between discourse participants must ensure that no one party can assert power over others.

These process conditions seek to enforce two basic elements of discourse-based valuation: competence and fairness (Renn *et al.*, 1995). Yet competence and fairness cannot be neatly separated. A broad-based, diverse group of discourse participants for example, may assure a degree of fairness, but it may not guarantee the intersubjective understanding necessary to advance competence. What is needed in addition is the willingness to uncover hidden value biases and to expose them to the scrutiny of conflicting cognition.

CONFRONTING INVISIBLE BARRIERS

Two challenges of discourse-based valuation become evident: institutional barriers associated with 'fairness', and cognition barriers associated with 'competence'. Since institutions are invariably linked to societal assumptions about knowledge and knowledge creation, the two barriers are connected (Douglas, 1986). The subordination of nature in Western industrial thinking, for example, is reflected in institutional arrangements that ignore or even undermine ecosystems' structures and functions, and make it impossible to protect river systems, old-growth forests or coastal areas effectively.[8] Expectations of labour market flexibility disregard social needs for establishing long-term relationships or ecological needs for acquiring long-term intimate knowledge of one's surroundings. The time demands of an economy where 'time is money' are in conflict with the time demands of biological care or of discursive interaction. The emphasis on competition and knowledge as power communicated in educational institutions fosters the ability to operate in isolation rather than to cooperate. And the primacy of private property ownership discourages regard for broadly accessible public space where uncoerced discourse can take place. These examples illustrate the ties between established institutional arrangements and the underlying conceptual conditions which hinder the forming of a discursive ethic and the commitment to intersubjective understanding.

To overcome the barriers to fair and competent discourse, existing valuation biases must be made explicit. This requires, first, that particularly those whose voices have been marginalized be admitted to the discourse process: those whose biocentric or multigenerational ethic is vastly different from the dominant ethic expressed in the economic, scientific or political mainstream, who represent indigenous knowledge, gendered knowledge or a place-based relational concept of historicity. Fair and competent discourse must also mean giving particular attention to the differences in verbal skill among discourse participants. The distribution of verbal skill can become just as much a source of power and distortion as the distribution of wealth in price-based valuation. The broader rationality of discursive reason may not at all be supported by featuring culturally rewarded skills like articulate speech, deductive logic or abstract thinking to the exclusion of less articulate, empathetic or traditional thinking.

Secondly, fair and competent discourse must be intent on uncovering epistemological biases. Admitting marginalized views to the discourse table is no assurance of a discourse that overcomes cognition barriers and improves understanding of the valuation process. The contributions of marginalized voices who often represent local, experiential or traditional knowledge must also be acknowledged as competent. This is no easy feat. George Tinker, Professor at Iliff School of Theology in Denver, Colorado, and a member of the Osage Nation, tells the story of how he took a small group of students up into the Colorado mountains to conduct a ceremony of preparing a place for a retreat in Native spirituality. The group hiked up a mountain, found a suitable place, and Tinker and one of the students, a Navajo, conducted the ceremony in which they offered prayers, burned incense and distributed the smoke using an eagle feather. After the ceremony they made their way back down the mountain in silence. Finally, one of the Western students could not contain himself any longer. Tinker recounts:

> He said: 'That was beautiful', and after a long pause and more silence, he chimed in – 'What did it mean?' The meaning question is always prevalent for Euroamericans. How are we going to categorize it? How are we going to explain this so it can become part of our world? If we can't explain it, it can't be a part of our world.... You see, my children understand the ceremony. They know what to do when it happens. They understand its sacredness, so that explaining the ceremony isn't an important part of the Indian learning system. Rather our young are expected to watch the elders in everything that they do, whether it's planting corn or telling stories or conducting a ceremony of prayer. They learn by watching. They learn by watching the relationship between their elders and the earth and the different people in the community. (Tinker, 1994, p. 9)

Despite well-meaning attempts at creating 'formal' equality, discourse processes invariably carry the mark of participants' conception of reality and of 'meaning giving'; that is, of placing observations into an accepted framework of reality and its constructed value. As Gould (1978), Lewontin (1982), Roth (1982) and others have pointed out, organisms do not simply adapt to their environments: they also construct them out of bits and pieces of information about the external world. We do not simply perceive the world as it really is, but we perceive pieces and construct the rest, thus giving meaning to the whole. Valuation is therefore more than assigning value gradations to observed parameters, structures or functions. It also involves a process of boundary drawing, of establishing categories of sameness and difference (Douglas, 1986, 1992). Such boundaries serve to establish notions of logical meaning, knowledge and value. Only after the boundaries are defined can classification schemes be devised that allow us to identify 'valid' measures, weigh them and evaluate trade-offs between different validated measures. The quasi-factual intake of information is as much shaped by culture, history and perception as more obvious normative judgments. The process of 'meaning giving', of making sense of and attributing significance to observations, therefore, becomes a selection mechanism to inquiry itself. Observations that 'make sense' are admitted to the data set while those that do not fit into established categories of meaning are discarded. This is particularly evident for quantitative valuation methods which tend to force responses into predetermined categories. In contrast, the competence needed for successful discourse-based valuation involves the ability to suspend existing classification schemes and uncover underlying valuation biases (O'Hara, 1996). Competence thus does not simply imply a form of predefined 'expertise', but connotes personal development, context experience, social interaction skills and the ability to be self-reflective.

Different discourse techniques tend to be able to overcome barriers to discursive valuation and meet the standards of competence and fairness to a different degree (Renn *et al.*, 1995; Selman, 1996; Sexton *et al.*, 1999).[9] Citizen Advisory Councils, for example, are relatively restricted to a selected group of participants who are generally expected to contribute a particular 'formal' expertise to the valuation process. Advisory councils thus tend to limit participation to the 'invited' and underscore institutional as well as cognition barriers. Citizen juries and planning cells tend to be less exclusive than citizen councils. Both processes generally represent a broad cross-section of the affected public and thus may ensure broad participation. However, citizen juries in particular restrict the valuation process to evaluating a limited number of preselected policy options and assess acceptance barriers and other transaction costs that may impede their implementation.

Focus groups are generally rather short-term and designed to gauge existing opinions or understanding of an issue, rather then seeking to improve understanding among focus group participants. Like citizen juries and planning cells, focus groups tend to select group participants from a broad spectrum of citizens. However, participants are grouped into small groups of six to 10, according to 'typical' characteristics representing a specific subgroup. As a result, focus groups tend to lack the multifaceted representation of viewpoints that facilitate the communicative reason of discursive interaction. Study groups, on the other hand, are designed to increase understanding about specific environmental or development issues. They tend to be longer-term and can offer a forum for expanding existing knowledge systems, as well as encouraging broad-based participation. However, it is often difficult for study groups to maintain a level of participation if the learning process is devoid of institutional power and does not translate into action.

Citizen initiatives tend to be more action-oriented. They are generally open and inclusive of a wide variety of perspectives. Initiatives generally view it as their responsibility to inform as well as organize citizens on pertinent environmental and development issues. Because of this commitment to educating the public, citizen initiatives generally work hard at representing a spectrum of local, experiential and technical knowledge and thus can be a powerful force in overcoming competence barriers. Projects undertaken by citizen initiatives are often carried by the sheer energy of determined citizens with little institutional support. The Clean Annapolis River Project (CARP) in Nova Scotia, for example, has been part of Canada's Atlantic Coastal Program since 1991. Since then CARP has been involved in more than 30 initiatives, including public education programmes, voluntary water quality monitoring, fish habitat restoration and sustainable development planning (IREE, 1996; for additional examples, see also Rivervalleypartners, 1997; Douthwaite, 1996). Many similar initiatives have been particularly successful in strengthening public awareness of ecological boundaries and in moving the valuation and decision process from a focus on political boundaries to one more compatible with ecological space. Yet barriers do remain and may hinder the effectiveness of citizen initiatives. Decision makers and agencies representing environmental policies or official development agendas, for example, may dismiss citizen initiatives as 'biased' or representing limited 'local views'. If such barriers are overcome, and citizen initiatives become part of a more formal effort to implement a citizen-based valuation process, they can prove a very successful forum for selecting, evaluating and implementing sustainable development options.

So where does this leave us with respect to the potential for discourse-based valuation as an alternative way of giving expression to the multiple economic, social and environmental systems essential to ecological economics? Formal rules of fairness and broad-based participation may support but not necessarily guarantee acceptance of different modes of competence in the discourse process. Discourse that meets the basic characteristics of fairness and competence can therefore not simply be content with identifying and expressing disciplinary valuation categories, contrasting views between experts and practitioners, or technological versus organic approaches. To truly meet its goal of seeking understanding, discourse must also be intent on making value biases, assumptions and implicit power structures visible. This suggests that the discursive ethic formed in an open and uncoerced discourse process is an ethic critical of accepted assumptions and knowledge definitions. The Swiss economic ethicist Arthur Rich (1984) contrasts two essential aspects of ethics: ethic as familiar place, connoting common practice, custom or manners, and ethic as informed insight about what should be, connoting critical examination of accepted standards and a continuing critical redefinition as context conditions change. While the first aspect may form an important basis for discourse, the second aspect may be essential to reaching new insights and solutions to pressing social and environmental problems. Given the potential of discourse for broadening our awareness of what is as well as our perceptions of what can be, the biggest challenge to discourse-based valuation may also be its biggest opportunity.

CONCLUSIONS

It has not been easy for ecological economics to navigate its way between economics and science, markets and regulatory policy, impartial inquiry and engaged advocacy. Neither markets nor centralized economies have built-in mechanisms to value and respect social and ecological processes. And neither laboratory experiments nor field studies can guarantee certainty so as to establish policy guidelines beyond doubt. These challenges limit the effectiveness of standard valuation methods in all disciplines involved.

This chapter has suggested an alternative process to assess and manage the competing demands of interrelated economic, social and environmental systems. This process relies on the decentralized, open discourse of informed citizens. Discourse thus can be viewed as being situated between the two familiar pillars of environmental policy: markets and government regulation. Two points are intended with this placement of discourse. First, discourse has elements of both the decentralized structure of markets and the responsibility to society at large ideally expressed in regulatory measures. Secondly, discourse offers an integrated valuation framework which does not rely on any one subsystem's mechanism to express systems parameters, function and behaviour. Instead, discourse offers an assessment process in which multiple criteria and measures can be expressed. At the same time, discourse makes neither price-based nor regulation-based policies, neither quantitative nor analytical methods superfluous. It offers instead a valuation process that gives expression to quantitative and qualitative measures, positive and normative judgments, matter and meaning of the life world. Critical discourse places all these perspectives within a conceptual framework that makes the weakness of established valuation and policy measure explicit, including their hidden value biases and power assertions.

Many have pointed to the rapid loss of biodiversity as one of the most serious environmental problems we face today. I would add the loss of sociodiversity as equally disturbing (O'Hara, 1995). Its related problem is increased homogenization and the rapid loss of information, skill and intelligence. This homogenization is not simply the result of increasingly global markets or faster and more accessible transport and information systems. It is also the result of selectively excluding perceptions of reality from the valuation process as the reliance on market values increases. This exclusion invariably narrows the information from which we evaluate quantitative and qualitative changes in economic, social and environmental systems. Discourse expands common disciplinary methods to a broader, language-based rationality which invites multidisciplinary exchange, local participation and a participatory description of scenarios for a sustainable future. The fact that both the complexities of the life world and the uncertainties of coevolving systems can be articulated in a discursive valuation process does not make discourse less precise than more established assessment methods. Instead, it may well make valuation more honest as common boundaries of valid versus invalid, measurable versus intangible and accurate versus speculative are challenged. The real challenge to discourse, then, is not the multiple criteria it admits to the valuation process but the biases that enter the discourse process unconsciously, unspoken and unrecognized. Making such hidden biases visible requires first and foremost a meta discourse about disciplinary biases, expert biases and cultural biases that stand in the way of an ethical discourse free of coercive power.

In his book, *The End of Certainty*, Ilya Prigogine writes: 'Science is a dialogue with nature.' A discourse, one might say, not a monologue of restating what we already know, but a dialogue that allows the possible to become visible beyond our own limited cognition. Prigogine also writes: 'The possible is richer than the real. Nature presents us in effect with the image of creation, of the unforeseeable, or novel' (1997, p. 83) Dialogue, if it is to increase our understanding of the complexities of our world, needs to be open to the obvious as well as the seemingly irrelevant background noises of the conversation. Our commitment to this discourse may just be the most essential work we have to offer to claim the possibilities of a sustainable future.

ACKNOWLEDGMENTS

My sincere thanks to two anonymous reviewers and numerous participants in the 1996 ISEE conference for their helpful comments on an earlier draft of this manuscript. Any remaining errors or misunderstandings are my responsibility.

NOTES

1. The relationship of these four systems has been described as overlapping circles, or as the 'bio-physical sphere' encompassing the spheres of human activity and economic activity.
2. The 1993 report of the US Environmental Protection Agency (EPA)-sponsored Ecosystems Valuation Forum identified naturalist/recreational services, ecological services, scientific services, aesthetic services, utilitarian services and cultural, symbolic, moral and historic services of ecosystems.
3. Similar examples of the importance of social structures in animal populations are also known for wolves and foxes. They do not deny the significant impacts changes in habitat, climatic or hydrological patterns can have. They simply illustrate relational factors affecting biological/ecological systems change that are easily overlooked.
4. The economist McCloskey offers a somewhat different yet compatible argument for the usefulness of language in economics. According to McCloskey, language (or rhetoric, as she calls it) is not only a useful methodological tool but economic activity itself a reflection of language (McCloskey, 1994, McCloskey and Klamer, 1995).

5. Experiments conducted by the Swiss economists Bohnet and Frey (1995) focused especially on the impact of communication on cooperative behaviour. They concluded that communication is a far more important factor in achieving cooperative behaviour (77 per cent) than group identity (23 per cent).
6. A substantial literature on discursive and deliberative approaches to valuation and value formation can be found in philosophy and political science (see, for example, Fishkin, 1995).
7. Similar criteria were developed by Biesecker (1996). Renn and Webler suggest a somewhat different list of nine criteria (Renn, 1996, p. 1170; Renn and Webler, 1994).
8. In its 1995 report on ecosystems approaches to public policy, Environment Canada identifies five general characteristics of ecosystems-based decision making: (1) the geographic area has to be based on natural systems, not just political jurisdiction; (2) decision making has to be multisectoral to allow all stakeholders to participate in the decision process; (3) holistic and interdisciplinary approaches to decision making; (4) cross-scale (temporal and spatial) co-operation between government and community organizations; (5) adaptive and flexible management styles; (6) ethic of sustainability.
9. Renn *et al.* (1995) offer an extensive discussion of eight discourse models: Citizen Advisory Councils, Planning Cells, Citizen Juries, Citizen Initiatives, Regulatory Negotiation, Mediation, Voluntary Sitings of Waste Facilities, and The Dutch Study Group. These models are evaluated against three characteristics of 'fairness' and four characteristics of 'competence'.

REFERENCES

Apel, Karl-Otto (1973), *Diskurs und Verantwortung. Das Problem des Übergangs zur post-konventionellen Moral*, Frankfurt: Surkamp Verlag.
Ayers, Robert and A. Kneese (1969), 'Production, Consumption and Externalities', *American Economics Review* LIX, 282–97.
Biesecker, Adelheid (1994), 'Ökonomie als Raum sozialen Handelns – ein grundbe-grifflicher Rahmen', in Adelheid Biesecker and Klaus Grenzdörffer (eds), *Ökonomie als Raum sozialen Handelns*, Bremen: Donat Verlag.
Biesecker, Adelheid (1996), 'Power and Discourse. Some Theoretical Remarks and Empirical Observations', in Adelheid Biesecker, Wolfram Elsner, Klaus Grenzdörffer and Holger Heide (eds), *Bremer Diskussionspapiere zur Sozialoekonomie*, Nr. 14, October, Universitaet Bremen: Fachbereich Wirtschaftswissenschaft.
Bishop, Richard (1978), 'Endangered Species and Uncertainty: The Economics of a Safe Minimum Standard', *American Journal of Agricultural Economics*, 60, 10–18.
Bohnet, Iris and Bruno Frey (1995), 'Ist Reden Silber und Schweigen Gold? Eine Oekonomische Analyse', *Zeitschrift fuer Wirtschafts- und Sozialwissenschaften*, 2, 169–209.
Boulding, Kenneth (1993), 'The Coming of the Spaceship Earth', in A. Markandya and J. Richardson (eds), *Environmental Economics: A Reader*, New York: St Martin's Press.
Caporael, Linnda, Robyn Dawes, John Orbell and Alphons Van de Kragt (1989), 'Self-ishness examined: Cooperation in the absence of egoistic incentives', *Behavioral and Brain Sciences*, 12, 683–739.
Cobb, John (1992), 'Postmodern Christianity in Quest of Eco-Justice', in Dieter Hessel (ed.), *After Nature's Revolt*, Minneapolis: Fortress Press.
Cormik, Gerald (1987), 'The Myths, the Reality and the Future of Environmental Mediation', in Robert Lake (ed.), *Resolving Locational Conflict*, The State University of New Jersey – Rutgers: Center for Urban Policy Research.

Correia, Mary (1995), 'Institutionalizing Sustainable Land Development', paper presented at the 1995 Eastern Economic Association Conference, 17–19 March, New York City.

Daly, Herman (1991), *Steady State Economics*, 2nd. edn, New York: Island Press.

Dawes, Robyn, Alphons van de Kragt and John Orbell (1990), 'Cooperation for the Benefit of Us: Not Me, or My Conscience', in Jane Mansbridge (ed.), *Beyond Self-Interest*, Chicago and London: University of Chicago Press.

Douglas, Mary (1986), *How Institutions Think*, Syracuse: Syracuse University Press.

Douglas, Mary (1992), *Risk and Blame. Essays in Cultural Theory*, London and New York: Routledge.

Douthwaite, Richard (1996), *Short Circuit. Strengthening Local Economies for Security in an Unstable World*, Dublin: Lilliput Press.

Dryzek, John (1987), *Rational Ecology: Environment and Political Economy*, Oxford and New York: Basil Blackwell.

Dryzek, John (1997), *The Politics of the Earth: Environmental Discourses*, New York: Oxford University Press.

Duchin, Faye and Glenn-Marie Lange (1994), *The Future of the Environment: Ecological Economics and Technological Change*, New York: Oxford University Press.

Environment Canada (1995), 'Guiding Principles for Ecosystem Initiatives', Ecosystem Conservation Directorate, Environment Canada, Hull, QC.

Fishkin, John (1995), *The Voice of the People: Public Opinion and Democracy*, New Haven: Yale University Press.

Freeman, M. (1986), 'Renewable Resources, Economics and Native Communities', in *Native People and Renewable Resource Management*, Report of the 1986 Symposium of the Alberta, Canada, Society of Professional Biologists.

Geisler, Cheryl, Larry Honeycutt and Edwin Rogers (1996), 'Professionalization and Multidisciplinarity: The Reemergence of Public Discourse', paper presented at the annual meeting of the American Educational Reserach Association, New York.

Georgescu-Roegen, Nicholas (1971), *The Entropy Law and the Economic Process*, Cambridge and New York: Harvard University Press.

Georgescu-Roegen, Nicholas (1979), 'Methods in Economic Science', *Journal of Economics Issues*, XIII, 317–28.

Gould, Stephen (1978), *Ever since Darwin: Reflections in Natural History*, 2, London: Burnett Books.

Governor's Commission for a Sustainable South Florida (1995), Draft #2/25, Coral Gables, Florida.

Gowdy, John and Sabine O'Hara (1995), *Economic Theory for Environmentalists*, Delray, Fl.: St. Lucie Press.

Habermas, Jürgen (1982), *Theory des kommunikativen Handelns, Vol. 2*, Frankfurt am Main: Surkamp Verlag.

Habermas, Jürgen (1984), *The Theory of Communicative Action, Vol. 1, Reason and the Rationalization of Society*, Boston: Beacon Press.

IREE (Institute for Research on Environment and Economy) (1996), 'Community Empowerment in Ecosystem Management' (Philippe Crabbe, project director), University of Ottawa.

Kellert, Stephen (1993) 'Attitudes, Knowledge and Behavior Toward Wildlife Among the Industrial Superpowers: United States, Japan and Germany', *Journal of Social Issues*, 49(1), 53–69.

Krutilla, J. (1967), 'Conservation Reconsidered', *American Economic Review*, 57(4), 777–86.

Lewontin, R.C (1982) 'Organisms and Environment', in H.C. Plotkin (ed.), *Learning, Development and Culture: Issues in evolutionary epistemology*, New York: Wiley.

Martinez-Alier, Juan and Karl Schluepmann (1987), *Ecological Economics*, Oxford and New York: Blackwell.

McCloskey, Donald (1994), *Knowledge and Persuasion in Economics*, Cambridge: Cambridge University Press.

McCloskey, Donald and Arjo Klamer (1995), 'One Quarter of GDP is Persuasion', *American Economic Review Papers and Proceedings*, 85(2), 1991–5.

Norgaard, Richard (1994), *Development Betrayed: The End of Progress and a Coevolutionary Revisioning of the Future*, London and New York, Routledge.

O'Hara, Sabine (1995), 'Valuing Socio-Diversity', *International Journal of Social Economics*, 22(5), 31–49.

O'Hara, Sabine (1996), 'Discursive ethics in ecosystems valuation and environmental policy', *Ecological Economics*, 16, 95–107.

O'Hara, Sabine (1998), 'Internalizing Economics: Sustainability Between Matter and Meaning', Essays in Honor of Clement Allen Tisdell, Part IV, (ed.) John O'Brien, *International Journal of Social Economics*, 25 (2/3/4), 175–95.

Prigogine, Ilya (1997), *The End of Certainty. Time, Chaos and the Laws of Nature*, New York: The Free Press.

Pruitt, Dean and Kenneth Kressel (1985), 'The Mediation of Social Conflict: An Introduction', *Journal of Social Issues*, 41(2), 1–10.

Rees, William and Mathis Wackernagl (1996), *Our Ecological Footprint: Reducing Human Impact on the Earth*, Gabriola Island, BC and Philadelphia, PA. New Society Publishers.

Renn, Ortwin (1996), 'Moeglichkeiten und Grenzen diskursiver Verfahren bei umweltrelevanten Planungen', in Adelheid Biesecker and Klaus Grenzdoerfer (eds), *Kooperation, Netzwerk, Selbstorganisation: Elemente demokratischen Wirtschaftens*, Pfaffenweiler: Centaurus Verlag.

Renn, Ortwin and Thomas Webler (1994), 'Konfliktbewültigung durch Kooperation in der Umweltpolitik – theoretische Grundlagen und Handlungsvürschlüge', in Oikos: Umweltoekonomische Studenteninitiative an der HSG (eds), *Kooperationen für die Umwelt. Im Dialog zum Handeln*, Chur, Zürich: Verlag Ruegger.

Renn, Ortwin, Thomas Webler and Peter Wiedemann (1995) *Fairness and Competence in Citizen Participation. Evaluating Models for Environmental Discourse*, Dordrecht: Kluwer.

Rich, Arthur (1984), *Wirtschaftsethik. Grundlagen in theologischer Perspecktive*, Guetersloh: Guetersloher Verlagshaus Gerd Mohn.

Rivervalleypartners (1997), http://www.rivervalleypartners.com

Roth, G. (1982), 'Conditions of evolution and adaptation in organims as autopoietic systems', in D. Mossakowski and G. Roth (eds), *Environmental Adaptation and Evolution*, Stuttgart: Fischer Verlag.

Sagoff, Mark (1990), *The Economy of the Earth: Philosophy, Law and the Environment*, New York and Cambridge: Cambridge University Press.

Sagoff, Mark (1998), 'Aggregation and deliberation in valuing environmental public goods: a look beyond contingent pricing', *Ecological Economics*, 24 (2,3), 213–30.

Selman, Paul (1996), *Local Sustainability. Managing and Planning Ecologically Sound Places*, New York: St Martin's Press.

Sexton, Ken, Alfred Marcus, William Easter and Timothy Burkhardt (1999), *Better Environmental Decisions. Strategies for Governments, Businesses and Communities*, Washington, DC and Covelo, Calif.: Island Press.

Tinker, George (1994), 'Of place, creation and relations', in Sabine O'Hara (ed.) *Finding Our Place, Ecojustice Quarterly*, 14(2).

Tisdell, Clement (1995), 'Issues in Biodiversity Conservation Including the Role of Local Communities', *Environmental Conservation*, 22(3), 216–22.

Ulrich, Peter (1989), 'Lassen sich Oekonomie und Oekologie wirtschaftsethisch versoehnen?', in Eberhard Seifert and R. Pfriem (eds), *Wirtschaftsethik und ökologische Wirtschaftsforschung*, Berne and Stuttgart: Paul Haupt Verlag.

U.S. EPA Ecosystems Valuation Forum (1993), 'Issues in Ecosystem Valuation – Improving Information for Decision Making', Report to the U.S. Environmental Protection Agency, Washington, DC.

Wallerstein, Immanuel (1996), 'Social Science and the Quest for a Just Society', lecture presented at the Society for the Advancement for Socio Economics, Geneva.

Whorf, Benjamin (1963), *Sprache, Denken, Wirklichkeit. Beiträge zur Metalinguistik und Sprachphilosophie*, ed. and trans. Peter Krausser, Munich: Rowohlt Verlag.

PART II

The Economics of Nature

6. The need for a new growth paradigm

Robert U. Ayres

INTRODUCTION

The title of this chapter is obviously intended to provoke questions. Does the need for a new paradigm mean that an old one must be discarded? What does 'growth paradigm' mean? Is the chapter about the end of growth? Is it about 'limits to growth' in the sense of the 1970s debate? Or is it, perhaps, about the nature of a hypothetical 'no growth' or 'steady state' society, and some of the implications of such a society? The answer to all of these questions is no. Probably some readers will assume that this is another neo-Malthusian anti-growth tract. It is not. Quite the contrary, I believe that economic growth is both possible and essential for social and political reasons, if no other. The question I want to address is: what has gone wrong with the old formula and how can (must) it change?

The economic growth engine, as it operates today, is running amok. Economic growth in most of the world is so inequitable that by far the largest share of the benefits is being appropriated by a tiny group of those who were already rich or well-connected, or by corrupt military officers. The so-called 'Asian Miracle' was touted as growth with equity, but the collapse has revealed a very different reality. Worse, globalization led by the multinational corporations leaves an increasing part of the population – and *most* of the population in many parts of the world – with little prospect of benefit, either now or in the foreseeable future. Growth as measured by GDP, even where it is more than keeping up with population, is not producing comparable increases in real social welfare. In short, the present pattern of growth is socially unsustainable.

The present pattern of economic growth, which is based on increasing labour productivity by substituting physical capital based on fossil resources for human workers, is also ecologically and environmentally unsustainable. In fact, there are limits to growth as it is occurring today. However, while the earth's stock of fossil fuels and metal ores is finite and exhaustible, the immediate limits to growth are not imposed by physical scarcity of these commodities, at least for the next generation. The immediate economic problem for developing countries is the opposite: falling commodity prices resulting in falling export income.

The most binding limits are of so-called renewable and environmental resources. The two most immediate problems are water and wood. Economic growth in North China, Northern India, Pakistan and much of the Middle East will be constrained by the growing scarcity – and inequitable allocation – of water for irrigation and for the burgeoning populations of cities. Wood for domestic fuel and charcoal production (for many small-scale industries) is also becoming critically scarce in much of Asia and Africa. The inevitable consequence is uncontrolled deforestation, especially in hilly and mountainous areas, resulting in soil erosion and increasingly catastrophic floods. A third, and arguably more serious, problem is that the toxic waste-assimilative capacity of the earth is declining, as a consequence of the degradation and loss of topsoil, deforestation and loss of biodiversity, while the demand for this service of nature is rising. A fourth problem, much more widely known, albeit still difficult to evaluate quantitatively, is climate warming and its associated dangers.

Economic growth in the future must provide the resources to compensate for these problems, while not being short-circuited by them. Clearly, it must be technology-driven, but the technologies that are needed will have to substitute solar energy and non-material resources – especially information – for material resources. Of course, the ultimate resource is trained human intelligence, which is the main source of our prospects for long-term survival as a species. (This is one of my few points of agreement with the late Julian Simon (Simon, 1980).)

Unfortunately, politicians in all the countries of the West, but especially in continental Europe, have unwittingly compromised this one essential resource. They have sharply limited the possibility of investment in the needed education and scientific research by committing future 'growth dividends' to current consumption by, and subsidies to, all sorts of politically well-connected groups. The R&D and investment deficit is slowing growth when and where it is most needed. A day of reckoning is fast approaching.

To return to the focus of the chapter, then: the existing patterns of growth and the government policies, economic incentives and institutional mechanisms are now driving economic growth along unsustainable and ever more harmful paths. These policies, inconsistent as they are, are based partly on history and partly on theory. The history is relevant to where we are, but it will not help us make the U-turn that is necessary. The economic theory that supports present policies is faulty and misleading in several important ways. The standard economic models and their underlying assumptions must, therefore, be challenged and reconsidered, insofar as they apply to economic growth. In short, the growth *paradigm* must change.

THE COMING CRISIS

The vast majority of professional economists today are obsessed with trade, savings, investment, competitiveness and globalization. They do not concern themselves with equity, environment or technology. Equity is considered irrelevant to growth. Trade is universally supposed to be a primary cause of prosperity. Environmental services are everywhere treated by industry as a 'free good'. To be sure, economic theory generally acknowledges that environmental services are underpriced, but the prevailing 'free market' doctrines assume that government intervention is undesirable because it would be likely to create still greater distortions. Welfare is widely assumed to be just another word for GNP per capita. Technology is almost everywhere assumed – again, except by a few theorists – to be a free good, 'manna from heaven'. These assumptions are all so far off the mark that the future of our civilization is at risk.

The problem of inequity is near the core of the problem. Growth producing benefits only for the elite, the well-educated, the property owners, is socially intolerable and certainly unsustainable (Figure 6.1). Unemployment, especially of the youngest, less skilled, less educated and minority groups (and men), is a blight in the industrial world, particularly Europe. The rising tide of ethnic conflicts, religious fundamentalism and massive population displacements

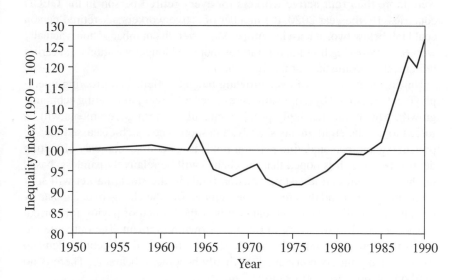

Source: Jackson & Marks, 1994

Figure 6.1   Index of inequality: income distribution in the UK

resulting from wars, environmental disasters and even 'successful' economic development programmes in some parts of the world are creating huge pools of potential refugees trying desperately to get into Europe and North America.

Those who succeed in passing the barriers (and quite a few do, thanks to a growth industry of immigrant smuggling) are driving down wages and displacing unskilled native workers. They also consume social services themselves, especially where such services are most generous. Finally, insecure, unassimilated, marginalized and 'ghettoized', they drive up social costs for all. Rising social costs have to be financed by present taxes or present debt (which must be financed by future taxes). Either of these alternatives reduces job-creating investment and cuts potential economic growth.

Moreover, governments in all of the industrialized countries, including Japan, are facing rising unemployment trends (notwithstanding periodic but ever-weaker 'cyclic recoveries') and ever-growing budget deficits due to past commitments for health care and pensions (so-called 'entitlements') that were expected to be financed out of a perpetual 'growth dividend' that has been overspent (Figure 6.2).

There are two basic reasons for rising costs. One is simple demographics. The fraction of workers living long enough to collect retirement benefits is rising every year, while the declining birth rate means that the number of younger workers available to pay the bills is declining. Forty years ago there were more than four active workers for every retired person in the OECD countries. By the year 2020, the number of active workers per retired person could fall below two, at least in Europe. Moreover, the number of hours actually worked per working lifetime is falling as more and longer vacations and earlier retirements become the norm (Figure 6.3).

Unless the problems of ever-growing budget deficits and growing unemployment are solved by a miraculous resurgence of real job-creating economic growth, which is increasingly problematic, all Western governments will be forced to cut the entitlements sharply, and soon. The much-discussed idea of privatizing and personalizing pension funds is, of course, one way of cutting defined benefits. It is hoped that the change will be relatively painless, based on the argument that investing pension funds in the stock market will spur economic growth and thus reap higher returns. But the changeover can hardly be painless for the generation that will bear the burden of paying for current pensioners while also saving to finance its own retirement. The only alternative is to allow government budget deficits to grow until the debt burden and its accompanying tax consequences finally become unbearable. There is no third option open to a democratic regime.[1]

It is an unpalatable choice. In one sense it is a choice between the young (and future generations) and the old in our society. To allow the present system to continue means continuously raising social security taxes. It also means

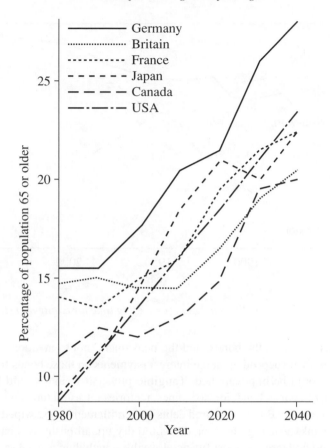

Figure 6.2   Soaring demand for pensions

cutting other expenditures, such as on education and research.[2] Higher taxes on workers means increasing immediate unemployment, the effect of which falls most harshly on the young, especially those who have never held a job. But if taxes are *not* raised, the only alternative left to governments will be to 'print money' to pay the bills that will grow year by year. This can only be done by selling ever more government bonds, thus competing with private sector credit needs. This will simultaneously drive up nominal interest rates and expand the money supply. Of course taxes will also have to rise, in the long run, to meet the cost of debt service.

The result of this strategy would be a gradually accelerating monetary inflation. As inflation eventually took hold, all savings and unsecured 'faith and credit' government debt would be devalued. Inevitably, the financial

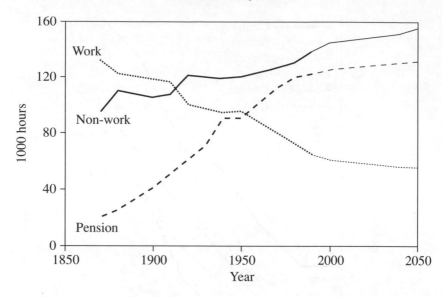

Figure 6.3   UK average lifetime hours (excluding time for eating and sleeping)

institutions who own the bonds, and the pensioners (not to mention widows and orphans) who depend upon the interest payments on those bonds for their incomes, would be impoverished. Tangible physical wealth would be left untouched, of course. Land, forests, mines, factories infrastructure, houses and cars would remain. But if unsecured debts and entitlements were wiped out by inflation, banks would go bust, credit would dry up, all businesses based on credit would collapse and most financial wealth – including private savings – would be lost in the debacle. The retired folks who kept their nominal entitlements would eventually be hurt even worse by a runaway inflation.

   To avoid this outcome, economic growth must continue. Indeed, it must accelerate. Is this possible?

IS GLOBALIZATION A RELIABLE DRIVER OF GROWTH?

Trade barriers have fallen dramatically in Europe and the United States, but very unevenly elsewhere. Asia takes full advantage of free markets for exported goods, but all the Asian countries still practise a high degree of protectionism at home. To be sure, trade liberalization has been good for the multinational firms and the financial sector (which supports it), but the uncomfortable truth is that liberalization has already moved millions of manufacturing jobs from

Europe and North America to East Asia, eastern Europe (and Mexico), with more and more such transfers to come. But increased trade has resulted in no compensating job growth in Europe, and probably none in America. The trade theorists and financial writers who formerly trumpeted huge but hypothetical gains are now reduced to claiming that the negative impact of trade liberalization on jobs is 'lost in the noise' of other macroeconomic effects.

The Southeast Asian 'meltdown' of 1997–8 is only the first evidence of deep-seated problems associated with globalization. One of the key problems is imbalance. Another is lack of effective regulation. Capital markets have been almost totally globalized and deregulated (except for China). And the consequences of huge inflows of portfolio capital into countries without adequate bank regulation or transparency have not been entirely beneficial, to put it mildly.

On the other hand, labour markets have not been globalized at all. Nor will they be. The above discussion of trade liberalization did not even mention the consequences of direct foreign investment (DFI) in contrast to portfolio investment. This is export of capital from the rich industrial countries to exploit cheap labour. In this case, the loss of potential growth in one area of the world is presumably compensated by faster growth among poorer countries. Nevertheless, this trend to export capital to places with cheap labour exacerbates unemployment in Europe, where unemployment is already far too high (Figure 6.4). It also contributes to declining wage rates among the unskilled workers in countries with less regulated labour markets, notably the United States. Both result in worsening social problems.

The fundamental imbalance between globalized capital flows and tightly restricted labour mobility is leading to increasing pressures for migration. Illegal immigrants are accumulating rapidly in countries with relatively liberal immigration policies and protection for victims of harsh and intolerant regimes. A number of the latter are learning how to dump their problem minorities in their neighbours' laps. In response, the recipients of hordes of penniless refugees are becoming less and less liberal.

The theory of free trade itself is flawed. In theory, trade benefits everybody by increasing efficiency and reducing prices for consumers. In theory, job losses are only temporary, at worst, because capital inflows will compensate for negative balances in current trade and investment will create new jobs. In theory, no country can have a negative (positive) balance of trade and a negative (positive) balance of capital flows at the same time. Yet, according to the published statistics, China is positive in both accounts and the United States is equally negative in both departments! The statistics are probably wrong or misleading, but the theoretical balancing effect of return flows does not always work out in practice.

The funds that flow out of Europe and America as portfolio or direct foreign investment or to pay for manufactured goods made in East Asia need not, and

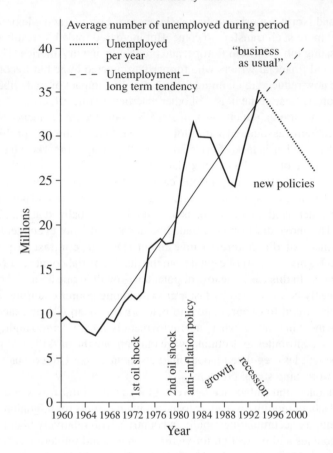

Figure 6.4   Unemployment in OECD countries, 1960–93

do not (for the most part), return as job-creating direct investments in America or Europe. They can be retained abroad indefinitely as official (or unofficial) monetary reserves, effectively increasing the local money supply,[3] or they can return in one of several other non-job-creating ways. The first is through purchases of government bonds to finance the government budget deficits (and, incidentally, to prevent currency devaluations that might help to rectify the trade balance). Or they can return as speculative investments in land, buildings or the booming stock market. The stock markets began rising in the 1980s, partly owing to increasing company profits thanks to 'downsizing' and lower wage bills. But in the last few years there have been clear indications of the 'bubble' phenomenon in the US stock market. Prices have been rising, to some extent, simply because funds keep pouring in. In recent years the most profitable investments have been in the stock market itself. (But bubbles always burst, eventually, as they did in Japan in 1987–9 and more recently in Southeast Asia.) More globalized capital markets mean that financial troubles in faraway places are increasingly felt in New York, London and Frankfurt.

Globalization has been good for some sectors (notably financial services) and for the large multinationals. The impact on growth in Asia was unquestionably powerful, at least for a time. But whether that growth will resume in the near future depends on reforms that most Asian governments seem very unwilling to make. In any case, Asian growth is unlikely to be an engine of growth for Europe or America.

GROWTH VERSUS WELFARE

As a matter of sober fact, economic growth in recent decades has been more apparent than real. In the first place, the statistical growth of GNP that has occurred in the twentieth century has been partly due to the monetization of activities that were formerly not exchanged in the market-place. Women's work at home and subsistence agriculture were two examples of unmonetized activity that have gradually been monetized in the Western world, but much less so in Asia and elsewhere.

But, more relevant to current problems, there has been a disproportionate increase in so-called 'defensive expenditures', such as personal security, transport to and from work, health insurance, accident insurance, legal costs and environmental protection costs. These expenditures add nothing to real welfare. They merely compensate or protect from threats to personal and environmental security and wellbeing that are consequences of urbanization and economic activity itself.

If the social safety net breaks decisively, and if Western democratic institutions prove incapable of responding adequately, the consequences will be catastrophic. I can think of no other suitable word. When poverty, unemployment, hopelessness and despair reach a certain point, which cannot be predicted with precision, the result is chaos. Africa is the precursor. I deeply fear the rise of a new generation of political extremists in both Europe and the United States (and Japan) and a rerun of the 1930s and 1940s – but with modern nuclear, chemical and biological weapons. In the immortal words of Mme Pompadour: 'Après nous, le déluge.' There will be no safe havens from the next flood, if it occurs.

Another reason for misleading statistical growth, in which current prosperity is being achieved at the expense of future generations, is the consumption of natural capital without any provision for replacement. Businesses are not allowed to consume capital and call it income, but governments do it all the time. Oil and gas are pumped and forests are clear-cut and the proceeds are counted as part of GNP, whereas any compensating investments (such as re-forestation) would equally be counted as income.[4] Pollution damages are not subtracted from GNP; on the contrary, the costs of treatment of pollution-related illness and other damages are also added to GNP. The result is that GNP no longer measures the real state of the economy (see, for example, Daly and Cobb, 1989; Jackson and Marks, 1994). (See Figures 6.5 and 6.6.)

Worse still, much of the depletion of natural capital is not even properly measured in economic terms. This includes loss of biodiversity, stratospheric ozone depletion, acidification and toxic build-up in soils, deforestation, erosion and desertification. A problem that is seldom even recognized is disruption of natural cycles, from the hydrological cycle to the carbon, oxygen, nitrogen and sulphur cycles. Human activity already mobilizes at least as much fixed nitrogen, and probably more sulphur, than natural processes (Ayres, 1998). As far as some toxic metals are concerned, human economic activity is already mobilizing several times as much as natural processes in a number of cases, notably arsenic, cadmium and lead (Azar *et al.*, 1996). (See Table 6.1.)

Table 6.1   Indicators of unsustainability

Metal	Ratio of anthropogenic to natural flow	Ratio of cumulative extraction to topsoil inventory
Antimony (Sb)	6.0	—
Arsenic (As)	0.33	—
Cadmium (Cd)	3.9	3.0
Chromium (Cr)	4.6	2.6
Copper (Cu)	24.0	23.0
Lead (Pb)	12.0	19.0
Mercury (Hg)	6.5	17.0
Nickel (Ni)	4.8	2.0
Selenium (Se)	2.0	—
Vanadium (V)	0.32	—
Zinc (Z)	8.3	6.9

The old link between economic growth and human welfare is nearly broken. Each one per cent of growth in GDP now yields, on average, only one-tenth of a one per cent increase in employment. In recent decades, the size of the US economy has grown modestly, but the social welfare of most citizens has not. The rich, the top few per cent, are indeed getting richer. But the condition of the middle class is stagnant and that of the poor, especially the inner city

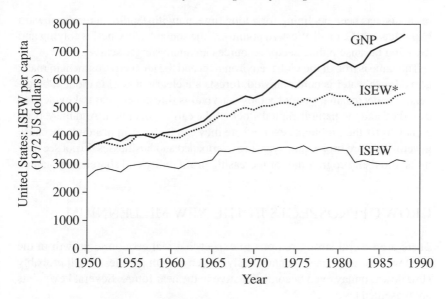

Source: Stockholm Environment Institute, 1994

Figure 6.5   GNP vs. ISEW: USA

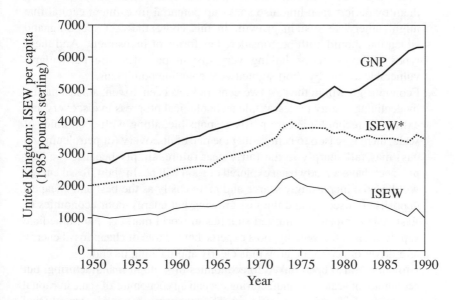

Source: Stockholm Environment Institute, 1994

Figure 6.6   GNP vs. ISEW: UK

residents, has been declining for a long time, notwithstanding a recent upward blip. Meanwhile, in all Western countries, the social 'safety net' is fraying and decaying because public sector resources are increasingly scarce.

The same is true of the global environment and the local environment in many areas. Fresh water is contaminated, forests are clear-cut, soil is eroded, biodiversity is decreasing, many species' survival is threatened, natural cycles are disturbed and the natural capital stock of the earth is depleted. And there is no money to fix the problems, even where they can be fixed in principle, because governments are broke, taxpayers are overloaded and businesses do not see how it fits into their programme for increasing profitability and shareholder value.

GROWTH PROSPECTS IN THE NEW MILLENNIUM

There are several strong reasons to expect that real economic growth in the West will not accelerate spontaneously. Given current policies, it will probably slow down. It may even become negative in the near future. Several key points are presented here.

1. Unfunded entitlements in most Western countries are clearly out of control. Financing them by taxation soaks up potential savings directly. Financing them by deficit spending also soaks up potential investment capital that might otherwise sustain growth. In this context, R&D spending and education should both be considered as forms of investment. And these types of investments, having very distant pay-offs, are particularly vulnerable to cuts by short sighted vote-counting politicians.
2. Economic growth in the past two centuries has been driven, at least partly, by declining energy prices. While technological progress in discovery and extraction technologies are partly responsible, along with economies of scale, there is reason to believe that the rate of discovery (of petroleum and gas) may fall sharply in the fairly near future, simply because the best prospects have already been explored or soon will be. In short, fossil energy will become increasingly scarce and more costly as the best and cheapest deposits are used up and the fast growing but energy-poor economies of East Asia compete for limited supplies in world markets. No immediate supply crisis is foreseen by most experts, but the role of cheap fossil energy as a driver of economic growth is clearly approaching its end.
3. Growth has also been linked to economies of scale in manufacturing, but economies of scale in manufacturing depend on economies of scale in capital equipment. Bigger is more efficient. Thus economic growth is strongly tied to increasing capital intensity. The more capital-intensive the economy, the more capital is needed to replace capital that depreciates. Replacing depre-

ciated fixed capital investments (including infrastructure) soaks up funds that might otherwise finance new projects. Depreciation is one of the causes of declining marginal productivity of capital.
4. Technological progress in information technologies tends to *increase* the rate of depreciation of both fixed and 'human' capital through obsolescence, in some sectors at least. The need to replace obsolescent human capital (such as obsolescent skills) obviously diverts capital away from new investment.
5. Even the GDP growth that is measured by the statisticians is mostly illusory, at least in the West. It does not reflect people being better off, merely greater monetization, more intensive trading activity and more 'defensive' expenditure to compensate for or protect against hazards that did not exist in a non-industrialized world. It also reflects consumption (without replacement) of natural capital.

This brings me to the last and hardest question. Will technological progress create the needed burst of job creation? This deserves a more extended response. In the first century and a half of the Industrial Revolution, technological change generally created more jobs than it cost. New industries were created, to produce new products and services. These new industries employed millions of workers. Even though technological change made labour more productive, the increased output of goods and services more than compensated, by forcing prices down and thus stimulating increased consumption.

Economists have always tended to assume that this synergy between technological innovation and job creation is automatic and 'built in'. In the past, however, it was assumed that all new technologies were subject to the rule of declining returns, so that each 'burst' of technological progress was self-limiting. However, the most active debate among economic growth theorists in the last decade has concerned whether or not information technology (IT) is an exception to the rule of declining returns. In other words, it is claimed by some that information technology has the capability of accelerating economic growth indefinitely by virtue of the (assumed) fact that it is characterized by 'increasing returns' to scale. The (presumed) reason is that the cost of production of an information product (such as software) is insignificant in relation to the cost of R&D. It follows that profits increase faster than sales. Profits can, of course, be invested in more R&D, thus accelerating the technology race.[5]

It is true that the pace of technological progress in the IT sector appears (by some measures) to have accelerated since the 1970s. While this is open to challenge, since there are no objective measures of technological progress per se, we may accept it for purposes of argument. But this fact (if it is a fact) does not prove that diminishing returns no longer apply in other sectors, or that economic growth overall can be accelerated indefinitely.

Recent indications from other sectors are discouraging. Technological improvements and declining costs in information technology have undoubtedly caused prices of information services to fall and demand for them to rise. In this respect the classical mechanism has operated according to classical economic theory. But, unfortunately, unlike previous technological revolutions, IT has not – up to now – resulted in significant new services to final consumers, except perhaps for personal computers (PCs) and computer games, for which consumers are willing to pay a lot more money. Instead, it has displaced enormous numbers of jobs in other industries, both in manufacturing and in services. Thus technological change, for the first time in history, has become a major direct contributor to unemployment.

This point deserves emphasis. When steam engines displaced sails on ships, they did not eliminate sailors. When steam railroads were introduced, steam engines displaced horses, not humans, while sharply cutting transport costs. (To be sure, carriage drivers and stable boys were replaced by engine drivers and mechanics, but the numbers were comparable.) The large-scale use of iron as an industrial material displaced wood and masonry to a minor extent, but it made possible many new machines and structures, and whole industries to produce them. Mechanization in agriculture did displace many agricultural labourers, but they were quickly put to work in city factories making textiles, kitchenware, clothing and other consumer goods. Electric motors displaced steam engines in factories, but few workers. The introduction of electric lighting and electrical household appliances (such as washing machines) displaced some laundry maids, but few other workers. Cars and trucks displaced horses, trams and railways, but employment in the car-manufacturing and car service sectors quickly compensated for the losses.

By contrast, the impact of IT on other industries has been pervasive. The number of jobs created by the IT industry and its satellites (such as the software sector) is not negligible. The software industry employs about 2 million people in the United States, a similar number in western Europe, and 1 million in Japan. But software products for final consumers, mainly games and PC software, account for only a small fraction of this total. Most software is used by business, mainly to operate computer systems that have been installed to increase productivity: that is, to cut employment. Labour-saving technology, formerly confined to the factory floor, has now reached the service sector and the managerial suite with a vengeance. Computers are now replacing literally millions of paper-shuffling and communications jobs in the industrialized world, while millions more are at risk. For example, shopping via the Internet may drive many retail shops out of business.

In fact, computers and IT are reducing the market value of human capital by making many skills obsolete. Already, huge numbers of clerical workers and stenographers have been displaced by computers. Those jobs are disappearing.

Data entry of all kinds is being automated. Telephone and switchboard operators are fast being replaced by voice mail. Programmable machines have eliminated large numbers of machine operators across the whole spectrum of manufacturing. Draughtsmen have been replaced by computer graphics. Bank tellers have been displaced in large numbers by cash machines. Optical scanners have sharply reduced the need for retail check-out clerks. Whole layers of middle management are now being eliminated as information is being passed back and forth between functions (for example, sales, finance, manufacturing, purchasing) with less and less need for human interfaces. Only the fact that lower *costs* of information processing have sharply increased the *demand* for information keeps the employment picture from being much worse than it is.

In short, technological progress, especially in computers and telecommunications, in recent decades has made life better for many, but it has also cost a lot of jobs. Computerization and trade liberalization have been good for the stockholders of multinational corporations (MNCs) and the financial community, but they offer little benefit to the workers. Many of the new jobs now being created, mainly in the service sector, are not good ones capable of supporting families at a decent standard of living. Mostly, they are in retail sales or personal services. The potential of IT for creating 'good' jobs in other sectors is unclear and the record to date is not especially promising. However, this issue cannot be pursued further here.

THE NEED FOR ECORESTRUCTURING

It is difficult to say when, or how, the current economic growth system will collapse; it has proved more resilient than many would have predicted. But, unless *job-creating* growth can be sharply accelerated, the choice facing governments is stark: either there will be very sharp and painful cuts in entitlements and social welfare or there will be a financial crisis, probably sudden (like the onset of the Great Depression) and probably within 20 years.

There is only one way to escape the coming crash ('coming' because it will surely come unless we take preventive action soon). Whereas labour-saving technology has contributed to our socioeconomic difficulties, new technology of another kind – resource-saving and depreciation-cutting rather than labour-saving – offers a possible way out of the economic troubles we now face. In fact, the only possible long-term strategy for global economic revival in the next two decades or so is what has been called 'ecoefficiency' or 'ecorestructuring'.

What is meant by ecorestructuring? It means shifting, on a massive scale, away from production of goods to production of services. It means de-emphasizing the use of labour-saving but resource-intensive technology, shifting to resource-saving technology and dematerialization. It means gradually closing the materials cycle, to reduce and finally eliminate the need for non-renewable extractive resources, especially fossil fuels, and focus instead on redesign to facilitate repair, re-use, renovation, remanufacturing and recycling. This shift is necessary, in any case, for long-term environmental sustainability, but, even if that were not the case, *it is the only way to combine economic growth with increasing employment opportunity.*

It is really elementary economics, although perhaps not so obvious to people with standard training. The starting point is to view economic output of goods and services, in the aggregate, as a function of certain inputs, known as 'factors of production'. These are usually identified as labour, capital and 'resources', usually interpreted as energy (fossil fuels, nuclear power and so on). Economic growth implies increased output. This can result from increases in the factor inputs themselves, or increases in their 'productivity' (output per unit of input).

Most economic growth in the past two centuries has been due to increased labour productivity, resulting from extensive substitutions of physical capital and fossil fuel energy for human labour. To get economic growth without further increases in labour productivity, two things are needed: first, either capital or resources, or both, must become more productive; second, new industries must be created to utilize human labour without utilizing more natural resources. Increasing labour productivity generated economic growth in the late nineteenth and early twentieth centuries because it released labour to work in the new industries that were being created at the time: cars, electrical goods, household appliances, aircraft, and so on.

But increased labour productivity is no longer increasing employment because very few new jobs are being created, even by newly created businesses (of which there are very few in Europe or Japan). This is partly because new businesses at the moment are mostly being created in two areas, information technology and biotechnology, neither of which is very labour-intensive. Moreover, these two new sectors tend to replace labour in other sectors. But it is also because the major manufacturing industries of today, which were mainly established over a century ago, are now mature. They are good at making gradual improvements in existing products but they introduce no radically new and different products or services. Nor will they ever do so.

From the perspective of the private sector, dematerialization in the long run means converting products into services. After all, products are consumed because of the services they provide. But a company that makes its profits by selling products must keep its factories as busy as possible to maximize profits. The profit motive works to maximize production of goods. Because goods are made of materials, this, in turn, tends to maximize the use of natural resources. But materials used do not vanish; they are merely converted into wastes at some stage. Thus the profit motive also tends to maximize the generation of pollution and waste, which eventually degrades the environment.

The way out of this cul de sac is for companies to sell the *services* of products rather than the products themselves. If the manufacturer continues to be the owner (or must take the product back at the end of its useful life), the profit motive works differently. Then, profits are maximized when material inputs are minimized. The incentives are to conserve, not to waste.

Needless to say, this massive transformation will not occur of its own accord, at least not soon enough. There are too many powerful industries heavily invested in the status quo. Government intervention of a very forceful kind will be needed to help new 'sunrise industries' to compete with the established 'sunset' industries. It is essential to disconnect the latter from their subsidies and special access to government regulatory authorities. It would be better to eliminate large existing subsidies on budgetary grounds. The key policy levers we have available are (1) new technology and (2) resource/pollution taxes or (3) exchangeable consumption or emissions quotas.

Tax policy is a tool to accelerate dematerialization via the introduction of new technology. Green taxes should be 'employment-friendly' without being 'growth-unfriendly' by cutting labour costs vis-à-vis resource costs. The idea is to shift the existing tax burden away from labour and capital, which are both far too heavily taxed, and onto non-renewable resources, especially fossil fuels, forest products and metals. Exchangeable quotas, especially consumption quotas, are non-tax mechanisms for income redistribution. They have the further advantage of attacking environmental problems directly and efficiently while simultaneously increasing social equity. The same strategy could also be applied internationally with respect to dealing with truly global problems such as ozone depletion, acidification and climate warming. The first step, of course, would be to negotiate international agreement on national emission quotas for ozone-depleting substances like chlorofluorocarbons (CFCs), acidifying effluents (SO_2 and NO_x) and substances contributing to climate warming (CO_2, methane, N_2O, CFCs and so on). This negotiation would be no easy task, since it involves fundamental ethical issues, but if it could be achieved, the next step would combine environmental protection with development assistance: industrial countries contributing more heavily to these problems would pay the less developed countries for their underused emission quotas.

SURVIVING ECONOMICALLY IN THE GREENHOUSE

I now focus briefly on just one environmental problem, which is a consequence of human interference with the natural carbon–oxygen cycle by converting buried fossil carbon into atmospheric carbon dioxide. The result is climate warming. The probable consequences include increasing disease threats, increased storminess, with accompanying floods and droughts that may make recent episodes seem tame by comparison, and irreversible melting of glaciers and permafrost. The sea level can be expected to rise, during the next half century, by anywhere from 30 centimetres to as much as a metre. Thereafter, glacier melting in the Antarctic and Greenland will kick in and the process will accelerate. This is already happening.

The Kyoto agreement of 1997, with its binding targets on CO_2 emissions reduction for the year 2008, poses a serious challenge to governments, both in the EU and elsewhere. It is generally recognized that 'business as usual' will not achieve the needed results. It is doubtful that the international exchange of tradeable permits, as advocated by the United States, will suffice. That device surely has limited potential at best. Some cynics assume that the targets in question will simply not be achieved, forcing governments to abandon efforts to achieve the impossible. Many of those who resist government intervention of any kind believe that 'technology' will somehow come to the rescue if, indeed, there is a real problem at all. However, for the less cynical, and for those, like the present writer, who believe that the Kyoto targets are already far too modest, failure is not an acceptable option.

Unfortunately a Pigouvian carbon tax – the approach that has been 'on the table' in Europe for some time (see, for example, von Weizsäcker and Jesinghaus, 1992) – has three serious drawbacks. One is, simply, that it is perceived by most industry groups to be just another tax on top of an already excessive tax burden, and a likely drag on productivity and 'competitiveness'. The possibility of fiscal neutrality has been suggested, but most such suggestions remain theoretical. They have not been accompanied by specific and convincing proposals for linking the carbon tax to social security (or some other) tax relief.

The second drawback is that the tax is only a 'second-best' solution to a problem of resource misallocation. It would create new price distortions. Moreover, it is argued that any such tax will inevitably be regressive and inequitable. It would hurt some elements of society (such as low-income consumers, coal miners and coal-burning electric utilities) and offer undeserved windfalls to others (for example, nuclear and hydroelectric power producers). Attempts to shield the first groups and to tax the windfall gains of the second group would inevitably be difficult and contentious.

The third serious drawback of a carbon tax also arises from the fact that economists cannot calculate, in advance, precisely what price a functional market would attach to the rights to consume carbon, how much of a tax would be required to achieve a given reduction in carbon consumption, or how rapidly the adjustment would take place. In practice, any tax rate fixed by a legislature or government agency will be either too high or (much more likely) too low to hit the target.

To compensate for this, any tax programme should be somewhat flexible, even experimental, in nature. But this, in turn, would make it very difficult for firms to plan, and equally difficult for finance ministries to forecast revenues. The difficulty applies equally, if not more, to a carbon tax that is programmed to increase gradually over time, so as to minimize disruption. There are many reasons why the tax would be likely to err on the side of optimism (that is, being set too low), but in that case it might have to be increased much faster than the original plan in order to achieve the target result. This would be traumatic (and politically difficult) and could even trigger a recession.

TRADEABLE CARBON QUOTAS: A POSSIBLE 'WIN–WIN' PROPOSAL

The foregoing catalogue of economic and environmental problems poses a formidable challenge. Nevertheless, there is an opportunity to ameliorate several of them at the same time. In brief, this would involve the waste-assimilative capacity of the earth, specifically for carbon, being treated as a global resource. Until now, access to this resource has been free to all-comers. This means that the greatest benefits have gone to the greatest polluters. (In the case of carbon emissions, this means the United States, although western Europe is not far behind.)

To simplify the argument, I assume that the problem of international allocation among nations has been solved by negotiation. Suppose that each nation has an internationally agreed carbon emissions target, decided several years in advance. This would correspond to a per capita consumption quota. Let these individual quotas be exchangeable.[6] This means the quotas would have a market value because the available quotas would be set (intentionally) somewhat smaller than the quantity demanded in a 'business as usual' scenario.

There are three alternative allocation schemes that need to be assessed. One is for the government to sell quotas, by auction or some other formula, thereby obtaining revenue that would be available for other purposes. One possibility would be to use the proceeds to reduce social security taxes on labour; another would be to finance technological research development on alternatives to hydrocarbon-based energy technologies. The private market for quotas, in this case, would be rather small, inasmuch as most users in a given time period would buy directly from the government. The private market would only match marginal short-term deficits and surpluses. Thus the market price might fluctuate significantly, and the transaction costs (per unit) might be fairly large.

The second alternative is for the government to allocate the quotas free of charge to selected groups. A major question arises in this connection, namely whether it is essential to allocate some or all of the quotas to firms, or whether all quotas should be allocated initially to individual citizens. The argument for allocation to firms is largely based on political expediency. It is widely believed that industry could successfully prevent the adoption of any scheme that did not include 'grandfathering' allocations at no cost. This approach has already been used in the case of sulphur dioxide quotas currently exchanged by electric power utilities in the United States. However, since such allocations have market value, as mentioned already, this would be tantamount to a subsidy for past energy users. In fact, it would be both inequitable and economically inefficient: it would reward inefficient firms that had not cut their fuel usage, while punishing both efficient and growing firms.

The third basic alternative allocation scheme would be to give carbon quotas to citizens (not firms) at no cost. This is an alternative 'first best' approach which is very much in the spirit of internationally tradeable permits, but operates at the national level.[7] (The idea could obviously be extended to some other materials, such as sulphur or chlorine or toxic heavy metals, and perhaps others.) The argument for allocation to individuals is based on fundamental equity considerations. In the first place, it properly reflects the fact that carbon quotas constitute a kind of 'right' and that this fundamental right should belong in the first instance only to persons, not firms or their stockholders. From this perspective, it can be argued – and probably would be argued in court – that any other allocation (for example, to firms) would constitute an unwarranted 'giveaway' of public property to existing property owners. The fact that public property has been allocated to private interests in the past, with respect to mineral rights, water rights and rights to use the electromagnetic spectrum, among others, could be cited as a legal precedent for the practice. But it also provides evidence of just how large and unjustified some of the past giveaways have been.

A further advantage of the individual allocation is that it would not be distributionally regressive in impact. In fact, low-income people are quite likely to be underconsumers of energy and therefore of carbon. Such persons would thus receive a significant net addition to income (albeit of uncertain amount) for selling their unused carbon quotas. High-income individuals with above average energy consumption, on the other hand, would forgo potential income from the sale of carbon quotas or even (in some cases) be forced to buy more on the open market. But one feature of this allocation scheme is that *everyone* (above a certain age) would receive a quota with monetary value.

Since most fuels are purchased in the first instance by utilities and industry, not by individuals, *most individuals would be able to sell a significant fraction of their quotas, and receive money income for it*. Underconsumers, especially the poor and elderly, would receive the most benefits, and the benefits would increase over time. The extra costs to industry would, of course, be reflected in higher prices for energy-intensive goods and services. In that regard, the effect would be similar to that of a carbon tax. It would have all the beneficial effects of a carbon tax and few of the disadvantages.

The mechanics of the system would be very straightforward in the age of information technology. In brief, the national carbon quota for each year (or quarter, or month) would be set, well in advance, by an independent government authority with the specific legislative mandate to set quotas that will achieve the Kyoto target as smoothly as possible. This authority would also have to be responsible for collecting data, monitoring compliance and supervising the exchange mechanism. National carbon quotas would be allocated according to a formula set by the legislature.

Each individual would receive his or her carbon quota in the form of a bank deposit of carbon entitlements – a kind of second currency. The consumer would also receive a debit card, similar to the 'smart cards' that have been available for many years in some countries (such as France). All *direct* purchases of carbon fuels such as heating oil or petrol would require appropriate carbon deductions from the consumer's carbon bank account, as well as the usual money payment. The accounting could easily be done by a modest extension of the existing payment system. *Indirect* purchases of carbon in the form of other goods would not require any additional carbon entitlements since those entitlements would have already been bought and paid for by the producer of the good or service.

The market of quotas itself would be a computerized auction, conducted at regular intervals, perhaps weekly. Computerized centralized exchange markets already exist, and it would only be necessary to decide on the frequency of price setting and the allocation of brokerage rights and fees. Presumably, banks would be the main retail agents for purchase and sale, and each citizen and firm would have a personal carbon account with an instantaneous monetary value.

Each industrial user or electric power producer would, of course, include the price of purchased carbon quotas in its cost base. This would eventually add to the price of the product or service, but it would also create a very powerful incentive for industry to find and develop alternative low-carbon technologies. The end result for the industrial user would be quite similar to the impact of a carbon tax, except that, whereas the tax would be more predictable to the industry, its effect on carbon emissions would be less so.

The new source of income for individuals would, over time, permit the government to cut some social security outlays with less pain. One transparent way of doing this would be for the government to encourage individuals during their working years to credit this extra income directly to tax-deferred individual retirement accounts (IRAs). In time, as the value of saleable underconsumption quotas rose, the need for direct government income transfers would fall. That, in turn, would permit reduction in social security taxes on wages.

This is where the favourable impact on employment enters the picture. Just as in the case of a carbon tax, the result would change the relative prices of energy and capital goods vis-à-vis labour.[8] This would, over time, encourage greater use of labour and less use of labour-saving (but hydrocarbon fuel-consuming) machinery and equipment. It would also encourage re-use and remanufacturing, as compared to primary production, for the same reason.

Again, the exchangeable quota system would keep much of the money in the hands of the lowest-income consumers, thus answering the usual objection that a carbon tax would be regressive. In fact, it would redistribute income from high consumers to low consumers and thus create a fair and equitable income supplement or 'safety net'. It would simultaneously keep the money out of the reach of bureaucrats and politicians who might spend it on pet projects (such as subsidies for favoured constituents). This idea would not be especially welcome to finance ministries, but it would appeal to a lot of voters. That is important because it suggests the possibility of building a viable political constituency for the proposal.

To summarize and emphasize: the assimilative capacity of the environment is a resource that has significant monetary value. This resource should be allocated equitably among the residents of each country and, eventually, the planet. That would be a 'first'. If done right, the result would be to reduce the use of material resources and the cost of labour. Under these conditions, entrepreneurialism would flourish as never before, and truly sustainable economic development would follow.

NOTES

1. A political revolution could, of course, solve the problem with a repudiation of the debt burden, as the Bolsheviks did in 1917.
2. Defence expenditures have already been cut sharply during the past decade, which accounts for the current US budget surplus. But these cuts are unlikely to continue, given the political instabilities and ethnic conflicts around the world. It is noteworthy that the defence savings in Europe have been smoothly reabsorbed by the costly welfare apparatus in Europe, with no benefit to taxpayers.
3. China has reserves of nearly $200 billion.
4. Robert Repetto and his colleagues at the World Resources Institute have documented and quantified these inconsistencies (for example, Repetto *et al.*, 1989; Repetto, 1992).
5. There is another aspect of the problem that interests economic theorists, namely the fact that increasing returns promote oligopoly (because the market leader continues to gain on its competitors) and thus destroy competition. The rapid oligopolization of the software industry, with Microsoft far in the lead, appears to support this contention, and thus (indirectly) to support the increasing returns hypothesis. However, it must be recalled that the entire telecommunications sector, as well as the movie industry, have always been characterized by increasing returns for similar reasons. In fact, the same can be said of any industry in which advertising is extremely important.

6. Sale or purchase would be subject to certain restrictions, for example, on the sale of 'futures'. There could be other rules to protect the poor and unwary from exploitation by clever middlemen.
7. Ayres, Robert U., 'Environmental Market Failures: Are There Any Local Market-Based Corrective Mechanisms for Global Problems?', *Mitigation & Adaptation Strategies for Global Change*, 1997. Also Ayres op. cit. 1998.
8. The effect would also be very similar to the impact of the so-called 'Unitax proposal' presented briefly by Farel Bradbury at this symposium. It differs mainly in that it would apply only to carbon-based fuels (in proportion to their carbon content) rather than to all sources of energy. I would argue that a tax on all sources of energy that does *not* discriminate against carbon would, in fact, encourage continued use of hydrocarbon fuels, which are currently the cheapest, thus effectively discouraging the use of non-polluting sources of energy such as solar power. There was no opportunity to make this point at the symposium, unfortunately.

REFERENCES

Ayres, Robert U. (1997), 'Environmental Market Failures: Are There Any Local Market-Based Corrective Mechanisms for Global Problems?', *Mitigation & Adaptation Strategies for Global Change*.
Ayres, Robert U. (1998), *Turning Point: An End to the Growth Paradigm*, London: Earthscan Publications.
Ayres, Robert U. (1999), 'Industrial Metabolism & the Grand Nutrient Cycles', in Jeroen C.J.M. van den Bergh (ed.), *Handbook of Environmental and Resource Economics*, Cheltenham, UK and Lyme, US: Edward Elgar.
Azar, Christian, John Holmberg and Kristian Lindgren (1996), 'Socio-economic Indicators for Sustainability', *Ecological Economics*, **18**, 89–112.
Daly, Herman E. and John Cobb (1989), *For the Common Good*, Boston: Beacon Press.
Jackson, Tim and Nick Marks (1994), *Measuring Sustainable Economic Welfare – A Pilot Index: 1950–1990*, Stockholm: Stockholm Environmental Institute (in cooperation with the New Economics Foundation, London).
Repetto, Robert (1992), 'Accounting for Environmental Assets', *Scientific American*, 64–70.
Repetto, Robert, William Macgrath, Michael Wells, Christine Beer and Fabrizio Rossini (1989), 'Wasting Assets: Natural Resources in the National Income Accounts', World Resources Institute, Washington, DC.
Simon, Julian (1980), *The Ultimate Resource*, Princeton: Princeton University Press.
von Weizsäcker, Ernst Ulrich and Jochen Jesinghaus (1992), *Ecological Tax Reform: A Policy Proposal for Sustained Development*, London: Zed Books.

7. Implementing sustainable development: a practical framework

Mohan Munasinghe

INTRODUCTION TO SUSTAINABLE DEVELOPMENT

The degradation of the environment has become a serious issue worldwide in recent years. Decision makers are seeking more proactively designed projects and policies that will help anticipate and minimize environmental harm. In the early years of the twenty-first century, the concept of sustainable development has emerged which seeks long-run improvements in the quality of life while protecting productive assets (especially natural resources) for the benefit of future generations (WCED, 1987).

Past work has focused mainly on project level environmental effects through processes such as environmental impact assessments. Continued progress in this area is very important given that conventional development projects often have serious environmental consequences. However, policies that go beyond the local project level frequently have even more potent effects. In particular, for many decades policy reforms contained in the adjustment process, particularly in sector adjustment lending, have included elements that affect natural resource use and the environment. For example, rationalizing of electricity and water prices and removing subsidies for pesticides have been standard objectives of project and sector lending.

More generally, conventional economywide reform efforts (including structural adjustment programmes) have been guided mainly by efficiency and income distribution objectives, without specifically seeking to influence the quality of the natural environment. However, to the extent that they have major impacts on relative prices or on incomes, such reforms hold significant potential either to help or to harm the environment. Therefore analysing links between economywide policies and environment is as important as studying the environmental impacts of projects.

This chapter seeks to provide a comprehensive approach to addressing sustainable development issues. The overall theme focuses on the integration of environmental concerns into conventional economic analysis at all levels of analysis, ranging from the local or project level to the international level, but with special emphasis on the environmental impacts of economywide policies. In the rest of this section, the three main elements of sustainable development – economic, social and environmental – are explained. The second section describes a framework for sustainable development that integrates diverse viewpoints, with ecological economics as the key unifying element. A proactive multidisciplinary procedure is used to assess and quantify the ecological, social and physical impacts of both development policies and projects. Ecological economics helps to value these impacts and incorporate them into conventional economic analysis. Methods for tracing environmental impacts at the project level are set out in the third section, followed by a practical case study that illustrates how the technique might be applied. Three further sections follow the same pattern, describing examples of practical application of the integrated framework and effective articulation of policies and projects to make development more sustainable at the sectoral, national and international levels, respectively. Rather more emphasis is placed on the environmental effects of macroeconomic policies (fifth section), because this is a relatively new area. The main conclusions of the chapter, including areas for further work, are summarized in a final section.

The concept of sustainable development which emerged in the 1980s draws heavily on the experience of several decades of development efforts. Historically, the development of the industrialized world focused on production. Not surprisingly, therefore, the model followed by the developing nations in the 1950s and the 1960s was output- and growth-dominated, based mainly on the concepts of economic efficiency. By the early 1970s, the large and growing numbers of poor in the developing world, and the inadequacy of 'trickle-down' benefits to these groups, led to greater efforts to improve income distribution directly. The development paradigm shifted towards equitable growth, where social (distributional) objectives, especially poverty alleviation, were recognized as distinct from and as important as economic efficiency.

Protection of the environment has now become the third major objective of development. By the early 1980s, a large body of evidence had accumulated that environmental degradation was a major barrier to development. The concept of sustainable development has, therefore, evolved to encompass three major points of view, economic, social and environmental, as shown in Figure 7.1 (Munasinghe, 1993).

Lindahl and Hicks developed the concept of the maximum flow of income that could be generated from a non-declining stock of assets (or capital), which is the basis of the economic approach to sustainability (Solow, 1986; Mäler, 1990). There is an underlying concept of optimality and economic efficiency applied to the use of scarce resources. Problems of interpretation arise in identifying the kinds of capital to be maintained (for example, manufactured, natural and human capital) and their substitutability, as well as in valuing these assets, particularly ecological resources. Uncertainty, irreversibility and catastrophic collapse also introduce additional difficulties (Pearce and Turner, 1990). The social concept of sustainability is people-oriented, and seeks to maintain the stability of social and cultural systems, including the reduction of destructive conflicts (Munasinghe and McNeely, 1994). Intragenerational equity (especially elimination of poverty), pluralism, grassroots participation and the preservation of cultural diversity across the globe are important aspects of this approach (Dasgupta, 1993; Hanna and Munasinghe, 1995a, 1995b). The ecological view of sustainable development focuses on the stability of biological and physical systems (Munasinghe and Shearer, 1995). The emphasis is on preserving the resilience and dynamic ability of such systems to adapt to change, rather than conservation of some 'ideal' static state. Protection of biological diversity is a key aspect (Goodland, 1999).

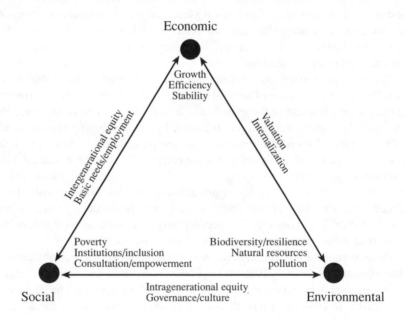

Source: Munasinghe (1993).

Figure 7.1   Elements of sustainable development

Reconciling these various concepts and operationalizing them as a means to achieve sustainable development is a formidable task, since all three elements of sustainable development must be given balanced consideration. The interfaces among the three approaches are also important. Thus the economic and social elements interact to give rise to issues such as intragenerational equity (income distribution) and targeted relief for the poor. The economic–environmental interface has yielded new ideas on valuation and internalization of environmental impacts. Finally, the social–environmental linkage has led to renewed interest in areas like intergenerational equity (rights of future generations) and popular participation.

Sustainable development implies a set of actions adopted to achieve long run improvements in human wellbeing, rather than short-term gains which cannot be sustained. In order to understand sustainable development, it is important to formulate a definition of 'sustainability' in terms of a physical state, rather than a set of activities. The concept of sustainability as applied to ecological and social systems has both spatial and temporal dimensions; in particular, sustainable states of such systems have key characteristics based on persistence, viability and resilience over their 'normal' life spans (see, for example, Munasinghe, 1996). In the hierarchy of such living systems the larger ones (such as a forest ecosystem) generally have greater longevity than smaller ones (such as individual trees).

AN INTEGRATED FRAMEWORK FOR IMPLEMENTING SUSTAINABLE DEVELOPMENT

In seeking an implementable framework that integrates the three different elements of sustainable development in a practical way, it is useful to recognize that most development decisions continue to be based on economic efficiency criteria. An ecological economics framework for integrating environmental considerations into economic decision making is summarized below (for details, see Munasinghe, 1993). The methodology seeks to make development more sustainable by eliminating unsustainable activities – this incremental approach is more practical than trying to define the ideal status of sustainable development.

Ecological Economics and Decision Making

Economic decisions are made at various hierarchical levels of modern society, including the local/project, subnational/sectoral, national/economywide and transnational/global levels. Unfortunately, such a socioeconomic structuring is not compatible with the holistic approach used in environmental analysis to study a physical or ecological system in its entirety. The techniques of environmental assessment (EA) help to identify the impacts of projects and policies on natural systems, but complications arise when such systems cut across the structure of human society. For example, a complex forest ecosystem (like the Amazon) or a physical resource system (like a large river) could span several countries, and also interact with many economic sectors within each country. Furthermore, forest destruction may be caused by hydroelectric dams (energy sector policy), roads (transport policy), slash and burn farming (agriculture sector policy), mining of minerals (industrial sector policy), land clearing encouraged by land tax incentives (fiscal policy), and so on. Disentangling and prioritizing these multiple causes and their impacts will involve a complex analysis. Formulating and implementing remedial measures will be equally difficult.

Ecological economics plays a crucial bridging role. By assigning values to physical and social impacts, ecological economics techniques help to integrate the EA results into the framework of conventional economic analysis at the different hierarchical levels of decision making. Ideally, environmental costs and benefits could be treated like any other costs and benefits of an economic activity.

More broadly, the field of ecological economics encompasses an integrated conceptual approach in which the net benefits of economic activities are maximized, subject to maintaining the stock of productive assets over time, and providing a social safety net to meet the basic needs of the poor. Some analysts support a 'strong sustainability' rule which requires the separate preservation of each category of critical asset (for example, manufactured, natural, sociocultural and human capital), assuming that they are complements rather than substitutes (Daly and Cobb, 1994). Other researchers have argued in favour of 'weak sustainability', which seeks to maintain the aggregate monetary value of the total stock of assets, assuming a high degree of substitutability among the various asset types. At the same time, the underlying basis of economic valuation, optimization and efficient use of resources may not be easily applied to ecological objectives such as protecting biodiversity, or to social goals such as promoting public participation and empowerment – thereby forcing reliance on other techniques such as multi-criteria analysis (see below) to facilitate tradeoffs among a variety of such non-commensurable objectives. The above approach implies that renewable resources, especially if they are scarce, should be utilized at rates less than or equal to the natural rate of regeneration. The efficiency with which non-renewable resources are used ought to be optimized on the basis of the substitutability between these resources and technological progress. Waste should be generated at rates less than or equal to the assimilative capacity of the environment, and efforts should be made to protect intragenerational and intergenerational equity. Finally, the implementation of sustainable development requires a pluralistic and consultative social framework that protects cultural diversity and encourages information exchange with hitherto marginalized groups, to identify less material and pollution-intensive paths for human progress.

One important role of ecological economics is to establish a systematic procedure to improve the design and articulation of (a) sectoral and macro-economic policies, (b) investment projects, and (c) complementary environmental measures. The *first step* towards incorporating environmental concerns into conventional economic decision making is to determine the environmental and social impacts of a project or policy. Economically valuing environmental and social impacts is the *second step* in taking these issues into account. Once the foregoing steps are completed, the *final step* involves redesigning projects and policies to reduce adverse impacts, thereby shifting the development process towards a more sustainable path.

Determining environmental and social impacts of policies and projects requires multidisciplinary expertise. For example, epidemiological studies are used to determine the impact of policies and projects on human health, while sociological studies and analyses provide information on the relevant social impacts. Similarly, ecological impacts of development activities are established by means of ecological analyses. The credibility and effectiveness of the subsequent steps depends on the successful completion of the first step. Hence it is crucial that the environmental and social impacts of policies are both thorough and well documented. Very often uncertainty and poor information tend to hamper the estimation of impacts of projects and policies.

Valuing Environmental Impacts

Economic valuation – the second step in the implementation process outlined earlier – poses significant problems. There has been some modest progress in recent years, in both the theory and application of valuation methods. The conceptual basis for valuation and various practical techniques described in detail in Munasinghe (1993) are briefly summarized below.

Valuation concepts
The basic purpose of valuation is to determine the *total economic value* (TEV) of a resource. TEV consists of two broad categories: use value (UV) and non-use value (NUV); that is, TEV = UV + NUV. *Use values* may be broken down further into (1) direct use value (DUV), (2) indirect use value (IUV) and (3) potential use value or option value (OV). Direct use value is the immediate contribution an environmental asset makes to production or consumption (for example, food or recreation). Indirect use value includes the benefits derived from functional services that the environment provides to support production and consumption (for example, recycling nutrients or breaking down wastes). Option value is the willingness to pay now for the future benefit to be derived

from an existing asset. *Non-use values* are based generally on altruistic, non-utilitarian motives (Schechter and Freeman, 1992) and occur even though the valuer may have no intention of using a resource: one important category, called 'existence value', arises from the satisfaction of merely knowing that the asset exists (as with a rare and remote species).

For the practitioner, what is important is not necessarily the precise conceptual breakdown of economic value, but rather the various empirical techniques that permit us to estimate a monetary value for environmental assets and impacts. However, the results derived from some of these techniques are uncertain even in developed economies and, therefore, their use in developing countries should be tempered by caution and sound judgment.

The willingness to pay (WTP) of individuals for an environmental service or resource is the economic basis for a variety of available valuation techniques (Kolstad and Braden, 1991). WTP is strictly defined as the area under the compensated or Hicksian demand curve which indicates how demand varies with price while keeping the user's utility level constant. Equivalently, the difference between the values of two expenditure (or cost) functions could be used to measure the change in value of an environmental asset. The former are the minimum amounts required to achieve a given level of utility (for a household) or output (for a firm) before and after varying the quality and price of, and/or access to, the environmental resource in question. All other aspects are kept constant. However, the commonly estimated demand function is the Marshallian one, which indicates how demand varies with the price of the environmental good, while keeping the user's income level constant. In practice, it has been shown that the Marshallian and Hicksian estimates of WTP are comparable under certain conditions (Willig, 1976). Furthermore, in a few cases, once the Marshallian demand function has been estimated, the equivalent Hicksian function may be derived in turn. The payments people are willing to accept (WTA) in the way of compensation for environmental damage is another measure of economic value that is related to WTP. WTA and WTP could diverge significantly (Cropper and Oates, 1992). In practice either or both measures are used for valuation.

Valuation techniques

Valuation methods may be categorized according to which type of market they rely on, and by considering how they make use of actual or potential behaviour (see Table 7.1). The most useful methods are based on the way environmental quality changes affect directly observable actions, valued in conventional markets.

Table 7.1 Techniques for valuing environmental impacts

	Type of Market		
Type of behaviour	Conventional market	Implicit market	Constructed market
Acutal behaviour	Effect on production Effect on health Defensive or preventive costs	Travel cost Property values Wage differences Proxy marketed goods	Artificial market
Intended behaviour	Replacement cost Shadow project		Contingent valuation

Effect on production An investment decision often has environmental impacts, which in turn affect the quantity, quality or production costs of a range of productive outputs that may be valued readily in economic terms.

Effect on health This approach is based on health impacts caused by pollution and environmental degradation. One practical measure related to the effect on production is the value of human output lost owing to ill health or premature death. The loss of potential net earnings (called the human capital technique) is one proxy for forgone output, to which the costs of health care or prevention may be added.

Defensive or preventive costs Often costs may be incurred to mitigate the damage caused by an adverse environmental impact. For example, if the drinking water is polluted, extra purification may be needed. Then such additional defensive or preventive expenditures (ex post) could be taken as a minimum estimate of the benefits of mitigation.

Replacement cost and shadow project If an environmental resource that has been impaired is likely to be replaced in the future by another asset that provides equivalent services, the costs of replacement may be used as a proxy for the environmental damage – assuming that the benefits from the original resource are at least as valuable as the replacement expenses. A shadow project is usually designed specifically to offset the environmental damage caused by another project. For example, if the original project was a dam that inundated some forest land, the shadow project might involve the replanting of an equivalent area of forest elsewhere.

Travel cost   This method seeks to determine the demand for a recreational site (such as number of visits per year to a park), as a function of variables like price, visitor income and socioeconomic characteristics. The price is usually the sum of entry fees to the site, costs of travel and opportunity cost of time spent. The consumer surplus associated with the demand curve provides an estimate of the value of the recreational site in question.

Property values   In areas where relatively competitive markets exist for land, it is possible to decompose real estate prices into components attributable to different characteristics such as house and lot size, air and water quality. The marginal WTP for improved local environmental quality is reflected in the increased price of housing in cleaner neighbourhoods. This method has limited application in developing countries, since it requires a competitive housing market, as well as sophisticated data and tools of statistical analysis.

Wage differences   As in the case of property values, the wage differential method attempts to relate changes in the wage rate to environmental conditions, after accounting for the effects of all factors other than environment (age, skill level, job responsibility and so on) that might influence wages.

Proxy marketed goods   This method is useful when an environmental good or service has no readily determined market value, but a close substitute exists which does have a competitively determined price. In such a case, the market price of the substitute may be used as a proxy for the value of the environmental resource.

Artificial market   Such markets are constructed for experimental purposes, to determine consumer WTP for a good or service. For example, a home water purification kit might be marketed at various price levels, or access to a game reserve might be offered on the basis of different admission fees, thereby facilitating the estimation of values.

Contingent valuation   This method puts direct questions to individuals to determine how much they might be willing to pay (WTP) for an environmental resource, or how much compensation they would be willing to accept (WTA) if they were deprived of the same resource. The contingent valuation method (CVM) is more effective when the respondents are familiar with the environmental good or service (for example, water quality) and have adequate information on which to base their preferences. Recent studies indicate that CVM, cautiously and rigorously applied, could provide rough estimates of value that would be helpful in economic decision making, especially when other valuation methods were unavailable.

For more detail on these valuation techniques, see Munasinghe (1993).

Multi-criteria analysis

Multi-criteria analysis (MCA) or multi-objective decision making is particularly useful in situations when a single criterion approach like cost–benefit analysis (CBA) falls short (owing, for example, to problems in valuing environmental impacts such as biodiversity loss). In MCA, desirable objectives are specified, usually within a hierarchical structure. The highest level represents the broad overall objectives (for example, improving the quality of life), often vaguely stated and, hence, not very operational. Some of these, however, can be broken down into more operational lower-level objectives (such as to increase income) so that the extent to which the latter are met may be practically assessed. Sometimes only proxies are available (for example, if the objective is to enhance recreation opportunities, the attribute number of recreation days can be used). Although value judgments may be required in choosing the proper attribute (especially if proxies are involved), measurement does not have to be in monetary terms. More explicit recognition is given to the fact that a variety of concerns may be associated with planning decisions.

Trade-off curves and screening

Figure 7.2 illustrates the basic concepts underlying MCA. Consider a hydro-electric project which could potentially cause biodiversity loss. Objective Z_1 is the additional project cost required to protect biodiversity, and Z_2 is an index indicating the loss of biodiversity. The points A, B and C in the figure represent alternative projects (for example, different designs for the dam). In this case, project B is superior to (or dominates) A in terms of both Z_1 and Z_2 because B exhibits lower costs as well as biodiversity loss relative to A. Thus alternative A may be discarded. However, when we compare B and C the choice is more complicated since the former is better than the latter with respect to costs but worse with respect to biodiversity loss. Proceeding in this fashion, an optimal trade-off curve or curve of best options may be defined by all the non-dominated feasible project alternatives such as B, C and D.

Further ranking of alternatives is not possible without the introduction of value judgments (for an unconstrained problem). Typically, additional information may be provided by a family of equipreference curves that indicate the way in which the decision maker or society trades off one objective against the other (see Figure 7.2). The preferred alternative is one which yields the greatest utility, that is, at the point of tangency D of the best equipreference curve, with the trade-off curve.

Since the equipreference curves are usually not known, other practical techniques may be used to narrow down the set of feasible choices on the trade-off curve. One approach uses limits on objectives or 'exclusionary screening'. For example, the decision maker may face an upper bound on costs (that is, a budgetary constraint), depicted by *CMAX* in the figure. Similarly, ecological

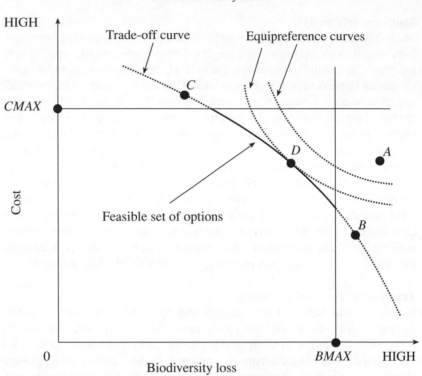

Figure 7.2   A simple two-dimensional example of multi-criteria analysis

experts might set a maximum value of biodiversity loss *BMAX* (for example, a level beyond which the ecosystem suffers catastrophic collapse). These two constraints help to define a more restricted portion of the trade-off curve (darker line), thereby narrowing and simplifying the choices available to the single alternative *D* in the figure.

Decision Making Using MCA

In the somewhat more complicated case shown in Figure 7.3, MCA helps policy makers make strategic decisions when progress towards multiple objectives cannot be measured in terms of a single criterion (that is, monetary values). Take the case of drinking water (an essential element of sustainable development) illustrated in this figure. While the economic value of water is measurable, its contribution to social and environmental goals is not easily valued monetarily. Outward movements along the axes trace gains in three indicators: economic efficiency (monetary benefits), social equity (service to the poor) and environmental pollution (water quality).

Let us assess the policy options. First, triangle *ABC* describes the existing water supply where economic efficiency is moderate, social equity is low and overall water quality is worst. Next, triangle *DEF* indicates a 'win–win' future option in which all three indices improve, as could occur with a new water supply scheme that provided cleaner water, especially to the poor. The economic gains would include cheaper water and increased productivity from reductions in waterborne diseases; social gains would come from helping the disadvantaged; and wastewater treatment would reduce impure water discharges and overall water pollution.

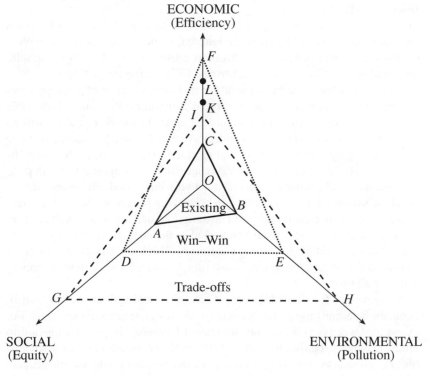

Source: Munasinghe (1993).

Figure 7.3 Decision making using MCA

After realizing such 'win–win' gains, other available options would require trade-offs. In triangle *GIH*, further environmental and social gains are attainable only at the expense of sharply increasing costs. In sharp contrast to the move from *ABC* to *DEF*, which is unambiguously desirable, a policy maker may not make a further shift from *DEF* to *GIH* without knowing the relative weights that society places on the three indices. Such preferences are often difficult to determine explicitly, but it is possible to narrow the options. Suppose a small economic cost, *FL*, yields the full social gain *DG*, while a large economic cost, *LI*, is required to realize the environmental benefit *EH*. Here, the social gain may better justify the economic sacrifice. Further, if budgetary constraints limit costs to less that *FK*, then sufficient funds exist only to pay for the social benefits, and the environmental improvements will have to be deferred.

Complicating Factors

Discount rate

In economic decision making, a forward-looking approach is used in which past (or sunk) costs and benefits are ignored, while a discount rate is applied to future costs and benefits to yield their present values (see, for example, Dasgupta *et al.*, 1972; Little and Mirrlees, 1974; Harberger, 1976).

Starting from the theoretically ideal (or first-best) situation of perfectly functioning, competitive markets and an optimal distribution of income, it is possible to show that the discount rate should be equal to the marginal returns to investment (or marginal yield on capital) which will also equal the interest rate on borrowing by both consumers and producers (Lind, 1982). More specifically, there are three conditions to ensure an efficient (or optimal) growth path. First, the marginal returns to investment between one period and the next should equal the rate of interest (i) charged to borrowing producers. Second, the rate of change of the marginal utility of consumption (or satisfaction derived from one extra unit consumed) from one period to the next should be equal to the interest rate (r) paid out to lending consumers. Third, and finally, the producer and consumer rates of interest are equal (that is, $i = r$), throughout the economy and over all time periods.

As we deviate from the ideal market conditions and optimal income distribution, the determination of the discount (or interest) rate becomes less clear. For example, taxes (subsidies) may increase (decrease) the borrowing rate to producers above (below) the interest rate paid to consumers on their savings (that is, i unequal to r). More generally, if the three conditions do not hold because of economic distortions, then efficiency may require project or sector-specific discount rates that would include second-best corrections to compensate for the economic imperfections. In extreme cases, there is no theoretical basis for linking observed market interest rates to the social rate of discount. However, market behaviour would still provide useful information on the social rate of discount.

Practically speaking, there are two main approaches to determining a value of the social rate of discount (SRD) for climate change analysis: one based on the social rate of time preference (SRTP), which seeks to estimate how consumption is valued today relative to the future, and the other on actual market returns to investment (MRI). While the concepts underlying the two approaches may appear to diverge, when practical adjustments are made they tend to produce estimates for the social discount rate that are comparable: typically, SRTP varies from 1 to 5 per cent and MRI (for risk-free projects) lies in the range 4 to 8 per cent, for long-run investment decisions (for applications to climate change, see Jepma and Munasinghe, 1998).

The long-term perspective required for sustainable development suggests that the discount rate might play a critical role in intertemporal decisions concerning the use of environmental resources (Lind and Arrow, 1982). The rate of capital productivity is very high in many developing countries, because of capital scarcity, and the rate of time preference also is elevated because of the urgency of satisfying immediate food needs rather than ensuring long-term food security (Pearce and Turner, 1990). Projects with social costs occurring in the long term and net social benefits occurring in the near term will be favoured by higher discount rates. Conversely, projects with benefits accruing in the long run will be less likely to be undertaken under high discount rates. Thus some environmentalists have argued that discount rates should be lowered to facilitate environmentally sound projects meeting the CBA criteria. This would lead, however, to more investment projects of all types, thereby possibly threatening fragile environmental resource bases. Norgaard (1991) argues that lowering discount rates can in fact worsen environmental degradation: by lowering the cost of capital and thereby lowering the cost of production, more is consumed in the near term relative to the case where discount rates were higher. Further, using a very low discount rate to protect future generations is inequitable, since it would penalize the present generation, especially when the present contained widespread poverty (Pearce, 1991).

In order to facilitate such intergenerational transfers, one option is to impose a sustainability constraint, whereby current wellbeing is maximized without reducing the welfare of future generations below that of the current generation. In practice, this would entail monitoring and measurement of capital stocks (man-made, human and natural) and a broad investment policy which sought to ensure that compensating investments offset depreciation of existing assets. Theoretically, the aim would be to ensure that the overall stock of assets is preserved or enhanced for future generations, but practical application would be difficult.

For routine project cost–benefit analysis, the normal range of opportunity cost of capital (for example, 4–12 per cent) may be used as the discount rate. Efforts should be made to ensure that compensating investments offset capital stock degradation arising from policy and project decisions; and in the case of projects leading to irreversible damage, CBA should (to the extent possible), include the forgone benefits of preservation.

There is some basis in traditional discount rate analysis for arguing in favour of using declining (and even negative) discount rates for evaluating costs and benefits over very long (or multigenerational) time periods, when welfare and returns on investment may be falling. Consider the social rate of time preference which has components $SRTP = a + bg$. Here a represents the preference of an individual for consumption today rather than in the future – it may be based on the myopic notice of 'pure' preference, as well as the risk perception that future consumption may never be realized; b is the elasticity of marginal welfare and g is the growth rate of consumption. The second term (bg) reflects the fact that the declining marginal welfare of consumption combined with increases in expected future consumption will make future consumption less valuable than present-day consumption: since we are likely to be richer in the future, today's consumption is more highly valued.

The general consensus is that a is close to zero, usually 0 to 3 per cent, and b may be in the range of 1 to 2. Thus, if g is large (high expected economic growth rates), then SRTP could be quite large too. On the other hand, if we consider a long-range scenario in which growth and consumption are falling (for example, catastrophic global warming in 100 years), then g could become negative and consequently SRTP might be small or even negative. In this case, with SRTP as the discount rate, future costs and benefits would loom much larger in present value terms than if the conventional opportunity cost of capital (say, 8 per cent) was used, thereby giving a larger weight to long-term, intergenerational concerns. The key point is that it may be misleading to choose discount rates without assuming some consistent future scenario (see Uzawa, 1969, for a case where the discount rate is endogenized). Thus an optimistic future would be associated with higher discount rates than a gloomy one, which is consistent since the risk of future catastrophes should encourage greater concern for the future.

Risk and uncertainty
All economic decisions about the future entail risk and uncertainty. Risk is usually defined as the likelihood of occurrence of an undesirable event (such as an oil spill) and estimated by its probability of occurrence. In standard CBA, the risk probability and severity of damage may be used to determine an expected value of potential costs. However, the degree of variability in outcomes or the range of values that might be expected is not captured by the use of a single number (or expected value of risk). Furthermore, it does not allow for individual perceptions of risk. No such quantification is possible for uncertainty, where (by definition) the future outcome is unknown. Here, since the future cannot be perceived clearly, the speed of advance should be tailored to the distance over which the clarity of vision is acceptable. As more understanding of an unknown phenomenon is gained, the uncertainty may be gradually transformed into estimates of future risk probability.

Sensitivity analysis is the conventional way of incorporating risk and uncertainty considerations into project-level CBA. In this approach, both optimistic and pessimistic values are used for different variables to determine how sensitive project benefits and costs are to such variables. Sensitivity analysis is useful for determining which variables are most critical to the success or failure of a project, although the upper or lower values of variables need not reflect their actual probability of occurrence. More sophisticated approaches to analysing risk and uncertainty are available (Kolstad and Braden, 1991). For example, a range of values helps identify more robust options, whereas a single deterministic point value could be quite misleading. Other criteria such as mini-max and minimum regret may be used. The issue of uncertainty plays an important role in environmental valuation and policy formulation – for example, because option values and quasi-option values are based on the existence of uncertainty (for details, see Pearce and Turner, 1990; Freeman, 1993).

PROJECT OR LOCAL LEVEL APPLICATIONS

Analytical Framework

If the economic valuation exercise is successful, these results could be incorporated directly into cost–benefit analysis (CBA). CBA seeks to assess project costs and benefits using a common yardstick. Benefits are defined in relation to the way in which a project improves human welfare. Costs of scarce resources used up by the project are measured by their opportunity costs: the benefit forgone by not using these inputs in the best alternative application. One basic criterion for accepting a project compares the flow of discounted costs and benefits over time to ensure that the net present value (NPV) of benefits is positive.

Efficiency-related problems arise in measuring costs and benefits because some project inputs and outputs have incorrect market prices. A general remedy is to use shadow prices, usually based on economic opportunity costs (Dasgupta *et al.*, 1972; Little and Mirrlees, 1974; Squire and Van der Tak, 1975; Munasinghe, 1990). In simpler cases, existing market prices may be adjusted directly (for example, by eliminating distorting taxes and duties or subsidies), or pre-calculated conversion factors could be used to estimate shadow prices for relevant goods and services. A more difficult example that is more specific to environmental assets involves a typical class of market failures called externalities; they are defined as beneficial (or harmful) effects imposed on others, for which the originator of these effects cannot charge (or be charged). Unfortunately, many externalities are not only difficult to quantify in physical terms, but even harder to convert into monetary equivalents. Another example, equally difficult to value, involves open access resources, typically those goods and services that are accessible to everyone without payment, such as a lake or public highway. They tend to be overexploited since user charges are negligible.

If the value of a damaging externality can be estimated on the basis of its shadow price, appropriate charges may be imposed on the source. When such valuation and pricing are difficult, often the approach taken is either to impose regulations and standards that set physical limits on perceived external damages or to better define property rights, thereby encouraging improved natural resource management. Techniques such as multi-criteria analysis (described earlier), are also helpful to decision makers when economic valuation is difficult.

Asymmetries in the incidence of project costs and benefits also have equity implications. The issues are particularly acute if the principal beneficiaries are relatively wealthy, while costs (frequently related to environmental degradation) have to be borne by poorer groups. In theory, if total benefits exceeded total costs, the gainers could compensate the losers and still remain better off. In practice, such schemes are often difficult to implement. For example, in a number of hydroelectric schemes, local residents whose dwellings were inundated by the dams received quite inadequate resettlement benefits, even though specific measures were included in the original project design (Guggenheim, 1994). A more difficult case might involve a polluting industry discharging toxic chemicals into a river, which in turn results in a diffuse and hard-to-measure external health hazard downstream (Carlin *et al.*, 1992).

Case Study: Rainforest Management in Madagascar

Madagascar is one of the economically poorest and ecologically richest countries in the world, and it has been designated by the international community as a prime area for biodiversity whose ecosystems are also at great risk. The government of Madagascar is taking steps to control forest degradation and to protect biodiversity. The results summarized below are from the first stage in the analysis to arrive at a rational decision concerning the proposed creation of the Mantadia National Park in Madagascar (see Kramer *et al.*, 1992).

The creation of a national park generates many indirect and direct costs and benefits. Costs arise from land acquisition (if the land had been previously privately owned), the hiring of park personnel and the development of roads, visitors' facilities and other infrastructure. Another important set of costs that are often ignored are the opportunity costs associated with the forgone uses of park land. Benefits include both use values and non-use values. Tourism can generate considerable revenues for the country from entrance fees and travel expenditures. National parks also generate a number of non-use benefits, among which existence value and option value are important. Other benefits may include reduced deforestation, watershed protection and climate regulation. This study seeks to measure some of the more important and difficult-to-measure economic effects, that is, the impact of the park on local villagers and the benefits of the new park for foreign tourists.

Local people use the park area for rice cultivation and for gathering forest products. The creation of the park results in an opportunity cost in terms of lost production, as summarized in Table 7.2, based on detailed surveys of 351 households in 17 villages within a 7.5 km radius of the proposed park. The forgone benefit net of inputs used is $91 per household per year. A comprehensive contingent valuation survey of the same villages indicated that the WTP for access denied to the park area amounted to $108 per household per year.

Table 7.2   Value of agricultural and forestry activities (in US dollars)

Activity	Number of observations	Total annual value for all villages	Annual mean value per household
Rice	351	44 928	128
Fuelwood	316	13 289	38
Crayfish	19	220	12
Crab	110	402	3.7
Tenreck	21	125	6
Frog	11	71	6.5

A novel international travel cost (or recreation demand) model was used to determine the value of the proposed park to international tourists. The average tourist earned about $60 000 per year, had 15 years of education, and spent about $2900 per trip. Two empirical models – random utility (RU) and typical trip (TT) – were used to measure value, yielding estimates of $24 and $45 per trip. A separate contingent value survey of ecotourists yielded a mean willingness-to-pay of $65 per trip.

Conclusions
All these results, and the total present value of benefits from these alternative uses of the rainforest (by local villagers or tourists), are summarized in Table 7.3. Several tentative conclusions can be drawn from the early results of this study. Non-market valuation techniques can provide useful information for economic evaluation of national parks. A major strength of this study is the opportunity to compare valuation techniques. For the village component, the estimated benefits from park use based on two entirely different methods, opportunity cost analysis and contingent valuation method, were remarkably similar ($91 and $108, respectively, per household per year). The estimates of tourist benefits based on the travel cost method and contingent valuation method were somewhat more disparate ($24 to $65 per trip) but it is noteworthy that the benefit estimates are of the same order of magnitude. We note that the higher

contingent valuation estimate may reflect some non-use values, while the recreation demand method is mainly for use value only.

Table 7.3   Summary of economic analysis of Mantadia National Park

Estimates of Welfare Losses to Local Villagers from Establishment of Park		
Method used	Annual mean value per household (in US$)	Total present value[1] (in US$)
Opportunity cost	91	673 078
Contingent valuation	108	566 070

Estimates of Welfare Gains to Foreign Tourists from Establishment of Park		
Method used	Annual mean value per trip (in US$)	Total present value[1] (in US$)
Recreation demand 1 (RU)	24	936 000
Recreation demand 2 (TT)	45	1 750 000
Contingent valuation	65	2 530 333

[1]   Discount rate = 10 per cent.

This type of analysis would have implications for policy, investment decisions, resource mobilization and project design and management. It can help governments decide how (a) to allocate scarce capital resources among competing land use activities; (b) to choose and implement investments for natural resource conservation and development; (c) to determine pricing, land use and incentive policies; (d) to determine compensation for local villagers for forgone access to forest areas designated as national parks; and (e) to value the park as a global environmental asset for foreigners (thus attracting external assistance for conservation programmes at the local level).

At the same time, the findings indicate future issues. Reliance on WTP is fundamental to the economic approach, but tends to overemphasize the importance of value ascribed to richer foreign visitors. Assuming mutually exclusive alternative uses of the park, the costs (represented by the forgone benefits of villagers) are significantly less than potential benefits to tourists. If conflicting claims to park access were to be determined purely on this basis, residents (especially the poor local villagers) are more likely to be excluded. Therefore, as indicated in the introduction to this chapter, the sociocultural concepts of sustainable development (especially intragenerational equity and distributional concerns) would need to be invoked to protect the basic rights of local residents, perhaps in the form of a 'safe minimum' degree of access to park facilities.

SECTORAL OR SUBNATIONAL-LEVEL APPLICATIONS

Analytical Framework

Actions that affect an entire sector or region of a country often have more significant and pervasive environmental and social impacts than individual projects; examples include policies concerning the pricing of water or transport, investment programmes involving a series of energy projects, and administrative measures such as improving land tenure. The basic rule for economically efficient pricing of a scarce resource (or service) like energy, water or transport is that price should equal the marginal opportunity cost of supply (Munasinghe, 1990). In many countries, such resources are subsidized – an example of a policy distortion. Raising resource prices closer to efficient levels and strengthening market forces are essential prerequisites for reducing the wasteful use of resources, thereby realizing both economic savings and environmental gains. At the same time, efficient investment planning at the sector level implies determining least-cost supply facilities that meet the demand. A typical example is the optimal long-run development plan for a power supply system, involving a series of projects (Munasinghe, 1992).

Environmental economic analysis of such sectoral measures has helped to improve efficient resource use. For example, the use of a resource may have external impacts, such as automobile exhausts causing respiratory problems. In this case, pollution taxes should be imposed on energy users, corresponding to the marginal environmental or health damage that occurs. Such charges are additional to the conventional marginal cost of supply, and therefore reinforce the desirability of efficient pricing. Environmental economists also adopt a long-run perspective, thereby facilitating comprehensive planning and the sustainable exploitation of resources. Sectoral policies such as energy price reforms have such broad effects that they are better analysed in the same context as other economywide policies (see below).

The widespread nature of policies in a given sector emphasizes the need explicitly to take account of their impact on other sectors of the economy (that is, to treat them as economywide policies). This requires an integrated, multisectoral analytic framework. Such an integrated decision-making approach is described here, within the context of a case study involving the energy sector and emphasizing the hierarchical conceptual framework for analysis of sustainable energy development. But the framework can be easily adapted to other sectors as well.

The core of the framework is the integrated multi-level analysis shown in the middle column of Figure 7.4 (drawing on the example of the energy sector). The framework can accommodate issues ranging from the global level down to the local or project level. At the global level it is recognized that there are energy–environmental issues. Individual countries constitute elements of an international matrix. Economic and environmental conditions imposed at this level constitute exogenous inputs or constraints on national-level decision makers.

The next level of hierarchy focuses on the multisectoral national economy, of which the energy sector is one element. The framework suggests that planning within the energy sector requires analysis of the links between the energy sector and the rest of the economy. At the intermediate level the framework focuses on the energy sector as a separate entity composed of subsectors such as electricity, petroleum products and so on. This permits detailed analysis, with special emphasis on interactions among different energy subsectors. The most disaggregate and lowest hierarchical level pertains to energy analysis within each of the energy subsectors. At this level most of the detailed energy planning and implementation of projects is carried out by line institutions (both public and private).

In practice, the various levels of analysis merge and overlap considerably, requiring that (inter) sectoral linkages should be carefully examined. Energy–environmental interactions (represented by the vertical bar) tend to cut across all levels and need to be incorporated into the analysis as far as possible. Such interactions also provide important paths for incorporating environmental considerations into national energy policies.

Case Study: Improving Energy Sector Decision Making in Sri Lanka

The incorporation of environmental externalities into decision making is particularly important in the power sector, where environmental concerns abound. It is also clear that in order for environmental concerns to play a real role in power sector decision making, one must address these issues early: at the sectoral and regional planning stages, rather than later, at the stage of project environmental assessment. Many of the valuation techniques discussed earlier are most appropriate at the micro level, and may therefore be very difficult to apply in situations involving a potentially large number of technology, site and mitigation options. Therefore the multi-criteria analysis (MCA) may be applied, since it allows for the appraisal of alternatives with differing objectives and varied costs and benefits, which are often assessed in differing units of measurement. Such an approach is used by Meier and Munasinghe (1994) in a study of Sri Lanka, to demonstrate how environmental externalities could be incorporated into power system planning in a systematic and efficient manner. Sri

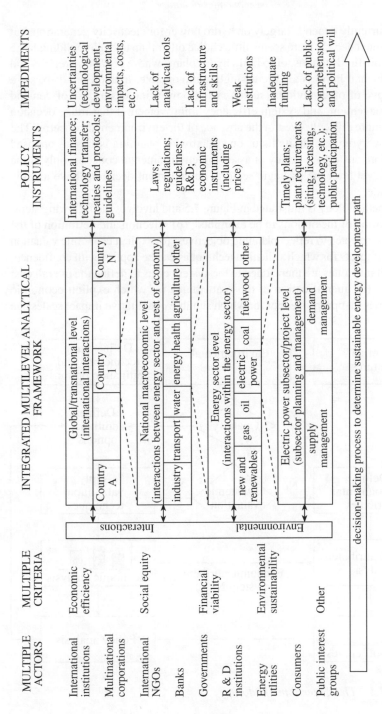

Figure 7.4 A conceptual framework for sustainable development

155

Lanka currently depends largely on hydro power for electricity generation, but over the next decade there seems little choice other than to begin building large coal- or oil-fired stations, or to build hydro plants whose economic returns and environmental impacts are increasingly unfavourable. In addition, there are a wide range of other options (such as wind power, increasing use of demand side management, and system efficiency improvements) that make decision making quite difficult, even in the absence of the environmental concerns. The study is very unusual in its focus on systemwide planning issues, as opposed to the more customary policy of assessing environmental concerns only at the project level after the strategic sectoral development decisions have already been made.

The methodology is illustrated in Figure 7.5 and involves the following steps: (a) definition of the options to be examined; (b) selection and definition of the attributes, selected to reflect planning objectives; (c) explicit economic valuation of those impacts for which valuation techniques can be applied with confidence; the resultant values are then added to the system costs to define the overall cost attribute; (d) quantification of those attributes for which explicit economic valuation is inappropriate, but for which suitable quantitative impact scales can

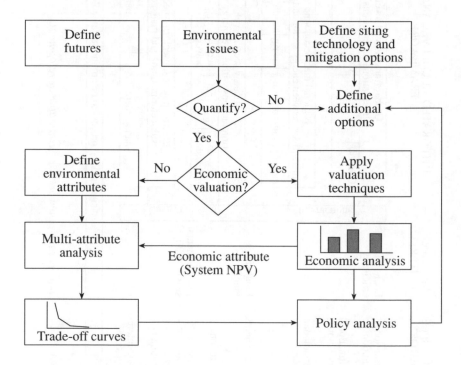

Figure 7.5   The general methodology

be defined; (e) translation of attribute value levels into value functions (known as 'scaling'); (f) display of the trade-off space, to facilitate understanding of the trade-offs to be made in decision making; and (g) definition of a candidate list of options for further study; this also involves the important step of eliminating inferior options from further consideration.

Main results

Policy options The main set of sectoral policy options examined included (a) variations in the currently available mix of hydro and thermal (coal and oil) plants; (b) demand side management (using the illustrative example of compact fluorescent lighting); (c) renewable energy options (using the illustrative technology of wind generation); (d) improvements in system efficiency (using more ambitious targets for transmission and distribution losses than the base case assumption of 12 per cent by 1997); (e) clean coal technology (using pressurized fluidized bed combustion (PFBC) in a combined cycle mode as the illustrative technology); and (f) pollution control technology options (illustrated by a variety of fuel switching and pollution control options such as using

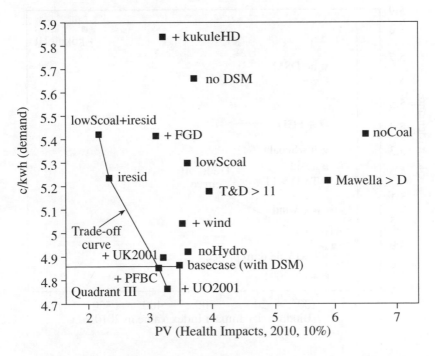

Figure 7.6   The health impact trade-off curve

imported low sulphur oil for diesels, and fitting coal-burning power plants with flue gas desulphurization (FGD) systems).

Attributes   Great care needs to be exercised in criteria or attribute selection; they should reflect issues of national (as opposed to local project-level) significance, and ought to be limited in number. To capture the potential impact on global warming, CO_2 emissions were defined as the appropriate proxy. Health impacts were measured through population-weighted increment in fine particulates and NO_x attributable to each source. To capture the potential biodiversity impacts, a probabilistic index was derived. As an illustrative social impact, employment creation was used.

Trade-off curves   Figure 7.6 illustrates a typical trade-off curve, in this case for health impacts. The 'best' solutions are those that lie closest to the origin, and the so-called 'trade-off curve', defined by the set of 'non-inferior' solutions, represents the set of options that are superior, regardless of the weights assigned to the different objectives. For example, on this curve, the option defined as

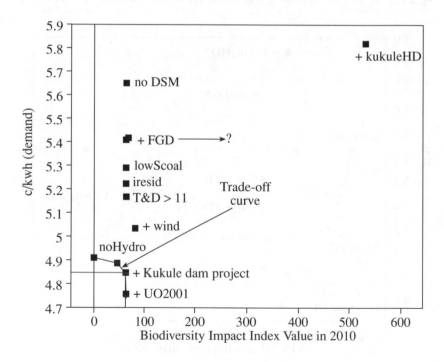

Figure 7.7   The biodiversity index trade-off curve

'iresid' (which calls for the use of low sulphur imported fuel oil at diesel plants) is better than the use of flue gas desulphurization systems (point FGD) in terms of both cost and environment.

A quite different trade-off curve was derived between biodiversity index value and average incremental cost, as illustrated in Figure 7.7. Most of the options have an index value that falls in the range of 50–100; the no hydro option has an essentially zero value, because the thermal projects that replace hydro plants in this option tend to lie at sites of poor biodiversity value (either close to load centres or on the coast). For example, while wind plants would require rather large land area, the vegetation of the area on the south coast has relatively low biodiversity value, and therefore the overall increase in biodiversity impact of this option is small. Thus the best options (or non-inferior curve) include the no hydro option, and run-of-river hydro options that require essentially zero inundation. Note the extreme outlier at the top right-hand corner, which is the Kukule hydro dam: it has a biodiversity loss index ($B = 530$) that is an order of magnitude larger than for other options ($B = 50$ to 70).

Conclusions

The case study draws several useful conclusions. First, the results of the case study indicate that those impacts for which valuation techniques are relatively straightforward and well-established – such as valuing the opportunity costs of lost production from inundated land, or estimating the benefits of establishing fisheries in a reservoir – tend to be quite small in comparison to overall system costs, and their inclusion in the benefit–cost analysis does not materially change results. Second, even in the case where explicit valuation may be difficult, such as in the case of mortality and morbidity effects of air pollution, implicit valuation based on analysis of the trade-off curve can provide important guidance to decision makers. Third, the case study indicated that certain options were in fact clearly inferior, or clearly superior, to all other options when one examines all impacts simultaneously. For example, the high dam version of the Kukule hydro project can be safely excluded from all further consideration as a result of poor performance on all attribute scales (including the economic one). Fourth, the results indicate that it is possible to derive attribute scales that can be useful proxies for impacts that may be difficult to value. For example, use of the population-weighted incremental ambient air pollution scale as a proxy for health impacts permitted a number of important conclusions that are independent of the specific economic value assigned to health effects.

Finally, with respect to the practical implications for planning, the study came to a series of specific recommendations on priority options, including (1) the need to systematically examine demand side management options, especially fluorescent lighting; (2) the need to examine whether the present transmission and distribution loss reduction target of 12 per cent ought to be further reduced;

(3) the need to examine the possibilities of pressurized fluidized bed combustion (PFBC) technology for coal power; (4) replacement of some coal-fired power plants (on the south coast) by diesel units; and (5) the need to re-examine cooling system options for coal plants.

ECONOMYWIDE OR NATIONAL-LEVEL APPLICATIONS

Analytical Framework

The oil price increases of the 1970s, and the worldwide recession and developing country debt crisis of the 1980s, led to the adoption of so-called 'structural adjustment policies' (SAPs). These economic reform packages, which included stringent monetary and fiscal measures, sought to restore conditions for growth and development with a combination of short-term 'stabilization' and more medium-term 'adjustment' policies for the macroeconomy. The term 'economywide policies' used in this chapter is broader and includes SAPs as a subset. Table 7.4 contains a summary of the main economywide policies, and the broad objectives of decision makers.

Economywide policy reforms are designed primarily to achieve broad economic objectives (for example, improving macroeconomic stability, enhancing efficiency and growth, and alleviating poverty) and, therefore, it is not surprising that their environmental and social consequences could be either positive or negative. Accordingly, we summarize below the results of key recent studies, focusing on three broad categories of countrywide policy impacts on various indicators of sustainability: beneficial, harmful and less well-defined. In the first group are the so-called 'win–win' policies, where it is possible to achieve simultaneous gains in all three areas of sustainable development (economic, social and environmental) when economywide reforms are implemented. The second category recognizes important exceptions where such potential gains cannot be realized unless the macro reforms are complemented by additional environmental and social measures which protect both the environment and the poor. The third category consists of less predictable impacts, mainly because of the complexity of the links, and the long-run time perspective.

In this context, economic–environmental–social interactions may be identified and analysed, and effective sustainable development policies formulated, by linking and articulating these activities explicitly. One tool that would facilitate the implementation of such an approach is the action impact matrix (AIM); a simple example is summarized in Box 7.1, although an actual AIM would be much larger and more detailed (Munasinghe and Cruz, 1994).

Table 7.4 Typical examples of economywide concerns and policy tools to address them

Macroeconomic Concerns	
Issues	**Policy tools and strategies**
Trade imbalance (usually a deficit)	Exchange rate adjustment
Inflation	Monetary policy (money supply, interest rate, etc.)
Government budget deficits	Reductions in government spending
Unemployment	Fiscal policy (e.g. increased taxes)
Poverty	Economic liberalization (trade, prices, etc.)
	Privatization/decentralization

Sectoral Concerns	
Issues	**Policy tools and strategies**
Low productivity	Pricing policy reforms
Unprofitability and chronic deficits	Economic incentives
Inefficient use of resources	Building human resource capacity
Institutional weaknesses	Strengthening institutions
	Liberalization/privatization/ decentralization

Case Studies: Examples of Various Impacts

Case studies of the environmental and social impacts of countrywide policies (including structural adjustment programmes) have been presented in a number of recent articles and volumes (see for example, Reed, 1992; Munasinghe and Cruz, 1994; Abaza, 1995; Young and Bishop, 1995; Munasinghe, 1996; Reed, 1996; Opschoor and Jongma, 1996; Cruz *et al.*, 1997; Warford *et al.*, 1997). The linkages tend to be extremely complex and country-specific. Thus, even the purely economic impacts of structural adjustment programmes are difficult to trace comprehensively.

Beneficial impacts

Macroeconomic reforms Liberalizing reforms which seek to make desirable alterations to the structure of the economy will often contribute to both economic and sustainability gains. Such changes include the removal of price distortions, promotion of market incentives, and relaxation of trade and other constraints (which are among the main features of adjustment-related reforms).

BOX 7.1   ACTION IMPACT MATRIX (AIM): A TOOL
           FOR POLICY ANALYSIS, FORMULATION
           AND COORDINATION

Table 7.5 shows an action impact matrix to promote an integrated
view, meshing development decisions with priority economic, environmental and social impacts. The left-hand column of the table
lists examples of the main development interventions (both policies
and projects), while the top row indicates some of the main sustainable development issues. Thus the elements or cells in the
matrix help (a) to identify explicitly the key linkages, (b) to focus
attention on valuation and other methods of analysing the most
important impacts, and (c) to suggest action priorities. At the same
time, the organization of the overall matrix facilitates the tracing of
impacts, as well as coherent articulation of the links between a
range of development actions: that is, policies and projects. A
stepwise procedure, starting with readily available data, has been
used effectively to develop the AIM in several country studies that
have been initiated recently (for instance, Ghana, Nepal, the Philippines and Sri Lanka). This process has helped to harmonize views
among those involved (economists, environmental specialists and
others), thereby improving the prospects for successful implementation (see Munasinghe and Cruz, 1994).

Screening and Problem Identification
One of the early objectives of the AIM-based process is to help in
screening and problem identification by preparing a preliminary
matrix that identifies broad relationships and provides a qualitative
idea of the magnitudes of the impacts. Thus the preliminary AIM
would be used to prioritize the most important links between policies
and their sustainability impacts. For example, the row corresponding to exchange rate in Table 7.5, a currency devaluation aimed at
improving the trade balance may make timber exports more
profitable and lead to deforestation of open access forests. The
appropriate remedy might involve complementary measures to
strengthen property rights and restrict access to the forest areas.
   A second example might involve increasing energy prices closer
to marginal costs to improve energy efficiency and decrease
pollution (row corresponding to energy pricing). A complementary
measure involving the addition of pollution taxes to marginal energy

costs will further reduce pollution. Increasing public sector account-ability will reinforce favourable responses to these price incentives by reducing the ability of inefficient firms to pass on cost increases to consumers or to transfer their losses to the government. In the same vein, a major hydroelectric project is shown in the row cor-responding to Project 1 in the table as having two adverse impacts – inundation of forested areas and of villages – as well as one positive impact, the replacement of thermal power generation (thereby reducing air pollution). A reafforestation project coupled with adequate resettlement efforts may help address the negative impacts.

This matrix-based approach therefore encourages the systematic articulation and coordination of policies and projects to achieve sus-tainable development goals. Using readily available data, it would be possible to develop such an initial matrix for many countries. Furthermore, a range of social impacts could be incorporated into the AIM, using the same approach.

Analysis and Remediation
This process may be developed further to assist in analysis and remediation. For example, more detailed analyses and modelling may be carried out for each matrix element in the preliminary AIM which represented a high priority linkage between economywide policies and environmental impacts that had already been identified in the cells of the preliminary matrix. This, in turn, would lead to a more refined and updated AIM, which helps to quantify impacts and determine additional measures to enhance positive linkages and mitigate negative ones.

The types of more detailed analyses which could help to determine the final matrix would depend on planning goals and available data and resources. As discussed in the next section, they may range from the application of conventional sectoral economic analysis methods (appropriately modified in scope to incorporate environmental impacts) to fairly comprehensive system or multi-sector modelling efforts, including computable general equilibrium (CGE) models that include both conventional economic, as well as environmental or resource, variables. Sectoral and partial equilib-rium analyses are more useful for tracing details of direct impacts, whereas CGE modelling provides a more comprehensive but aggregate view, and insights into indirect linkages.

Table 7.5   A simplified preliminary action impact matrix[1]

Activity/ Policy	Main Objective	Impacts on Key Sustainable Development Issues			
		Land degradation	*Air pollution*	*Resettlement*	*Other impacts*
Macroeconomic & sectoral policies	Macroeconomic and sectoral improvements	Positive impacts due to removal of distortions Negative impacts mainly due to remaining constraints			
Exchange rate	Improve trade balance and economic growth	(–H) (deforest open-access areas)			
Energy pricing	Improve economic and energy use efficiency		(+M) (energy efficiency)		
Other policies					
Complementary measures[2]	Specific/local social and environmental gains	Enhance positive impacts and mitigate negative impacts (above) of broader macroeconomic and sectoral policies			
Market-based	Reverse negative impacts of market failures, policy distortions and institutional constraints		(+M) (pollution tax)		
Non-market-based		(+H) (property rights)	(+M) (public sector accountability)		
Investment projects	Improve efficiency of investments	Investment decisions made more consistent with broader policy and institutional framework			
Project 1 (Hydro Dam)	Use of project evaluation (cost–benefit analysis, environmental assessment, multi-criteria analysis, etc.)	(–H) (inundate forests)	(+M) (displace fossil fuel)	(–M) (displace people)	
Project 2 (Reafforest and relocate)		(+H) (replant forests)		(+M) (relocate people)	
Other projects					

Two recent studies highlighted in Munasinghe and Cruz (1994) illustrate win–win situations. In a case involving Zimbabwe, currency devaluation would produce economic gains while also promoting wildlife management activities that are environmentally beneficial. More indirect or systemic effects of economic policies on the environment have been analysed using a computable general equilibrium (CGE) model for Morocco, which showed that a combination of trade liberalization and water pricing reforms would not only increase economic growth rates, but also conserve water and help limit emerging water deficits. Similarly, an earlier CGE model of Thailand showed that combined economic and environmental gains would be possible with adjustment policies coupled with complementary measures, including the clear delineation of property rights in rural areas, and use of regulatory or economic instruments to limit urban pollution (Panayotou and Susangkarn, 1991). Although the quantitative results of CGE models should be interpreted with care, the qualitative results provide valuable insights and highlight the kinds of information needed to be able to anticipate with greater accuracy the environmental consequences of policy reform (Devarajan, 1990; Robinson, 1990).

Other illustrative examples of the role of macroeconomic policies include the investigation of links between adjustment policy and environment in the agriculture sector in Sub-Saharan Africa (Stryker *et al.*, 1989). Important contributions have also been made by environmental organizations through studies on the environmental impact of the adjustment process in Thailand, the Ivory Coast, Mexico and the Philippines (Reed, 1992; Cruz and Repetto, 1992). Another study suggests that trade policies which encourage greater openness in Latin America have tended to be associated with a better environment, primarily due to environmentally benign characteristics of modern technologies (Birdsall and Wheeler, 1992).

Sectoral reforms   Reforms which improve the efficiency of industrial or energy-related activities could reduce economic waste, increase the efficiency

Notes:
1. A few examples of typical policies and projects as well as key environmental and social issues are shown. Some illustrative but qualitative impact assessments are also indicated; thus + and – signify beneficial and harmful impacts, while H and M indicate high and moderate intensity. The AIM process helps to focus on the highest priority environmental issues and related social concerns.
2. Commonly used market-based measures include effluent charges, tradeable emission permits, emission taxes or subsidies, bubbles and offsets (emission banking), stumpage fees, royalties, user fees, deposit-refund schemes, performance bonds and taxes on products (such as fuel taxes). Non-market-based measures comprise regulations and laws specifying environmental standard (such as ambient standards, emission standards and technology standards) which permit or limit certain actions ('dos' and 'don'ts').

Source: Munasinghe and Cruz, 1994.

of natural resource use and limit environmental pollution. Similarly, improving land tenure rights and access to financial and social services not only yields economic gains but also promotes better environmental stewardship and helps the poor. Some examples are summarized below.

More specific or restricted policies affecting major sectors, such as *industry and agriculture*, or key resources, like *energy*, are also addressed in programmes of economywide policy reforms. For example, Meier *et al.* (1993) demonstrate that raising subsidized energy prices closer to the long-run marginal cost of electricity supply will not only improve the efficiency of power use and accelerate GNP growth, but also reduce both in-country air pollution and CO^2 emissions that contribute to global greenhouse warming (for details, see Munasinghe, 1996). More generally, World Bank (1993a) estimates that non-OECD countries spend more than $250 billion annually on subsidizing energy. The countries of the former USSR and Eastern Europe account for the bulk of this amount ($180 billion) and it is estimated that more than half of their air pollution is attributable to such price distortions. Removing all energy subsidies would produce large gains in efficiency and fiscal balances, sharply reduce local pollution and cut carbon emissions by up to 20 per cent in some countries and by about 7 per cent worldwide.

The negative environmental effects of industrial protection policies in Mexico also suggest the potential for 'win–win' industrial policy reforms (for details, see Munasinghe and Cruz, 1994). Between 1970 and 1989, industrial pollution intensity (per unit of value added) in Mexico increased by 25 per cent, induced by government subsidies and investments in the petrochemical and fertilizer industries, while the energy intensity of industry also increased by almost 6 per cent in the same period. Broad subsidies for fuels and electricity absorbed $8–13 billion, or 4–7 per cent of GDP, from 1980 to 1985. Thus removing such subsidies and distortionary incentives to energy-intensive industries would result in large economic savings and reductions in industrial pollution.

Experience in *water and sanitation* shows that both targeting and reducing subsidies would have beneficial economic, social and environmental impacts. They would help to reduce wasteful use of water, improve cost recovery in a resource-scarce sector, eliminate the large subsidies that are captured mainly by the wealthy, expand facilities to low-income areas and reduce water pollution. A number of recent projects illustrate these points, including the Water Quality and Pollution Control Project in Brazil (World Bank, 1992b), the Karnataka Rural Water Supply and Environmental Sanitation Project in India (World Bank, 1993b) and the Changchun Water Supply and Environmental Project in China (World Bank, 1992c).

As regards *land use*, the negative effects of underpricing resources can also be seen in the agricultural sector of Tunisia, where the government's concern with ensuring sufficient supply and affordability of livestock products has resulted in a web of pricing and subsidy interventions which have encouraged herd maintenance at levels beyond rangelands' carrying capacity (for details, see Munasinghe and Cruz, 1994). Removal of livestock subsidies would produce significant economic gains and also improve the sustainable use of rangelands. Studies done for the Zambia Marketing and Processing Infrastructure Project (World Bank, 1992c) show that restructuring public expenditures for agriculture by eliminating maize, fertilizer and transport subsidies would improve the efficiency of food production, increase farm output and encourage more sustainable farming practices. In the past few years, several additional examples have emerged, showing how eliminating perverse subsidies would simultaneously yield economic, environmental and social benefits. In the Amazon region, Mahar (1989) and Binswanger (1991) have analysed the role of subsidies to agricultural and livestock expansion as the key factor leading to deforestation. Schneider (1993) focuses on institutional barriers at the economic frontier that prevent the emergence of land tenure services, such as titling and property rights enforcement, and thus undermine the potential for sustainable land use. Other studies have addressed similar adverse impacts of agricultural policies on the environment in Indonesia (soil erosion), Sudan (deforestation) and Botswana (pasture land degradation) (Barbier, 1988; Larson and Bromley, 1991; Perrings, 1993).

Stabilizing inflation Price, wage and employment stability encourage a longer-term view on the part of firms and households alike. Lower inflation rates not only lead to clearer pricing signals and better investment decisions by economic agents, but also protect fixed income earners. The critical link between inflation and sustainability is illustrated in a case study of Costa Rica, using a CGE model to examine the deforestation implications of various macroeconomic factors (Persson and Munasinghe, 1995). The results demonstrate that lower real interest rates associated with a stable economy allow the logging sector to anticipate correctly the benefits from future returns to forestry, thereby leading to more sustainable logging practices.[1] Similarly, the establishment of better tenurial security over the resource (and future benefits from it) also promotes sustainable logging. This corresponds to the well-known result in renewable resource exploitation models, that open-access resource conditions influence economic behaviour the same way as having secure property rights with very high discount rates.

Other studies have indicated that low and stable discount rates favour the choice of sustainable farming rather than short-term cultivation practices (Southgate and Pearce, 1988). This is important since 'mining' of agricultural land resources is often the prevailing form of resource use in many tropical areas. Frontier farmers have to choose between a sustainable production system with stable but low yields and unsustainable practices which initially have high yields. Using farm models and data from Brazil, a recent study found that, if interest rates are very high, farmers will tend to use less sustainable methods (Schneider, 1994). The critical macroeconomic implication of this result is that attempts to resolve the land degradation problem solely by focusing on providing better agricultural technologies would probably be ineffective. To arrest land degradation, macroeconomic reforms which reduce the real interest rate would be needed – although this option may not be feasible in many developing countries where savings rates are inadequate and the opportunity cost of capital is high.

Harmful impacts

The results of a recent UNEP/World Bank workshop (Abaza, 1995) concluded that two major outcomes of structural adjustment programmes may have adverse consequences. First, strong substitution effects in favour of exports could lead to environmental harm, for example as a result of the increased profitability of export crops that may be more soil-erosive in the long run, or through the deforestation of open-access areas caused by export-oriented logging. Second, changes in both public expenditures and relative prices have often hurt the poor, and in turn led to further environmental degradation, especially when the landless poor have had no other alternative than to overexploit fragile lands. In this context, a typical economywide reform programme is handled in stages, with the initial adjustment package aimed at the most important macroeconomic issues. Often some distortions that policy makers intend to address later, or other constraints that have passed unnoticed in the initial screening, are the cause of environmental or social harm (Munasinghe *et al.*, 1993). The remedy will generally require the implementation of additional complementary measures (both economic and non-economic) that remove such policy, market and institutional imperfections, rather than the reversal of the original reforms. Munasinghe (1995c) presents an explicit microeconomic model that analyses the mechanisms involved.

Policy distortions Environmental gains can be realized by addressing remaining policy failures. In Poland, initial countrywide adjustments, including increases in energy prices, contributed to some improvements in energy use and pollution (Bates *et al.*, 1995). However, both environmental harm and economic losses persisted because of the remaining policy distortions resulting from the entire system of state ownership which placed little emphasis on financial discipline and managerial accountability. This means that price responsiveness is blunted, since financial losses are simply absorbed by the public budget, or passed on to consumers in the form of higher output prices. Similar challenges face the former Soviet Union (FSU) and other countries of Central and Eastern Europe as they attempt to restructure their economies and make a rapid transition to a market-oriented system. Basically, the reform of regulations and institutions should not be allowed to lag too far behind economic restructuring.

Market failures In the case of Indonesia, liberalization policies and industrial promotion have accelerated growth in the modern sector, expanded employment opportunities and contributed to reduced pollution through the use of more efficient production and better pollution control techniques (for details, see Munasinghe and Cruz, 1994). In addition, industry expanded rapidly outside densely populated Java, reducing the potential health impacts of industrial concentration. However, there are signs that pollution may increase as a result of the sheer scale of expansion coupled with market failures, because of inadequate price signals to address the externalities. Clearly, introducing complementary measures in the form of pollution taxes and environmental regulations is warranted to correct this emerging problem.

Institutional constraints The role of institutional constraints in macroeconomic reform programmes was examined in a case study of Ghana (for details, see Munasinghe and Cruz, 1994). In this example, the model predicted that trade liberalization, by reducing the taxation on agricultural exports, would lead to increased production incentives, while efforts to reduce the government wage bill would tend to increase the pool of unemployed. Thus the adjustment process helps to stimulate production of export crops and, combined with rapid population growth and lack of employment opportunities outside the rural sector, leads to increasing pressure on land resources, encroachment onto marginal lands, and soil erosion. In Ghana, as in many regions of Africa, agricultural lands are governed by traditional land use institutions, and farms are communally owned by the village or tribe. These common property regimes may have been sufficient in allowing sustainable use of agricultural lands when populations were much smaller, and sufficient fallow periods could allow land to regain its fertility. However, the analysis suggests that such traditional arrangements would be overwhelmed ultimately by economywide forces, resulting in reduced fallowing, loss of soil fertility and environmental decline. This suggests that better clarification of property rights may help to resist the pressures on common property resources, externally induced by the broad policy reforms.

Relevant laws and regulations governing resource access should be reviewed when economywide reforms are planned, especially when there is evidence that key resource sectors such as land, forests, minerals or marine resources will be affected. In a recent adjustment operation in Peru, it was determined that economywide reforms to promote economic recovery could increase harvesting pressures on Peru's overexploited fisheries through growth of demand for fish. Accordingly, complementary new fishing regulations to protect various fishing grounds were incorporated directly into the adjustment programme (World Bank, 1993c).

Stabilization, government deficit reduction and recession Early views on the social aspects of adjustment were motivated by the concern that adjustment programmes would focus on growth, at the expense of distributional objectives. A major issue was that the poor, who would be most vulnerable to the effects of macroeconomic contraction, also might be deprived of 'safety nets', especially if governments cut social services disproportionately. In this same vein, reduced government spending and its potentially adverse impact on environmental protection services have been the subject of criticism from environmental groups. In a study performed by ECLAC (1989), it was concluded that adjustment policies pursued in Latin America during the 1980s led to cutbacks in current expenditure allotments for managing and supervising investment in sectors such as energy, irrigation, infrastructure and mining. This limited the funds available for environmental impact assessments and the supervision of projects to control their environmental impacts. Miranda and Muzondo (1991), in an IMF survey, recognized this problem and suggested that high levels of government expenditure in other areas may lead to reduced funding of environmental activities. Recent case studies attributed increases in air pollution problems in Thailand and Mexico to reductions in expenditures for adequate infrastructure (Reed, 1992). Adverse impacts of stabilization programmes on low-income groups in Africa (especially women and children), have been noted, typically due to reduced government spending in areas such as health.

By contrast, a study of the social consequences of adjustment lending in Africa found that, although there have been declines in government expenditures, the budget proportion going to social expenditures and agriculture actually increased during the adjustment period (Stryker *et al.*, 1989). The results of similar studies focusing on social safety nets during adjustment programmes confirm that pursuing fiscal discipline and macroeconomic stability need not take place at the cost of increased hardship for the poor. In much the same way, specific environmental concerns can be incorporated in stabilization efforts. For example, in many countries in Sub-Saharan Africa, forestry departments and their activities have always been severely underfunded (World Bank, 1994). Thus targeted efforts to support forestry management activities could be included in reform packages as part of a proactive environmental response. In brief, both critical environmental and social expenditures could be protected if government budget cuts were made judiciously.

Longer-term and less predictable effects
In addition to the short- to medium-term concerns discussed earlier, the crucial long-term links between poverty and environmental degradation in developing countries are increasingly being recognized (see, for example, World Bank, 1992a). The need to break the 'cycle' of poverty, population growth and environmental degradation is also a key challenge for sustainable development. Given that capital and labour stocks are relatively fixed in the short run, a major objective of adjustment programmes is to increase factor mobility through both structural and financial reforms (creating new and more dynamic industries, increasing human resources and skills, reforming the banking sector, and so on). Thus both the economic and the environmental consequences of adjustment programmes will depend crucially on capital and labour mobility in the longer run.

An important result of examining the general equilibrium effects of macroeconomic policy is that indirect resource allocation effects become important and may dominate the more direct effects of some price or income policy changes. In the Costa Rica study, the economic and environmental implications of wage restraints in structural adjustment are examined with the use of a CGE model which highlights the economic activities and factors affecting deforestation (Persson and Munasinghe, 1995). Because the role of intersectoral resource flows is incorporated in the CGE model, the effects of changes in wages are different from partial equilibrium results. If the wage of unskilled labour were increased (for example as a result of minimum wage legislation), the model predicts that deforestation could worsen rather than decline: although logging declines owing to increased direct costs, this is more than made up by the indirect effect of intersectoral flows since the industrial sector (where minimum wage legislation is more binding) is much more adversely affected by the higher labour costs. Labour and capital thus tend to flow from industry to agriculture, leading to greater conversion of forest land for farming. This simulation exercise suggests the need for caution in attempting to 'legislate' income improvements by increasing minimum wages. Introducing higher wages initially improves labour incomes, but a resulting contraction of industrial and agricultural employment leads not only to more unemployment but to environmental degradation as well. The increase in unemployment results in greater pressures for expanding shifting cultivation in forest lands.

Beyond pricing and intersectoral environmental linkages that can be identified in general equilibrium approaches, another set of studies has looked at the environmental implications of rural poverty and unemployment within the broader context of the social and demographic problems of inequitable land access and rapid population growth (Feder *et al.*, 1988; Lele and Stone, 1989). Import substitution, industrial protection and regressive taxation are some economywide policies that have historically been associated with lagging employment generation, income inequality and poverty. Unequal distribution of resources and inappropriate tenure are institutional factors that also contribute to the problem. In the context of inequitable assignment of endowments and rapid population growth, the resulting unemployment and income inequality force the poor to depend increasingly on marginal resources for their livelihood. The result is pressure on fragile environments. This effect can be analysed in conjunction with the assessment of large migration episodes. These may occur as a result of resettlement programmes or inappropriate policies, such as land colonization programmes.

With regard to sustainable agriculture concerns, recent work explicitly links the related problems of rapid population growth, agricultural stagnation and land degradation in Africa (Cleaver and Schreiber, 1991). This study found that shifting cultivation and grazing in the context of limited capital and technical change cannot cope with rapid population growth. At the same time, the traditional technological solution of relying on high-yielding crop varieties is not available. Thus a mix of responses was identified, in terms of reforms to remove subsidies for inappropriate land uses, improve land use planning, recognize property rights, provide better education and construct appropriate rural infrastructure to promote production incentives. The importance of long-term links between adjustment programmes, trade and agriculture, and the difficulties of analysing them, are also emphasized by Goldin and Winters (1992).

A Philippines case study (Munasinghe and Cruz, 1994) evaluates the policy determinants of long-term changes in rural poverty and unemployment that have motivated increasing lowland to upland migration, and led to the conversion of forest lands to unsustainable agriculture. The inability of the government to manage forest resources is an important direct cause of deforestation, but the study also links deforestation induced by lowland poverty to agricultural taxation, price controls and marketing restrictions. At the same time, trade and exchange rate policies (dominated by an urban consumer and industrial sector bias) have played important roles in the Philippines. The agricultural sector was implicitly taxed by an average of about 20 per cent for several decades, worsening rural incomes and poverty, and forcing migration into environmentally fragile lands.

The foregoing evidence suggest that countrywide policy reforms may have counterintuitive environmental and social impacts, through longer-term and indirect mechanisms. Considerable new work will be required to trace these complex linkages and improve the long-run sustainability of economic policies.

Macroeconomic Issues

Up to now we have not seriously considered altering economywide policies merely to achieve sustainability objectives, but instead have chosen to rely on specific complementary measures to mitigate environmental and social harm. Here we examine whether circumstances exist under which even macro-economic policies might be tailored to satisfy environmental considerations.

Fine-tuning policy reforms

Second-best economic policies   In a recent paper, Mäler and Munasinghe (1996) developed a theoretical model in which they showed that following first-best macroeconomic policies to achieve a Pareto optimum will not maximize welfare, if an environmental externality exists. In such a case, it is possible to question whether second-best macroeconomic policies might be better: basically, to trade off between broad macroeconomic goals and environmental damage.

More specifically, their mathematical analysis confirms the empirical obser-vations made earlier in this chapter that it is the combination of growth-inducing economywide policies and residual imperfections such as policy distortions, market failures and institutional constraints which lead to environmental damage. The model also underlines the microeconomic analysis considered above, that such imperfections and resultant economic harm may well go unnoticed in a relatively stagnant economy, only to emerge quite visibly when growth rates begin to rise. Mäler and Munasinghe explain further that the first-best solution would be to correct the imperfections using complementary policies while pursuing the original macroeconomic reforms. However, if political or other constraints delay the correction of the policy, market or insti-tutional imperfections, then second-best macroeconomic policies may be justified – especially when the environmental harm could be significant.

Timing and sequencing policies   It is also relevant to examine the dynamics of the policy reform process. For example, such reforms might be intensified over a period of time (instead of being suddenly imposed), thereby allowing further time for residual imperfections that degrade the environment to be gradually phased out. In this context, suppose that the environmental damage due to an economic reform programme is likely to be rather large. Is it possible to adjust the timing and sequencing of macroeconomic and sectoral policy tools to avoid the worst environmental consequences? There is a growing body of literature which examines the pros and cons of timing and sequencing stabilization and adjustment measures to achieve economic goals, but not envi-ronmental ones (Munasinghe, 1998a).

Munasinghe (1995c) presents an example in which policy reforms are fine-tuned to meet environmental requirements. In this case, the economy under consideration requires an exchange rate devaluation and liberalization of trade and capital flows to correct a chronic current account deficit and restore the external balance. At the same time, an increase in the price of state-subsidized energy is warranted to reduce the government budget deficit, eliminate excess demand and restore the internal balance. Suppose the foreign exchange and trade reforms could be achieved first, for example if powerful domestic forces delayed the raising of energy prices. Then the opening up of the economy might lead to greater foreign investment and expansion of energy-intensive industries which were attracted by the low energy prices. However, this apparent economic gain would also result in wasteful use of (the still subsidized) energy and even more environmental pollution. Therefore it might be preferable to raise energy prices first, before liberalizing capital and trade flows.

Munasinghe (1995c) points out that the foregoing analysis is limited by its simple, static and short-term nature. Nonetheless, some environmentally related arguments such as the above could be used to re-examine fruitfully (and perhaps fine-tune) policy reforms.[2] Since hardly any work has been carried out in this area, and country circumstances vary widely, it would be difficult to generalize at present. At the same time, good judgment is required to avoid the temptation of making major changes in economywide policies merely to achieve minor environmental (and social) gains. Policy options that achieved 'win–win' gains would be the most desirable.

Effects due to the stage and structure of growth

Environmental Kuznets curve (EKC)   Over a period of time, economywide policies also influence the structure and stage of economic growth of a country, which could in turn also affect the state of the environment. In this context, the recent concern for the environment has revived interest in a generic concept proposed over 30 years ago by Simon Kuznets (1955): that, as countries develop and incomes rise, certain measures of the quality of life (such as income distribution) might initially deteriorate before becoming better. Recent studies explore whether the level of environmental degradation and per capita income (conventionally measured) might obey the inverted-U shaped relationship shown in Figure 7.8, dubbed the 'environmental Kuznets curve' or EKC (for a review, see Munasinghe, 1998b).

The EKC hypothesis is intuitively appealing. Thus, at the low levels of per capita income associated with pre-industrial and agricultural economies, one might expect rather pristine environmental conditions relatively unaffected by economic activities at the subsistence level. As development and industrialization progressed, the increasing use of natural resources and emission of pollutants, less efficient and relatively 'dirty' technologies, high priority given to increases in material output and disregard for or ignorance of the environmental consequences of growth would all have contributed to increasing environmental damage. This argument might be relevant for middle-income or newly industrializing countries (NICs), especially where growth rates of GNP exceeding 5 per cent per annum are commonplace. In the final post-industrial

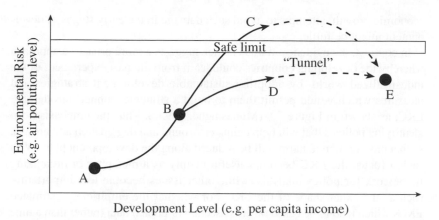

Source: M. Munasinghe (1995c)

Figure 7.8   Environmental risk versus development level

stage (corresponding to the mature Western economies), cleaner technologies and a shift to information and service-based activities, the growing ability and willingness to pay for a better environment, improved internalization of environmental externalities and greater financial surpluses that could be used to pay for a more pre-emptive approach to environmental protection might be expected to result in reduced environmental degradation.

Tunnelling through the EKC   A major motivation for more systematically examining the links between economywide policies and the environment, based on analysis of past growth patterns, is the search for environmentally sustainable development paths in the future. The EKC diagram (Figure 7.8) provides a convenient framework to represent some of the lessons of experience. First, if the EKC hypothesis holds true, the early to middle stages of economic growth could be quite detrimental from both the environmental and social viewpoints of sustainable development. In particular, poorer groups might be even more adversely affected than Kuznets had originally predicted on the basis of income inequality alone, to the extent that the poor also suffer more as a result of environmental degradation. This would require appropriate policy responses, especially on the social side. Second, the extent to which decision makers ought to devote their limited time and resources to designing and implementing policies for sound environmental management could well depend on the extent to which the driving forces underlying the EKC are susceptible to such policies. In other words, if environmental damage is an inevitable consequence of economic growth, attempts to avoid such damage in the early stages of development might be futile.

In contrast, the evidence in this chapter suggests a more proactive approach whereby the developing countries could learn from the past experiences of the industrialized world, by adopting sustainable development strategies and measures which would permit them to build a strategic 'tunnel' through the EKC, as shown in Figure 7.8 (Munasinghe, 1995c). Thus the emphasis is on identifying policies that will help delink environmental degradation and growth, so that environmental harm will be reduced along the development path. With such a focus, the EKC becomes useful mainly as a metaphor or organizing framework for policy analysis, while other issues become less important – such as the exact shape of the EKC,[3] or whether the empirically estimated EKCs which tend to be based on cross-section or pooled data (rather than a time series of observations) can adequately capture the growth characteristics of any single country.

A basic model developed by Munasinghe (1998b) shows how economic imperfections (which make private decisions deviate from socially optimal ones) could lead to the higher path *ABC* in Figure 7.8. Thus the adoption of corrective policies that reduce such divergences and thereby reduce environmental damage, permit movement through the tunnel ABD. Avoiding the path of greater environmental risk would help to prevent irreversible environmental harm (such as loss of biodiversity). In other words, the tunnel would enable developing countries to short-circuit more conventional development paths (such as ABCE in the figure), which merely mimicked the evolution of the Western market economies. This approach is quite consistent with the fundamental insight provided by the analysis and empirical results presented earlier, that imperfections in the economy could combine with growth-inducing economywide policies to cause environmental harm, and result in suboptimal development paths like ABCE. Therefore complementary policies that removed such imperfections would be needed to protect the environment and shift the path towards the more sustainable tunnel BDE.[4] In general, successful 'tunnelling' would require the following steps: (1) Every effort should be made to adopt 'win–win' policies that provide simultaneous economic, environmental and social gains – in particular, this will require more systematic analysis to identify the environmental and social impacts of economywide policies (see earlier section on the Action Impact Matrix); (2) unintended but harmful environmental and social impacts should be addressed through complementary measures, rather than by reversing successful economic reforms: and (3) if the threat to sustainability is serious enough, even economywide policies might be reshaped appropriately – for example by modifying the timing and sequencing of reforms.

Measuring wellbeing

Gross domestic product (GDP), the commonly used growth measure, relies on transactions in markets, and is the basis on which many aspects of macro-economic policy are determined. However, its shortcomings include neglect of income distributional concerns as well as non-market activities and environmental effects (see below). Furthermore, one serious criticism raised in the 'green' national accounting literature is that currently used measures of national output (especially conventionally measured national income) do not adequately reflect either the depletion of natural resource stocks as in deforestation, or environmental damage – such as that due to pollution (see, for example, Atkinson *et al.*, 1997).[5]

Green national income accounting   Currently, several countries are exploring different types of environmental adjustments to the conventional system of national accounts (SNA). First, *natural resource (stock) accounts* emphasize balance sheet items, the opening and closing stocks of various natural resources (like forests) and the flows that add to and subtract from the balance sheet position; these accounts are in physical quantities (and sometimes values) and may or may not be linked to the SNA through the national balance sheet. Second, there are the *resource and pollutant flow accounts* that typically embody considerable sectoral detail and often are explicitly linked to the input–output accounts, as part of the SNA; these accounts are therefore de facto satellite accounts in physical quantities. Third, the *environmental expenditure accounts* are valued in monetary units, and can be viewed as classical satellite accounts (if they are separated from the conventional SNA data). Finally, *alternative national accounts aggregates* such as green measures of national product and wealth are being considered, but no countries are at present planning to alter their usual national accounts to reflect resources and the environment, beyond what is in the 1993 revision to the SNA.

The first step towards standardizing this multitude of accounting approaches is provided by the United Nations' integrated system of environmental and economic accounting, the System of Environmental Economic Accounts, or SEEA (United Nations Statistical Office, 1993). The SEEA is designed to be a *satellite* account to the conventional system of national accounts, in that it is an adjunct to (rather than a modification of) the core accounts. The SEEA is highly complex, involving disaggregation of the standard accounts to highlight environmental relationships, linked physical and monetary accounting, imputations of environmental costs, and extensions of the production boundary of the SNA. A comprehensive framework like the SEEA may be used to estimate national accounts aggregates such as 'green GNP', which are adjusted downwards to reflect the costs of net resource depletion and environmental pollution.

The foregoing discussion highlights the distinction between conventional income per capita as an indicator of development, and a more complex set of measures that might better capture the essence of sustainable development. For example, as discussed earlier (see Figure 7.1) sustainable development has been defined in terms of three key elements: economic, social and environmental. Some researchers have sought to compute a composite index of human welfare and to show that the relationship between 'true' welfare and conventional income per capita is positive in the early stages of development, but becomes negative later on – in contrast to the EKC effect (see, for example, Daly and Cobb, 1994; Max-Neef, 1995). They estimate that one such measure, based on the Index of Sustainable Economic Welfare (ISEW), had already reached its peak in the 1970s or 1980s and is now declining for the United States, the United Kingdom, Germany, Austria and the Netherlands.

Modern concepts of wealth and genuine savings   Recently, several practical suggestions have been made concerning different indicators of sustainable development, including true national savings (for an overview, see Atkinson *et al.*, 1997). If the greening of national accounts includes the expansion of the measure of national wealth (see, for example, Scott, 1956) – including the value of stocks of not only manufactured capital, but also living and non-living resources – then total wealth per capita becomes a useful indicator of sustainability. If this ratio is non-decreasing, development is sustainable (or *weakly* sustainable, since it is assumed that produced assets are highly substitutable for natural assets). That is, for total wealth W and population P, the sustainability criterion is: $S = [d(W/P)/dt]/[W/P] \geq 0$. This index has several desirable properties, including the possibility of separately accounting for the changes in the level of natural assets for which substitution possibilities are low.

The rate of change of wealth (dW/dt) may be considered as 'genuine savings' or savings net of resource depletion: that is, the depreciation of manufactured capital and that of natural resources are treated symmetrically (Hamilton, 1994). Because weak sustainability aggregates all forms of capital, a single numeraire is needed, and monetary units serve this purpose. If an economy saves less than the level necessary to cover depreciation then it is, prima facie, unsustainable in the weak sense. Genuine savings is a one-sided indicator of sustainability, because positive genuine savings is a necessary but not sufficient condition for long-term sustainability. In other words, consistent negative savings is unsustainable. However, non-negative genuine savings at any given point in time does not guarantee a sustainable development path, since the latter depends on non-negative growth of welfare which is related to per capita consumption. Some estimates of both wealth and savings for a range of countries are presented in Atkinson *et al.* (1997) and World Bank (1997).

Current work has focused on methods of incorporating environmental aspects in national income accounts. However, severe data constraints limit the applicability of such a comprehensive approach in many developing countries. 'Short-cut' methods therefore need to be developed. For example, easily applicable rules-of-thumb (calibrated by well-chosen national studies) could be used to devise baseline estimates of national wealth in the form of natural resources, human capital and produced assets. Environmental indicators of land, water and air quality could supplement economic measures, in the same way as social indicators (for example, literacy and health).

INTERNATIONAL-LEVEL APPLICATIONS

Transnational impacts (such as acid rain) and global issues (such as ozone layer depletion, global warming, biodiversity loss and pollution of international waters) give rise to difficult issues of external impacts, cost and benefit sharing and free-riding (Munasinghe and King, 1992; Munasinghe, 1995b). Measures to reduce emissions of greenhouse gases (GHG) and ozone depleting substances (ODS) provide illustrative examples of recent applications of ecological economics to these global issues.

Climate Change Mitigation Targets: Globally Efficient Optimization

Economic activity in the post-industrial period has caused a sharp increase in the accumulation of GHGs (chiefly carbon dioxide) above historic levels. There is growing evidence to indicate that a continuation of this trend will lead to changes in the global climate, including an increase of about 2.5 degrees Celsius in the global mean temperature and a rise of about 50 centimetres in the global mean sea level (IPCC, 1996). Even though the impacts are uncertain, sustainability suggests that limits should be imposed on resource degradation, particularly if future consequences could be irreversible and catastrophic. This precautionary approach underlies the emerging consensus on limiting GHG emissions to avoid possible global warming. Efforts are also under way to improve mitigation mechanisms to mobilize and allocate resources efficiently and equitably.

Global optimization of GHG emission levels is based on cost–benefit analysis (CBA) and the concept of maximizing the net benefits (NB) of emissions reduction; that is, finding a strategy which maximizes the benefits (B) of reduced climate change, net of the costs (C) associated with GHG abatement efforts (for details, see Munasinghe, 1995b). If we measure benefits in terms of the avoided costs (D) of greenhouse damages, then maximizing net benefits is equivalent to minimizing total costs (TC) or the sum of the costs of damages and abatement. In other words, since we can also write $NB = [B - C]$ $= [-D - C] = -[TC]$, then maximizing net benefits is equivalent to minimizing total costs. Using R to represent the level of emissions reduction, we may write: $TC(R) = -[C(R) + D(R)]$. Thus TC is minimized when the first derivative equals zero, or $[dTC/dR] = [(dC/dR) - (dD/dR)] = 0$.

We might identify (dC/dR) and (dD/dR) respectively, as the marginal abatement cost (MAC) or change in C per additional unit of GHG abated, and the marginal avoided damages (MAD) or change in damages per unit of GHG abated. We would expect that MAC increases and MAD decreases with higher levels of abatement. TC is minimized at the point where the slope of the abatement cost (MAC) curve equals the negative slope of the damage cost (MAD) curve: that is, abatement should be pursued up to the level where MAC = MAD or $(dC/dR) = -(dD/dR)$.

Setting targets under uncertainty
An important practical handicap is the likelihood that the costs and benefits curves may exhibit great uncertainty (for the reasons set out earlier), especially the marginal avoided damage costs (MAD). Figure 7.9 indicates how such uncertainty will affect the global optimization process. In Figure 7.9(a), both the marginal avoided damages and the abatement costs are economically undefined. Nevertheless, it may be possible to use scientific judgment to determine the target level of emissions reduction R_{AS} , beyond which the risk of damage is unacceptably high. The cross hatching shows the extent of uncertainty in defining the two zones. Indeed, the dividing line at R_{AS} has been drawn closer to the error margin on the right, to indicate a cautious viewpoint (see also the discussion below on the *precautionary* approach). The target level R_{AS} is based on an *absolute standard*, because the obligation to avoid harm is absolute. It implies that the underlying MAD curve (if available) would have been quite low in the acceptable risk zone to the right of R_{AS}, but rising sharply in the zone of unacceptable risk. In other words, the potential damages are so high within the unacceptable risk zone that the cost of abatement carries very little weight in this decision.

In Figure 7.9(b), the marginal abatement costs (MAC) are available while the marginal avoided damage costs are still undefined. The cross-hatching on the MAC curve indicates the degree of uncertainty on either side of its expected (or mean) value. In this case, the target level of emissions reduction R_{AM} reflects the judgmental balance between the affordable level of abatement costs and the acceptability of damage risk. This approach is termed the *affordable safe minimum standard*. The relevant total affordable cost is the area under the MAC curve, up to the vertical line. One difficulty is that affordability is not well

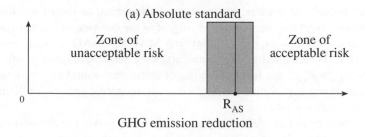

(a) Absolute standard

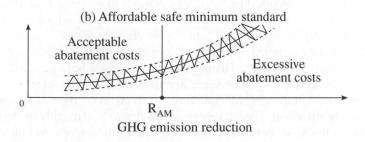

(b) Affordable safe minimum standard

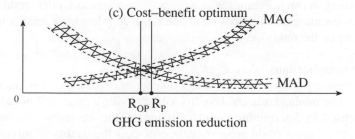

(c) Cost–benefit optimum

Source: Adapted from IPCC (1996c, Figure 5.10)

Figure 7.9 Determining abatement targets

defined and subject to different interpretations. This also implies that the underlying MAD curve is still quite low in the zone to the right of R_{AM}.

Finally in Figure 7.9(c), the optimal level of emissions reduction is defined in terms of the CBA framework presented earlier. In this case, either both the marginal avoided damage cost and abatement cost functions are known with certainty, or the expected values of these curves are used (in the absence of risk aversion), with the cross hatching again indicating the margin of error around the mean value. Then the globally desirable degree of emissions reduction is indicated by R_{OP}, at the point where MAC = MAD.

The benefits of greater information are apparent, to the extent that the abatement target may become less stringent as the decision making progresses through the three cases, in which (a) both MAC and MAD are undefined, (b) only MAD is undefined, and (c) both curves are defined. In other words, since $R_{AS} > R_{AM} > R_{OP}$, the level and costs of abatement would be progressively reduced as one approached the optimal point, reflecting greater confidence in the information available.

The attitude to risk plays a key role in decision making under uncertainty. Great weight is placed on the *precautionary* approach to decision making (which is in fact endorsed by the United Nations Framework Convention on Climate Change), when *risk aversion* interacts with the uncertainty associated with potentially irreversible and catastrophic climate change impacts.[6] As an example of the precautionary approach, consider Figure 7.9(c). Here, although the uncertainty in the avoided damages curve is likely to be large, the decision need not be delayed. A risk-averse decision maker would select the more stringent target emissions reduction level R_P (lying to the right of R_{OP}, which is currently unknown). The relevant point B is determined roughly by the intersection of the MAC curve and some estimate of the upper envelope of the avoided damages (MAD) line. Furthermore, in the face of the greater level of uncertainty shown in Figure 7.9(a), a precautionary approach might result in the even more stringent emissions reduction target R_{AS}, leaving a smaller margin for error on the right side.

Some complications

The foregoing analysis gives rise to a number of corollaries. First, uncertainties in determining costs and benefits would require a great deal of judgment to be used in determining target emissions reduction levels. Second, the decision criterion could progressively evolve as the quality of information improved: from the absolute standard, through the affordable safe minimum standard, to the precautionary and optimal approaches. Third, there may be significant returns to investing in better research and information gathering on climate change.

There are many difficulties that would complicate the analysis. For example, the emission of a unit of GHG may give rise to a varying stream of environmental costs which must be discounted over time to yield a present value aggregate. The environmental damage function may be discontinuous and non-linear. Abatement costs may change over time, depending on when the technologies are applied, because of technological progress. Similarly, abatement costs may exhibit economies of scale (for example, mass production of solar photovoltaic cells), resulting in a marginal cost curve that actually declines beyond a certain point. Such costs may also differ across countries, for various reasons. Moreover, the abatement costs are net costs, to the extent that some technologies (such as renewables) may produce other (non-climate-related) benefits and costs: the joint products complication discussed below.

Finally, costs and benefits accrue to so many diverse individuals, groups and nations that simple aggregation raises equity issues. It is possible to incorporate elements of 'equity' into the globally optimal solution, for example by weighting costs and benefits in inverse proportion to the income levels of the respective victims and beneficiaries. However, determining such weights has proved to be highly contentious, even in the much simpler context of development projects. To conclude, it is more practical to focus on the efficient solution (subject to some judgment) at the global optimization stage, and to introduce equity later.

Sharing Climate Change Burdens: Combining Equity and Efficiency

Suppose that the analysis of climate change yielded a target level of desirable worldwide GHG emissions in the future (see the global optimization process, described above). To illustrate the issue more clearly, we will take a single constant level of emissions that will achieve some desired emissions target. The principles of allocation discussed below would apply in exactly the same way to any other case involving an alternative emissions profile. One method of allocating constant emissions might be based on ethics and basic human rights, that is, equal per capita (EPC) emission rights for all human beings. The total national 'right to emit' would then be the product of the population and the basic per capita emissions quota. An alternative allocation rule is based on equiproportional reductions (EPR) of emissions. In this case, all countries would reduce emissions by the same percentage amount relative to some previously agreed baseline year, to achieve the desired global emissions target.

Equal Per Capita Emissions Rights versus Equal Percentage Reductions

Figure 7.10 illustrates the dynamics of two allocation rules in simplified form. The line *EPC* indicates the constant level of per capita emissions, if the total global emissions target were allocated equally to all human beings during the decision-making time horizon. If we assume a total permissible accumulation of 800 gigatons of carbon (GtC) during the 100-year period 2000–2100, shared equally among the global population of about 6 billion (in 2000), then the constant average per capita emission right would amount to 1.33 tons of carbon (TC) per year, up to 2100, as shown by the solid line *EPC* in the figure. A more precise calculation might seek to aggregate both past and future emissions (using discounting techniques that further penalize near-term emissions which would cause damage over a longer period) to yield the grand total over any given period of time.

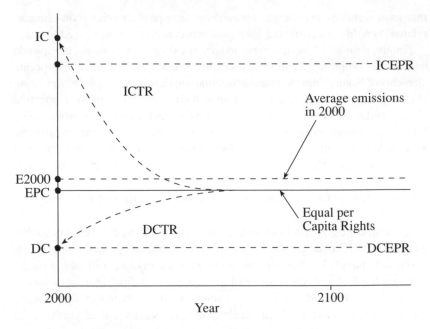

Source: Munasinghe (1996).

7.10   Allocating emission rights

The points IC and DC represent the average current per capita GHG emissions of the industrialized (that is, OECD nations, Eastern Europe and former Soviet Union) and developing countries, respectively. Although the figure is not exactly to scale, IC (about 3.5 TC per capita per year) is both above EPC and considerably larger than DC (about 0.5 TC per capita). Thus the industrialized countries would need to cut back GHG emissions significantly if they were to meet the EPC criterion, which would entail economic costs (depending on the severity of the curtailment in each country). On the other hand, the developing countries have considerable room to increase their per capita emissions as incomes and energy consumption grow.

Next, consider the EPR rule, where all nations reduce their emissions equipro-portionally. Assuming a global average emission rate of about 1.47 TC per capita per year in 2000 (indicated by the broken line E2000 in the figure), this implies that all countries would need to curtail carbon emissions by about 10 per cent to meet the EPR criterion (as shown by the broken lines ICEPR and DCEPR in the figure). Clearly, given the primary impetus provided by energy to economic development, such a solution would severely restrict growth prospects in the developing world, where per capita energy consumption is low to begin with (Munasinghe, 1995a).

Achieving a practical balance

The foregoing analysis indicates that the EPC and EPR approaches would result in some hardship and inequity for the developed and developing countries, respectively. Another related equity issue is whether past emissions should be considered also or ignored in deciding the current and future quotas. Suppose we assume that the future global atmospheric concentration of CO_2 must be stabilized at 550 parts per million by volume (ppmv). Over 80 per cent of carbon accumulated up to 1990 has resulted from fossil fuel use in the industrialized world. Clearly, the industrialized countries have used up a significant share of the 'global carbon space' available to humanity while driving up atmospheric CO_2 concentrations from the pre-industrial norm of 280 ppmv to the current level of about 360 ppmv. Therefore the developing countries argue that responsibility for past emissions should be considered when future rights are allocated. Correspondingly, it would be in the industrialized countries' interest to use a fixed base year population (for example, in the year 2000) as the multiplier of the per capita emissions right (such as EPC) in determining total national emission quotas. This would effectively penalize countries with high population growth rates, since their national quota (determined by base year population) would have to be divided up among more people in the future.

In practice, it is possible that some intermediate requirement which falls between EPC and EPR might emerge eventually from the global collective decision-making process. For example, EPC may be set as a long-term goal. In the shorter run, pragmatic considerations suggest that both the industrialized and transition countries be given a period of time to adjust to the lower GHG emissions level, in order to avoid undue economic disruptions and hardship, especially for poorer groups within those countries (see transition emissions paths ICTR and DCTR in Figure 7.10). Even if some industrialized nations might argue that the goal of EPC emissions rights for all individuals is too idealistic or impractical, the directions of adjustment are clear. Net CO_2 emissions per capita in industrialized countries should tend downwards, while such emissions in developing countries will increase with time. This result emerges even if the goal is a more equitable distribution of per capita emissions, rather than absolute equality of per capita emissions.

Another adjustment option might be the facilitation of an emissions trading system. For example, once national emissions quotas have been assigned, a particular developing country may find that it is unable to utilize fully its allocation in a given year. At the same time, an industrialized country might find it cheaper to buy such 'excess' emissions rights from the developing nation, rather than undertake a much higher cost abatement programme to cut back emissions and meet its own target. More generally, the emissions trading system would permit quotas to be bought and sold freely on the international market, thereby establishing an efficient current price and even a futures market for GHG emissions (burden reallocation is also possible through activities implemented jointly).

SUMMARY AND CONCLUSIONS

Sustainable development has economic, social and environmental components. Given the key role played by economics in development decision making, this chapter has set out a practical framework for better integrating the different elements of sustainability, based on ecological economics. This approach may be used at various hierarchical levels of decision making: project/local, sectoral/subnational, economywide/national and global/transnational. Case studies illustrate specific methods of application.

Traditionally, the economic analysis of projects and policies (including the techniques of shadow pricing), has helped countries make more efficient use of scarce resources. 'External effects', especially those arising from adverse environmental consequences, have often been neglected in the past. This chapter has focused on concepts and techniques for valuation of environmental impacts of projects and policies that enable such environmental considerations to be explicitly considered in the conventional cost–benefit calculus used in economic decision making. The process of internalizing these environmental externalities may be facilitated by extending the techniques of neoclassical economic theory, with particular reliance on willingness-to-pay as a measure of value. (Problems caused by discounting, risk and uncertainty have been discussed.) When economic valuation of environmental impacts is difficult, reliance may have to be placed on broader methods such as multi-criteria analysis.

Economywide policies (both sectoral and macroeconomic) often have significant environmental effects. Broad policy reforms which usually promote efficiency or reduce poverty should also be generally beneficial for the environment. However, some of these reforms may have negative environmental effects, depending on pre-existing (and often localized) imperfections, including policy distortions, market failures and institutional constraints. The solution is not necessarily to modify the original broader policies (which have conventional economic or poverty-related goals), but rather to design more specific and complementary environmental measures that would address the more specific policy, market or institutional imperfection and thereby help mitigate negative effects or enhance positive impacts of the original policies on the environment. Such environmentally focused remedial actions would include both market-based approaches (such as Pigouvian taxes on environmental externalities, or allocation of limited pollution rights coupled with marketable permits) and non-market methods (such as command-and-control techniques, or better definition of property rights). In cases where environmental harm may be severe, even fine-tuning of economywide policies might be considered to limit such damage, both economic planners and environmental analysts need to cooperate closely in this process.

Overall, the case studies suggest that economic techniques exist – and for most countries, so does natural resource information – to improve the way environmental issues are addressed at the project, sector and macro levels. While significant data problems remain, the studies illustrate the feasibility of making rough assessments, not simply of environmental impacts of projects, but also of economic policies (and in particular economywide policies), thereby hastening the integration of environment into the mainstream of economic decision making. The action impact matrix-based approach outlined here may be applied at varying levels of sophistication to improve the coordination and articulation of policies and projects, thereby addressing the economic, social and environmental goals of sustainable development in a more systematic way. At the global level, ecological economics facilitates the combined use of efficiency and equity criteria to develop practical policies.

At the same time, it is clear that more experience is required in applying the ecological economics concepts and techniques presented in this chapter to real-world problems in developing countries. Such work can indicate orders of magnitude of impacts, eliminate gross environmental errors and help identify the critical environmental indicators to which decisions should be sensitive. In particular, estimates of non-use values are rare in the developing world, and multi-objective decision methods also need to be explored more systematically. In the case of economywide reforms, areas of current interest such as trade reform and privatization policies should receive early attention. The significance of role of global environmental issues and how they might be integrated into country-level sustainable development strategies is another key area which it would be fruitful to study.

The incidence of environmental costs and benefits, distributional, political economy and institutional issues also need to be addressed in future work, because the nature of environmental problems is heavily dependent on the allocation of political and institutional power, and policy reforms that have substantial implications for redistributing income and wealth will be resisted by vested interests. Finally, the need for a more systematic way of monitoring the impacts of policies and projects suggests that better environmental and social indicators should be developed.

ACKNOWLEDGMENTS

The author wishes to thank Sanath Ranawana, Noreen Beg and Arati Belle for assistance in preparing this chapter. The opinions expressed herein are those of the author and should not be attributed to any institution.

NOTES

1. If real interest rates were too low (for example, close to zero), the low cost of capital might lead to overinvestment, which could then exacerbate deforestation, for example through the availability of better roads and mechanized logging equipment. (For further discussion, see Munasinghe, 1993.)
2. Extending this line of reasoning, it might be reasonable to consider avoiding certain macro-economic policies altogether in extreme cases where irreversible and catastrophic environmental damage would occur.
3. In the case of some forms of environmental degradation and pollution, the EKC is more S-shaped.
4. Given that policy regimes vary widely across countries and over time, an EKC estimated using cross-section (or pooled) data is likely to be a composite of many paths. Even an EKC based on time series data for one country will reflect the effects of a range of time-varying policies.
5. Such an approach suggests that, if the system of national accounts (SNA) was adjusted to correctly reflect the status of the environment, the shape of the resulting EKC might be quite different (Munasinghe, 1998b).
6. More specifically, Article 3.3 of the UNFCCC states that the Parties to the UNFCCC should 'take precautionary measures to anticipate, prevent or minimize the causes of climate change and mitigate its adverse effects. Where there are threats of serious or irreversible damage, lack of full scientific certainty should not be used as a reason for postponing such measures, taking into account that policies and measures to deal with climate change should be cost effective so as to ensure global benefits at the lowest possible cost. To achieve this, such policies and measures should take into account different socio-economic contexts, be comprehensive, cover all relevant sources, sinks and reservoirs of greenhouse gases and adaptation, and comprise all economic sectors. Efforts to address climate change may be carried out cooperatively by interested Parties.'

REFERENCES

Abaza, H. (1995), 'UNEP/World Bank workshop on the Environmental Impacts of Structural Adjustment Programmes – New York, 20–21 March 1995', *Ecological Economics*, 14(1), 1–5.

Arrow, K.J., W. Cline, K.G. Mäler, M. Munasinghe and J. Stiglitz (1995), 'Intertemporal Equity, Discounting, and Economic Efficiency', in M. Munasinghe (ed.), *Global Climate Change: Economic and Policy Issues*, Washington, DC: World Bank.

Atkinson, G., R. Dubourg, K. Hamilton, M. Munasinghe, D. Pearce and C. Young (1997), *Measuring Sustainable Development*, Cheltenham, UK and Lyme, US: Edward Elgar.

Barbier, E.B. (1988), 'The Economics of Farm-Level Adoption of Soil Conservation Measures in the Uplands of Java', Environment Department Working Paper 11, Washington, DC: World Bank.

Bates, R., S. Gupta and F. Boguslaw (1994), 'Economywide Policies and the Environment: A Case Study of Poland', Environment Department Working Paper 63, Washington, DC: World Bank.

Binswanger, H. (1991), 'Brazilian Policies that Encourage Deforestation in the Amazon', *World Development*, 19, 821–9.

Birdsall, N. and D. Wheeler (1992), 'Trade Policy and Industrial Pollution in Latin America: Where are the Pollution Havens?' in P. Low (ed.), *International Trade and the Environment*, Discussion Paper 159, Washington, DC: World Bank.

Carlin, A., P.F. Scodari and D.H. Garner (1992), 'Environmental Investments: The Cost of Cleaning Up', *Environment*, 34(2).

Cleaver, K. and G. Schreiber (1991), *The Population, Environment and Agriculture Nexus in Sub-Saharan Africa*, Africa Region Technical Paper, Washington, DC: World Bank.

Cropper, M.L. and W.E. Oates (1992), 'Environmental Economics: a Survey', *Journal of Economic Literature*, XXX, 675–740.

Cruz, Wilfredo, Mohan Munasinghe and Jeremy Warford (1997), 'The Greening of Economic Policy Reform, 2. (Case Studies)', Washington, DC: World Bank.

Cruz, Wilfredo and R. Repetto (1992), *The Environmental Effects of Stabilization and Structural Adjustment Programs: The Philippines Case*, Washington, DC: World Resources Institute.

Daly, Herman E. and John B. Cobb (1994), *For the Common Good*, 2nd edn, Boston: Beacon Press.

Dasgupta, P. (1993), *An Enquiry into Poverty and Destitution*, Oxford: Oxford University Press.

Dasgupta, P., S. Marglin and A.K. Sen (1972), *Guidelines for Project Evaluation*, New York: UNIDO.

Devarajan, S. (1990), 'Can Computable General Equilibrium Models Shed Light on the Environmental Problems of Developing Countries', Paper prepared for WIDER Conference on the Environment and Emerging Development Issues, Helsinki, September, 1990.

Economic Commission for Latin America and the Caribbean (ECLAC) (1989), 'Crisis, External Debt, Macroeconomic Policies and Their Relation to the Environment in Latin America and the Caribbean', paper prepared for the Meeting of High-Level Government Experts on Regional Co-operation in Environmental Matters in Latin America and the Caribbean, United Nations Environmental Programme, Brasilia.

Feder, G., T. Onchan, Y. Chalamwong and C. Hongladarom (1988), *Land Policies and Farm Productivity in Thailand*, Baltimore: Johns Hopkins University Press.

Freeman, A.M. (1993), *Measurement of Environmental and Resource Values*, Washington, DC: RFF.

Goldin, I. and A. Winters (1992), *Open Economies: Structural Adjustment and Agriculture*, London: Cambridge University Press.

Goodland, Robert (1999), 'The Biophysical basis of Environmental Sustainability', in Jeroen C.J.M. van den Bergh (ed.), *Handbook of Environmental and Resource Economics*, Cheltenham, UK and Lyme, US: Edward Elgar.

Guggenheim, S. (1994), 'Involuntary Resettlement: An Annotated Reference Bibliography for Development Research', World Bank Environment Department Working Paper 64, Washington DC: World Bank.

Hamilton, K. (1994), 'Green Adjustments to GDP', *Resources Policy*, 20, 155–68.

Hanna, S. and M. Munasinghe (1995a), 'Property Rights and the Environment', Stockholm and Washington DC: Beijer Institute and the World Bank.

Hanna, S. and M. Munasinghe (1995b), 'Property Rights in Social and Ecological Context', Stockholm and Washington DC: Beijer Institute and the World Bank.

Harberger, A.C. (1976), *Project Evaluation: Collected Papers*, Chicago: University of Chicago Press.

Intergovernmental Panel on Climate Change (1996), *Second Assessment Report*, General: IPCC.

Jepma, Catrinus J. and Mohan Munasinghe (1998), *Climate Change Policy*, Cambridge: Cambridge University Press.

Kolstad, C. and J. Braden (eds) (1991), *Measuring the Demand for Environmental Quality*, New York: Elsevier.

Kramer, R.A., M. Munasinghe, N. Sharma, E. Mercer and P. Shyamsundar (1992), 'Valuing and Protecting Tropical Forests: A Case Study of Madagascar', paper presented at the IUCN World Parks Congress, Caracas.

Kuznets, Simon (1955), 'Economic Growth and Income Inequality', *American Economic Review*, 49, 1–28.

Larson, B. and D. Bromley (1991), 'Natural Resource Prices, Export Policies and Deforestation: The Case of Sudan', *World Development*.

Lele, U. and S. Stone (1989), 'Population Pressure, the Environment and Agricultural Intensification', MADIA Discussion Paper 4, Washington, DC: World Bank.

Lind, R.C. (1982), *Discounting for Time and Risk in Energy Policy*, Baltimore: Johns Hopkins University Press.

Little, I. and J. Mirrlees (1974), *Project Appraisal and Planning for Developing Countries*, New York: Basic Books.

Mahar, D. (1989), 'Government Policies and Deforestation in Brazil's Amazon Region', Washington, DC: World Bank.

Mäler, K-G. (1990), 'International Environmental Problems', *Oxford Review of Economic Policy*, 6(1), 80–108.

Mäler, K.G. and M. Munasinghe (1996), 'Macroeconomic Policies, Second-Best Theory and the Environment', *Environment and Development Economics*, 1(2), 149–63.

Max-Neef, M. (1995), 'Economic Growth and Quality of Life: A Threshold Hypothesis', *Ecological Economics*, 15, 115–18.

Meier, P. and M. Munasinghe (1994), 'Incorporating Environmental Concerns into Power Sector Decisionmaking', Washington, DC: World Bank.

Meier, P., M. Munasinghe and T. Siyambalapitiya (1993), 'Energy Sector Policy and the Environment: A Case Study of Sri Lanka', Workshop on Economywide Policies and the Environment, Washington, DC: World Bank.

Miranda, K. and T. Muzondo (1991), 'Public Policy and the Environment', *Finance and Development*, 28(2), 25–7.

Munasinghe, M. (1990), *Energy Analysis and Policy*, London: Butterworths.

Munasinghe, M. (1992), *Water Supply and Environmental Management*, Boulder, Col.: Westview Press.

Munasinghe, M. (1993), 'Environmental Economics and Sustainable Development', Washington, DC: World Bank.

Munasinghe, M. (1995a), 'Sustainable Energy Development', Environment Paper 16, Washington, DC: World Bank.

Munasinghe, M (ed.) (1995b), *Global Climate Change: Economic and Policy Issues*, Washington, DC: World Bank.

Munasinghe, M. (1995c), 'Making Economic Growth More Sustainable', *Ecological Economics*, 15(1), 121–4.

Munasinghe, M. (ed.) (1996), *Environmental Impacts of Macroeconomic and Sectoral Policies*, Washington, DC and Solomons, MD: World Bank, UNEP and ISEE.

Munasinghe, M. (1998a), 'Countrywide Policies and Sustainable Development: Are the Linkages Perverse?', in T. Teitenberg and H. Folmer (eds), *The International Yearbook of International and Resource Economics*, London: Edward Elgar.

Munasinghe, M. (1998b), 'Is Environmental Degradation an Inevitable Consequence of Economic Growth?', *Ecological Economics*, December.

Munasinghe, M. and W. Cruz (1994), 'Economywide Policies and the Environment', Washington, DC: World Bank.

Munasinghe, M. and K. King (1992), 'Accelerating Ozone Layer Protection in Developing Countries', *World Development*, 20 (April), 609–18.

Munasinghe, M. and J. McNeely (eds) (1994), *Protected Area Economics and Policy*, Geneva and Washington, DC: World Conservation Union (IUCN) and the World Bank.

Munasinghe, M., W. Cruz and J. Warford (1993), 'Are Economywide Policies Good for the Environment?', *Finance and Development*.

Munasinghe, M. and W. Shearer (eds) (1995), *Defining and Measuring Sustainability: The Biogeophysical Foundations*, Tokyo and Washington, DC: UN University and World Bank.

Opschoor, J.B. and S.M. Jongma (1996), 'Structural Adjustment Policies and Sustainability', *Environment and Development Economics*, 1, 183–202.

Panayotou, T. and C. Sussangkarn (1991), 'The Debt Crisis, Structural Adjustment and the Environment: The Case of Thailand', paper prepared for the WWF Project on Impact of Macroeconomic Adjustment on the Environment.

Pearce, D.W. (1991), 'Economic Valuation and the Natural World', paper prepared for World Development Report 1992: Development and the Natural World, Washington, DC: World Bank.

Pearce, D.W. and K. Turner (1990), *Economics of Natural Resources and the Environment*, London: Harvester Wheatsheaf.

Perrings, C. (1993), 'Pastoral Strategies in Sub-Saharan Africa: The Economic and Ecological Sustainability of Dryland Range Management', Environment Working Paper 57, Environment Department, Washington, DC: World Bank.

Persson, A. and M. Munasinghe (1995), 'Natural Resource Management and Economywide Policies in Costa Rica', *World Bank Economics Review*.

Petry, F. (1990), 'Who is Afraid of Choices? A Proposal for Multi-Criteria Analysis as a Tool for Decisionmaking Support in Development Planning', *Journal of International Development*, 2, 209–31.

Reed, David (ed.) (1992), *Structural Adjustment and the Environment*, Boulder, Col.: Westview Press.

Reed, David (1996), *Structural Adjustment, the Environment and Sustainable Development*, London: Earthscan.

Robinson, S. (1990), 'Pollution, Market Failure and Optimal Policy in an Economywide Framework', Working Paper No. 559, Department of Agricultural and Resource Economics, University of California at Berkeley.

Schecter, M. and S. Freeman (1992), 'Some Reflections on the Definition and Measurement of Non-Use Value', Natural Resources and Environmental Research Center and Department of Economics, University of Haifa.

Schneider, R. (1993), 'Land Abandonment, Property Rights and Agricultural Sustainability in the Amazon', LATEN Dissemination Note 3, Washington, DC: World Bank.

Scott, A. (1956), 'National Wealth and Natural Wealth', *Canadian Journal of Economics and Political Science*, 22, 373–8.

Solow, R. (1986), 'On the Intergenerational Allocation of Natural Resources', *Scandinavian Journal of Economics*, 88(1), 141–9.

Southgate, D. and D.W. Pearce (1988), 'Agricultural Colonization and Environmental Degradation in Frontier Developing Economies', Working Paper 9, Environment Department, Washington, DC: World Bank.

Stryker, J.D. *et al.* (1989), 'Linkages Between Policy Reform and Natural Resource Management in Sub-Saharan Africa', Unpublished paper, Fletcher School, Tufts University, and Associates for International Resources and Development.

Squire, L. and H. van der Tak (1975), *Economic Analysis of Projects*, Baltimore: Johns Hopkins University Press.

United Nations Statistical Office (1993), *Integrated Environmental and Economic Accounting*, New York: United Nations.

Uzawa, H. (1969), 'Time Preference and the Penrose Effect in a Two-Class Model of Economic Growth', *Journal of Political Economy*, 77, 628–52.

Warford, Jeremy, Mohan Munasinghe and Wilfredo Cruz (1997), 'The Greening of Economic Policy Reform, 1. (Principles)', Washington, DC: World Bank.

Willig, Robert D. (1976), 'Consumer's Surplus Without Apology', *American Economic Review*, 66(4), pp. 589–97.

World Bank (1992a), *World Development Report 1992*, New York: Oxford University Press.

World Bank (1992b), 'Water Quality and Pollution Control Project in Brazil. Staff Appraisal Report', Washington, DC: World Bank.

World Bank (1992c), World Bank Structural and Sectoral Adjustment Operations: The Second OED Review, Operations and Evaluation Department, Washington, DC: World Bank.

World Bank (1993a), 'Energy Efficiency and Conservation in the Developing World', Policy Paper, Washington, DC: World Bank.

World Bank (1993b), *The World Bank's Role in the Electric Power Sector*, A World Bank Policy Paper, Washington, DC.

World Bank (1993c), 'Peru: Privatization Adjustment Loan, Report No. P-5929-PE, Washington, DC: World Bank.

World Bank (1997), 'Measuring Environmental Progress', Environment Department, Washington, DC: World Bank.

World Commission on Environment and Development (WCED) (1987), *Our Common Future*, Oxford: Oxford University Press.

Young, C.E.F. and J. Bishop (1995), 'Adjustment Policies and the Environment: A Critical Review of the Literature', CREED Working Paper Series 1, London: International Institute for Economic Development.

8. The environmental Kuznets curve: a review

David I. Stern

INTRODUCTION

The environmental Kuznets curve (EKC) hypothesis proposes that there is an inverted U-shape relation between various indicators of environmental degradation and income per capita. This has been taken to imply that economic growth will eventually redress the environmental impacts of the early stages of economic development and that growth will lead to further environmental improvements in the developed countries. Far from being a threat to the environment in the long term, as argued in *The Limits to Growth* and *Beyond the Limits*, by Meadows *et al.* (1972, 1992) among others, economic growth is seen as necessary in order for environmental quality to be maintained or improved. This is an essential part of the sustainable development argument as put forward in *Our Common Future* by WCED (1987). The EKC literature constitutes an evaluation of these arguments. The EKC is named after Simon Kuznets (1955, 1963) who hypothesized that the relationship between a measure of inequality in the distribution of income and the level of income is an inverted U-shape curve. Figure 8.1 illustrates the typical shape of the EKC.

Proponents of the EKC hypothesis argue that at very low levels of economic activity environmental impacts are generally low, but as development proceeds the rates of land clearance, resource use and waste generation per capita increase rapidly. However, 'at higher levels of development, structural change towards information-intensive industries and services, coupled with increased environmental awareness, enforcement of environmental regulations, better technology and higher environmental expenditures, result in levelling off and gradual decline of environmental degradation' (Panayotou, 1993). Thus there are both proximate causes of the EKC relationship – changes in economic structure or product mix, changes in technology and changes in input mix – as well as underlying causes such as environmental regulation, awareness and education. These effects act to counteract or exaggerate the gross impact of economic growth or the scale effect.

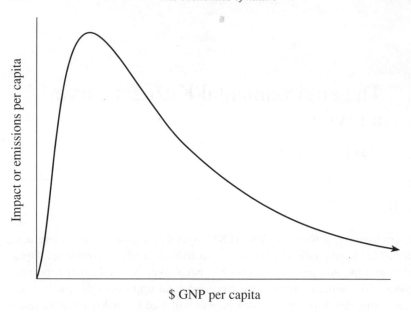

Figure 8.1   Environmental Kuznets curve

The EKC theme was promoted by the World Bank's *World Development Report 1992* (IBRD, 1992). The authors noted that 'The view that greater economic activity inevitably hurts the environment is based on static assumptions about technology, tastes and environmental investments' (p. 38) and that 'As incomes rise, the demand for improvements in environmental quality will increase, as will the resources available for investment' (p. 39). Some expounded this position even more forcefully: 'there is clear evidence that, although economic growth usually leads to environmental degradation in the early stages of the process, in the end the best – and probably the only – way to attain a decent environment in most countries is to become rich' (Beckerman, 1992).

These views have been countered by critics of the EKC concept and literature (for example, Arrow *et al.*, 1995; Stern *et al.*, 1996). The main arguments against the EKC are the following: much of the empirical evidence is weak and statistical techniques inappropriate, the static relationship between rich and poor countries does not necessarily tell us about dynamics as countries experience economic growth and EKC relationships been found for only a subset of indicators; growth might improve these but would lead to worsening levels of others. In addition, even where EKC relationships might hold true, projections (Stern *et al.*, 1996; Selden and Song, 1994) show that global levels of impacts are likely to rise over the next few decades.

In the several years since Grossman and Krueger's (1991) pathbreaking study, a large literature has developed estimated EKCs and discussed their implications. Several papers on the EKC were presented at the ISEE conference in Boston. Several of those papers will be published in a special edition of *Ecological Economics*, together with an introductory paper. Therefore, though this chapter reviews the ISEE conference papers, it does not focus on them exclusively. Instead, a general review of the literature is attempted.[1] The principal criterion used to evaluate the contributions is 'Do developments in the literature represent advances in terms of our knowledge about the existence of such relations, our understanding of their determinants and implications and in terms of the methods used to investigate them?'

There have been four main types of contributions to the literature: estimation of 'basic' EKCs, studies of the theoretical determinants of the EKC, studies of the empirical determinants of the EKC and critique of EKCs. The chapter is organized so that theoretical studies that build on the basic background discussed above are reviewed in the next section, followed by a survey of estimates of basic EKCs. These sections are followed by a review of the critiques of these basic EKCs and their interpretation. The fifth section surveys studies that have examined empirical determinants of the EKC, while the final two sections of the chapter examine whether progress is being made in our understanding of the EKC and suggest directions for further research.

THEORETICAL DETERMINANTS OF THE EKC

A few papers have built on the heuristic theory of the EKC described in the previous section to mathematically relate plausible assumptions about technology and preferences to the shape of the time path of environmental impacts.

Lopez (1994) provides a theoretical analysis of environment–growth relationships at a fairly high level of generality. His model has two production sectors, weak separability between pollution and the conventional factors of production, constant returns to scale, quasi-fixed inputs of capital and labour, exogenous technical change and exogenous output prices. Preferences are a function of revenue, pollution and the output price vector. If producers pay a zero or fixed pollution price, increases in output unambiguously result in increases in pollution in this system, irrespective of the features of the technology or preferences. However, when producers pay the social marginal cost of pollution, the relation between emissions and income depends on the properties of the technology and preferences. If preferences are homothetic, increasing output again results in increasing pollution. However, when preferences are non-homothetic, as is likely in reality (Pollak and Wales, 1992), the response of pollution to growth depends on the elasticity of substitution in production between pollution and the conventional inputs and the degree of relative risk aversion: that is, the rate at which marginal utility declines with rising consumption of produced goods.[2] The faster marginal utility declines, and the more substitution is possible in production, the less pollution will tend to increase with production. For empirically reasonable values of these two parameters, pollution may increase at low levels of income and fall at high levels: the inverted U. This result is interesting, but its relevance is limited if the price of pollution is not socially optimal. Command and control measures on pollutants that show inverted Us may result in effective prices that are close to being socially optimal while the effective price of pollutants such as carbon dioxide is generally close to zero. Also in the latter case the elasticity of substitution is probably lower and the apparent damage less evident to consumers, both implying a higher turning point. Lopez also constructs a model for deforestation, where, as might be expected, if the stock effects of the forest on agricultural production are internalized, growth results in less deforestation and vice versa.

Selden and Song (1995) derive an inverted U curve for the optimal path of pollution using Forster's (1973) growth and pollution model. The latter model is similar to Lopez's model but assumes a priori that utility is additively separable in consumption and pollution. It therefore corresponds to Lopez's non-homothetic preferences case. Optimal abatement is zero until a given capital stock is achieved, whereafter it rises sharply at an increasing rate. As a result the optimal pollution path is an inverted U in the capital stock.

While Lopez (1994) and Selden and Song (1995) both develop models based on infinitely lived agents, John and Pecchenino (1994) and John *et al.* (1995) develop models based on overlapping generations (McConnell, 1997). In these models, the externality of pollution is, therefore, only partially internalized. Also pollution is generated in these latter models by consumption rather than production activities. All these models can generate inverted U-shape curves under appropriate conditions. McConnell (1997) develops a model of consumption pollution.[3] He uses this model to argue that there is no defining role in the EKC theory for the income elasticity of environmental quality. While a higher elasticity will lead, *ceteris paribus*, to a faster reduction in pollution, pollution can decline even if the elasticity is non-positive.

In summary, it seems fairly easy to develop models that generate EKCs under appropriate assumptions. The challenge would appear to be to find empirical evidence as to which of these stories, if any, is more plausible.

BASIC EKCs

This section surveys studies whose primary purpose is to estimate the relationship between environmental impact indicators and GDP. Several of these studies also examined the effects of possible conditioning variables such as trade intensity, but that seems a secondary focus of these papers.

The first empirical EKC study appears to have been the NBER working paper by Grossman and Krueger (1991)[4] that estimated EKCs as part of a study of the potential environmental impacts of the North American Free Trade Agreement (NAFTA). The authors estimated EKCs for SO_2, dark matter (fine smoke) and suspended particles (SPM) using the GEMS data set. This data set comprises ambient measurements from a number of locations in cities around the world. Each regression involves a cubic function of PPP (purchasing power parity) per capita GDP and various site-related variables, a time trend and a trade intensity variable. The turning points for SO_2 and dark matter are at around $4000–5000. The concentration of suspended particles appeared to decline even at low-income levels. Both the time trend and the trade intensity variables had a significant negative coefficient in the SO_2 regression. Neither the time trend nor the trade variable was significant in the equation explaining the concentration of dark matter. The time trend was significant in the suspended particles regression but again the trade variable was insignificant. At income levels over $10 000–15 000, Grossman and Krueger's estimates show increasing levels of all three pollutants. Though economic growth at middle income levels would improve environmental quality, growth at high-income levels would be detrimental. This result may either reflect the type of phenomenon raised by Pezzey (1989) (see below) or simply be the result of an inappropriate functional form that is a dependent variable in levels rather than logs.

Shafik and Bandyopadhyay's (1992)[5] study was particularly influential, as the results were used in the 1992 World Development Report (IBRD, 1992). They estimated EKCs for 10 different indicators: lack of clean water, lack of urban sanitation, ambient levels of suspended particulate matter, ambient sulphur oxides, change in forest area between 1961 and 1986, the annual rate of deforestation between 1961 and 1986 (that is, observations for each year), dissolved oxygen in rivers, faecal coliforms in rivers, municipal waste per capita and carbon emissions per capita. Data coverage and sources varied between the different indicators.

They used three different functional forms: log-linear, log-quadratic and, in the most general case, a logarithmic cubic polynomial in PPP GDP per capita, a time trend and site-related variables. In each case the dependent variable was untransformed.[6] Lack of clean water and lack of urban sanitation were found to decline uniformly with increasing income and over time. Both measures of deforestation were found to be insignificantly related to the income terms. River quality tended to worsen with increasing income. Shafik and Bandyopadhyay suppose that this is because the external costs imposed by this form of pollution may decline as water supply systems improve. The two air pollutants, however, conform to the EKC hypothesis. The turning points for both pollutants are found for income levels of between $3000 and $4000. The time trend is significantly positive for faecal coliform and significantly negative for air quality. Finally, both municipal waste and carbon emissions per capita increase unambiguously with rising income. The broader range of indicators examined by Shafik and Bandyopadhyay shows a much more ambiguous picture of the relationship between environment and development than indicated by Grossman and Krueger's more limited study.

Subsequent studies have moved to use pollution emissions data rather than ambient concentrations, include population density as an explanatory variable for a number of indicators, calculate future projections based on the estimated EKCs and investigate further indicators such as energy use.

Panayotou (1993, 1995) estimated EKCs for SO_2, NO_x, SPM and deforestation. In contrast to most other studies Panayotou employed only cross-sectional data, and GDP is in 1985 US dollars converted at market exchange rates. The three pollutants were measured in terms of emissions per capita on a national basis. Data for developing countries were estimated from fuel use and fuel mix data. Deforestation was measured as the mean annual rate of deforestation in the mid-1980s, plus unity. There are 68 countries in the deforestation sample and 54 in the pollution sample. The fitted equations for the three pollutants are logarithmic quadratics in income per capita. For deforestation, Panayotou fitted a translog function in population density and income per capita, with the addition of a dummy variable for tropical countries. All the estimated curves are inverted Us. For the sample mean population density, the turning point for deforestation is $823 per capita. Deforestation rates were significantly greater in tropical countries. Deforestation was also higher in countries with higher population densities. For SO_2 emissions, the turning point is around $3000 per capita (see Figure 8.1), for NO_x around $5500 per capita and for SPM around $4500. The market exchange rates used by Panayotou tend to lower the income levels of developing countries and raise those of the developed countries (apart from the United States) relative to the PPP values. Despite this, the turning points for the pollutants are in a similar range to those reported by Grossman and Krueger and Shafik and Bandyopadhyay. This is probably because Panayotou uses emissions per capita rather than ambient concentrations.

Selden and Song (1994) estimated EKCs for four airborne emissions series: SO_2, NO_x, SPM and CO on longitudinal data from World Resources (WRI, 1991). These primarily represent developed countries. Here we concentrate on the results they present for a fixed effects model including a population density variable. The authors suggest that in countries with low population densities there will be less pressure to adopt stringent environmental standards, and emissions due to transport will be higher. The estimated turning points are all very high compared to the three studies discussed above: SO_2, $8709; NO_x, $11 217; SPM, $10 289; and CO, $5963. Selden and Song suggest that this is because ambient pollution levels are likely to decline before aggregate emissions. The paper also contains projections for these pollutants for the next few decades, which show a monotonic increase in global emissions.

Holtz-Eakin and Selden (1995) estimate quadratic EKCs for carbon dioxide emissions on panel data confirming the very high ($35 000 in a levels regression, $8 million in a logarithmic regression) turning points for this pollutant found by Shafik (1994). They utilize a wide range of diagnostic tests and statistics. They also produce projections for emissions over the next century under a number of different assumptions and a convergence-based economic growth model. Schmalensee *et al.* (1995) also look at carbon dioxide and make projections using a more extensive version of the Holtz-Eakin and Selden database. The innovation is the use of a spline regression in place of the conventional polynomials. They choose the spline regression in place of higher-order polynomials which, though they fit the data better than a quadratic, have varying out-of-sample properties. The spline estimate has 10 piecewise segments. Carbon elasticities with respect to income are negative for both the segment associated with the lowest level of income and that associated with the highest level of income (below PPP$(1985) 629 and above PPP$(1985) 9799) but positive for middle-income levels. Therefore per capita carbon emissions decline with rising income well within the sample range. The time effects from the fixed effects estimator show rising emissions from 1950 to 1980 and level thereafter. As in most panel regression estimates of the EKC, the country effects explain the vast majority of the variance in the data. Despite the inverted U-shape curve, emission projections using IPCC population and economic growth assumptions show a more rapid rise in emissions than assumed by the IPCC. Dijkgraaf and Vollebergh (1998) also found an inverted U relationship for carbon emissions using only data from OECD countries. Schmalensee *et al.* (1995) effectively also only use developed country data to estimate the high-income part of the EKC. The shape of EKCs for other pollutants such as sulphur may also depend on the sample used (Stern *et al.*, 1998).

Horvath (1997) estimates an EKC for energy use per capita for a sample of 114 countries using cross-sectional and longitudinal data. Per capita energy use is increasing with rising per capita income. As suggested by Stern *et al.* (1996) and Suri and Chapman (1998) energy use might serve as an indicator of overall environmental impact.

Cole *et al.* (1997) add a number of novel indicators to those examined in previous studies, including specific transport emissions for SO_2, SPM, NO_2 and total energy use, nitrates in water, CFC emissions, traffic volumes and methane. Again local pollutants had inverted U-shape curves, as did CFCs. Traffic volumes, nitrates and methane did not have within-sample turning points.

Cropper and Griffiths (1994) estimate three regional (Africa, Latin America and Asia) EKCs for deforestation using panel data for 64 countries over a

30-year period. The dependent variable is the negative of the percentage change in forest area between two years. The independent variables in each regression are rural population density, percentage change in population, timber price, per capita GDP and percentage change in per capita PPP GDP, square of per capita PPP GDP, a dummy variable for each country and a time trend. Neither the population growth rate nor the time trend was significant in either Africa or Latin America and the price of tropical logs was insignificant in Africa. Otherwise, the coefficients in these regressions were significantly different from zero. None of the coefficients in the Asian regression were significant. For Africa, the turning point is $4760 and, for Latin America, $5420. These levels are very much higher than either Panayotou's or Shafik and Bandyopadhyay's results. In contrast to Shafik and Bandyopadhyay and, to a lesser degree, Panayotou, Cropper and Griffiths conclude that economic growth will not solve the problem of deforestation. Antle and Heidebrink (1995) estimate EKCs for afforestation and national parks on cross-sectional data. They find a U-shape curve for both indicators (that is an inverted U for environmental impact) with turning points of 2000 and 1200 (1985) US dollars, respectively, a result closer to that of Shafik and Panayotou. All these three studies use cross-sectional data rather than the panel data used by Cropper and Griffiths.

CRITIQUE OF THE EKC

Identification of Problems

Stern *et al.* (1996), Arrow *et al.* (1995), Ekins (1997), Pearson (1994) and Ansuategi *et al.* (1998) provide a series of reviews and critiques of the EKC studies. Rothman (1998) reviews the critiques, and numerous articles in special editions of *Ecological Economics* (1995), *Environment and Development Economics* (1996) and *Ecological Applications* (1996) discuss the Arrow *et al.* paper.

Stern *et al.* (1996) identified seven major problems with some of the basic EKC estimates and their interpretation: the assumption of unidirectional causality from growth to environmental quality and the reversibility of environmental change; the assumption that changes in trade relationships associated with development have no effect on environmental quality; econometric problems; ambient concentrations v. emissions; asymptotic behaviour; the mean–median income problem; and the interpretation of particular EKCs in isolation from EKCs for other environmental problems. Most of the criticisms of other authors can be fitted into this framework. The remainder of this section reviews these problems, integrating the insights from other critiques and indicating where progress has been made in empirical studies since the writing of Stern *et al.* (1996).

Simultaneity and Irreversibility

The EKC hypothesis derives from a model of the economy in which environmental damage is reversible and there are special assumptions regarding the impact of environmental damage on growth. For example, in the McConnell (1997) and Ansuategi *et al.* (1998) models, consumption pollution affects output negatively, but neither abatement activities nor production itself generate any pollution. In the Lopez (1994) pollution model, pollution does not affect production. In the absence of feedback to production or irreversibilities, uncontrolled economic growth would maximize economic output and environmental quality in the long run. But, given such feedback, and/or irreversibility, attempting to grow fast in the early stages of development when environmental degradation is rising may prove unsustainable. There is clear evidence of this from many developing countries (Barbier, 1994).

Generally, the economy and its environment are jointly determined (Perrings, 1987). Estimating single equation relationships by ordinary least squares where simultaneity exists produces biased and inconsistent estimates. In practice, this criticism is most likely to be of relevance for samples including very poor countries where land degradation and the like are having a current impact on GDP (Barbier, 1994) and for regressions where the dependent variable is a general indicator such as energy use which enables broad economic growth. The simultaneity issue was directly addressed by Cole *et al.* (1997) and Holtz-Eakin and Selden (1995), who used Hausman tests for regressor exogeneity and found no evidence of simultaneity.

Trade and the EKC

Several of the early EKC studies included trade variables. These variables were indicators of openness to trade rather than measures of actual physical trade. Whereas, *ceteris paribus*, openness might be expected to reduce environmental damage in both developing and developed countries (Grossman and Krueger, 1991), trade itself is likely to increase impacts in developing countries and reduce them in the developed countries. This may be one of the determinants of the EKC relationship (see the discussion of Suri and Chapman, 1998). The Hecksher–Ohlin trade theory suggests that, under free trade, developing countries would specialize towards the production of goods that are intensive of the factors that they are endowed with in relative abundance: labour and natural resources. The developed countries would specialize towards human capital and manufactured capital-intensive activities. Part of the reduction in environmental degradation levels in the developed countries and increases in environmental degradation in middle-income countries may reflect this specialization (Lucas *et al.*, 1992; Hettige *et al.*, 1992; Suri and Chapman,1998).

Environmental regulation in developed countries might further encourage polluting activities to gravitate towards the developing countries (Lucas *et al.*, 1992; Ekins *et al.*, 1994).

These effects would exaggerate the apparent decline in pollution intensity with rising income along the EKC. In our finite world, the poor countries of today would be unable to find further countries from which to import resource-intensive products. When the poorer countries apply similar levels of environmental regulation they will face the more difficult task of abating these activities rather than hiving them off to other countries (Arrow *et al.*, 1995; Stern *et al.*, 1996). Suri and Chapman (1998) and Liddle (1996) have now attempted to capture the effects of actual trade flows.

Econometric Problems

As discussed above, there are a number of simultaneity issues that make iden-tification of alternative structures difficult, if not impossible, within a single equation OLS/GLS framework. Also none of the early EKC studies presented diagnostic statistics of the regression residuals. Stern *et al.* (1996) raised the issue of two forms of heteroscedasticity in the context of cross-sectional re-gressions of grouped data. Schmalensee *et al.* (1995) found that regression residuals from OLS were heteroscedastic with smaller residuals associated with countries with higher total GDP and population, as predicted by Stern *et al.* (1996). Ekins (1997) points out that different researchers have found different results for the same pollutant by investigating different data sets, using different functional forms (for example logarithmic v. levels) and different estimation techniques. This seems to indicate that the relationship, if any, is fragile.[7] Stern and Common (in press) find that the EKC for sulphur emissions is very poorly specified and that the results are highly contingent on the subsample of countries examined.

Ambient Concentrations v. Emissions

Data on environmental problems are notoriously patchy in coverage or poor in quality. Those studies that have attempted to estimate the EKC have faced these problems. The available data are not necessarily appropriate data on which to base policy conclusions. Grossman and Krueger and Shafik and Bandyopad-hyay both used ambient pollution data from urban areas. This is appropriate insofar as the effects on human health in urban areas are concerned. However, the estimated EKC relationship can be misleading in projecting the expected change in the acid burden on natural and agricultural ecosystems from nitrogen and sulphur oxide emissions. As is well known, societies tend to go through a process of increasing and then falling urban population densities and concentrations of population as they develop (see Stern, 1992, for references). The concentration of pollution sources is therefore also likely to go through a similar process. Declining ambient concentrations of pollutants do not mean that the overall pollution burden is necessarily declining. Many more studies have now been carried out using emissions data. As predicted, EKC estimates based on emissions show much higher turning points than do ambient concentration EKCs.

Asymptotic Behaviour

Economic activity inevitably implies the use of resources, even if some activities require less resource input per unit of value than other activities. In the long run, the share of low resource input activities in economic output can rise, resulting in a lower resource to GDP ratio. But food and other basic needs which have given minimum necessary resource inputs will always be consumed, so that resource use per capita definitely has a lower bound. Per capita use is the relevant variable, as the EKC is expressed in per capita terms. By the laws of thermodynamics, use of resources inevitably implies the production of waste. Regressions that allow levels of indicators to become zero or negative are inappropriate, except in the case of deforestation, where afforestation can occur.[8] This restriction can be applied by using a logarithmic dependent variable. De Bruyn and Opschoor (1994) present evidence that the 'delinking' of GDP from material use in the 1970s and early 1980s was partially reversed in the late 1980s. Pezzey (1989) proposes that the optimal level of environmental degradation may be monotonically increasing with the level of development. Initially, property rights are not established and environmental degradation increases more rapidly than the optimal rate. As environmental degradation and the level of development increase, property rights are established and the level of environmental degradation declines until it 'catches up' to the optimal path and the increase in environmental degradation recommences. As total impacts cannot eventually tend to zero in the very long run (Common, 1995), rising income, if it could be sustained, would inevitably mean rising degradation. Grossman and Krueger's results and some of Shafik and Bandyopadhyay's results present a similar picture. Because they do not use a logarithmic dependent variable, it is not clear whether these results simply imply that the rate of decline slows at higher income levels, rather than reversing.

Mean v. Median Income

Some studies show that EKC estimates for a number of indicators – SO_2 emissions, NO_x and deforestation – reach their peak at income levels around the current world mean per capita income. So a cursory glance at the available econometric estimates might lead one to believe that, given likely future levels of mean income per capita, environmental degradation should decline. This interpretation is evident in the 1992 World Bank Development Report (IBRD, 1992). However, income is not normally distributed but very skewed, with much larger numbers of people below mean income per capita than above it. Therefore it is median rather than mean income that is the relevant variable. This means that, assuming that the EKC relationship is valid, global environmental degradation is set to rise for a long time to come (Stern *et al.*, 1996; Ekins, 1997; Selden and Song, 1994). On the other hand some other studies (for example, Cropper and Griffiths, 1994; Selden and Song, 1994; Stern and Common (in press)) found much higher turning points for some of these indicators, which reduces the chance of this misinterpretation.

Aggravation of Other Environmental Problems

It is clear that the levels of many pollutants per unit of output in specific processes have declined in the developed countries over time with increasingly stringent environmental regulations and technical innovations. However, the mix of effluent has shifted from sulphur and nitrogen oxides to carbon dioxide and solid waste, so that aggregate waste is still high and per capita waste may not have declined. Economic activity is inevitably environmentally disruptive in some way (see above). Satisfying the material wants and needs of people requires the use and disturbance of energy flows and materials. The enhanced greenhouse effect is one of the most serious threats to global sustainability (Common, 1995), but almost no one suggests that an inverted U-shaped curve applies for the greenhouse gases,[9] or for energy use per capita (Suri and Chapman, 1998). EKCs for global pollutants with long-term costs and perhaps for some resource stocks tend to be monotonically increasing, while those with local impacts tend to have the inverted U shape (Arrow *et al.*, 1995). Therefore, even if economic growth could greatly lower the current rates of per capita emissions of other pollutants and deforestation in developing countries, it would be likely to increase these countries' contribution to global warming. Estimation of EKCs for total energy use are an attempt to capture environmental impact whatever its nature (see, for example, Suri and Chapman, 1998).

Alternative Approaches

Stern *et al.* (1996) argued that 'the examination of the historical experience of individual countries, using econometric and also qualitative historical analysis.' (p. 1159) could be a more fruitful approach to investigate the environment–development relationship. So far there have been four studies of individual countries. Vincent (1997) examines the experience of Malaysia and

Carson *et al.* (1997) the United States, while de Bruyn *et al.* (1998) examine the experience of four OECD countries (see below). Unruh and Moomaw (1998) use a qualitative historical approach to look at events in individual countries around the oil price shocks (see below). Vincent (1997) compared Selden and Song's predictions for a country with the income level of Malaysia, with mixed results. In particular, sulphur emissions fell sharply in the 1980s, rather than rising as predicted. This was due to a sudden shift to power generation using domestic natural gas. Ambient measurements of total suspended particulates and various water pollution indicators are available for about 15 years for most of the states of peninsular Malaysia, whose income levels vary widely but overlap temporally owing to rapid economic growth. All the indicators show rising monotonic or insignificant relations with income and population density. Shafik (1994) and Grossman and Krueger (1991) both found declining concentrations over this income range.

Carson *et al.* (1997) argue that a study of a single country eliminates the problems associated with comparing data from different countries. The richest US states have more than double the income of the poorest. The variation among US counties is even greater. On the other hand, institutional factors and other variables are fairly common across the states. All EKCs for a variety of pollutants for both US states and counties were declining in income. This relationship was significant even when industrial employment mix variables were added to the regression. As mining and mineral processing are very capital-intensive activities, this is not so surprising and perhaps gross product originating on an industry basis should have been used. It turns out that the poorest US states such as Louisiana, West Virginia, New Mexico and Utah are often states with important resource extraction and processing industries, while the richest states such as Connecticut, New Jersey, Massachusetts and New York are states with an orientation towards the service sector and high tech industry. Trade specialization among these states might explain even more of the variation of emissions across states than worldwide trade specialization might explain of variation in emissions among countries.

Pearson (1994) reiterates the points in the Stern *et al.* (1996) critique, but emphasizes the need for empirical work to investigate the determinants of the EKC relationship in terms of structural change, policy variables and so on, even if in a single equation framework. This is the direction in which most of the recent literature seems to be moving. As will be seen below, though the second stage of EKC studies has looked at the role of additional explanatory variables, this has not been a systematic effort to explain the underlying determinants of the EKC relationship, but rather, each study examines separately the role of possible conditioning variables in influencing the EKC relationship. Though these studies are interesting and useful as initial explorations, there is the danger of omitted variables bias.

EMPIRICAL DETERMINANTS OF THE EKC

Many of the most recent EKC studies have focused on examining possible determinants of the EKC relationship or on investigating the impact of various conditioning variables on the EKC relationship. This section is organized according to the variables investigated.

Trade

Rock (1996) estimates EKCs for two indicators of toxic intensity of GDP also used by Lucas *et al.* (1992). The independent variables include the quadratic function in income per capita, the share of manufacturing in GDP and four different indicators of trade orientation. A separate regression was estimated for each of the latter indicators. The inverted U is present and pollution is rising with the share of manufacturing in GDP. A dummy variable for closed v. open economies shows that closed economies had lower toxic intensities of GDP, while the growth rate of exports and the growth rate of the share of exports in GDP are both positively related to the pollution indices. The Dollar (1992) index of trade orientation has an insignificant coefficient.

Liddle (1996) examines changes in the consumption/production ratio of various metals and paper in the OECD countries. In most cases there is no clear trend over time. This result could be evidence against a major role for trade in determining the EKC. In contrast to Liddle, Suri and Chapman (1998) argue for an important role for trade in generating the EKC relationship. They show that the ratio of manufacturing exports to manufacturing imports has increased in many developing countries while it has decreased in many developed countries. They estimate an EKC for energy use per capita for the period 1970–91 for 34 countries, ranging from Bangladesh to the United States in income levels. The EKC is a logarithmic quadratic with the addition of the following variables: M/MFG – imports of all manufactures as a share of domestic manufacturing production; X/MFG – exports of all manufactures as a share of domestic manufacturing production; and MFG/GDP – share of manufacturing in GDP. The estimates indicate an inverted U (turning point more than $50 000) with the expected coefficient signs for the auxiliary variables, but among the auxiliary variables only the coefficient for X/MFG is significant. Exclusion of the quadratic term results in all the coefficients being significant, showing that these variables covary strongly with squared GDP per capita. A number of variant models are also estimated. A model with an interaction term M GDP/MFG investigates whether the effect of imports on lowering energy use is greater as income rises. This seems to be the case, and the M/MFG coefficient falls to zero. A third version with a dummy variable for high-income countries in the interaction term provides a better fit. This is the best evidence so far that trade effects are one of the causes of the flattening or downward slope of the EKC, but this result was not found for a different sample of countries with carbon dioxide as the dependent variable (Cooke, 1997).

Rothman (1998) argues that one way to avoid the trade issue is to look at the environmental impacts generated by consumption rather than by the production activities in a country. To this end he estimates EKCs for expenditure on different categories of consumption goods. Only expenditure on food, beverages and tobacco shows an inverted U within the sample range of income. The other categories of expenditure are monotonically increasing, including a number of resource-intensive categories such as rent, fuel and power. The data are calculated on the basis of international PPP prices but there is no guarantee that the prices of individual commodities within groups reflect their environmental impact or that the impacts from goods consumed in the developed countries are equal to those in the developing countries.

R & D

Komen *et al.* (1997) estimate an EKC for public R&D expenditures on environmental protection in a group of OECD countries. The main result of the paper is that the elasticity of these expenditures with respect to income is approximately unity. The authors recognize that public expenditures are only a small part of total environmental R&D expenditures. Also R&D is only a small part of total expenditure on environmental protection and may or may not actually result in improved environmental quality. Nonetheless, this is one of the links in an investigation of the empirical determinants of the EKC.

Political Freedom

Torras and Boyce (1998) look at various indicators of democracy which presumably mediate between private preferences and public policy, as well as influencing the formation of preferences. They estimate cubic EKCs using the GEMS data analysed by Grossman and Krueger (1994) and data on access to safe water and access to sanitation at the national level from the Human Development Report. In addition to the GDP terms, the following explanatory variables are included in the regression: the Gini coefficient of income distribution, literacy, an index of civil liberties and control variables similar to those used by Grossman and Krueger. On the whole, coefficients for the three 'democracy' indicators have the expected negative sign and are significant, especially for the developing countries. Literacy and rights have a more consistent effect than the Gini index, possibly reflecting difficulties in measuring and comparing this index across countries. For the three atmospheric pollutants from the GEMS data the significance of the income terms declines when the democracy variables are added, showing that they explain variation previously modelled by the EKC relationship. The pattern is mixed for the other dependent variables.

Density of Economic Activity

Kaufmann *et al.* (1998) and Shukla and Parikh (1992) examine the influence of the spatial intensity of economic activity (GDP/area) and city size, respectively, on ambient concentrations. Kaufmann *et al.* use ambient SO_2 concentrations for a panel of mostly developed and middle-income countries (but including China) between 1974 and 1989. The estimated equation is:

$$C_{jt} = \alpha + \beta_1(Y/P)_{jt} + \beta_2(Y/P)_{jt}^2 + \beta_3(Y/A)_{jt} + \beta_4(Y/A)_{jt}^2$$
$$+ \beta_5(S/GDP)_{jt} + \beta_6 t + \varepsilon_{jt} \qquad (8.1)$$

where Y/P is GDP per capita, Y/A is GDP per area and S/GDP is steel exports as a percentage of GDP which is intended to capture the effects of trade. The authors argue that this approach is superior to including population density as a RHS variable because the impact of population density would be expected to vary with the level of income per capita. Increases in density would have less impact when overall emissions were low than when they were high. This could be easily addressed by putting all variables in logarithms or using the multiplicative approaches of Panayotou (1993) or Vincent (1997). The model is estimated for both national average levels of Y/A and city-specific levels of Y/A. The authors find that concentrations are a U-shape function of income per capita and an inverted U function of income per area. The former result is obviously diametrically opposed to the standard EKC results for sulphur dioxide concentrations. However, in (8.1) the derivative of emissions with respect to Y/P is dependent on Y/A as the area of individual countries is fixed and therefore national Y/A cannot be held constant as Y/P increases:

$$\frac{\partial C_j}{\partial (Y/P)_j} = \beta_1 + 2\beta_2(Y/P)_j + \beta_3(P/A) + 2\beta_4(Y/P)_j(P/A)_j^2 \qquad (8.2)$$

The signs of the estimated parameters in (8.2) are $\beta_1 < 0$, $\beta_2 > 0$, $\beta_3 > 0$, $\beta_4 < 0$. This implies a reverse shape N cross-section as Y/P is increased, so that at high income levels emissions are declining.

Shukla and Parikh (1992) were primarily interested in the relationship between city size and ambient pollution levels for SO_2, particulates and smoke. Using cross-sectional data from WRI (1989) they found that pollution rose with city size. However, when they added GDP per capita and its square to the regression, an inverted U was found with respect to city size. The EKC relationship holding city size constant was, however, U-shaped, though few coefficients are significant at conventional levels except for those in the particulates regression. This finding is similar to the results of Kaufmann *et al.*

Economic Structure

Westbrook (1995), Suri and Chapman (1998), Rock (1996) and Cooke (1997) all examined aspects of the output structure. This is one of the proximate determinants listed above and noted in several papers (for example, Panayotou, 1993; Shafik and Bandyopadhyay, 1992). Westbrook and Cooke both estimated models for carbon dioxide emissions and used a systematic breakdown of GDP into three or four major sectors. Suri and Chapman and Rock looked at the influence of the share in GDP of manufacturing on energy consumption and pollution intensity, respectively.

Westbrook (1995) used a panel of 56 developing countries between 1971 and 1991. Of most interest is a regression of log emissions per capita on GNP per capita and its square and the shares of GNP in agriculture and services. All the coefficients in the regression are significantly different from zero. The income relationship is an inverted U and, as would be expected, the signs of the industrial structure coefficients are negative, reflecting the lower emissions of agriculture and services relative to the industrial sector. The implication is that, though industrial structure is a significant explanatory factor, other factors also contribute towards the inverted U relationship. Cooke's (1997) results (including both developed and developing countries) are very similar. Suri and Chapman (1998) and Rock (1996) also find a positive coefficient for manufacturing.

Historical Events and Structural Change

A couple of studies have begun to examine the role of price shocks and other events in individual countries. De Bruyn *et al.* (1998) estimate the following regression individually for West Germany, the Netherlands, the United Kingdom and the United States for groups of 17 to 29 observations over the period 1960–93:

$$\Delta \ln E_{jt} = \beta_{0j} \Delta \ln Y_{jt} + \beta_{1j} + \beta_{2j} \ln Y_{jt-1} + \beta_{3j} \Delta \ln P_{jt} + \varepsilon_{jt} \qquad (8.3)$$

for CO_2, NO_x and SO_2. E is emissions, Y is income and P is an energy price index. The authors interpret β_{0j} in terms of the scale effect. If $\beta_{1j} < 0$ and $\beta_{2j} = 0$ then they would attribute declining emissions to exogenous technical change.

If, however, $\beta_{2j} < 0$ then they would attribute the change to structural change and increased R&D efforts as income levels rise. β_{3j} would be expected to be negative and less than unity in absolute value. The results show that β_{0j} is positive and except in one case it is significantly different from zero. β_{1j} is mostly zero or negative. β_{2j} is zero or negative and more significantly so for NO_x, and for all three pollutants in Germany. β_{3j} is insignificant except for carbon dioxide in the United States. Therefore they conclude that structural change related to the income level is of importance. They argue that the decline in pollution seen in developed countries since the early 1970s is due to the slow rate of economic growth during this period. The continuing effects of the level of income in reducing pollution have not been overcome by the effects of growth in raising it. The authors also calculate the economic growth rates that are compatible with zero emissions growth. For CO_2 these are 1.8 per cent in the United Kingdom and the Netherlands, 2.9 per cent in Germany and 0.3 per cent in the United States where the price effect has had most influence in reducing emissions. Zero emissions growth rates are much higher for the other two pollutants, but lowest for the United Kingdom, which has the least effective legislation.

This model can also be interpreted as a type of error correction model (see Cuthbertson *et al.*, 1992), though there is no tendency to return to an equilibrium between income and emissions if emissions are perturbed by exogenous shocks. The price and growth effects have the effect of permanently shifting the emissions–income relationship. When $Y_{jt-1} = \exp(-\beta_{1j}/\beta_{2j})$ and growth and price inflation are zero, there is no tendency for emissions to change. Below this income level emissions tend to increase irrespective of the growth rate and above this level they tend to decline. The interpretation of β_{1j} and β_{2j} as technical and structural change parameters is therefore dubious.

Unruh and Moomaw (1998) also look at the effect of prices, but they use plots of the time paths of CO_2 emissions per capita in various countries rather than econometrics. They find that the transition to lower per capita emissions levels can happen at varying income levels and tends to happen fairly abruptly. In particular, the major changes in countries as different as Spain and the United States happened shortly after the oil price shocks of the 1970s.

PROGRESS ON THE EKC?

There are several promising signs in recent EKC papers. In particular, there is a concentration on investigating empirical determinants of the EKC. Also a few studies have looked at historical events (Unruh and Moomaw, 1998) or estimated EKCs for individual countries (Vincent, 1997; de Bruyn *et al.*, 1998). Econometric practice does seem to have improved (see below). In particular,

Table 8.1 Econometric techniques

Authors	Date	Data type	Estimation technique	Dependent variable	Exchange rate	Cubic term	Regression diagnostics
Antle and Heidebrink	1995	C-S	OLS	Levels	Market	No	No
Cole *et al.*	1997	Panel, C-S	FE/GLS, OLS	Logs and levels	PPP	No	*
Cropper and Griffiths	1994	Panel	FE	Logs	PPP	No	No
Dijkgraaf and Vollebergh	1998	Panel	FE, RE	Logs	PPP	No	Yes
Grossman and Krueger	1991	Panel	RE	Levels	PPP	Yes	No
Holtz-Eakin and Selden	1995	Panel	FE	Logs and levels	PPP	No	*
Horvath	1997	Longitudinal	FE	Levels	PPP	Yes	No
Kaufmann *et al.*	1998	Panel	OLS, FE, RE	Levels	PPP	No	Yes
Komen *et al.*	1997	Panel	OLS, FE, RE, AR	Levels	PPP	No	Yes
Liddle	1996	Panel	FE	Logs and levels	PPP	No	Durbin–Watson
Panayotou	1993	C-S	OLS	Logs	Market	No	No
Rock	1996	C-S	OLS	Levels	Market	No	No
Rothman	1998	C-S	OLS	Levels	PPP	No	No
Schmalensee *et al.*	1995	Panel	FE, Spline Regression	Logs	PPP	n.a.	Yes
Selden and Song	1994	Panel	OLS, FE, RE	Levels	PPP	No	Yes
Shafik	1994	Panel, C-S	FE	Levels	PPP	Yes	No
Shukla and Parikh	1992	C-S	OLS	Levels	Market	No	No
Suri and Chapman	1998	Panel	FE, AR	Logs	PPP	No	No
Torras and Boyce	1998	Panel	OLS	Levels	PPP	Yes	No
Westbrook	1995	Panel	FE, RE	Logs	Market	No	No

Notes:
C-S: cross-section; OLS: ordinary least squares; GLS: generalized least squares; FE: fixed effects; RE: random effects; AR: autocorrelation correction applied; PPP: purchasing power parity.
* results available from authors.

the paper by Cole *et al.* (1997) claims to address the statistical issues raised by Stern *et al.* (1996) such as investigating the simultaneity issue in a statistical sense. However, the deeper issues of irreversibility raised by Arrow *et al.* (1995) have not been adequately addressed. EKCs for energy use have been estimated which address the issue of the shifting nature of environmental impact. The different natures of EKCs and impact projections seem to be better understood than was shown by the World Bank Development Report in 1992 (for example Rothman, 1998). Differences between EKCs for ambient concentrations and emissions have also been extensively discussed.

Econometric technique is one aspect of the many studies that can be summarized quantitatively. Table 8.1 summarizes the key points concerning the econometric techniques used by the 20 studies discussed in this chapter that employ econometrics of multi-country databases. Studies involving single country regressions (de Bruyn *et al.*, 1998; Carson *et al.*, 1997; Vincent, 1997) and Stern and Common (forthcoming) are omitted. None of the remaining studies uses all of the more sophisticated methods (Stern *et al.*, 1996). Table 8.2 summarizes these data in terms of the proportion of studies using the more sophisticated techniques. In the entire sample, use of panel data and PPP exchange rates is the most widely adopted technique, while testing of cubic terms is the least adopted. Only three techniques increased in uptake from the pre-1996 sample to the 1996 and post-1996 sample. The use of logarithmic dependent variables and cubic terms declined between the two time periods.

CONCLUSIONS

There has been progress on understanding the EKC in the last few years and some progress in methods of investigation. Evidence continues to accumulate that the inverted U-shape relation only applies to a subset of impacts and that overall impact, perhaps approximately indicated by per capita energy use (Suri and Chapman, 1998), rises throughout the relevant income range. The current crop of studies shows surprisingly little interest in looking at whether impacts begin to rise again at high income levels for those indicators where a mid-income turning point has been identified.

Knowledge has advanced furthest in terms of understanding the determinants of the EKC. It is clear that structural change and technological progress are of importance. Torras and Boyce (1998) show the importance of 'democracy' – a variable that is also a correlate of development – in lowering emissions. There is, however, increasing evidence that the EKC is partly determined by trade relations. If this is so, the poorest countries of today will find it more difficult than today's developed countries to reduce environmental impact as income rises. Some studies present more disaggregated evidence that is of interest in evaluating the performance of individual countries and the influence of particular events. Change may occur quite rapidly in crisis periods such as the oil price shocks of the 1970s or the CFC negotiations of the 1980s. Some of the empirical relationships that have been uncovered may not be robust, though this is not yet known – the issue of omitted variables bias has not been adequately raised.

Table 8.2 Summary of econometric techniques

Time period	Panel or longitudinal data (%)	FE, RE, GLS (%)	Logarithmic dependent variable (%)	PPP exchange rate (%)	Cubic term (%)	Regression diagnostics (%)
All studies	75	70	45	75	25	40
Pre-1997	70	70	50	60	30	30
1997 and post 1997	80	70	40	90	20	50

Note: For each variable the figure is the percentage using the technique in question of all the relevant papers.

Despite such progress we know little about other issues. For example, no empirical study has been carried out which decomposes the EKC into the four proximate variables noted above, though the de Bruyn *et al.* (1998) study represents a move in this direction. Neither has there been any explicit empirical testing of the theoretical models surveyed in the second section of the chapter.

ACKNOWLEDGMENTS

I thank the authors of the Boston ISEE Conference papers and Dale Rothman for making copies of those papers available to me. Charles Perrings provided me with preprints of the papers in the special issue of *Environment and Development Economics* on the EKC. Charles Perrings, Mick Common and Dale Rothman and an anonymous referee made very useful comments on draft versions of this chapter.

NOTES

1. The EKC papers presented at the conference and reviewed in this chapter are de Bruyn *et al.* (1998), Horvath (1997), Kaufmann *et al.* (1998), Liddle (1996), Rothman (1998), Suri and Chapman (1998), Unruh and Moomaw (1998).
2. This specific result depends on a Constant Elasticity of Substitution revenue function. For other aggregators, the path could depend on further parameters.
3. A similar model is developed by Ansuategi *et al.* (1998).
4. The paper was later published as Grossman and Krueger (1994). See also Grossman and Krueger (1995).
5. See also Shafik (1994).

6. Shafik and Bandyopadhyay (1992) also carried out a number of additional regressions adding various policy variables such as trade orientation, electricity prices and so on. The results for these are rather ambiguous and difficult to interpret and are not reported in Shafik (1994).
7. See Levine and Renelt (1992) for a possible approach to investigating this problem.
8. For some pollutants one could imagine future technologies where emissions are essentially zero, for example, for sulphur dioxide. A 100 per cent efficient pollutant recovery process is either physically infeasible or just uneconomic given the energy and material expenditures involved. So eliminating sulphur dioxide emissions means that no metals would be processed from sulphate ores using technologies that generate sulphur gases, and no coal, oil and so on would be burnt. Such a state of technology is way off in the future, so the average impact will not be zero any time soon. The marginal impact can well be negative at least for a range of incomes until abatement costs start rising sharply. From then on total impact will again start to rise. Also all services require large expenditures of energy and materials, so that a shift to consumption of services will only partially aid in averting an upturn in environmental impacts. A referee suggested that carbon emissions can be negative if carbon sequestration activities such as afforestation take place. The carbon emissions data used in EKC studies have not taken sequestration into account.
9. Schmalensee *et al.* (1995) present results showing a within-sample turning point for the carbon dioxide EKC, as do Dijkgraaf and Vollebergh (1998). In both cases the estimates use developed country data only or allow parameters for developed countries to differ from those for developing countries. These papers are discussed in the third section of this chapter.

REFERENCES

Ansuategi, A., E.B. Barbier and C.A. Perrings (1998), 'The environmental Kuznets curve', in J.C.J.M. van den Bergh and M.W. Hofkes (eds), *Theory and Implementation of Economic Models for Sustainable Development*, Dordrecht: Kluwer.

Antle, J.M. and G. Heidebrink (1995), 'Environment and development: theory and international evidence', *Economic Development and Cultural Change*, 43, 603–25.

Arrow, K., B. Bolin, R. Costanza, P. Dasgupta, C. Folke, C.S. Holling, B-O. Jansson, S. Levin, K-G. Mäler, C. Perrings and D. Pimentel (1995), 'Economic growth, carrying capacity and the environment', *Science*, 268, 520–21.

Barbier, E.B. (1994), 'Natural capital and the economics of environment and development', in A. Jansson, M. Hammer, C. Folke and R. Costanza (eds), *Investing in Natural Capital: The Ecological Economics Approach to Sustainability*, New York: Columbia University Press.

Beckerman, W. (1992), 'Economic growth and the environment: whose growth? whose environment?', *World Development*, 20, 481–96.

Carson, R.T., Y. Jeon and D.R. McCubbin (1997), 'The relationship between air pollution emissions and income: U.S. data', *Environment and Development Economics*, 2(4).

Cole, M.A., A.J. Rayner and J.M. Bates (1997), 'The environmental Kuznets curve: an empirical analysis', *Environment and Development Economics*, 2, 401–16.

Common, M.S. (1995), *Sustainability and Policy: Limits to Economics*, Cambridge: Cambridge University Press.

Cooke, K. (1997), 'An Empirical Investigation of the Relationship between Economic Development and Carbon Dioxide Emissions', Masters Research Essay, National Centre for Development Studies, Australian National University, Canberra.

Cropper, M. and C. Griffiths (1994), 'The interaction of population growth and environmental quality', *American Economic Review*, 84, 250–54.

Cuthbertson, K., S.G. Hall and M.P. Taylor (1992), *Applied Econometric Techniques*, Ann Arbor: University of Michigan Press.

de Bruyn, S.M. and J.B. Opschoor (1994), 'Is the Economy Ecologizing?', Discussion Paper TI 94-65, Tinbergen Institute, Free University, Amsterdam.

de Bruyn, S.M., J.C.J.M. van den Bergh and J.B. Opschoor (1998), 'Economic growth and emissions: reconsidering the empirical basis of environmental Kuznets curves', *Ecological Economics*, 25, 161–76.

Dijkgraaf, E. and H.R.J. Vollebergh (1998), 'Growth and/or (?) Environment: Is There a Kuznets Curve for Carbon Emissions?', paper presented at the 2nd biennial meeting of the European Society for Ecological Economics, 4–7 March, Geneva.

Dollar, J. (1992), 'Outward oriented countries really do grow more rapidly: evidence from 95 LDCs: 1976–85', *Economic Development and Cultural Change*, 40, 523–44.

Ekins, P. (1997), 'The Kuznets curve for the environment and economic growth: examining the evidence', *Environment and Planning, A.*, 29, 805–30.

Ekins, P., C. Folke and R. Costanza (1994), 'Trade, environment and development: The issues in perspective', *Ecological Economics*, 9, 1–12.

Forster, B.A. (1973), 'Optimal capital accumulation in a polluted environment', *Southern Economic Journal*, 39, 544–7.

Grossman, G.M. and A.B. Krueger (1991), 'Environmental Impacts of a North American Free Trade Agreement', National Bureau of Economic Research Working Paper 3914, Cambridge, Mass.: NBER.

Grossman, G.M. and A.B. Krueger (1994), 'Environmental impacts of a North American Free Trade Agreement', in P. Garber (ed.), The US–Mexico Free Trade Agreement, Cambridge, Mass.: MIT Press.

Grossman, G.M. and A.B. Krueger (1995), 'Economic growth and the environment', *Quarterly Journal of Economics*, 112, 353–78.

Hettige, H., R.E.B. Lucas and D. Wheeler (1992), 'The toxic intensity of industrial production: global patterns, trends and trade policy', *American Economic Review*, 82(2), 478–81.

Holtz-Eakin, D. and T.M. Selden (1995), 'Stoking the fires? CO_2 emissions and economic growth', *Journal of Public Economics*, 57, 85–101.

Horvath, R.J. (1997), 'Energy Consumption and the Environmental Kuznets Curve Debate', Department of Geography, University of Sydney.

IBRD (1992), *World Development Report 1992: Development and the Environment*, New York: Oxford University Press.

John, A. and R. Pecchenino (1994), 'An overlapping generations model of growth and the environment', *Economic Journal*, 104, 1393–1410.

John A., R. Pecchenino, D. Schimmelpfennig and S. Schreft (1995), 'Short-lived agents and the long-lived environment', *Journal of Public Economics*, 58, 127–41.

Kaufmann, R.K., B. Davidsdottir, S. Garnham and P. Pauly (1998), 'The determinants of atmospheric SO_2 concentrations: reconsidering the environmental Kuznets curve', *Ecological Economics*, 25, 209–20.

Komen, M.H.C., S. Gerking and H. Folmer (1997), 'Income and environmental R&D: empirical evidence from OECD countries', *Environment and Development Economics*, 2, 505.

Kuznets, S. (1955), 'Economic growth and income inequality', *American Economic Review*, 49, 1–28.

Kuznets, S. (1963), 'Quantitative aspects of the economic growth of nations, VIII: the distribution of income by size', *Economic Development and Cultural Change*, 11, 1–92.

Levine, R. and D. Renelt (1992), 'A sensitivity analysis of cross-country growth regressions', *American Economic Review*, 82, 942–63.

Liddle, B.T. (1996), 'Environmental Kuznets Curves and Regional Pollution', paper presented at the 4th biennial conference of the International Society for Ecological Economics, Boston University.

Lopez, R. (1994), 'The environment as a factor of production: the effects of economic growth and trade liberalization', *Journal of Environmental Economics and Management*, 27, 163–84.

Lucas, R.E.B., D. Wheeler and H. Hettige (1992), 'Economic development, environmental regulation and the international migration of toxic industrial pollution: 1960–1988', in P. Low (ed.), *International Trade and the Environment*, World Bank Discussion Paper No. 159, Washington, DC.

McConnell, K.E. (1997), 'Income and the demand for environmental quality', *Environment and Development Economics*, 2, 383–99.

Meadows, D.H., D.L. Meadows and J. Randers (1992), *Beyond the Limits: Global Collapse or a Sustainable Future*, London: Earthscan.

Meadows, D.H., D.L. Meadows, J. Randers and W. Behrens (1972), *The Limits to Growth*, New York: Universe Books.

Panayotou, T. (1993), 'Empirical Tests and Policy Analysis of Environmental Degradation at Different Stages of Economic Development', Working Paper WP238, Technology and Employment Programme, International Labour Office, Geneva.

Panayotou, T. (1995), 'Environmental degradation at different stages of economic development', in I. Ahmed and J.A. Doeleman (eds), *Beyond Rio: The Environmental Crisis and Sustainable Livelihoods in the Third World*, London: Macmillan.

Pearson, P.J.G. (1994), 'Energy, externalities and environmental quality: will development cure the ills it creates?', *Energy Studies Review*, 6, 199–216.

Perrings, C.A. (1987), *Economy and Environment: A Theoretical Essay on the Interdependence of Economic and Environmental Systems*, Cambridge: Cambridge University Press.

Pezzey, J.C.V. (1989), 'Economic Analysis of Sustainable Growth and Sustainable Development', Environment Department Working Paper No. 15, World Bank, Washington, DC.

Pollak, R.A. and T.J. Wales (1992), *Demand System Specification and Estimation*, New York: Oxford University Press.

Rock, M.T. (1996), 'Pollution intensity of GDP and trade policy: can the World Bank be wrong?', *World Development*, 24, 471–9.

Rothman, D. (1996), 'Basic economic indicators', in L. Roberts *et al.* (eds), *World Resources: A Guide to the Global Environment*, New York: Oxford University Press.

Rothman, D.S. (1998), 'Environmental Kuznets curves – real progress or passing the buck? A case for consumption-based approaches', *Ecological Economics*, 25, 177–94.

Schmalensee, R., T.M. Stoker and R.A. Judson (1995), 'World Energy Consumption and Carbon Dioxide Emissions: 1950–2050', Sloan School of Management, Massachusetts Institute of Technology, Cambridge, Mass.

Selden, T.M. and D. Song (1994), 'Environmental quality and development: Is there a Kuznets curve for air pollution?', *Journal of Environmental Economics and Environmental Management*, 27, 147–62.

Selden, T.M. and D. Song (1995), 'Neoclassical growth, the J curve for abatement and the inverted U curve for pollution', *Journal of Environmental Economics and Environmental Management*, 29, 162–8.

Shafik, N. (1994), 'Economic development and environmental quality: an econometric analysis', *Oxford Economic Papers*, 46, 757–73.

Shafik N. and S. Bandyopadhyay (1992), 'Economic Growth and Environmental Quality: Time Series and Cross-Country Evidence', Background Paper for the World Development Report 1992, The World Bank, Washington, DC.

Shukla, V. and K. Parikh (1992), 'The environmental consequences of urban growth: cross-national perspectives on economic development, air pollution and city size', *Urban Geography*, 12, 422–49.

Stern, D.I. (1992), 'Population distribution in an ethno-ideologically divided city: The case of Jerusalem', *Urban Geography*, 13, 164–86.

Stern, D.I., M.S. Common and E.B. Barbier (1996), 'Economic growth and environmental degradation: the environmental Kuznets curve and sustainable development', *World Development*, 24, 1151–60.

Stern, D. I. and M. S. Common (in press), Is There an Environmental Kuznets Curve for Sulfur?, *Journal of Environmental Economics and Management*.

Suri, V. and D. Chapman (1998), 'Economic growth, trade and the energy: implications for the environmental Kuznets curve', *Ecological Economics*, 25, 195–208.

Torras, M. and J.K. Boyce (1998), 'Income, inequality and pollution: A reassessment of the environmental Kuznets curve', *Ecological Economics*, 25, 147–60.

Unruh, G.C. and W.R. Moomaw (1998), 'An alternative analysis of apparent EKC-type transitions', *Ecological Economics*, 25, 221–9.

Vincent, J.R. (1997), 'Testing for environmental Kuznets curves within a developing country', *Environment and Development Economics*, 2, 417–31.

WCED (1987), *Our Common Future*, Oxford: Oxford University Press.

Westbrook, T. (1995), 'An Empirical Examination of the Relation Between Carbon Dioxide Emissions and Economic Development, and Carbon Dioxide Emissions and Economic Structure', MSc Dissertation, Department of Environmental Economics and Environmental Management, University of York.

WRI (1989), *World Resources 1988–89*, Washington, DC: World Resources Institute.

WRI (1991), *World Resources 1990–91*, Washington, DC: World Resources Institute.

9. Alternatives to gross domestic product: a critical survey

Richard W. England

INTRODUCTION

Efforts to measure a nation's aggregate income date back to the seventeenth century, when Sir William Petty devised one of the first national income estimates. After Petty's time, the national income concept evolved slowly as economists developed their understanding of the way economic systems operate and as the key economic issues faced by society changed. It is widely recognized, however, that the economic crisis of the Great Depression, the political and military conflict of the Second World War and the emergence of Keynesian macroeconomic theory prompted the creation of modern national income accounting (Carson, 1975; Ruggles, 1993). As Robert Eisner (1989) correctly observed, 'The national income and product accounts ... have been among the major contributions to economic knowledge over the past half century.'

Since 1945, national income statistics have found a variety of practical uses. For instance, they help to inform the design of government fiscal and monetary policies, influence corporate investment plans and are commonly used to assess economic development strategies in less developed nations. From their inception, however, the national income and product accounts have also been used to make international comparisons of wellbeing and to track changes in a country's level of welfare. Simon Kuznets, one of the architects of national accounts, certainly intended this use: 'National income may be defined as the net value of all economic goods produced by the nation ... Any claim to significance such a total would have would lie in its presumptive usefulness as an appraisal of the contribution of economic activity to the welfare of the country's inhabitants, present and future' (1941, pp. 3–4).

During the past quarter-century, national income, gross domestic product and allied accounting concepts have been sharply criticized by a wide array of commentators. Many of those critics have questioned whether national income data adequately measure the level of or changes in economic wellbeing. A typical defence of gross domestic product and its conceptual siblings has been

218

to simply deny that they serve as measures of economic welfare. Juster (1973, p. 26), for example, declared, 'economists generally have no desire to turn the accounts into some sort of happiness index ... [There] may well be more important considerations than mere material goods and services, but they are not within the purview of the economist or the social accountant.'

This defence is too facile, however. Leading economic historians and macro-economists readily cite data on real per capita gross domestic product (GDP) *as though* they can provide insights into standards of living and economic progress. In their influential text on economic growth, for example, Barro and Sala-i-Martin (1995, pp. 1, 4) observe that real per capita GDP in the United States grew by a factor of 8.1 from 1870 to 1990. They then conclude, 'Even small differences in [annual GDP] growth rates, when cumulated over a generation or more, have much greater consequences for standards of living than ... short-term business fluctuations.'[1]

Because of welfare-tinged interpretations of GDP data by many economists and politicians, the critics of GDP deserve a serious hearing, especially by those who seek to understand the sources of human wellbeing. Consequently, this chapter critically surveys a number of quantitative measures which have been proposed as complements to or substitutes for GDP. These alternatives typically raise some combination of the following issues:

- the need to specify properly the distinction between intermediate and gross final output,
- the need to account for asset depreciation in a comprehensive manner,
- the need to divide net final output between consumption and capital accumulation on a reasonable basis, and
- the need to take account of the welfare implications of various forms of social inequality.[2]

INTERMEDIATE VERSUS FINAL GOODS

From the earliest days of modern national income accounting, deciding what products of human activity belong in GNP has been a contentious issue. Kuznets (1941, pp. 6–8) argued for inclusion of goods which are scarce and alienable sources of satisfaction to their users and which are legally exchanged in the market-place.[3] He acknowledged that this accounting criterion was an arbitrary one and that many sources of human satisfaction would remain undetected and unmeasured by national income accountants if his criterion were officially adopted.[4]

At the same time, Kuznets (ibid., pp. 36–40) also noted that not all commodities currently produced, exchanged and consumed are a source of final satisfaction to their users. Rather, they are intermediate inputs required to produce other useful goods. Thus one of the authors of national income accounting reluctantly conceded that work clothing and commuting expenses should probably be treated as intermediate expenses of production and not as final consumption yielding subjective utility to employees.

In his later assessment of national income accounting, Juster (1973, pp. 72–4) took this argument a step further: 'At present we classify everything purchased by households as final consumption ... and most of the things purchased by business enterprise as intermediate products ... [However,] most of what we now call final product is really intermediate in the more fundamental sense.' What exactly is the fundamental distinction between intermediate and final output? Juster argued that all products used to maintain the flow of services from existing assets be excluded from final output, and that products be included in final output only to the degree that they increase the flow of services from tangible and intangible assets via net investment. Application of this criterion would sharply reduce empirical measures of a nation's net final output, a consequence that Kuznets had anticipated and opposed.[5] However, Juster (ibid., p. 76) was correct when he concluded, 'we can provide a better set of distinctions between intermediate and final product than the ones now embedded in ... our existing accounts ... Converting some but not all of our present final outputs to intermediate outputs should represent an improvement in what we now measure as net output'.

More recently, Christian Leipert has adjusted GNP data in order to account more reasonably for intermediate costs of production. He proposes that we measure 'defensive expenditures ... made to eliminate, mitigate, neutralize, or anticipate and avoid damages and deterioration that industrial society's process of growth has caused to living, working, and environmental conditions' (Leipert 1989, p. 28). These defensive outlays presumably do not belong in a measure of aggregate final output.

Leipert identifies six spheres in which major defensive costs occur: the environment, transport, housing, personal security, health and the workplace. Outlays for car repairs and medical treatment resulting from road accidents, for example, should not be treated as final consumption but rather should be seen as unfortunate intermediate costs associated with provision of transport services. Even outlays on extending metropolitan highway networks do not 'increase the quality of life, but rather ... can be regarded as a cost factor stemming from a specific type of development in the transport system and regional structure' (ibid., pp. 35–6).

Although one might quibble with the details of his estimates, Leipert has certainly shown that intermediate expenses for defensive purposes comprise a substantial portion of GNP as currently measured. In his estimates for the former West Germany, he found that defensive expenditures exceeded 10 per cent of

GNP, 'only the tip of the iceberg' in Leipert's view. (See Table 9.1.) It would seem, then, that GDP figures typically overestimate the aggregate value of final output currently available to satisfy either current wants (via consumption) or future wants (via asset accumulation).[6]

Table 9.1 Defensive expenditures as percentage of GNP, Federal Republic of Germany, 1985

Environmental protection services of industry and government	1.33
Environmental damages	0.80
Costs of road accidents	1.1
Costs of extended travel routes	2.2
Higher housing costs due to urban agglomeration	0.75
Costs of personal security	1.26
Defensive health care costs	2.6

Source: Leipert (1989, p. 41).

ACCOUNTING FOR ASSET DEPRECIATION

Excluding intermediate costs of production from GDP in a more thorough fashion would certainly result in a more accurate measure of a nation's gross final output. However, even this improved version of GDP would fail as a measure of economic welfare since it would include newly produced durable assets (new vehicles and computers, for example) which will serve only to replace worn out or obsolete assets of an earlier vintage. In other words, final output *net* of asset depreciation is a better measure of society's capacity to service the present and future needs of its members.[7]

A severe defect of national income accounting, as commonly practised by various central governments, is that asset depreciation is not fully accounted for. Consider two cases. Depreciation of tangible durable assets owned by private business enterprises is typically estimated and then used to calculate net output; depreciation of the human capacity to work productively resulting from domestic violence, highway accidents and prolonged unemployment is not. Because of this asymmetry, various adjustments to national income accounts have been proposed so that asset depreciation would be measured more comprehensively, thereby allowing a more realistic estimate of the net output available for current consumption and asset accumulation.

Robert Repetto and his associates at the World Resources Institute (WRI) have proposed a depreciation adjustment to take account of various forms of natural resource depletion. As they have noted,

> there is a dangerous asymmetry today in the way we measure ... the value of natural resources. Man-made assets ... are valued as productive capital, and are written off against the value of production as they depreciate ... Natural resource assets are not so valued, and their loss entails no debit charge against current income that would account for the decrease in potential future production. (Repetto *et al.*, 1989, p. 2)

Particularly in developing nations dependent on natural resource production and exports, this exclusion of resource depletion from their national income accounts results in exaggerated official numbers for both net output and capital formation.

In a widely cited case study of Indonesia, the WRI found that accounting for soil erosion, deforestation and petroleum extraction lowered estimates of Indonesian domestic output quite significantly from its official level. In 1984, for example, the Indonesian government reported the nation's GDP to be 13.5 trillion rupiah (deflated to 1973). After taking into account the market value of net changes in the physical stocks of forest, soil and petroleum resources, the WRI researchers estimated that the official data ignored 2.3 trillion rupiah of natural resource depletion, a sum equal to 17.3 per cent of GDP. During the period from 1971 to 1984, the annual WRI adjustment for these three forms of resource depletion averaged 9 per cent of GDP (ibid., p. 6).

The methodology employed by WRI to derive these estimates has been criticized, however. Salah El Serafy (1993, p. 14) questions the use of annual changes in the market value of proven reserves of natural resources as an adjustment to GDP: 'Since the resource stocks are normally much larger than annual extraction, re-estimation of their [physical] size, as well as incorporation of changes in their value ... following price fluctuations, can dwarf the adjustment specifically due to extraction.' As El Serafy points out, discovery of new physical reserves in excess of the current extraction rate would even suggest a positive adjustment to GDP.[8] From the perspective of long-run sustainability, discovery of large reserves of an exhaustible resource is not impressive if previously discovered reserves are currently being consumed at a rapid pace.

El Serafy (1993, 1996) has proposed that the user cost of natural resource depletion be used to adjust GDP. User cost is that portion of the receipts from selling a non-renewable resource, net of extraction costs, which must be reinvested in other assets in order to maintain a flow of future income after the resource stock has been completely depleted. El Serafy demonstrates that user cost as a fraction of net receipts equals $1/(1+r)^{n+1}$, where r is the interest rate for investment purposes and *n* the remaining life of the resource stock at the current extraction rate. (See Table 9.2 for an application of the user cost approach to the WRI data on Indonesia.)

This user cost methodology suggests that nations which rely heavily on natural resource exploitation to boost their GDP growth rates suffer from a variety of illusions. Net product and net capital formation are overestimated. Fiscal deficits of central governments which own natural resource enterprises are underestimated. Current account deficits in a nation's balance of payments may be masked by unsustainable sales of natural assets.

Table 9.2   Adjustments by El Serafy for natural resource depletion, Indonesia, 1971–84 (percentage of official GDP)

	Deforestation	Soil erosion	Petroleum user cost	Total
1975 (minimum)	–3.3	–1.1	–5.6	–10.1
1979 (maximum)	–9.3	–0.7	–9.8	–19.8
1971–84 (annual average)	–6.8		–7.8	–14.6

Sources: Repetto *et al.* (1989, p. 6), El Serafy (1993, p. 24).

CONSUMPTION, INVESTMENT AND NET OUTPUT

For two decades, Robert Eisner (1978, 1985, 1989) championed major reform of national income accounting systems. In his view, we need to develop 'better measures of economic activity contributing to social welfare ... measures which capture as fully and distinctly as possible both the flow of current consumption and the accumulation of capital contributing to future welfare' (Eisner 1989, pp. 2, 7).

Eisner's total incomes system of accounts (TISA) aims to extend and revise the official national income accounts in a variety of ways. First, it questions the practice of treating government and household purchases as expenditures on final output and business purchases on current account as intermediate outlays.[9] It also argues that a large portion of government purchases (on roads, police, the military and the courts) are intermediate in nature and should be excluded from GDP (ibid., p. 9). Furthermore, work-related spending by households, commuting expenses for instance, are an intermediate cost of production and not a source of consumer satisfaction. Finally, TISA shifts some consumption services which are provided by businesses to their employees and clients from the intermediate to final output category.

Another area of accounting reform addressed by TISA is the need to acknowledge that some products make a contribution to social wellbeing and deserve to be counted as final output, but are currently excluded from GDP because those outputs are not exchanged in the market-place. These non-market outputs, many of which are produced within the household sector, include meal preparation, house cleaning and painting, care of the young and elderly, and services of household durables.[10] If one makes imputations for these various forms of production within the home, the household sector's share of GNP in the United States exceeds one-third (ibid., p. 36).

A third issue raised by TISA is the need to assign net output between current consumption and capital accumulation on a reasonable basis. The GDP accounts of some nations assume that private businesses undertake all of society's investment activity and that capital accumulation consists of building up business holdings of plant, equipment and inventories. This highly skewed perspective on social investment ignores all acquisitions of tangible assets by government and households, with the possible exception of new home purchases. It also excludes investments in intangible assets such as new technologies and literacy skills. If one attempts to measure accumulation of both tangible and intangible assets by all sectors of society, not just business investment in physical assets, one arrives at a much larger estimate of social investment. Eisner (ibid., p. 49) found, for example, that the US Commerce Department's gross private domestic investment figure for 1981 included only 26 per cent of his extended estimate of total gross investment in the United States for that year.

Eisner's TISA proposal invites us to question several premises embedded in the national income and product accounts. One is that business enterprises exist only to produce and invest on behalf of ultimate consumers. Another is that households are unproductive and exist merely to enjoy commodities purchased from the business sector. Still another is that government property is unproductive and that government purchases make no contribution to a nation's wealth.

Despite these strengths, however, the TISA framework has several limitations, especially if one wants to trace all of the links between economic activity and social wellbeing. As Ruggles (1991, pp. 455–6) has noted, Eisner declined to include the value of leisure time in his estimate of non-market output. In addition, TISA ignores issues associated with employment (both the personal satisfaction of being productive and also dissatisfaction with poor working conditions) and eschews analysis of income distribution issues. Finally, TISA does not address Repetto's concerns about depreciation of natural capital assets, soil erosion and fossil fuel depletion, for example.[11]

FACING UP TO SOCIAL INEQUALITY

Up to this point, this critical survey of national income accounting has con-
centrated on identifying final uses of gross output and on measuring asset
depreciation and depletion properly. Although that discussion is highly relevant
to human wellbeing, we have not yet faced the question of who benefits from
the use of net output. As we shall see, raising the question of who benefits
immediately leads us to issues of poverty, sexism and ethnic discrimination.

An eminent economist who has persistently addressed the issue of social
inequality and its implications for human welfare is Amartya Sen (1981, 1992).
As Sen (1993, p. 40) has framed the issue,

> Economics is not solely concerned with income and wealth but also with using those
> resources as means to significant ends, including the promotion and enjoyment of
> long and worthwhile lives. If ... the economic success of a nation is judged only by
> income ... as it so often is, the important goal of well-being is missed.

Mortality data, which are simple to use and readily accessible, are valuable
indicators of the way a nation's net output has been used. Sri Lanka, for
example, promoted mass literacy early in the twentieth century. Its government
expanded medical care in the 1940s and also began to distribute rice to the
hungry. In 1940 the Sri Lankan death rate was 20.6 per 1000; by 1960 it had
fallen to 8.6 per 1000. Similar changes took place in the Indian state of Kerala.
Despite a per capita GNP considerably lower than the Indian average, longevity
in Kerala now exceeds 70 years (ibid., p. 45). The lesson is clear: not only the
level of net income per capita but also how that income average is distributed
and utilized helps to determine society's level of wellbeing.

This insight has been explored by the authors of the Human Development
Index (HDI). Created by the United Nations Development Programme
(UNDP),[12] the HDI builds upon the following premise:

> People are the real wealth of a nation. The basic objective of development is to create
> an enabling environment for people to enjoy long, healthy, and creative lives ...
> Human development is a process of enlarging people's choices ... at all levels of
> development, the three essential ones are for people to lead a long and healthy life,
> to acquire knowledge and to have access to resources needed for a decent standard
> of living. (UN 1990, pp. 9–10)

Thus the HDI 'emphasizes sufficiency rather than satiety' (UN, 1994, p. 91)
and views the expansion of output and wealth as a means to promoting human
development, not an end in itself (UN, 1990, p. 10). Human development, in
turn, has two sides: 'the formation of human capabilities – such as improved
health, knowledge and skills – and the use people make of their acquired

capabilities – for leisure, productive purposes or being active in cultural, social and political affairs' (ibid.).

Since income is necessary but not sufficient to achieve human development, the UNDP uses real per capita GDP as one component of its Human Development Index. Recognizing that low incomes typically satisfy basic needs, whereas high incomes are spent in part on luxuries, the UN transforms per capita GDP to take account of the declining contribution of a higher average income level to human development.[13] Since 1991, an Atkinson-style utility function has been used to transform a nation's income level into a measure of social welfare:

(W): $$W(y) = \frac{1}{1-\varepsilon} \cdot y^{1-\varepsilon},$$

where

y = a country's per capita income,
y^* = global per capita income,[14]
ε = $\alpha/(\alpha+1)$ with α a non-negative integer, and $\alpha y^* \le y \le (\alpha+1)y^*$.

Thus, for a nation with a per capita GDP below the global average, $\varepsilon = 0$ and hence $W(y) = y$. For a nation with an income level more than twice but less than three times the global average, $\varepsilon = 2/3$ and thus $W(y) = 3 \cdot y^{1/3}$. The claim implied by this specification is that continued economic growth in an already affluent nation contributes little to the human development of its citizens.

If extra GDP is necessary but not sufficient for human development and subject to rapidly diminishing returns, what other factors encourage 'a process of enlarging people's choices'? The HDI focuses on longevity and access to education.[15] For each of the three component indicators of the HDI (transformed income, life expectancy at birth and educational access), a country is given a deprivation score:

$$I_{ij} = (\overline{X} - X_{ij})/(\overline{X}_i - \underline{X}_i),$$

where

X_{ij} = the ith indicator of the jth nation, $i = 1, 2, 3$,
I_{ij} = the ith deprivation score of the jth nation,
$\overline{X}_i$ = a fixed maximum value for the ith indicator, and
$\underline{X}_i$ = a fixed minimum value for the ith indicator.[16]

A country's overall deprivation score (I_j) is the unweighted average of its three I_{ij}. Since human development is the antithesis of human deprivation, $HDI_j = 1 - I_j$.

Table 9.3 Maximum and minimum values for component indicators of HDI

Indicator	Maximum value $\overline{X}_i$	Minimum value $\underline{X}_i$
Educational access		
Adult literacy (2/3 weight)	100%	0%
Combined enrolment ratio (1/3 weight)	100%	0%
Life expectancy at birth	85 years	25 years
Per capita GDP	$40 000	$200

Source: UN (1995, p. 134).

How useful is the HDI as a measure of wellbeing? If one's goal is to detect differences among the developed nations, it is not a discriminating tool, despite the UN (1990, p. 2) claim that it 'applies equally to less developed and highly developed countries'. As Table 9.4 demonstrates, the HDI scores of the top 10 nations scarcely differ from one another. Further inspection reveals why: all enjoy nearly universal adult literacy, and the transformation procedure for income levels essentially equalizes their adjusted per capita GDP data. Only the combined school enrolment ratios of the top 10 countries differ to a significant degree. It is doubtful, however, that a set of nations including the United States, Japan, Spain and Sweden is as homogeneous as the HDI scores suggest.[17]

Despite the UNDP claim of universal applicability, the HDI is probably best used as a measure of the welfare effects of economic development strategies in the less affluent nations of the world. The stark differences among developing nations are suggested by Table 9.5. Brazil, Costa Rica and Turkey are at similar stages of economic development as measured by (unadjusted) per capita GDP. However, Costa Rica receives a substantially higher human development rating because its average citizen will live a decade longer and is far more likely to be literate. Among even poorer nations, similar differences are revealed by the HDI methodology. Sri Lanka, Congo and Pakistan have similar average incomes, but Sri Lanka clearly outranks the other two in longevity and schooling.

Of course, these HDI data provide only fragmentary evidence about the extent and sources of wellbeing within particular nations. They do, however, invite both political debate on national development strategy and international dialogue on development assistance policy (UN 1994, p. 101). Furthermore, HDI-based research has revealed 'large disparities within developing countries

– between urban and rural areas, between men and women, between rich and poor' (UN 1990, p. 2). These social and economic disparities are concealed within national averages and can depress the wellbeing of a substantial portion of a nation's population.[18] In sum, despite several critical reviews (for example, Kelley 1991; Srinivasan, 1994), it seems that the UNDP has made a useful contribution to the measurement of wellbeing and the identification of its sources.

Table 9.4   Top ten HDI scores, 1992

Nation	Life expectancy (years)	Adult literacy (%)	School enrolment ratio (%)	Transformed per capita GDP ($)	HDI score
Canada	77.4	99	100	5359	0.950
USA	76.0	99	95	5374	0.937
Japan	79.5	99	77	5359	0.937
Netherlands	77.4	99	88	5343	0.936
Finland	75.7	99	96	5337	0.934
Iceland	78.2	99	81	5343	0.933
Norway	76.9	99	88	5345	0.932
France	76.9	99	86	5347	0.930
Spain	77.6	98	86	5307	0.930
Sweden	78.2	99	78	5344	0.929

Source: UN (1995, p. 155).

Table 9.5   HDI scores, selected developing nations, 1992

Nation	Life expectancy (years)	Adult literacy (%)	School enrolment ratio (%)	Unadjusted per capita GDP ($)	HDI score
Costa Rica	76.3	94.3	66	5480	0.883
Brazil	66.3	81.9	70	5240	0.804
Turkey	66.5	80.5	61	5230	0.792
Sri Lanka	71.9	89.3	66	2850	0.704
Congo	51.3	70.7	56	2870	0.538
Pakistan	61.5	35.7	25	2890	0.483

Source: UN (1995, pp. 156–7).

ACCOUNTING FOR NATURE AND SOCIAL EQUITY

Various authors have urged us to take account of intermediate and defensive costs of production, accumulation and depreciation of both natural and government capital, and social issues such as poverty and discrimination. Only recently, however, have we witnessed an effort to integrate all of these issues into a single accounting scheme and to measure the welfare effects of macro-economic activity and social inequality in a comprehensive manner. That ambitious effort has been led by Herman Daly and John Cobb (Daly and Cobb, 1989, 1994).[19] Their proposed substitute for GDP is the Index of Sustainable Economic Welfare (ISEW).

They begin the difficult task of constructing an aggregate welfare measure by arguing that it is the current flow of services to humanity from all sources, not the current output of marketable commodities, which is relevant to economic welfare. Hence Daly and Cobb start with personal consumption expenditure and then perform a lengthy series of adjustments to officially measured consumption in order to estimate the sustainable flow of useful services. (See Table 9.6.)

The first adjustment, one for income distribution, recognizes that 'an additional thousand dollars in income adds more to the welfare of a poor family than it does to a rich family' (Daly and Cobb, 1994, p. 445). Although this inter-personal utility comparison might seem obsolete to many neoclassical economists, I would agree with the authors that 10 dollars distributed to an unemployed Detroit carworker will contribute more to social wellbeing than the same amount of cash flowing to the CEO of General Motors.[20] Thus, the greater the degree of income inequality, the lower the flow of economic welfare associated with a particular aggregate flow of consumption services.[21]

After adjusting consumption expenditure for income inequality, Daly and Cobb take account of four service flows currently omitted from the official US consumption measure and derived from four sources: household labour, the existing consumer durable stock, public streets and highways, and public spending on health and education. The authors admit, and rightly so, that their imputation for household labour is too low, since each hour is valued at the wage rate of paid domestic workers (and hence no value is placed on managerial functions within the home). Although they might disagree, Daly and Cobb (1994, p. 467) also underestimate the services of government programmes since they claim that 'government expenditures ... are largely defensive in nature ... [and do] not so much add to net welfare as prevent the deterioration of wellbeing by maintaining security, environmental health, and the capacity to continue commerce'. This claim that government programmes are largely defensive even extends to public (and, for that matter, private) education. Despite decades of scholarly research on the economics of education, the authors contend that schooling mainly serves to ration job vacancies by making credentials scarce and hence qualifies as neither consumption nor capital formation. Eisner (1994, p. 99), on the other hand, has identified 'the almost complete exclusion of human capital' as the most serious defect of the ISEW accounting framework.

Table 9.6   Index of Sustainable Economic Welfare, USA, 1990 (1972 $billions)

personal consumption	1266
income distribution – adjusted personal consumption	1164
+services of household labour	+ 520
+services of consumer durables	+ 225
+services of highways and streets	+ 18
+consumption portion of public spending on health and education	+ 45
–spending on consumer durables	– 235
–defensive private spending on health and education	– 63
–cost of commuting and car accidents	– 67
–cost of personal pollution control	– 5
–cost of air, water and noise pollution	– 39
–loss of wetlands and farmland	– 58
–depletion of non-renewable resources	– 313
–long-term damages from nuclear wastes, greenhouse gases and ozone depletion	– 371
+net capital growth	+ 29
±change in net international investment position	– 34
Index of Sustainable Economic Welfare	818

Note: Total differs from sum of items because of rounding errors.

Source: Daly and Cobb (1994, Table A.1).

Daly and Cobb continue their journey from personal consumption expenditure to sustainable economic welfare by deducting current spending on consumer durables. Since it is the entire stock of consumer durables which provides services, not newly purchased durables, this is an appropriate adjustment. (As Table 9.6 shows, however, imputed services of the consumer durable stock and spending on new household durables roughly cancel one another.) The authors also try to account for personal spending of a defensive or intermediate, not welfare-producing, nature by deducting household costs of commuting, car accidents and pollution control. Personal expenditures on education and medical care are also assumed to be in large measure defensive and not a net contributor to human wellbeing.

Still another deduction from personal consumption is an estimate of the current cost of air, water and noise pollution. For 1990, this amount equalled

$39 billion (in 1972 dollars), a surprisingly low figure. Daly and Cobb (1994, pp. 471–7) mention several reasons for believing that their estimate of current pollution damages is too low. One is that their water pollution estimate includes the effects of siltation and point discharges into waterways but not the impact of non-point emissions. Another is that their estimate of air pollution cost includes damages to crops, forests and durable equipment but excludes human health effects. Thus the ISEW deduction for pollution cost is probably too low in any particular year.

The depletion of natural assets is another set of concerns addressed by Daly and Cobb. Following the example of Repetto et al. (1989), they estimate and then deduct the annual loss of productive services associated with the past and present conversion of wetlands and farmland to urban uses. A marsh area converted to airport runway, for example, no longer provides present and future benefits of flood protection, groundwater purification and storage, wildlife preservation and scenic vistas. The loss of high-quality farmland to suburban development or soil erosion requires that crops be grown on less fertile fields with heavier doses of chemical fertilizers.[22] Because Daly and Cobb assume that land development is irreversible, that substitutes for the services of wetlands and farmland are not readily available, and that the marginal annual loss of benefits rises with cumulative land conversion, their accounting methodology ensures escalating aggregate costs of land development as time unfolds.

Extraction of non-renewable energy in the forms of oil, coal, natural gas and nuclear fuel is another category of natural capital depletion incorporated in ISEW. As Daly and Cobb (1994, p. 482) correctly observe, 'depletion of non-renewable resources ... [is] a cost borne by future generations that should be subtracted from (debited to) the capital account of the present generation'.

But what economic value should be placed on this debit entry in society's ledger? Although the architects of ISEW express qualified appreciation for the user-cost approach of El Serafy (1993), they opt instead for valuing the annual depletion of non-renewable energy reserves at the hypothetical marginal cost of a renewable substitute, ethanol. Because they assume that the real marginal cost of producing ethanol rises by 3 per cent annually, their estimate of the aggregate value of energy depletion would escalate rapidly even if the physical flow of non-renewable energy extraction were to stagnate. (See Table 9.7 for their US estimate.)

Having deducted various forms of natural capital depletion from society's current flow of consumption services, Daly and Cobb (1994, pp. 487–91) next try to account for the environmental damages imposed on future generations because of past economic activity. In particular, the ISEW methodology acknowledges that fossil fuel combustion, nuclear energy production and CFC use result in the accumulation of stocks of persistent pollutants within the global environment. These stocks include atmospheric methane and carbon dioxide, stratospheric chlorine and spent nuclear fuel.

Although Daly and Cobb are absolutely correct that transferring expanding stocks of hazardous materials to future generations is inconsistent with sustainable development, their method for estimating these long-term environmental damages is incomplete at best. In the case of greenhouse gases and nuclear wastes, they assume that the long-term environmental damages resulting from non-renewable energy use and suffered by US citizens are proportional to the cumulative consumption of fossil fuels and nuclear power within the United States since 1900.[23] This methodology has several serious flaws, however. First, it assumes that there is a fixed proportion between current non-renewable energy use and current emissions of persistent pollutants even if the mixture of non-renewable fuels evolves over time.[24] Second, it assumes that energy-related pollutants persist indefinitely once emitted into the environment. This premise ignores the lengthy, but nonetheless finite, half-lives of many environmental pollutants. Finally, since greenhouse gases circulate throughout the atmosphere regardless of their country of origin, the long-term damages from fossil fuel consumption suffered by US citizens depend upon past trends in global energy consumption, not just those in the United States.

Table 9.7   ISEW estimate of US non-renewable energy depletion

Year	Actual US non-renewable energy output (billions of barrels)	Assumed marginal cost of ethanol (1972 $ per barrel)	Estimated non-renewable energy depletion (billions of 1972 $)
1950	5.6	8.3	46.8
1970	10.2	15.3	157.0
1990	11.1	28.1	312.6

Note: The BTU content of coal, ethanol, natural gas and nuclear fuel has been converted to an equivalent number of barrels of petroleum.

Source: Daly and Cobb (1994, p. 501).

When they account for the long-term damages to stratospheric ozone resulting from CFC production and use, Daly and Cobb employ a somewhat different methodology: ISEW assigns an environmental cost of $5 per year to each kilogram of cumulative world production of CFC-11 and CFC-12. The use of global output is entirely appropriate since the welfare loss from ozone depletion suffered by US residents is indifferent to the country of origin of CFC molecules. As with fossil fuels and nuclear energy, however, ISEW ignores the eventual depreciation of a persistent pollutant, in this case the stratospheric chlorine associated with CFC use. Furthermore, the ISEW estimate ignores the lengthy time lags from CFC production to CFC discharge into the troposphere to CFC arrival in the stratosphere. These lags are important determinants of the time pattern of damages associated with CFC production.

These criticisms are raised, not in an effort to discredit the ISEW methodology, but rather in order to alert the reader to a crucial point. Daly and Cobb have transformed officially measured consumption into ISEW via a sequence of 20 specific adjustments. In the end, however, most of those adjustments are too small to explain the growing divergence between per capita GNP and per capita ISEW which seems to have occurred in various countries since 1970. As Table 9.8 shows, personal consumption expenditure in the United States grew by $928 billion between 1950 and 1990. During that same period, ISEW grew by only $438 billion. Hence the total adjustments to BEA consumption shifted in a negative direction by $490 billion between 1950 and 1990, thereby ensuring divergent time paths for the measures of official consumption and sustainable welfare. Over 58 per cent of that change in total adjustments to personal consumption – more than $285 billion – is accounted for by the estimated long-term damages from non-renewable energy and CFC use. For various reasons already noted, however, the ISEW estimates of those damages are highly speculative and very preliminary. Hence the growing gap between GNP and ISEW could be an artifact of the ISEW methodology and not an accurate measure of empirical trends.[25]

Table 9.8   Components of the gap between official consumption and ISEW (1972 $billions)

Year	BEA consumption (1)	Total adjustments to consumption (2)	ISEW (1) + (2)	Long-term environmental damages
1950	337.3	+ 42.9	380.2	−85.1
1990	1265.6	−447.4	818.2	−370.6
Change, 1950–90	+ 928.3	−490.3	+438.0	−285.5

Source: Daly and Cobb (1994, Table A.1).

Daly and Cobb complete their computation of ISEW by taking account of changes in the domestic and international capital position of the US economy. They argue, quite properly, that the current level of economic wellbeing can be sustained only if growth in the domestic capital stock matches population growth, thereby equipping workers with the same amount of capital per head in the future as in the past. Their measure of net capital growth is far too narrow, however, since it focuses on business investments in tangible plant and equipment and ignores social investments in human skills, scientific knowledge and ecological restoration. Their final adjustment, for changes in the net inter-national investment position of a nation's economy, is a compelling one. No country, not even the United States, can indefinitely sustain a particular level of domestic economic welfare by selling its manufactured and natural assets to foreigners and by accumulating financial liabilities abroad.

In sum, Daly and Cobb have successfully synthesized many of the criticisms of national income accounting within a single welfare-oriented framework. As they readily admit, however, many of their numerical estimates are prelimi-nary and based upon highly speculative assumptions.[26] Hence ISEW should be seen as a springboard for future research on national accounting and not as a completed framework filled with accurate data.

CONCLUSION

By this point it should be clear that the quest for an alternative to GDP is far from over. A variety of conceptual and data-gathering problems still remain to be solved. Perhaps the goal of a single numerical measure of human wellbeing is a chimera and will never be achieved. What this critical survey has demonstrated, however, is that we should reject the temptation, often un-conscious, to accept gross domestic product as an objective measure of social wellbeing and economic progress. As Lintott (1996, p.180) has correctly reminded us, 'statistics are social products: they are constructed with certain purposes in view, and... [are influenced] by social and political factors'. If measurement of social wellbeing and sustainable development is our purpose, we still face a challenging construction job.

NOTES

1. In a similar vein, see Maddison (1991, pp. 5–8).
2. For earlier discussions of this set of issues, see Kuznets (1941) and Juster (1973). More recent treatments can be found in Mäler (1991) and Asheim (1994).
3. He did, however, weaken this criterion by including foodstuffs consumed on the farm and services of owner-occupied housing (Kuznets, 1941, p. 9).
4. Kuznets mentioned services produced within the household which could have been purchased in the market-place (clothes washing, shaving and so on), but one might also add conversa-tions with one's friends and viewing a beautiful sunset as other sources of satisfaction excluded from GDP.

5. His reluctance seems rooted in a commitment to some combination of humanist philosophy and neoclassical economics: '[Widening] the scope of intermediate consumption ... reduces the net national product ... to that exceedingly minor magnitude that may be considered as *not* involved in the replacement of all goods, human capacity included, consumed in the process of economic production. No purely analytical or empirical consideration can invalidate this extension ... [However, we] do not look upon human beings ... as units for the production of other goods; consequently, we do not view the raising and education of the younger generation or the sustenance of the working population as intermediate consumption destined to produce or sustain so many [human] machines ... It is this idea of economic goods existing for men, rather than men for economic goods, that gives point to the concept of ultimate consumption' (Kuznets, 1941, pp. 37–8).

6. Repetto *et al.* (1989, p. 17) worry, however, that the 'notion of "defensive" expenditures is elusive, since spending on food can be considered a defence against hunger, clothing a defence against cold, and religion a defence against sin'.

7. Although net domestic product is a better measure of welfare than GDP, it is still an imperfect one, for reasons to be discussed in later sections of this chapter.

8. In the WRI study of Indonesia, domestic output adjusted for resource depletion actually *exceeded* official GDP in 1974 by 35.7 per cent because of significant discoveries of new oil reserves (Repetto *et al.*, 1989, pp. 4, 39).

9. An exception in the official accounting scheme is that business purchases to increase inventories of finished products count as capital expenditure.

10. The US Commerce Department accounts do, of course, include an imputation for the market value of services produced by owner-occupied housing units. Otherwise, the household sector is assumed to consume, not produce, final goods and services.

11. For a description of recent UN accounting reforms which do incorporate depreciation of natural assets, see Bartelmus (1992, 1994).

12. A panel of outside consultants including Gustav Ranis, A.K. Sen, Keith Griffin, Meghnad Desai and Paul Streeten assisted the UNDP (UN, 1990, p. iv).

13. In the original 1990 UN report, the transformed income figure was the log of real per capita GDP levels up to $4861 (the average official poverty line for nine industrial nations). Above $4861, it was assumed that extra per capita real GDP yielded *no* additional human development. This stringent assumption was relaxed in later reports, probably in reaction to criticism. For a survey of criticisms of the original HDI specification, see UN (1991, pp. 88–91).

14. In UN (1994), $y^* = \$5120$ of purchasing power parity dollars.

15. The original HDI used adult literacy to measure educational access (UN, 1990). From 1991 to 1994, the UNDP reports used a weighted average of adult literacy and mean years of schooling. Since 1995, the combined enrolment ratio for primary, secondary and tertiary education has replaced mean years of schooling (UN, 1995).

16. Until its 1994 report, the UNDP used the actual maximum and minimum values for each indicator within the sample of nations surveyed during a year. That practice led to a 'moving goalpost' problem. From year to year, $\bar{X}$ and X values changed and thus it was impossible to track a nation's human development progress over time using HDI scores. Those scores are now available for 1960–92 using 'fixed goalposts' in UN (1994, p. 105). See Table 9.3 for the fixed component indicators.

17. One fact revealed by the HDI methodology is the poor life expectancy of the average US citizen compared to the average Canadian. That difference reflects, in large measure, the poor life prospects of Afro-Americans (Sen, 1993, pp. 44–5). Thus, despite a higher unadjusted average income, the United States ranks below Canada in HDI score.

18. In UN (1992), the UNDP introduced a gender-sensitive version of the HDI. Taking account of gender differences in life expectancy, schooling, wages and labour force participation lowers the HDI ranks of the United States and Canada but raises the Scandinavian countries to the top of the list. The 1992 report also introduced the use of Gini coefficients to calculate income distribution-adjusted HDI scores.

19. They acknowledge their intellectual debt to Nordhaus and Tobin (1972). It should also be pointed out that Clifford Cobb, son of John, played a crucial role in the development of ISEW. The Genuine Progress Indicator (GPI) is an offspring of ISEW.

20. Eisner (1994, p. 100) does not object to Daly and Cobb's declining marginal utility of income assumption but argues that their adjustment for income inequality should take place after all other adjustments to official consumption have occurred. The authors note, but fail to pursue, the self-criticism that 'our calculus of economic well-being has failed to take in account ... that happiness is apparently correlated with relative rather than absolute levels of wealth or consumption' (Daly and Cobb, 1994, p. 460).
21. The authors considered several indexes of distributional inequality (harmonic mean of quintiles, Gini coefficient and so on) but chose an index based on the share of income accruing to the lowest quintile of households. This approach, they argue, 'gives special weight to the plight of the poorest members of society, which fits well with the theory of justice propounded by John Rawls' (Daly and Cobb 1994, p. 465).
22. Since the production of chemical fertilizers relies heavily on petroleum feedstocks, it is doubtful that this shift to less fertile land is sustainable. See Cleveland (1995).
23. The factor of proportionality assumed is $0.50 of future annual damages per barrel-equivalent of non-renewable energy consumption, in 1972 real dollars.
24. During the twentieth century, petroleum and natural gas replaced coal in many nations. Since coal is a dirtier fuel, that substitution has lowered the emissions propensity of non-renewable energy use.
25. It follows that the data suggesting declining sustainable welfare in several industrial countries offered by Max-Neef (1995) may simply reflect repeated application of the same imperfect methodology, not irrefutable empirical evidence that economic growth lowers the quality of life.
26. As Herman Daly has said in a personal communication, 'ISEW is like putting a filter on a cigarette. It's better than nothing.'

REFERENCES

Asheim, G.B. (1994), 'Net National Product as an Indicator of Sustainability', *Scandinavian Journal of Economics*, 96, 257–65.
Barro, R.J. and X. Sala-i-Martin (1995), *Economic Growth*, New York: McGraw-Hill.
Bartelmus, P. (1992), 'Accounting for Sustainable Growth and Development', *Structural Change and Economic Dynamics*, 3(2), 241–60.
Bartelmus, P. (1994), *Environment, Growth and Development*, London: Routledge.
Carson, C.S. (1975), 'The History of the United States National Income and Product Accounts: The Development of an Analytical Tool', *Review of Income and Wealth*, 21(2), 153–81.
Cleveland, C. (1995), 'Resource Degradation, Technical Change and the Productivity of Energy Use in U.S. Agriculture', *Ecological Economics*, 13(3), 185–201.
Daly, H.E. and J.B. Cobb (1994), *For the Common Good*, Boston: Beacon Press.
Eisner, R. (1978), 'Total Incomes in the United States, 1959 and 1969', *Review of Income and Wealth*, 24(1), 41–70.
Eisner, R. (1985), 'The Total Incomes System of Accounts', *Survey of Current Business*, 65(1), 24–48.
Eisner, R. (1989), *The Total Incomes System of Accounts*, Chicago: University of Chicago Press.
Eisner, R. (1994), 'The Index of Sustainable Welfare: Comment', in C. Cobb and J. Cobb (eds), *The Green National Product*, Lanham: University Press of America.
El Serafy, S. (1993), 'Country Macroeconomic Work and Natural Resources', Environment Working Paper No. 58, World Bank, Washington, DC.

El Serafy, S. (1996), 'Weak and Strong Sustainability: Natural Resources and National Accounting', *Environmental Taxation and Accounting*, 1(1), 27–48.

Juster, F.T. (1973), 'A Framework for the Measurement of Economic and Social Performance', in M. Moss (ed.), *The Measurement of Economic and Social Performance*, New York: Columbia University Press.

Kelley, A.C. (1991), 'The Human Development Index: "Handle with Care"', *Population and Development Review*, 17(2), 315–24.

Kuznets, S. (194), *National Income and Its Composition, 1919–1938*, New York: National Bureau of Economic Research.

Leipert, C. (1989), 'Social Costs of the Economic Process and National Accounts: The Example of Defensive Expenditures', *Journal of Interdisciplinary Economics*, 3, 27–46.

Lintott, J. (1996), 'Environmental accounting: useful to whom and for what?', *Ecological Economics*, 16, 179–90.

Maddison, A. (1991), *Dynamic Forces in Capitalist Development*, Oxford: Oxford University Press.

Mäler, K.-G. (1991), 'National Accounts and Environmental Resources', *Environmental and Resource Economics*, 1, 1–15.

Max-Neef, M. (1995), 'Economic Growth and Quality of Life: A Threshold Hypothesis', *Ecological Economics*, 15(2), 115–18.

Nordhaus, W. and J. Tobin (1972), 'Is Growth Obsolete?', in NBER, *Economic Growth*, Research General Series, No. 96E, New York: Columbia University Press.

Repetto, R., W. Magrath, M. Wells, C. Beer and F. Rossino (1989), *Wasting Assets: Natural Resources in the National Income Accounts*, Washington, DC: World Resources Institute.

Ruggles, R. (1991), 'Review of The Total Incomes System of Accounts by Robert Eisner', *Review of Income and Wealth*, 37(4), 455–60.

Ruggles, R. (1993), 'National Income Accounting: Concepts and Measurement. Economic Theory and Practice', *Economic Notes by Monte dei Pashi di Siena*, 22(2), 235–64.

Sen, A.K. (1981), *Poverty and Famines*, Oxford: Oxford University Press.

Sen, A.K. (1992), *Inequality Reexamined*, Cambridge, Mass.: Harvard University Press.

Sen, A.K. (1993), 'The Economics of Life and Death', *Scientific American*, 268(5), 40–47.

Srinivasan, T.N. (1994), 'Human Development: A New Paradigm or Reinvention of the Wheel?', *American Economic Review*, 84(2), 238–43.

UN Development Programme (1990–96), *Human Development Report*, Oxford: Oxford University Press.

10. Natural resource scarcity indicators: an ecological economic synthesis

Cutler J. Cleveland and David I. Stern

INTRODUCTION

In this chapter we review the literature on natural resource scarcity indicators, develop a synthesis based on the ideas of the institutionalist economist John Commons, and a method of decomposing a generalized unit cost indicator into more fundamental determinants of natural resource productivity. This generalized unit cost indicator is compared to alternative indicators using data from the US agricultural sector. Our thesis is that the various approaches to measuring natural resource scarcity are complementary, not contradictory. However, they represent a starting point rather than an endpoint in the investigation of resource scarcity. Hence our decomposition methodology.

An increase in natural resource scarcity is defined as a reduction in economic wellbeing due to a decline in the quality, availability or productivity of natural resources. Simple in concept, the measurement of natural resource scarcity is the subject of significant debate about which of the alternative indicators of scarcity, such as unit costs, prices, rents, elasticities of substitution and energy costs, is superior (for example, Brown and Field, 1979; Fisher, 1979; Hall and Hall, 1984; Cairns, 1990; Cleveland and Stern, 1993). Most neoclassical economists argue that, in theory, price is the ideal measure of scarcity (for example, Fisher, 1979) though some argue in favour of rents (Brown and Field, 1979; Farzin, 1995). Barnett and Morse (1963) developed the unit cost indicator from their reading of Ricardo as an alternative to the neoclassical indicators. Some ecological economists favour a biophysical model of scarcity and derive energy-based indicators (for example, Cleveland et al., 1984; Hall et al., 1986; Cleveland, 1991a, 1992; Ruth, 1995).

The scarcity of agricultural products has received considerable attention due to the obvious importance of food production and the very vocal argument that degradation is undermining the bioproductivity of the agricultural resource base. A number of analysts argue that soil erosion, groundwater depletion, reduced genetic diversity and other forms of resource degradation are severe threats to the long-run productivity of US agriculture (Brown, 1984, 1994; Ehrlich and Ehrlich, 1991; Pimentel, 1993). These claims seem to be supported by the results of field experiments and statistical analyses by agronomists and agricultural engineers who find significantly reduced crop yields on eroded land relative to non-eroded land (American Society of Agricultural Engineers, 1985; Follett and Stewart, 1985). Resource degradation in agriculture is a key driving force in some dynamic models of the United States (Gever *et al.*, 1986) and world economy (Meadows *et al.*, 1992) and in conceptual models of agricultural development in the tropics (Hall and Hall, 1993). In various ways, these models project increasing scarcity of food in the future.

Other analysts argue that, while degradation is important, there is little evidence to indicate it is undermining the future of US agriculture. Crosson (1991) finds that the on-farm costs of degradation over the next 100 years are small. Every analysis of multi- and total factor productivity in the United States shows a substantial overall increase since the 1940s (Trueblood and Ruttan, 1995), suggesting that the US agricultural resource base has not undergone pervasive, irreversible, long-term damage, and/or that technical change and factor substitution have more than offset any effects of degradation (Ball *et al.*, 1995). These conclusions are buoyed by the 24 per cent decline in sheet and rill erosion in the United States from 1982 to 1992 (USDA, 1994).

The purpose of this chapter is to review the different methods used to analyse resource scarcity, including their underlying theories, methodologies and principal empirical results. We attempt to put the issue in perspective by stepping back and asking the question, 'What do we actually mean by scarcity?', a question rarely addressed in the literature. We propose the terms *use scarcity* and *exchange scarcity* to distinguish between two broad approaches to measuring scarcity. These terms relate to the classical concepts of use and exchange value. Definitions of use and exchange value have varied among different economic paradigms, but broadly speaking use value is the value derived from consumption of a good, while exchange value is the value of goods or money that can be obtained in exchange for the good in an actual or potential market. Our usage of 'use value' is not the same as that of some environmental economists, who use it to describe value derived from active use of the resource in consumption or production, as juxtaposed to 'non-use values' of environmental resources that contribute to utility through, for example, knowledge of their existence.

As proposed in this chapter, exchange scarcity is commonly measured by price or rent, depending on whether the scarcity of in situ natural resources or resource commodities is being measured. Use scarcity refers to the ability of natural resources to generate use value and is typically measured in terms of the balance between the productivity and availability of the resource base and the level of technology (Cleveland and Stern, 1993). We call the most general indicator of the latter type 'generalized unit cost' (GUC). Barnett and Morse's (1963) unit cost is a special case of this indicator. It is possible to decompose such indicators into more fundamental components that reflect the driving forces behind changes in scarcity. This theoretical analysis shows the superiority of the GUC indicator for general unknown technologies of production. The various indicators are illustrated using data for the US agricultural sector between 1948 and 1993.

THE CLASSICAL MODEL OF SCARCITY

Ricardo, together with Karl Marx, argued that the labour cost of production could be used as a common unit of measurement of the exchange value of commodities.[1] Ricardo also saw nature, not as a factor of production, but rather as a force resisting the efforts of labour to produce use values (Commons, 1934). The poorer the quality of the resource stock, the more it resists the efforts of labour. Barnett and Morse (1963) take the meaning of increased scarcity to be an increase in the resistance of nature to the efforts of people to produce resource commodities, as in Ricardo's classic case of the declining fertility of land at the extensive margin. Therefore, naturally, we measure such scarcity by the labour required to produce a unit of the commodity. Rising resistance or rising scarcity means that more labour is required. This is the source of the unit cost measure, which in its simplest form is the inverse of labour productivity. Ricardo would have seen unit cost as an indicator of exchange value just like price. As discussed later in this chapter, Commons argues that this is a mistaken belief and that in fact unit cost is an indicator of use value or, as he would have said, efficiency.

The term 'unit cost' is somewhat unfortunate. Some analysts (for example, Farzin, 1995; Uri and Boyd, 1995) erroneously assume that unit cost is the average cost of extraction. Barnett and Morse also combine the Ricardian model with a neoclassical production function to derive a more comprehensive measure of scarcity that accounts for capital inputs.[2] In this case, unit cost is the inverse of multi-factor productivity defined with respect to labour and capital. Hall *et al.* (1984) expanded the definition to also include some materials.

Barnett and Morse (1963) defined unit cost as:

$$UC_t = \frac{\alpha(L_t/L_b) + \beta(K_t/K_b)}{Q_t/Q_b} \tag{10.1}$$

where:

UC_t = unit cost of extraction at time t,

Q_t = net output (value added) in constant dollars,

L_t = labour cost measured as number of persons employed,

K_t = capital cost measured as net fixed capital stock in constant dollars,

Q_b, L_b, K_b = output, labour and capital inputs in the base year b,

α_t = I^{Lt} / I^{Tt} where I^L is total labour compensation and I^T is value added originating in the industry in question (other indexation procedures such as Divisia aggregation can be used).

The classical model from which Barnett and Morse derive the unit cost index assumes that resources are used in order of descending quality. With unchanging technology, cumulative extraction will be associated with an increase in the quantity of labour and capital required to extract a unit of the resource. Technological innovations work in the opposite direction, reducing required labour and capital inputs per unit output. In real-world cases, where resources are not used in strict order of quality, new discoveries of higher-quality resources can also lower unit cost. Barnett and Morse argued that unit cost reflects the net effect of these opposing forces, and thus measures the long-run productivity of the resource base. As we show below, the overall quantity of resource stock under exploitation also affects unit cost: using more natural capital with given inputs of capital and labour will normally raise the productivity of the latter inputs.

Empirical Results of the Classical Model

Barnett and Morse calculated the unit cost index for aggregate resource industries (agriculture, forestry, fisheries and mining) and individual resource commodities in the United States from 1870 to 1957. They found an almost universal decline in unit cost, which they viewed as a rejection of the classical school's 'iron law of diminishing returns'. The lone exception was the forest products sector, which showed an overall increase in labour cost per unit output.

Johnson *et al.* (1980) used regression analysis to update Barnett and Morse to 1966, and used a dummy variable to test for a significant change in the trend in scarcity after 1957. They found that the cost of aggregate agricultural and mineral commodities fell at a *faster* rate from 1957 to 1966 compared to the period before 1957. Johnson *et al.* also found an overall increase in the cost of forestry products from 1870 to 1970, although costs generally declined after 1957. This trend was confirmed by Cleveland and Stern (1993) for the subsequent years to 1990 as well.

Hall and Hall (1984) updated the unit cost analysis for a number of resources, and used regression analysis to test for a significant change in scarcity between 1960 and 1980, and for the possible effects of the energy price shocks on unit cost. They found that the unit cost of petroleum and coal began to increase in the 1970s, but not for agriculture, electricity and metals. The authors emphasized that costs turned upwards prior to the energy price increases, indicating that the actions of the OPEC (Organization of Petroleum Exporting Countries) cartel were not the principal cause of the increase in cost.

The cost of oil resources in the United States has attracted considerable attention. Cleveland (1993) calculated the unit cost index for petroleum (oil and gas) extraction in the United States from 1880 to 1990. He found a precipitous decline in cost through the 1960s, followed by a sharp increase in cost up to 1990. As with the Hall and Hall (1984) results, costs turned upwards prior to the energy price shocks. Cleveland (1991b) also calculates the average (not unit) cost of oil discovery and production in the United States from 1936 to 1988. He finds that the time path for both are consistent with Slade's (1982) U-shaped time path for scarcity. The cost of oil discovery has increased steadily since the 1930s, while the cost of production began to increase in the 1960s. Like Hall and Hall (1984), Cleveland's econometric analysis indicates that the actions of the OPEC cartel accelerated – but did not cause – the cost increase.

Critique of the Classical Model

Barnett and Morse (1963) argued for the use of unit costs and against the use of rents as a scarcity indicator because changes in rent may be due to 'changes in interest rates, relative demand, and expectations concerning future resource availability' (p. 225) – in other words, forces that obscure the issue of productivity. As Smith (1980) stated, 'Their objective would seem to call for measuring resource scarcity without judging the legitimacy of society's ends ... Thus [Barnett and Morse] implicitly accepted the notion that there was an objective measure of scarcity independent of consumer preferences' (p. 261). Neoclassical economists criticize Barnett and Morse's unit cost measure because, inter alia, 'Whether a resource is becoming scarce or not, for example, ought to depend in part on expectations about future supplies' (Brown and Field, 1979, p. 230). In other words, an indicator that excludes any factor that determines exchange value is inadmissible.

One significant shortcoming is that unit cost excludes all inputs other than capital and labour, and output is measured in value added terms. Fuel, water and other purchased inputs are excluded, though this problem is addressed by Hall *et al.* (1984) and is not a fundamental problem. The most serious computational issue is that unit cost is a constructed index, which requires assumptions about the best way to measure output, inputs and the weighting factors (Brown and

Field, 1979; Howe, 1979). Particularly troublesome is the measurement of capital input and how the capital stock is depreciated over time. The weighting factors are also problematic because the return to capital is typically unobserved and combined with the compensation for land in a single measure of total profit.

Brown and Field (1979) showed that labour only unit cost would rise in the face of an increase in the price of the resource stock relative to wages. But, they argued, the impact would be greater the greater the ease of substitution between resources and labour in producing resource commodities. This relationship makes sense, as the optimal ratio of labour use to resource use will shift more the easier substitution is. Innovations that make it easier to substitute away from the resources base will accelerate the rate of increase in unit cost. This, they state, is perverse.

The more general point is that, contrary to Barnett and Morse's assertions, unit cost does depend on factor and output prices and all the variables that drive those prices. As discussed below, similar problems affect the biophysical indicators. It is, however, possible to calculate a unit cost indicator that is more independent of price movements. The GUC indicator that we develop later in the chapter is relatively free of these sorts of distortions.

THE NEOCLASSICAL MODEL OF SCARCITY

The neoclassical view of scarcity begins with the theory of optimal depletion (Hotelling, 1931) in which resource owners are assumed to maximize the discounted profits from the extraction and sale of the resource. Solution of the model suggests two possible scarcity indicators: price and rent. Fisher (1979) demonstrates this with a simple optimal control problem for non-renewable resource extraction in which the private profit-maximizing resource owner faces the following problem.

Maximize $\int_0^\infty [PY - WE]e^{-rt}dt$

subject to: $dX/dt = -Y$

$$Y = f(E,X,t) \tag{10.2}$$

where P is market price, W is the price of hiring a unit of effort E, Y is the quantity of the resource commodity produced from the stock X, and $f()$ is the production function. In equilibrium the following condition is met:

$$P = W/(\partial Y/\partial E) + q \tag{10.3}$$

where q is the costate variable attached to the constraint in the Hamiltonian. Market price, therefore, has the attractive feature of capturing the sum of direct sacrifices such as the cost of hiring labour, and indirect sacrifices such as the change in the net present value of future profits caused by reducing the size of the remaining resource stock. The quantity q is known as the shadow price of the stock, user cost, or rent. If we are only interested in the direct and indirect sacrifices associated with depleting the stock, rather than producing the commodity, q is a better indicator. Therefore market prices are the appropriate scarcity indicator for resource commodities and rents for resource stocks.

Several authors have developed theoretical time paths for rent and price as a resource is depleted (for example, Hotelling, 1931; Fisher, 1979; Lyon, 1981; Sedjo and Lyon, 1990; Slade, 1982; Farzin, 1992, 1995). In Hotelling's simple model, both price and rent rise monotonically at the rate of interest. In Fisher's model, price still rises monotonically but rent may follow a non-monotonic path. Slade (1982) developed a more complex model where the path of prices over time may follow a U shape, implying that declining prices may be a misleading signal for long-run scarcity. Farzin (1992, 1995) derives a variety of time paths under varying assumptions. The theoretical literature indicates that, for sufficiently general models, any time path may be possible. Lyon (1981) and Sedjo and Lyon (1990) derived specific models for forest products. The resulting time path is an S-curve, a path that both rents and prices followed remarkably closely in the United States in the last couple of centuries (Cleveland and Stern, 1993).

Empirical Results of the Neoclassical Model

The empirical analysis of price and rent is characterized by applying more sophisticated econometric tools to time series data. Barnett and Morse's (1963) visual inspection of prices from 1870 to 1957 led them to reject the hypothesis of increasing scarcity for agriculture and minerals (metals, non-metals and fuels) and accept it in forestry. The trend for fisheries was indeterminate.

Smith (1979) uses Brown–Durbin CUSUM (cumulative sum of squares) and Quandt log-likelihood tests to examine the stability of the coefficients from a simple linear regression of real prices as a function of time for four broad industry groups from 1900 to 1973. He finds significant instability, and concludes that any judgments as to a consistent pattern of change in the price series would be 'hazardous'.

Devarajan and Fisher (1982) develop a two-period model of optimal depletion, which indicates that marginal discovery cost is a close proxy of rent. They find that the average cost of oil discovery in the United States showed a statistically significant increase from 1946 to 1971, indicating a clear increase in scarcity.

Slade (1982, 1985) develops a model of optimal depletion in which the long-run path of price is U-shaped owing to changes in the effects of depletion and technical change. She tested the U-shaped model by estimating a quadratic time trend model for 12 non-renewable resources in the United States from 1870 to 1978. She found significant U shapes for 11 of the 12 resources, and noted that all had passed the minimum points on their fitted U-shaped curves, indicating growing scarcity.

Ozdemiroglu (1993) updated Slade's (1982) analysis by fitting a quadratic model to time series price data for 39 resources in five categories from a number of developed and developing nations. Of the nine resources that have significant trend coefficients, five show an inverted U shape, contrary to Slade's finding of a pervasive U shape for the US extractive sector. Ozdemiroglu's series are much shorter (as short as 12 years in the case of coal) than those used by Slade. Given that Slade's hypothesis is about long-run trends, it is doubtful that Ozdemiroglu's analysis really tests Slade's hypothesis.

Hall and Hall (1984) estimated a time trend model for 14 resource commodities in the United States from 1960 to 1980, and tested for the possible effects of the energy price shocks on price. They found that the real price of fuels and electricity increased in the 1970s, and the actions of the OPEC cartel accelerated – but did not cause – the observed increase in price.

Forest products in the United States have received considerable attention. Brown and Field (1979) found the rental value of Douglas fir (as measured by its stumpage price) relative to its lumber price increased significantly from 1930 to 1970. They noted that this increase occurred at the same time that the unit cost of forest products (L/Q) declined. Brown and Field also found that the stumpage price of Douglas fir relative to a quality-adjusted wage rate increased from 1920 to 1970. Cleveland and Stern (1993) tested econometrically for trends in lumber prices from 1800 to 1990 and for trends in stumpage prices from 1910 and 1989 in the United States. They found that both series are explained by a logistic function. Prices for lumber products and rental rates for timberland are much higher today than in the past, but have levelled off in recent decades.

An issue ignored in most studies of scarcity indicator trends, whether classical, neoclassical or biophysical, is the time series properties of the series in question. Recently, Uri and Boyd (1995) and Berck and Roberts (1996) have addressed this question. Berck and Roberts (1996) revisit Slade's (1982) results. They find that most of the series are difference stationary rather than trend stationary: that is, they can be represented by unit root processes. This result was confirmed by Uri and Boyd (1995) for the average cost of extraction and real resource price series for a group of metals. Berck and Roberts (1996) find that when forecasting 1991 prices using a model estimated on 1940 to 1976 data an ARIMA model is found to give more accurate predictions than Slade's quadratic model for all commodities except copper. The prices forecast by the ARIMA model are also lower for all commodities except copper. Using the quadratic model to predict 2000 prices from a 1991 base gives a probability of an increase in price of more than 75 per cent for every commodity and a mean probability of 87 per cent. The ARIMA model has a mean probability of increase of 57 per cent with only one commodity having a probability of less than 50 per cent. So, while price rises are seen to be less likely when a more appropriate model is fitted, the odds are still above even for an increase in prices in the future.

Critique of the Neoclassical Model

Price has a number of practical advantages relative to unit cost (Cleveland, 1993). First, the prices of most natural resources are readily observable, and that avoids the pitfalls of having to construct an index from secondary data. Second, the joint effects of the physical, technological and market factors that influence scarcity are subsumed in a single index. Third, price is not hampered by the joint product problem in industries such as oil and gas extraction, which complicates measurement of unit cost. Natural gas and crude oil have separate and distinct market prices. Rent does not, however, have many of these advantages.

There also are numerous caveats to the theoretical properties of price and rent. Most importantly, market prices and rents only indicate *private* scarcity (Fisher, 1979). In the presence of market imperfections or market failure, social indicators of scarcity will diverge from the private indicators.

The arguments for price are based on highly simplified models of optimal resource depletion that rest on restrictive assumptions about market structure, technical change, uncertainty about future cost and market conditions, and other factors that determine price. In the real world, there are many practical problems with price that negate some of its theoretical advantages. The price of natural resources is determined in markets that are far more complex than those described in many of the theoretical models. Furthermore, the trend in scarcity suggested by price is sensitive to the benchmark that nominal prices are compared to (Brown and Field, 1979).

Rent faces similar problems as a scarcity indicator. Mattey (1990) shows that stumpage prices, the resource rent in the forestry sector, are influenced more by short-term government policy and economic forecasts than by changes in the difficulty of production. Fisher (1979) describes the possibility of rent falling to zero as a low grade backstop resource is substituted for a depleted higher-quality resource, thus sending perverse signals about the impact on social wellbeing.

Norgaard (1990) presented what he argued was a logical fallacy in the empirical scarcity literature. The argument boils down to two points: imperfect information means that price or rent is not an accurate scarcity indicator for a resource owner, and that in addition imperfect or non-existent markets mean that price or rent are not indicators of social scarcity. Neither of these points is new, and they are explicit in earlier studies (for example, Barnett and Morse, 1963; Fisher, 1979). Norgaard also argues that if resource owners actually did have perfect information about resource scarcity then economists could ask them directly for this information. Yet economists generally prefer to use market data to investigate people's preferences rather than asking them directly. Stated preference methods such as contingent valuation are normally only used in the absence of markets for the resource. So, even if resource owners had perfect information, it might be useful to exploit market data where available.

THE BIOPHYSICAL MODEL OF SCARCITY

The biophysical approach begins by redrawing the conventional boundaries of the economic system. The economic process is a work process and, as such, it is sustained by a flow of low entropy energy and matter from the environment. As materials and energy are transformed in production and consumption, higher entropy waste heat and matter are ultimately released to, and assimilated by, the environment. Analysis of exchange in markets, which grabs the limelight in conventional economic analysis, is given less attention and is seen as an intermediate step in the process of fulfilling human needs and desires by the flow of energy and materials from resources to production, pollution and environmental assimilation.

The biophysical approach defines the resource transformation process as one that uses energy to upgrade the organization of matter to a more useful state (Ayres, 1978; Cook, 1976; Gever *et al.*, 1986; Hall *et al.*, 1986; Cleveland, 1991b; Ruth, 1993). In their natural state resources are not useful inputs to the production process. They must be located, extracted, refined, transported and upgraded in other ways into useful raw materials or products. By definition, lower-quality resources require more energy to be upgraded to a given state. The same fundamental relationship exists for renewable and non-renewable natural resources (Hall *et al.*, 1986). Just as more energy is required to isolate copper metal from a lower grade ore, more energy is required to pump oil from deeper and smaller fields, harvest food from less fertile soil and catch fish from smaller and more remote areas.

A second tenet of the biophysical model emphasizes the role that energy plays in implementing technical innovations in the extractive sector. Technical improvements have tended to be energy-using and labour-saving, achieved through the use of more powerful energy converters (Georgescu-Roegen, 1975). Empirical research demonstrates a significant relationship between labour productivity, the quantity of installed horsepower (Maddala, 1965) and fuel use (Hall *et al.*, 1986) per worker in the US extractive sector. Energy converters have also evolved towards the use of higher-quality forms of energy. Animate energy converters such as human labour and draught animals were replaced by inanimate energy converters burning wood and coal, then oil and natural gas, and eventually electricity.

The energy used to extract a resource is mirrored by the additional use of renewable resources and ecosystem services, such as clean water and air, and the land used to support the extraction process. The increase in throughput of energy and materials also increases the generation of wastes which, in turn, increases the use of natural capital in various forms for waste assimilation. The increase in the overall scale of extraction that accompanies the cumulative depletion of a resource increases the demand for natural capital inputs because that expansion often diverts larger portions of the landscape to extraction activities. Changes in the quality of the resource base affect all of these costs, just as they affect the energy cost of extraction. For example, the decline in quality of the US oil resource base has increased the energy cost of oil extraction. In turn, this has increased the amount of CO_2 released by the fuel burned to extract the oil, and the amount of water used per barrel of oil (Kaufmann and Cleveland, 1991; Cleveland, 1993). In surface metal and coal mines, a decline in resource quality increases the stripping ratio and hence the amount of waste produced per unit of the product (Gelb, 1984).

Empirical Results of the Biophysical Model

The energy cost of extracting a unit of resource in the United States shows some important differences relative to the trends in unit cost and price. The most thoroughly examined resources are fossil fuels (Cleveland *et al.*, 1984; Hall *et al.*, 1986; Gever *et al.*, 1986; Cleveland, 1991b; Cleveland, 1992; Cleveland, 1993). The energy cost of extracting oil and gas increased by 40 per cent from 1970 to the 1990s, indicating a significant increase in scarcity. The energy cost of coal extraction increased by a similar magnitude.

The energy cost of agricultural output increased steadily from 1910 until the late 1970s as the direct and indirect use of fossil fuels replaced labour and draught animals (Cleveland, 1991a; Cleveland, 1995a, 1995b). Since the second energy price shock, energy costs have declined owing to a reduction in the rate of energy use per hectare, a reduction in the number of harvested hectares and larger farms. Cleveland (1995a) finds no evidence that resource degradation has diminished the productivity of energy use in US agriculture.

The energy cost of metals such as silver, bauxite and iron show increasing scarcity in the United States, while copper, lead and zinc show stable or decreasing scarcity (Cleveland, 1991a). Most non-metals show no signs of increasing scarcity measured by their energy cost.

Cleveland and Stern (1993) developed an index of energy cost of forest products in the United States that adjusts for energy quality by using a Divisia index to aggregate energy inputs. Unit energy costs of forest products showed a decrease in scarcity since 1947.

Critique of the Biophysical Model

Stern (1994) argues that a biophysical theory of production need not reduce to an energy theory of production. Low entropy energy and matter are not the only non-reproducible inputs to production.[3] According to Stern, information could be seen in an analogous way to energy as a non-reproducible input. This information is accumulated as knowledge. Technology consists of the designs for the products to be manufactured, the ideas for which come in part from human imagination and the techniques used in producing those products. These techniques consist purely of the application of the knowledge of physical laws and the chemical and biological properties of resources to the production process, though of course the techniques used at any one time are contingent on the path of knowledge accumulation to that date. This latter knowledge is the result of the extraction of information from the environment. Capital, labour, and energy are required to extract that knowledge from the environment and render it into an economically useful form. Capital, labour and other reproducible goods are produced within the economy by applying the two non-reproducible factors of production (low entropy energy and knowledge) to matter. From the perspective of Ricardo and Marx, the use value of the products is not a function of energy alone, but also of the knowledge employed. For example, knowledge is embodied in the physical arrangement of capital, such as the shape and design of machines. From a more neoclassical perspective, knowledge can be used either in an embodied form in the capital and labour inputs or in the combination of the factors of production in the production process. The implication is that the economic value of capital and labour is not a linear function of the energy used in their production alone, even if we ignore the fact that two different products embodying the same energy and knowledge may have different values in their use by people.

Stern (in press) shows that, unless we subscribe to an energy theory of value where the productivity of non-energy inputs is a linear function of the energy used in their manufacture, energy cost could be a misleading indicator of scarcity. In particular, for most reasonable estimates of the elasticity of substitution of energy for capital and labour, energy cost could rise, although no change has occurred in the productivity of the resource base or in the state of technology. This finding is supported by empirical studies (Cleveland, 1995a; Mitchell and Cleveland, 1992) that show rising energy cost as the relative price of energy to capital and labour declined.

That productivity is not a function of energy alone is clear from the issue of varying energy quality (Berndt, 1978; Kaufmann, 1994). Petroleum is considered a higher-quality fuel than coal because of the accompanying physical and chemical properties of the fuel vector and the technologies available for using the fuels. This difference cannot be explained purely in terms of the embodied environmental energy in the fuels: that is, petroleum has not undergone considerably more processing in the environment than has coal. This problem can be addressed by using quality-weighted indices of energy inputs (Cleveland, 1993; Cleveland and Stern, 1993; Stern, 1993), typically the relative prices of the fuels. This is only a partial solution, which implies certain separability conditions imposed on the production function.

TOWARDS A SYNTHESIS: USE AND EXCHANGE SCARCITY

Much of the debate about the strengths and weaknesses of various scarcity indicators ignores a fundamental point: different indicators measure different types of scarcity. We elaborate this point below using the concepts of *use scarcity* and *exchange scarcity*.

The two fundamental concepts of value in economics are use value and exchange value. The definition of scarcity in terms of exchange value is described in detail above. For a private person wishing to acquire a resource commodity, market price is a valid indicator of exchange value. Similarly, rent is the relevant indicator for a resource stock. However, measures of opportunity cost for owners of resource stocks or for society will diverge from their market prices except under unrealistic conditions. Exchange scarcity would properly be measured by unobserved shadow prices of commodities or resources.

Use value was always a problematic concept because either it was believed to be impossible to measure or the units of measurement were unclear. For Adam Smith, use value was utility: the happiness or satisfaction derived from using a commodity. The classical economists did not conceive of this utility as declining with increasing consumption. Therefore there was no relation between use value per unit and the abundance or consumption of the commodity. Use value did change with what neoclassical economists would now call changes in preferences, in household production functions, or in capital stocks associated with household production (Stern, 1997). The use value of a particular material object would also decline through wear and tear over time. Commons suggested that we measure use value in physical units, such as tons of steel and dozens of watches, but this is clearly unsatisfactory. Marx did at times use this physical measure of use values while at other times asserting that 'Use-values become a reality only by use or consumption' (Marx, 1867, p. 45).

There were two versions of the classical labour theory of value. Smith (and Malthus) had used labour as the numeraire commodity because they had no other method of adjusting for inflation (Commons, 1934). Value was measured by the quantity of labour that could be commanded in exchange for the commodity in question. On the other hand, Ricardo and Marx were interested in using the labour theory to investigate the source of value. As such their labour theory of value was one of the labour embodied in the production of the commodity. Ricardo argued that the natural prices – or the long-run equilibrium prices (Eltis, 1984) – of commodities were determined by the labour required in their production. Ricardo, together with Karl Marx, argued that the labour cost of production could be used as a common unit of measurement of the exchange value of commodities (Commons, 1934). In opposition to Quesnay, Ricardo did not view nature as being a source of value; rather, nature resisted the efforts of labour to produce use values. The poorer the quality of the resource, the greater the resistance of nature, the greater the quantity of labour required to produce a unit of the commodity, and therefore the higher the natural price or equilibrium exchange value of the commodity would be.

Commons paralleled the concepts of exchange and use value with his categories of 'scarcity' and 'efficiency'. Commons contrasts technical efficiency and its role in the production of use value with scarcity and its role in the production of exchange value, and documents the relationship of the scarcity and efficiency concepts throughout the history of economics.

> By efficiency is meant in terms of managerial transactions, the rate of output per unit of input, the man-hour, thus increasing the power over nature but regardless of the total quantity produced. By scarcity is meant, in terms of bargaining transactions, the rate of proprietary income from other persons relative to the rate of proprietary outgo, measured by the dollar. Inefficiency means a slower rate of output per unit of input, but weak bargaining power means a lesser rate of income per unit of outgo. (Commons, 1934, p. 259)

Efficiency is, therefore, a measure of productivity determined by the technical relations of production and is defined as the rate of production of use value by the factors of production, or output per unit input. The inverse of this output/input ratio is Barnett and Morse's unit cost. When there are several factors of production instead of just labour, it is impossible to identify a priori

the contribution of each to use value. Commons approves of the Marxian aggregation of inputs by accounting for the capital employed in terms of its embodied
labour. Barnett and Morse weight inputs by their shares in income. Similarly,
biophysical economists thought energy to be the source of all value and
accounted for capital and other inputs in terms of their embodied energy
(Kaufmann, 1987).

Scarcity (in Commons' sense) is ultimately determined by institutional
relations, while efficiency is determined by technical relations. Citing Veblen,
Commons describes efficiency as being the domain of the engineer, while
scarcity is the domain of the businessman. Engineers are always prepared to
find ways of producing more output, while the role of businessmen is to restrict
the activities of the engineers in order to maximize profits. Higher average use
value indicates more abundance, while higher average exchange value indicates
less abundance. The exchange value concepts that parallel input and output are
expenditure or cost and revenue. Commons' scarcity indicator is the ratio of
revenue to cost or, in his terminology, income to outgo.

So, while Ricardo would have viewed the output/input ratio as an indicator
of the natural price of the commodity or its exchange value in long-run equilibrium, Commons argues that he was mistaken. Instead, this output/input ratio
is an indicator of use value produced per unit input of labour or Commons'
efficiency. Similarly, Marx was mistaken according to Commons in believing
he had found a theory of the formation of exchange value. Instead, he had
developed a theory of efficiency. Therefore we can reinterpret the unit cost
indicator of Barnett and Morse and the biophysical energy cost indicator as
Commons' efficiency indicators or indicators of the scarcity of use value.

However, in the neoclassical view, unless utility functions are linear in commodities, use value also is a function of the quantities of other commodities
consumed. Calculation of the utility of consumers derived from natural resources
also needs to take into account the efficiency of production downstream from
the resource sector. The unit cost indicator is, therefore, an 'upstream indicator'
of scarcity. The prices of resource commodities do not necessarily move in the
same direction as rent (Fisher, 1979), and downstream use scarcity does not
necessarily move in the same direction as unit cost. To our knowledge, no one
has attempted to construct a 'downstream indicator' of use scarcity.

BEYOND SCARCITY INDICATORS: GENERALIZED TECHNICAL CHANGE

The problem with all natural resource scarcity indicators is that we can only
look at the historic time path of the indicator and guess what the trend will be
in the future. Without a clear understanding of what are the forces that drive the

changes in the indicator, this can be little more than a guess or extrapolation. The recent literature on the time paths of prices and rent (Farzin, 1992) indicates that many time paths are possible, and assuming that the trend will continue is problematic. In order to develop more effective forecasts of future resource scarcity we need to look beyond the crude indicators to the production technologies, natural resource stocks and market structures that determine the indicators. Though no one could accurately forecast any of these variables, it should be possible to constrain the possible changes to a greater degree, through additional research efforts, than is possible for the indicator itself in the absence of this knowledge. Future trends in use scarcity might be better understood if we could estimate each of these components separately. Most analyses of use scarcity assume that the net result of these opposing forces is reflected in the historical trend of the indicator, and they do not explicitly measure the effects of depletion and innovation. One exception is the analysis of the cost of oil extraction in the United States, for which sufficient data are available to describe or proxy depletion and innovation (Norgaard, 1975; Cleveland, 1991b).

In this section, we develop a decomposition into such underlying components of a generalized unit cost indicator. In principle, such a decomposition could also be carried out for exchange scarcity indicators. This example is not intended to promote the view that the use scarcity indicator is more relevant or important than the exchange scarcity indicators. As we describe below, one advantage is that it directly decomposes into a number of more fundamental trends, such as the effects of depletion, technical change and resource availability. Barnett and Morse (1963) attempted a simple version of this decomposition with their index of relative unit cost: the ratio of unit cost in the extractive sector to unit cost in the non-extractive sector. The idea was to remove the overall technical change trend in the economy from the use scarcity indicator so that it more accurately reflected the results of depletion alone.

We make the standard neoclassical assumption that there is smooth substitutability between different inputs so that technology can be represented by a differentiable production function for the gross output of a resource commodity Q. The energy analysis approach implies restrictions on this general model. The production function can be represented by:

$$Q = f(A_i X_i, ..., A_n X_n, A_R R, N) \qquad (10.4)$$

where R is the resource stock (for example the area of agricultural land) from which the resource is extracted, and N is a vector of additional uncontrolled natural resource inputs such as rainfall and temperature. The X_i are other factors of production controlled by the extractor (such as capital, labour, energy and materials), and the A_i are augmentation factors associated with the respective factors of production. A_R is the augmentation (or depletion) index of the resource base.[4] In theory, we could also allow the effective units per crude unit of N to vary, though in most applications it will be assumed that their augmentation indices are constant. Equation (10.4) can obviously be generalized to multiple outputs and multiple resource inputs. A useful simplifying assumption is that the production function exhibits constant returns to scale in all inputs including the resource inputs. Again, generalizations can be made. If N is measured in terms of rainfall, temperature and so on, rather than water, heat and so forth, the relevant constant returns relate to the expansion of X and R but not N. There are decreasing returns when more inputs X are applied to a constant amount of the resource stock R.

Taking the time derivative of $\ln Q$ yields:

$$\dot{Q} = \Sigma \sigma_i \dot{A}_i + \sigma_R \dot{A}_R + \Sigma \sigma_i \dot{X}_i + \Sigma \sigma_j \dot{N}_j + \sigma_R \dot{R} \qquad (10.5)$$

where the σ_i are the output elasticities of the various inputs. A dot on a variable indicates the derivative of the logarithm of the variable with respect to time. The change in the logarithm of a generalized unit cost indicator $U = X/Q$ is given by:

$$\dot{U} = \Sigma \sigma_i \dot{X}_i - \dot{Q} \qquad (10.6)$$

Typically, the change in $\ln U$ will be calculated using a Divisia index of input where σ_i is replaced by the relevant revenue share. This calculation makes the neoclassical assumption of competitive profit-maximizing price-taking behaviour where in equilibrium the marginal products of inputs are equated to their prices. Substituting (10.5) into (10.6) we find that generalized unit cost is also given by:

$$\dot{U} = \Sigma \sigma_i \dot{A}_i - \sigma_R \dot{A}_R - \Sigma \sigma_j \dot{N}_j - \sigma_R \dot{R} \qquad (10.7)$$

Thus moves in the generalized unit cost indicator are the sum of the four terms in (10.7), respectively:

1. technical change: $\Sigma \sigma_i \dot{A}_i$;
2. resource depletion or augmentation: $\sigma_R \dot{A}_R$;
3. change in uncontrolled natural resource inputs such as rainfall and temperature in agriculture: $\Sigma \sigma_j \dot{N}_j$;
4. change in the dimension of the resource stock, such as area farmed: $\sigma_R \dot{R}$.

These components seem to cover the dynamics that unit cost proponents have tried to capture without distortions caused by shifts in input or output prices. Traditional unit cost has an additional term on the right-hand side of (10.7) that is a weighted sum of variable factor inputs. Energy cost also has additional terms involving input quantities (Stern, 1999). Factor prices still affect our indicator because, in general, the output elasticities will be functions of input quantities. For the special case of the Cobb–Douglas production function, the indicator is completely independent of prices. Given suitable data, the subcomponents of (10.7) can be estimated econometrically. In the following section we develop and estimate such a model for the US agricultural sector.

An interesting corollary of (10.7) is that all previous studies of biased technical change in the extractive sector of the economy aggregate technical change, resource depletion and resource availability. For example, some studies (Abt, 1987; Constantino and Haley, 1988; Merrifield and Haynes, 1985) of the forest products industry indicate that technical change has tended to be wood-using. This has been taken to indicate that wood is relatively less scarce than the other factors of production (Stier and Bengston, 1992). However, the finding of a wood-using bias could indicate that the quality of the resource base declined, and a wood-saving bias could indicate an improvement in the quality of the resource base. In general, the bias of 'technological change' in an extractive industry does not provide useful information on the scarcity of the natural resources in question unless further information is available which allows the researcher to separate the effects of depletion from the effects of technological change.

APPLICATION TO US AGRICULTURE

Generalized Unit Cost

We calculated GUC for the US agricultural sector between 1948 and 1993 using Divisia aggregation and revenue shares. The index of input included all variable controlled inputs and the capital stock. The data set is described in Ball *et al.* (1995). We aggregated the Ball *et al.* data into the following indices:

- livestock output;
- crop output;
- labour input;
- fertilizer input;
- pesticide input;
- energy input;
- land input – not including structures; the Ball *et al.* index of land is adjusted for the changing coverage of land types in the cultivated area over time;

- capital stock – durable equipment, structures, and inventory;
- other intermediate inputs – lime; feed, seed and livestock; agricultural services, miscellaneous.

The revenue share of the capital stock is derived using the approach of Berndt *et al.* (1993). The total service flow of land and capital is derived using service prices and capital quantities from the Ball *et al.* data set. The share of capital in this potential service flow is calculated from those data. Actual profit is calculated as gross operating surplus, that is, revenue minus the cost of the five variable inputs above. The return to capital is the calculated capital share multiplied by the actual profit. The share in revenue is the negative of the return to capital divided by revenue. The GUC index is shown in Figure 10.1. The figure shows a steady decline in GUC over time.

Figure 10.1 also presents two other use scarcity indicators: energy cost (U_E), and Barnett and Morse's unit cost (U_B). U_B is calculated with value added as

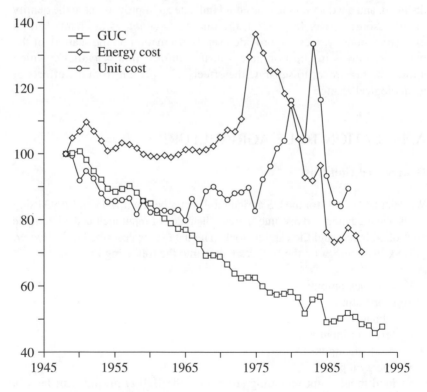

Figure 10.1   Generalized unit cost, unit cost and energy cost in US agriculture (1948 = 100)

the output and capital and labour as inputs. Data sources are described above. An increase in any of the indices indicates an increase in scarcity. The GUC indicator almost forms a lower envelope for the other indicators. Both U_E and U_B show large movements in both directions.

While energy cost and Barnett and Morse's unit cost show signs of rising scarcity in the late 1960s and 1970s, GUC does not. Similar results have been found by other studies. Researchers who made projections based on the energy cost trend at the time (for example, Gever *et al.*, 1986) have been shown to have been overly pessimistic (Cleveland, 1995b).

CONCLUSIONS

There is no 'correct' way to measure resource scarcity. To a large extent, arguments over the meaning and indicators of scarcity reflect fundamental disagreements among economists regarding the nature and purposes of economics (Cole *et al.*, 1983). However, we have tried to show how these different views are complementary. In our opinion, the argument that a particular indicator does not reflect the true movement in scarcity in most cases reflects a problem either with the question being asked or with the method of calculating the indicator, rather than with the type of indicator itself.

There are at least two meanings attached to the term 'scarcity' in the economic literature, which we name exchange scarcity and use scarcity. They relate to the Hotelling or Ricardian scarcity models. Rents and prices measure the private exchange scarcity of stocks and commodities, respectively, for those wishing to purchase them. They are not necessarily good measures of scarcity for society as a whole or for resource owners. Generalized GUC is a possible indicator of use scarcity, but it may not reflect downstream technical improvements in resource use, the possibility of non-linear utility functions or, as in the case of price, the impact of environmental damage associated with resource extraction on welfare. However, the calculated time series for GUC in US agriculture (Figure 10.1) does not show the fluctuations in response to economic events that are shown by the other indicators and so seems less problematic than the alternatives. Each indicator measures the aspect of scarcity for which it is designed.

ACKNOWLEDGMENTS

We thank V. Eldon Ball for providing us with the data.

NOTES

1. Barnett and Morse do not discuss the concept of value, whether use value or exchange value.
2. Throughout, 'capital' refers to manufactured capital; occasionally, we use the term 'natural capital' which can be understood as referring to the resource stock or resource base. Natural capital emphasizes the active contribution resource stocks play in production: for example, pressure in oil reservoirs forces oil to the surface.
3. Biophysical analysts have often argued that energy is the primary factor of production, and labour and capital are intermediate factors of production, while neoclassical economists are said to hold the opposing view. This is not a very good use of terminology. Capital stocks and labour are primary factors of production in the static production context because they are not produced within the production period. In most applications (with the exception of population economics and some recent endogenous growth theory), however, capital is treated as a reproducible factor and labour as a non-reproducible factor. However, the only truly non-reproducible factors are energy (energy vectors – fuels – are intermediate factors) and, as we argue here, information (in a certain sense).
4. Factor augmentation is a restriction on the nature of technological change. It specifies that technical change increases or decreases the effective quantity of each factor of production available per crude unit of the input used. The rates of change in the augmentation indices for different inputs can vary. Augmentation indices can be interpreted in terms of both qualitative changes in the inputs themselves and disembodied changes in the effectiveness of factor inputs. An example of a positive change of the former kind would be increases in the skills of workers and an example of a negative change would be land degradation. These changes could also be represented by changes in human capital or natural capital, respectively, if such direct data were available. Treating them as changes in technology is a neoclassical version of the way they would be treated in input–output analysis as changes in input–output coefficients.

REFERENCES

Abt, R.C. (1987), 'An analysis of regional factor demand in the U.S. lumber industry', *Forest Science*, 33, 164–73.

American Society of Agricultural Engineers (1985), *Erosion and Soil Productivity*, New Orleans: American Society of Agricultural Engineers.

Ayres, R.U. (1978) *Resources, Environment and Economics: Applications of the Materials/Energy Balance Principle*, New York: John Wiley.

Ball, V.E., J.-C. Bureau, R. Nehring and A. Somwaru (1995), 'Agricultural Productivity Revisited', United States Department of Agriculture, Washington, DC.

Barnett, H. and C. Morse (1963), *Scarcity and Growth: The Economics of Natural Resource Availability*, Baltimore: Johns Hopkins University Press.

Berck, P. and M. Roberts (1996), 'Natural resource prices: will they ever turn up?', *Journal of Environmental Economics and Management*, 31, 65–78.

Berndt, E.R. (1978), 'Aggregate energy, efficiency, and productivity measurement', *Annual Review of Energy*, 3, 225–73.

Berndt, E.R., C. Kolstad and J.K. Lee (1993), 'Measuring the energy efficiency and productivity impacts of embodied technical change', *Energy Journal*, 14, 33–55.

Brown, G.M. and B. Field (1979), 'The adequacy of scarcity measures for signaling the scarcity of natural resources', in V.K. Smith (ed.), *Scarcity and Growth Reconsidered*, Baltimore: Johns Hopkins University Press.

Brown, L.R. (1984), *Soil Erosion: Quiet Crisis in the World Economy*, Washington, DC: Worldwatch Institute.

Cairns, R.D. (1990), 'A contribution to the theory of depletable resource scarcity and its measures', *Economic Inquiry*, 28, 744–55.

Cleveland, C.J. (1991a), 'Natural resource scarcity and economic growth revisited: Economic and biophysical perspectives', in R. Costanza (ed.), *Ecological Economics: The Science and Management of Sustainability*, New York: Columbia University Press.

Cleveland, C.J. (1991b), 'Physical and economic aspects of resource quality: the cost of oil supply in the lower 48 United States, 1936–1988', *Resources and Energy*, 13, 163–88.

Cleveland, C.J. (1992), 'Energy quality and energy surplus in the extraction of fossil fuels in the U.S.', *Ecological Economics*, 6, 139–62.

Cleveland, C.J. (1993), 'An exploration of alternative measures of natural resource scarcity: the case of petroleum resources in the U.S.', *Ecological Economics*, 7, 123–57.

Cleveland, C.J. (1995a), 'Resource degradation, technical change, and the productivity of energy use in U.S. agriculture', *Ecological Economics*, 13, 185–201.

Cleveland, C.J. (1995b), 'The direct and indirect use of fossil fuels and electricity in USA agriculture, 1910–1990', *Agriculture, Ecosystems and the Environment*, 55, 111–21.

Cleveland, C.J. and D.I. Stern (1993), 'Productive and exchange scarcity: an empirical analysis of the U.S. forest products industry', *Canadian Journal of Forest Research*, 23, 1537–49.

Cleveland, C.J., R. Costanza, C.A.S. Hall and R. Kaufmann (1984), Energy and the U.S. economy: a biophysical perspective', *Science*, 255, 890–97.

Cole, K., J. Cameron and C. Edwards (1983), *Why Economists Disagree: The Political Economy of Economics*, New York: Longman.

Commons, J.R. (1934), *Institutional Economics*, New York: Macmillan.

Constantino, L.F. and D. Haley (1988), 'Wood quality and the input and output choices of sawmilling producers for the British Columbia coast and United States Pacific Northwest, west side', *Canadian Journal of Forest Research*, 18, 202–8.

Cook, E.F. (1976), 'Limits to the exploitation of nonrenewable resources', *Science*, 210, 1219–24.

Crosson, P.R. (1991), 'Cropland and soils: past performance and policy challenges', in K.D. Frederick and R.A. Sedjo (eds), *America's Renewable Resources*, Washington, DC: Resources for the Future.

Devarajan, S. and A.C. Fisher (1982), 'Exploration and scarcity', *Journal of Political Economy*, 90, 1279–90.

Ehrlich, P.R. and A.H. Ehrlich (1991), *Healing the Planet*, Reading, Mass.: Addison-Wesley.

Eltis, Walter (1984), *The Classical Theory of Economic Growth*, London: Macmillan.

Farzin, Y.H. (1992), 'The time path of scarcity rent in the theory of exhaustible resources', *Economic Journal*, 102, 813–31.

Farzin, Y.H. (1995), 'Technological change and the dynamics of resource scarcity measures', *Journal of Environmental Economics and Environmental Management*, 29, 105–20.

Fisher, A.C. (1979), 'Measures of natural resource scarcity', in V.K. Smith (ed.), *Scarcity and Growth Reconsidered*, Baltimore: Johns Hopkins University Press.

Follett, R.F. and B.A. Stewart (eds) (1985), *Soil Erosion and Crop Productivity*, Madison: Soil Science Society of America.

Gelb, B. (1984), 'A look at energy use in mining: it deserves it', International Association of Energy Economists, San Francisco.

Georgescu-Roegen, N. (1975), 'Energy and economic myths', *Southern Economic Journal*, 41, 347–81.

Gever, J., R. Kaufmann, D. Skole and C. Vorosmarty (1986), *Beyond Oil: The Threat to Food and Fuel in the Coming Decades*, Cambridge, Mass.: Ballinger.

Hall, C.A.S. and M.H.P. Hall (1993), 'The efficiency of land and energy use in tropical economies and agriculture', *Agriculture, Ecosystems and the Environment*, 46, 1–30.

Hall, C.A.S., C.J. Cleveland and R. Kaufmann (1986), *Energy and Resource Quality: The Ecology of the Economic Process*, New York: Wiley-Interscience.

Hall, D.C. and J.V. Hall (1984), 'Concepts and measures of natural resource scarcity with a summary of recent trends', *Journal of Environmental Economics and Management*, 11, 363–79.

Hall, D.C., J.V. Hall and D.X. Kolk (1984), 'Energy in the unit cost index to measure scarcity', *Energy*, 13, 281–6.

Hotelling, H. (1931), 'The economics of exhaustible resources', *Journal of Political Economy*, 39, 137–75.

Howe, C.W. (1979), *Natural Resource Economics*, New York: John Wiley.

Johnson, M.H., J.T. Bell and J.T. Bennett (1980), 'Natural resource scarcity: empirical evidence and public policy', *Journal of Environmental Economics and Management*, 7, 256–71.

Kaufmann, R.K. (1987), 'Biophysical and marxist economics: learning from each other', *Ecological Modelling*, 38, 91–105.

Kaufmann, R.K. (1994), 'The relation between marginal product and price in U.S. energy markets', *Energy Economics*, 16, 145–58.

Kaufmann, R.K. and C.J. Cleveland (1991), 'Policies to increase U.S. oil production: Likely to fail, damage the economy and damage the environment', *Annual Review of Energy and Environment*, 16, 379–400.

Lyon, K.S. (1981), 'Mining of the forest and the time path of the price of timber', *Journal of Environmental Economics and Management*, 8, 330–44.

Maddala, G.S. (1965), 'Productivity and technological change in the bituminous coal industry, 1919–1954', *Journal of Political Economy*, 73, 352–65.

Marx, K. (1867), *Capital: Volume I*; 1909 edition edited by Kerr (reference cited in Commons, 1934, p. 374).

Mattey, J.P. (1990), *The timber bubble that burst: government policy and the bailout of 1984*, New York: Oxford University Press.

Meadows, D.H., D.L. Meadows and J. Randers (1992), *Beyond The Limits*, London: Earthscan.

Merrifield, D.E. and R.W. Haynes (1985), 'A cost analysis of the lumber and plywood industries in two Pacific Northwest sub-regions', *Annals of Regional Science*, 19(3), 16–33.

Mitchell, C. and C.J. Cleveland (1992), 'Resource scarcity, energy use and environmental impact: A case study of the New Bedford, Massachusetts fisheries', *Environmental Management*, 17, 305–18.

Norgaard, R.B. (1975), 'Resource scarcity and new technology in U.S. petroleum development', *Natural Resources Journal*, 15, 265–82.

Norgaard, R.B. (1990), 'Economic Indicators of Resource Scarcity: A Critical Essay', *Journal of Environmental Economics and Management*, 19, 19–25.

Ozdemiroglu, E. (1993), 'Measuring natural resource scarcity: the study of the price indicator', working paper GEC 93-14, Centre for Social and Economic Research on the Global Environment, University of East Anglia, Norwich.

Pimentel, D. (ed.) (1993), *World Soil Erosion and Conservation*, Cambridge: Cambridge University Press.

Ruth, M. (1993), *Integrating Economics, Ecology and Thermodynamics*, Dordrecht: Kluwer Academic.

Ruth, M. (1995), 'Thermodynamic implications for natural resource extraction and technical change in U.S. copper mining', *Environmental and Resource Economics*, 6, 187–206.

Sedjo, R.A. and K.S. Lyon (1990), *The Long-Term Adequacy of World Timber Supply*, Washington, DC: Resources for the Future.

Slade, M.E. (1982), 'Trends in natural-resource commodity prices: An analysis of the time domain', *Journal of Environmental Economics and Management*, 9, 122–37.

Slade, M.E. (1985), 'Trends in natural-resource commodity prices: U-shaped price paths explored', *Journal of Environmental Economics and Management*, 12, 181–92.

Smith, V.K. (1979), 'Natural resource scarcity: a statistical analysis', *Review of Economics and Statistics*, 61, 423–7.

Smith, V.K. (1980), 'The evaluation of natural resource adequacy: elusive quest or frontier of economic analysis?', *Land Economics*, 56, 257–98.

Stern, D.I. (1993), 'Energy use and economic growth in the USA: a multivariate approach', *Energy Economics*, 15, 137–50.

Stern, D.I. (1994), 'Natural Resources as Factors of Production: Three Empirical Studies', PhD dissertation, Department of Geography, Boston University.

Stern, D.I. (1997), 'Limits to substitution and irreversibility in production and consumption: A neoclassical interpretation of ecological economics', *Ecological Economics*, 21, 197–215.

Stern D.I. (1999), 'Is energy cost an accurate indicator of natural resource quality?', *Ecological Economics*, 31, 381–94.

Stier, J.C. and D.N. Bengston (1992), 'Technical change in the North American forestry sector: A review', *Forest Science*, 38, 134–59.

Trueblood, M.A. and V.W. Ruttan (1995), 'A comparison of multifunction productivity calculations of the US agricultural sector', *Journal of Productivity Analysis*, 6, 321–31.

Uri, N.D. and R. Boyd (1995), 'Scarcity and growth revisited', *Environment and Planning A*, 27, 1815–32.

US Department of Agriculture (1994), 'Summary Report 1992 National Resources Inventory', Government Printing Office, Washington, DC.

11. Green national accounting: goals and methods

Robert Costanza, Steve Farber, Beatriz Castaneda and Monica Grasso

ECONOMIC INCOME, ECONOMIC WELFARE AND HUMAN WELFARE

The requirements for an aggregate accounting system depend upon the goals and objectives it is intended to serve. These goals and objectives include measuring (1) the level and pattern of economic activity; (2) sustainable economic income: the amount that can be consumed without depleting capital stocks (Hicks, 1946); (3) economic welfare: the net economic component of total welfare (Daly and Cobb, 1989); and (4) human welfare: the degree to which human needs are fulfilled (Max-Neef, 1992). This range of goals is arrayed in Figure 11.1 and Table 11.1. Economic income is a measure of the production and use of goods and services. There are variations (between columns 1–3 in Table 11.1) which have to do with the way environmental services, natural capital and other non-marketed items are dealt with. Figure 11.1 makes clear that economic income ultimately is generated from the stocks of both human-made and natural capital (the 'wealth' accounts) and that this income includes both marketed and non-marketed items. But conventional measures of marketed economic income and expenditure (GNP) do not adequately pick this up. Measures of *sustainable* economic income attempt to incorporate non-marketed natural capital changes. If it is assumed that natural and human-made capital are substitutable, the goal is to measure *weakly* sustainable income (Table 11.1, column 2). If it is assumed that natural and human-made capital are not substitutable in all cases, the goal is to measure *strongly* sustainable income (column 3).

But increases in economic *income* may not correlate with increases in economic *welfare*, especially if the income measures do not adequately distinguish 'costs' from 'benefits'. Economic welfare (column 4 of Table 11.1) attempts to look not just at how much income is generated, but also at how much economic welfare is produced. As shown in Figure 11.1, these measures

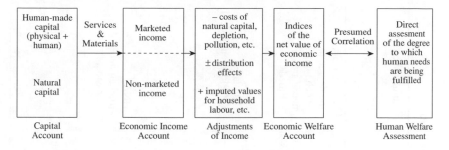

Figure 11.1   Distinctions between economic income, economic welfare and human welfare

generally adjust income to better reflect which items in the income measures are costs and benefits. They do this by subtracting costs (such as natural capital depletion and pollution), imputing values to missing services (such as household labour) and adjusting for income distribution effects using indices of income distribution.

Finally, economic welfare measured as the production of net benefits may still not correlate with overall human welfare, since many human needs are not related to consumption of economic products or services (Max-Neef, 1992). Human welfare (column 5 of Table 11.1) looks directly at the degree to which human needs are being met, the economic production involved being only one of many possible means to these ends. These distinctions and the specifics of measuring economic income, sustainable economic income, economic welfare and human welfare are further elaborated below.

DEFINING SUSTAINABLE ECONOMIC INCOME

The simplest objective for an aggregate accounting system is to develop an indicator of the production of goods and services in the economy for comparisons across either space or time. In order to avoid double counting, one can focus only on 'final' goods and services; that is, those which attain their final point of use during the accounting period, and are not intermediate in the sense of being destined for incorporation into further goods and services. As an accounting procedure, if production activity is fully compensated by monetary payments, either aggregate incomes obtained from production activity or aggregate expenditures can be used as an indicator. These two ways of measuring the total (income or expenditure) should be equal. This measure is referred to as gross national product (GNP: Table 11.1, column 1).

Table 11.1 A range of goals for national accounting and their corresponding frameworks and measures

Goal	Marketed (1)	Economic Income Weak sustainability (2)	Strong sustainability (3)	Economic Welfare (4)	Human Welfare (5)
Basic framework	Value of marketed goods and services produced and consumed in an economy	1 + non-marketed goods and services consumption	2 + preservation of essential natural capital	Value of the wefare effects of income and other factors (including distribution, household work, loss of natural capital, etc.)	Assessment of the degree to which human needs are fulfilled
Non-environmentally adjusted measures	GNP (gross national product) GDP (gross domestic product) NNP (net national product)			MEW (measure of economic welfare)	HDI (Human Development Index)
Environmentally adjusted measures	NNP' (net national product including non-produced assets)	ENNP (environmental net national product) SEEA (system of environmental economic accounts)	SNI (sustainable national income) SEEA (system of environmental economic accounts)	ISEW (Index of Sustainable Economic Welfare)	HNA (human needs assessment)

'Accounting income' is simply the sum of monetary payments to owners of the inputs used in production during an accounting period. This income concept is distinguished from 'Hicksian income', defined as 'the maximum value which [a man] can consume during a week, and still expect to be as well off at the end of the week as he was at the beginning' (Hicks, 1946). While both income concepts are flows, the Hicksian concept is a flow of consumption value which is sustainable, and not simply a measure of accounting income flowing into the household. When we interpret capital, K, as the total stock of productive capacity which generates flows of goods and services, the value of the flow of consumable goods and services, G, during a given accounting period is:

$$G = rK, \qquad (11.1)$$

where r is the rate of return, or productivity, of that capital stock. The maximum *sustainable* flow of consumables, Hicksian income, H, requires the maintenance of the productive capacity of the capital stock. Sustainable income is then:

$$H = G - R, \qquad (11.2)$$

where R represents the cost of capital stock maintenance. This cost may include a variety of defensive actions which maintain effective capital stock, such as replacement, repair and maintenance. It also includes avoidance costs which are designed to avoid losses in capital productivity. Replacing a worn-out machine is included in R, but so are medical expenditures for repairing worn-out human capital, food and shelter expenses necessary to maintain human capital, crime costs necessary for the repair and avoidance of degradation in cultural capital, the pollution control costs necessary to avoid destruction of natural capital, such as air and water, or the costs of replacing harvested timber stocks or depleted mineral resources. This suggests that R is a very broad concept not limited to reconstitution of traditional human-made, physical capital.

Goods and services are produced and used for a variety of purposes. For simplicity, they are divided between consumption (C) and gross investment in the capital stock (I), where the latter is undertaken for maintenance and growth of capital stock. Capital stock can be interpreted most broadly as the complete source of the flows of goods and services produced; that is, both human-made (buildings, machines and so on), human (knowledge and structure), cultural and natural (resources and environment). Consumption can be interpreted most broadly as the final use of any type of good or service produced within the human economy, but not limited to marketed items. Then the gross national product of the economy is:

$$G = C + I. \qquad (11.3)$$

The highest level of C which is permanently sustainable under a competitive economy with perfect foresight[1] has been shown by Weitzman (1976) to equal:

$$H = C + p\Delta K, \tag{11.4}$$

where ΔK is the *net* change in capital stock, that is, new capital minus loss of old capital, and p is the price of capital goods relative to consumption goods. The essence of the proof is that ΔK reflects annualized, optimized consumption opportunities in the future obtained from the net increases in capital stocks under competitive economy conditions. Under Weitzman's assumptions, H is a measure of Hicksian income. Both (11.2) and (11.4) can be used as a conceptual basis for estimating Hicksian income.

H (sustainable income) is a welfare indicator only insofar as welfare is correlated with the consumption of goods and services, C. It is a net income indicator in the sense of reflecting net benefits from production activity since costs of replacing or avoiding wearing out capital stock, including human capital, are included. Furthermore, it is an indicator of maximum sustainable income only insofar as all the conditions for Weitzman's (1976) proof hold, namely:

1. all capital stocks that affect the production of C must be included in measures of ΔK;
2. p must reflect the productivity, or shadow, value of capital;
3. the optimality conditions which underlie a competitive economy must hold, including equalities on the margins between the relative values of capital stocks and their productivities, and between interest rates and price changes in capital stocks.

Real economies are far from satisfying these conditions.

'Green Accounting' has emerged to address deficiencies in using traditionally measured GNP and NNP (net national product) to reflect the availability and production of goods and services and sustainable income, respectively. GNP measures only market-transacted goods and services. GNP is less than G, insofar as goods and services are produced which are not transacted in markets. This misrepresentation is especially troublesome for a variety of environmental and ecological goods and services (Costanza *et al.* 1997). Exclusion of these goods not only leads to an underestimate of available goods and services, it is also likely to lead to misrepresentations of the change in availability over time: overestimating change when ecological destruction diminishes their natural production, and underestimating change as the relative values of these unmarketed ecologically based goods and services increase with economic development and scarcity.

NNP has many problems as an indicator of sustainable income. First, since it is derived from GNP it suffers from the same exclusion of non-marketed goods and services. Second, it is a poor sustainability indicator since it does not fully account for the costs related to degradation of all capital forms. This is especially troublesome for human and natural capital. Third, it is deficient as a welfare indicator since it does not allow for the distinction between production of 'bads' and 'goods'. A welfare indicator would subtract the value of 'bads', such as unremediated adverse pollution-related health costs, or include as costs of capital replacement or maintenance the cost of offsetting adverse effects on natural capital. Costs incurred to offset 'bads' can be considered necessary to repair potentially degraded capital: human, cultural or natural. As a welfare measure, these costs should be deducted from gross production to establish net welfare. For example, both medical and police expenditures create benefits, but the benefits are to offset or avoid some of the potential costs of the activities that induce them, these potential costs being interpretable as losses in human and cultural capital. For this reason, it is useful in developing a welfare indicator to distinguish 'defensive' goods and services from other final goods and services, and to deduct defensive expenditures as costs of maintaining capital stocks (see the following sections).

The problem in adjusting for defensive expenditures is distinguishing between 'offensive' and 'defensive' expenditures. For example, medical expenses may be purely to offset adverse consequences of economic activity, and to permit the maintenance of original welfare levels; that is, to fully repair or avoid degrading human capital. On the other hand, some medical expenses may truly result in improvements in welfare above original levels; that is, they may create a net investment in human capital stock. In practice, distinguishing between these two types of expenditures, one welfare-enhancing and the other welfare-maintaining, is difficult, to say the least. Furthermore, there may be costs associated with economic activities that are not mitigated by defensive expenditures. For example, untreated health costs from pollution, or work days lost from pollution, are not explicit defensive expenditures. Increased time costs necessary to catch recreational fish, or diminished recreational enjoyment attributable to a degraded watershed, do not have explicit defensive expenditures that can be observed and used for adjusting GNP. These costs would have to be deducted from income to obtain a net income measure, since they do not reflect positive utility-creating consumables. Explicitly defensive expenditures, such as the increased travel time costs necessary to use an adequate recreational facility when a previously used one becomes too degraded for use, should be deducted from income as costs. However, traditional accounting would add them into income, erroneously suggesting welfare improvements.

Even if adjustments to income can be made to include natural capital, and the shadow values of that capital for valuation purposes are known, there is an additional important theoretical problem associated with using NNP as a sustainable income indicator. The competitive economy conditions necessary for $H = C + p\Delta K$ to reflect maximum sustainable consumption do not hold if those shadow values are not explicitly considered in production and use decisions. Weitzman's (1976) proof that NNP measures sustainable income requires these conditions. This is important since there is no assurance that $p\Delta K$ would reflect future consumption opportunities. While the necessary conditions may hold for some types of natural capital, especially those which are privately owned and sold in markets (oil, gold, timber and so on), they are not likely to hold for 'public goods'-type natural capital stocks or stocks which have public goods service flows. The latter stocks are unlikely to have use prices that reflect their values. Unless there is public restriction on use, they are not likely to be managed to sustain a maximum flow of production. Open access capital without sufficient property rights limitations represents this class of problem. In these cases, even if C and ΔK are comprehensive, and a shadow value of capital goods, p, was correctly employed in (11.4), NNP overstates maximum sustainable consumption. An adjustment to measured NNP must be made for the current overuse of natural capital stocks relative to future use, and this is above and beyond any adjustments simply for the depreciation or degradation of that capital (Hartwick, 1991).

Weitzman's (1976) concept of welfare is consumption-based and increases one-for-one (monotonically) with increases in the magnitude of consumables, C. Another potential welfare concept is net benefit, defined approximately as the sum of producer and consumer surpluses arising from the production and consumption of C. This concept reflects the net surplus, that is, the difference between benefits and costs, from C. This surplus depends on both the value of goods and services produced and their costs of production. Although the concept can be made analytically rigorous, implementation as a real-world measurement is problematic. One has to know the full range of both demand and supply functions, when we are likely to know only the prices and quantities around equilibrium and, at most, elasticities around equilibrium. Furthermore, some essential or critical goods, such as air and water, will have infinite total value, although on the margin their value may be finite. Perhaps the closest realistic approximation to the net benefit concept of welfare is GNP itself: cost of production. Since GNP is effectively the aggregation of prices times quantities, this approximation assumes no consumer surplus. Although it would not be a good indicator of the level of net benefit, changes in this welfare concept may be a reasonable indicator of welfare change over time as long as quantities of essential or critical goods do not fall below their threshold levels. But using net benefit as an indicator of sustainable welfare would require that cost of production include the same types of capital repair, replacement and maintenance cost adjustments as estimation of NNP. In addition, it would also require special adjustments when natural capital stocks fall below threshold levels for maintaining a flow of critical goods or services. In this case, Hueting's (1980) cost of preserving a sustainable level of ecosystem function might provide the necessary adjustment measure.

MEASURING SUSTAINABLE ECONOMIC INCOME

To summarize, within the goal of measuring sustainable economic income, we can distinguish three measurement situations. The first arises when we wish to focus solely on incomes generated through marketed goods and services. The basic framework is simply the aggregate of market values of these goods and services. The gross measure is traditional GNP; its sustainable counterpart is NNP = GNP: human-made capital depreciation. Human-made capital depreciation is measurable as the decline in market value of capital, or the cost of replacing comparable capital, the two being equalized by capital markets. Of course, NNP is not necessarily a measure of sustainable incomes, for all the reasons noted above. An adjustment to NNP can be made for the net depreciation of marketed natural capital stocks, such as minerals, timber and fisheries: NNP' = NNP – Net Depreciation and Depletion of Marketed Natural Capital. This adjustment would equal the difference in the value of additions to natural capital stock minus depletions of natural capital stock; it could be positive or negative.

We can distinguish between two types of marketed natural capital: depletables and non-depletables. These terms are both slightly misleading, since depletables, such as oil, can be replaced by new discoveries, and non-depletables, such as trees, can be exhausted. The essence of adjustment for sustainable income estimation purposes is to deduct from current values of production of goods and services an amount sufficient to cover the costs of maintaining that income. This is relatively simple for human-made capital since it requires a deduction for the value of goods and services necessary to replicate, repair or maintain potentially degraded capital stocks. While the principle of adjustment is the same for human-made and natural capital stock depreciation and depletion, the actual adjustment is more complicated for natural capital stocks.

The method of adjustment depends on the cheapest manner in which the lost productive capacity of the natural capital stock can be replaced. Take oil, for example. Several options exist for replacement of depleted oil stocks: new discoveries, replacement by other capital forms such as renewable energy, and increased energy efficiencies of human-made capital. In principle, even substitution across consumables of varying energy intensities will offset depletion, albeit at a cost of reduction in utility. All options require the shifting of productive capacities away from non-oil-related goods if the existing capital stock is to sustain production levels. The cheapest method of replacement of depleted capital stock will vary across time and resource endowments of various countries. A practical method for this adjustment assumes that the income-creating potential of depleted oil stocks equals their net price (price minus extraction cost), and that the net depletion of this value can be replaced elsewhere in the economy. This is referred to as the net price adjustment method.

If depletions of capital stock equalled new discoveries (with extraction costs constant) over a period, there would be no need to adjust currently for capital depletion. This means that, when resources are abundant relative to usage rates, there is no practical necessity of adjusting for natural capital depletion. Short of this extreme case, if there were anticipated reductions in incomes from potential exhaustion, the current account adjustment would be the value of production shifts necessary to offset that reduction. For example, using renewable energy replacement, a cost of planting trees sufficient to offset future depleted fossil fuel would be the necessary adjustment. This is the user cost adjustment suggested by El Serafy (1989).

Non-depletable capital yields a sustainable product under proper use. Timber and fishery harvests are potentially sustainable if forest and fishery capital stocks remain intact. Harvesting beyond the sustainable yield depletes the capital stock, which may take some time to regenerate itself, even if depletion is not extreme. Reductions in yields can be replaced by allowing time for regeneration. When trees are harvested beyond their sustainable yields, the stumpage value (in situ price excluding harvest cost) of net reductions in forest stock can be used as the adjustment to NNP. Alternatively, the discounted value of forgone income during the time it would take for the tree stock to be replaced up to pre-depletion levels can be the adjustment.[2] The first adjustment is a net price and the second a user cost method. Green accounting adjustments for full income require valuations of income flows from natural capital. A variety of methods can be used for this estimation, depending on the type of income received. Table 11.2 outlines some of these valuation methods.

Substitution of Capital Forms and Income Accounting

The estimation of sustainable incomes depends on the cost adjustments for losses in capital used in generating that income. Cost adjustments are relatively simple for human-made capital since it is, by definition, replicable at a cost. Observations on the decline in its market value are sufficient for estimating its cost of replacement since price of capital and replacement cost will be roughly similar. Green accounting, however, is particularly concerned with loss of natural capital during use. The adjustment measure for sustainable income is always some type of future incomes lost or cost necessary to replace or avoid the loss or degradation of capital productivity. In the case of natural capital, these costs are more difficult to measure. This is true for several reasons.

1. There are no well-functioning markets for measuring prices of all natural capital forms.
2. There are no well-functioning markets that would equate price of natural capital with replacement cost.
3. Natural capital productivity is more complex and less amenable to measurement than human-made capital.
4. The productive state, or health, of natural capital is more difficult to measure than that of human-made capital.

Table 11.2   Valuation techniques for some environmental functions

Functions	Valuation technique

System values
  Erosion control
  Local flood reduction
  Regulation of streamflows
	Change in productivity, preventive expenditure, trade-off games, cost effectiveness analyses, replacement cost

Ecological values
  Fixing and cycling nutrients
  Soil formation
  Cleansing air and water
	Change in productivity, loss of earnings, opportunity cost, trade-off games, cost-effective analysis, replacement cost

Biodiversity
  Gene resource
  Species protection
	Opportunity cost, cost-effective analysis, replacement cost, shadow project, relocation cost

Aesthetic	Property value, wage differential
Recreational	Travel cost
Cultural	Travel cost

Source: Modified from Dixon (1990).

Of course, these difficulties of measurement vary across natural capital forms, being less problematic when the predominance of goods and service flows from capital are marketable and that capital has well-defined markets which fully capture these marketable flows. This is most likely the case for mineral resources, although even they suffer from problems of measuring depletion. These difficulties are most severe for ecosystems, which provide a variety of goods and services in a complex manner. Forests and wetlands are good examples, both representing complex ecosystems where measurements of health and productivity are complicated, where some goods and service flows are marketable and others are not, and where private market values of the capital forms do not necessarily reflect their value or cost of replacement (Daily, 1997; Costanza *et al.*, 1997).

Adjustments to income for sustainability can be of two types: costs required and benefits lost. The most intuitive adjustment is cost-based and presumes a portion of income necessary either to mitigate actual or to avoid potential income losses due to capital loss or degradation. This can be for replacement, repair or maintenance of any forms of capital stock sufficient to replace potential income losses. It can include actions on the same type of capital as that which is being lost or degraded (replace a tree with a tree), or substitute capital forms which would yield the same types of incomes (replace lost oil reserves with trees for energy), or substitute capital forms which yield different types of incomes (replace fish used for food with trees used for shelter). These substitutabilities may appear to ease the burden of mitigation and avoidance adjustment estimation.

The second type of adjustment is benefits-based; it presumes that a portion of income is not sustainable owing to the loss or degradation of capital. In this case, estimates must be made of the benefits lost from non-sustainable capital conditions. For example, suppose a fishery is harvested at 140 tons per year and existing stock will only support a sustained yield of 100 tons per year. Forty tons of current income is not sustainable and a benefits-based adjustment requires that the value of the excess be subtracted from current yield to obtain the sustainable catch of 100 tons per year. Alternatively, a cost-based adjustment would consider that the fish stock will be depleted by 40 tons and the cost of replacing that stock is the adjustment. If the capital was managed in a socially optimal manner, the replacement cost and the value of the fish harvested would be identical, so the cost-based and benefits-based adjustments would be the same. Replacement cost in this case would be the value of reduced catch necessary to build up the stock to its original level. Stock build-up may have to occur slowly over time, so discounted lost catch would be appropriate.

What type of adjustment is most appropriate when the two possible adjustment measures differ substantially? For example, suppose the fishery is exhausted through overharvesting and is irreplaceable through any other form of capital: that is, replacement costs are infinite. Income adjustment will have to be deductions for incomes from fisheries which are not sustainable; that is, a benefits-based adjustment. The essential principle of adjustment is that the lesser of the cost or benefits-based measures should be used for adjustment. This principle is required for the resulting income to reflect the *highest* level of consumption which can be sustained.

Weak v. Strong Sustainability

The sustainability of income requires replacement, or avoidance of loss, of some forms of capital sufficient to maintain consumption opportunities. This means substitutability plays a crucial role in implementing any sustainable income adjustments to GNP. 'Weak' sustainability requires maintenance of the total capital stock. It assumes a high degree of substitutability between all forms of capital. 'Strong' sustainability presumes limited substitutability between natural capital and other capital forms; therefore strong sustainability requires the maintenance of some natural capital separately from other capital forms (Costanza and Daly, 1992; Pearce, 1993; El Serafy, 1996).

A wide range of replacement cost options are available under the weak sustainability case, including the forms of capital lost or degraded as well as substitute forms of capital. In the case of strong sustainability, degraded natural capital must be replaced in comparable form. There is no well-defined line dividing the two cases of weak and strong sustainability. The essence of the distinction relies on the ability of various capital forms to provide a flow of income: that is, the degree of substitutability between capital forms. There are no reasonable substitute capital forms for those types of natural capital which provide basic life support functions on large spatial and temporal scales (such as availability of the proper mix of ambient gases, hydrologic flows and protection from ultraviolet rays), although there may be substitutability on small scales.

Identifying strong sustainability may be as much a social notion as a physical one. A society may need to identify a level of natural capital beyond which it will not substitute. For example, it will not accept any change in the global ecosystem that would alter temperatures more than x degrees; or it will not accept any degradation in forest health beyond some measurable level. Such constraints state that there are (or should be) no trade-offs beyond these levels. In these cases, society invokes strong sustainability by definition. Accounting adjustments for degradation beyond these points require estimates of costs of repair to acceptable levels. For example, if a minimum level of wetlands health is defined as a lower-bound measure of habitat suitability, any degradation below that level will require adjusting income for the cost of repair. This cost of repair may be engineering costs of wetlands mitigation. If engineering methods will not successfully repair the damages, and natural processes will, some accounting must be made for income losses attributable to not using those wetlands during their natural regeneration period.

Accounting for the cost of repair of natural capital degraded beyond the acceptable limit is complicated by the likely long period required for repair. If degradation can be remedied by a one-year sacrifice in use, or one year's engineering costs, the sustainability adjustment is simply a deduction from current incomes for those costs. However, suppose it takes many accounting periods for repair. The adjustment would then seek to establish the portion of current incomes which must be set aside and dedicated to repair: that is, the value of the sinking fund. This would be the present value of engineering costs if engineering is the most credible method of repair; or the present value of loss of use costs (reduced incomes) while waiting for the system to repair itself naturally.

The environmental net national product (ENNP) (Mäler, 1991; Hamilton and Lutz, 1996) and the United Nations' System of Environmental Economic Accounts (SEEA – Bartelmus, 1994) are both measures which account for weak sustainability. Accounting for strong sustainability requires adjusting for the cost of returning specific forms of degraded natural capital to their 'acceptable' conditions (Hueting 1989). The sustainable national income (SNI – Hueting, 1995) and some versions of the SEEA incorporate this perspective.

MEASURING ECONOMIC WELFARE

So far we have been discussing various measures of economic income, with various adjustments for the sustainability of that income. Column 4 of Table 11.1 moves from the goal of economic income assessment to the goal of economic welfare assessment. The latter goal is more complex and requires clearly distinguishing between costs and benefits. While this distinction between costs and benefits is absolutely essential if one wants to talk about welfare rather than income, it is inherently a difficult and at least to some extent subjective and arbitrary distinction.

Nordhaus and Tobin (1972) produced an early version of this kind of indicator in their measure of economic welfare (MEW). MEW starts with GNP and makes three types of adjustments: 'Reclassification of GNP expenditures as consumption, investment, and intermediate; imputation for the services of consumer capital, for leisure, and for the product of household work; and a correction for some of the disamenities of urbanization' (ibid., p. 5). Some expenditures are regrettable necessities rather than contributions to welfare. MEW subtracts the costs of police services, sanitation services, road maintenance and national defence from GNP. All of these costs lead to increases in traditionally measured GNP, but they do not mean that more human wants are being satisfied. Rather, we can think of them as portions of the production stream necessary to repair, replace, maintain and avoid the loss of various capital forms. MEW then makes appropriate imputations for capital services, leisure and non-market work. Finally, MEW recognizes that there are negative 'externalities' connected with economic growth, such as congestion and commuting, and that these are most apparent in urban life: 'Some portion of the higher earnings of urban residents may be simply compensation for the disamenities of urban life and work. If so, we should not count as a sign of welfare the full increments of NNP that result from moving a man from farm or small town to city' (ibid., p. 13). Commuting costs are deducted from incomes as a cost of economic activity.

MEW focuses on the aggregation of individual welfare; that is, it is 'atomistic'. It does not include any adjustments for distributional effects. Nor does it include any adjustments for environmental costs. Daly and Cobb (1989) developed an Index of Sustainable Economic Welfare (ISEW) which takes consumption as a starting point, but incorporates some of the environmental and distributional issues ignored by MEW. To summarize these changes, ISEW

1. allows for an income distribution adjustment;
2. includes changes in the stock of fixed reproducible capital but excludes land and human capital in this calculation;
3. includes estimates for the costs of air, water and noise pollution;
4. includes estimates of costs of the loss of wetlands and farmlands, depletion of non-renewable resources, commuting, urbanization, car accidents, advertising and long-term environmental damage;
5. omits any imputation of the value of leisure;
6. includes imputed values for unpaid household labour.

Daly and Cobb (1989) and Cobb and Cobb (1994) calculated ISEW for the US economy for the period 1950–93. Other researchers have estimated ISEW for several other countries. Indices of ISEW for these several cases are shown in Figure 11.2, along with GNP indices for the same countries. In most of these cases, ISEW and GNP per capita run parallel for some initial period, but separate during the 1970s and 1980s. Max-Neef (1995) has postulated that this separation is evidence for a 'threshold hypothesis' that growth of economic income increases welfare only until a threshold is reached where the costs of additional growth (which are counted as benefits in GNP) begin to outweigh the real benefits. Nordhaus and Tobin (1972) calculated their MEW in 1972 before the threshold was reached, concluding that GNP was an adequate proxy for economic welfare.

While ISEW is certainly far from being a perfect measure of economic welfare, it is decidedly better than GNP for this purpose. This is because, as we have pointed out, GNP is not a welfare measure at all, but only an income measure.

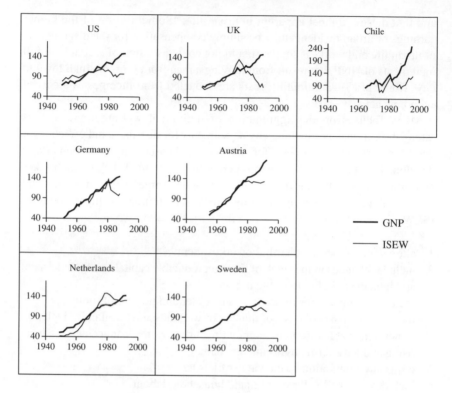

Figure 11.2   Indices of GNP and ISEW for several countries (1970 = 100 in all cases)

ASSESSING HUMAN WELFARE DIRECTLY

While the ISEW provides a measure of environmentally adjusted economic welfare, it is still based on measuring how much is being consumed, with the tacit assumption that more consumption leads to more welfare. ISEW at least adjusts for the desirability of this consumption, its negative impacts on natural capital, its distribution across income classes, and makes other reasonable adjustments. This is certainly an improvement on economic income measures like GNP and one that tells a very different story about recent changes in aggregate economic welfare.

A completely different approach, however, would be to look directly at the actual well-being that is achieved: to separate the means (consumption) from the ends (well-being) without assuming one is correlated with the other

(Figure 11.1). Some have begun to look at the problem from this perspective. The United Nations' Human Development Index (HDI) is a crude attempt to assess some of these basic needs with an index made up of generally available data on four variables at the country level: (1) life expectancy at birth, (2) literacy, (3) average number of years of schooling, and (4) GDP per capita (converted at purchasing power parity). These are combined into an overall index. Although this includes more than economic income by adding the other three elements, it is still based on 'means' assessment and excludes any measures of environmental degradation. Manfred Max-Neef (1992) has developed a matrix of human needs and has begun to address well-being more directly from the 'ends' perspective by involving people in interactive dialogues to perform a human needs assessment (HNA). The key idea is that humans do not have primary needs for the products of the economy; the economy is only a means to an end. The end is the satisfaction of primary human needs. Food and shelter are ways of satisfying the need for subsistence. Insurance systems are ways to meet the need for protection. Religion is a means to meet the need for identity. Max-Neef suggests:

> Having established a difference between the concepts of needs and satisfiers it is possible to state two postulates: first, fundamental human needs are finite, few and classifiable; second, fundamental human needs (such as those contained in the system proposed) are the same in all cultures and in all historical periods. What changes, both over time and through cultures, is the way or the means by which the needs are satisfied. (1992, pp. 199–200)

This is a very different conceptual framework from the others in Table 11.1, which assume that human desires are infinite and that, all else being equal, more consumption is always better. According to the alternative conceptual well-being framework, we should be directly measuring how well basic human needs are being satisfied since overall human well-being and consumption are not necessarily correlated and may in fact be going in opposite directions. Quantifying HNA is, however, even more difficult than HDI or ISEW or other 'means'-based measures, especially across time and between different countries – those conditions for which we would most like to have the quantifications for comparisons. This is obviously an area in need of much further research.

PRACTICAL LIMITATIONS, CASE STUDIES AND UNCERTAINTY

Several countries around the world have begun implementation of various versions of the indicators in Table 11.1. The ISEW has been calculated for the

United States, the United Kingdom, the Netherlands, Austria, Germany, Sweden, Australia and Chile. The UN's SEEA is being implemented in several countries including Mexico, Chile, Papua New Guinea, Japan, Korea, Indonesia, Colombia, Thailand, the Philippines and Costa Rica. In addition to conceptual matters,[3] practical limitations and data availability limit what can be done. In Chile, as in other countries where the SEEA is being implemented, the programme consists of four components: (1) creation of man-made and natural capital balance sheets, (2) creation of matrices of environmental externalities of economic activities and mitigation costs, (3) identification of defensive expenditures, and (4) economic valuation of natural resources and the environment. Initial implementation focused on the forestry, mining and fisheries sectors. These three sectors account for 50 per cent of total exports, 34 per cent of which are mineral exports, and together they contribute 16 per cent to total value added (Claude and Pizarro, 1995). Initial data on the changes in the volume of native forest indicate that Chile has lost between 400 000 and 900 000 ha. of native forest in the period 1985–94, mainly as a result of the substitution of monospecific plantations of pine and eucalyptus for native forest, clearing for agriculture and fires. The native forest is expected to be completely depleted in 20 to 25 years if current trends continue. Even this relatively straightforward physically based resource assessment caused controversy, largely because it exposed information about depletion rates of native forests. The indicators in Table 11.1 involve controversial valuation assumptions and uncertainties and will be even more difficult to implement in the existing institutional setting of many countries. What is needed are clear goals at the policy level taking account of the distinctions in Table 11.1, and a much more collaborative approach which can involve all the major stakeholder groups in a truly 'integrated assessment' (Costanza and Tognetti, 1999). This approach can illuminate and communicate the uncertainties involved, rather than ignoring them, and ultimately can help to build a broad consensus about the various goals of green accounting, the appropriate data collection and valuation methods, and practical steps towards implementation.

CONCLUSIONS

By arraying the range of possible goals for green accounting against the various frameworks which have been suggested, we have sought to clarify some of the confusion over these issues. All of the goals listed in Table 11.1 are important, but one must be clear about which goal one is pursuing. Economic income measures can certainly be improved, and some argue that this should be our first priority. As one moves to the right in Table 11.1, the suggested changes become more controversial and difficult, but also, many would argue, more relevant. We can make better decisions about our current status and future directions as a society using the whole array of green accounting indicators listed in Table 11.1 in an informed and intelligent way, being fully aware of the range of goals, methods and practical solutions.

We are still in the early stages of green accounting. Real progress is being made on several fronts, and the results have started to affect the policy debate in several countries, but we still have a long way to go before green accounting measures are being routinely used for informing public perception of economic performance and national policy. The technical barriers to making this change (while formidable) are not nearly as great as the political ones.

It must also be remembered that income accounting is only a static and retrospective picture of where the economy has been. It must be used in conjunction with more prospective techniques such as cost–benefit analysis, multi-criteria analysis and dynamic modelling in order for us to make intelligent choices about our common future.

ACKNOWLEDGMENTS

This chapter is a product of a workshop held at the World Bank in Washington, DC, 20–22 March 1996, with the following participants: Max Aguero, Edward Barbier, Peter Bartelmus, Beatriz Castaneda, Gerardo Castro, Clovis Cavalcanti, Robert Costanza, Marcel Claude, Herman Daly, John Dixon, Salah El Serafy, Steve Farber, Monica Grasso, Kirk Hamilton, Roefie Hueting, Mark Kenber, Ernst Lutz, Manfred Max-Neef, Peter May, Hans Opschoor, Olga Perez, Charles Perrings, Rodrigo Pizarro. The workshop was jointly sponsored by the International Society for Ecological Economics, the Indicators and Environmental Valuation Unit of the Environment Department of the World Bank, and the University of Maryland Institute for Ecological Economics, with funding support from the MacArthur Foundation. We also thank Peter Victor and one anonymous reviewer for helpful comments on an earlier draft. The authors are, of course, responsible for any errors or omissions.

NOTES

1. Ignoring for the moment that no such economy exists.
2. This, of course, assumes that one knows the appropriate discount rate for making these adjustments. There is much controversy on this issue and it is difficult (if not impossible) to determine what this rate should be.
3. One additional caveat should be mentioned as regards all proposed green accounting measures that include components that use market prices. This is that, if the problems that are being addressed by the various green accounting modifications did not exist, all market prices would be different, and to varying degrees. So making adjustments to GNP by adding and subtracting various quantities without also adjusting GNP itself to account for the expected price changes is a problem. Addressing this problem is required for theoretical consistency, but it is beyond the capabilities of most proposed green accounting systems.

REFERENCES

Aylward, B.A. and E.B. Barbier (1992), 'Valuing environmental functions in developing countries', *Biodiversity and Conservation*, 1, 34–50.

Barde, J-P. and D.W. Pearce (1991), *Valuing the Environment: Six Case Studies*, London: Earthscan.

Bartelmus, P. (1994), 'Towards a Framework for Indicators of Sustainable Development', Department for Economic and Social Information and Policy Analysis, Working Paper Series No. 7, New York: United Nations.

Bartelmus, P. and J. van Tongeren (1994), 'Environmental accounting: an operational perspective', DESIPA Working Paper 1, New York: United Nations.

Claude, M. and R. Pizarro (1995), 'The Chilean Environmental Accounts Project: Theoretical Framework and Results', unpublished manuscript, Banco Central de Chile.

Cobb, C. and J. Cobb (1994), *The Green National Product: A proposed Index of Sustainable Economic Welfare*, New York: University Press of America.

Costanza, R. and H.E. Daly (1992), 'Natural capital and sustainable development', *Conservation Biology*, 6, 37–46.

Costanza, R. and S. Tognetti (eds) (1999), *Ecological Economics and Integrated Assessment: a Participatory Framework for Including Fairness, Efficiency and Scale in Decision-making*, SCOPE.

Costanza, R., S.C. Farber and J. Maxwell (1989), 'The valuation and management of wetland ecosystems', *Ecological Economics*, 1, 335–361.

Costanza, R., R. d'Arge, R. de Groot, S. Farber, M. Grasso, B. Hannon, S. Naeem, K. Limburg, J. Paruelo, R.V. O'Neill, R. Raskin, P. Sutton and M. van den Belt (1997), 'The value of the world's ecosystem services and natural capital', *Nature*, 387, 253–60.

Daily, G. (ed.) (1997), *Nature's Services: Societal Dependence on Natural Ecosystems*, Washington, DC: Island Press.

Daly, H.E. and J. Cobb (1989), *For the Common Good: Redirecting the Economy Towards Community, the Environment and a Sustainable Future*, Boston: Beacon Press.

Dixon, J.A. and M.M. Hufschmidt (1986), *Economic valuation techniques for the environment: a case study workbook*, Baltimore: Johns Hopkins University Press.

Dixon, J. and P.B. Sherman (1990), *Economics of Protected Areas: A New Look at Benefits and Costs*, Washington, DC: Island Press.

Dixon, J.A. *et al.* (1994), *Economic Analysis of Environmental Impacts*, 2nd edn, London: Earthscan.

El Serafy, S. (1989), 'The proper calculation of income from depletable natural resources', in Y.J. Ahmad, S. El Serafy and E. Lutz (eds), *Environmental Accounting for Sustainable Development*, Washington, DC: World Bank.

El Serafy, S. (1996), 'In defense of weak sustainability: a response to Beckerman', *Environmental Value*, 5, 75–81.

Goulder, L.H. and D. Kennedy (1996), 'Valuing ecosystem services', in G. Daily (ed.), *Ecosystem Services: Their Nature and Value*, Washington, DC: Island Press.

Gregory, R., S. Lichtenstein and P. Slovic (1993), 'Valuing Environmental Resources: a Constructive Approach', *Journal of Risk and Uncertainty*, 7, 177–97.

Hamilton, K. and E. Lutz (1996), 'Green national accounts: policy uses and empirical experience', Environment Department Paper No. 039, Washington, DC: World Bank.

Hartwick, John M. (1991), 'Degradation of environmental capital and national accounting procedures', *European Economic Review*, 35 (2/3), 642–9.

Hicks, John R. (1946), *Value and Capital*, Oxford: Oxford University Press.

Hueting, R. (1980), *New Scarcity and Economic Growth*, Amsterdam: North-Holland.

Hueting, R. (1989), 'Correcting national income for environmental losses: toward a practical solution, in Y.J. Ahman, S. El Serafy and E. Lutz (eds), *Environmental Accounting for Sustainable Development*, Washington, DC: World Bank.

Hueting, R. (1995), 'Estimating sustainable national income', in W. van Dieren (ed.), *Taking Nature into Account: Toward a Sustainable National Income*, New York: Springer-Verlag.

Lutz, E. (ed.) (1993), *Toward Improved Accounting for the Environment*, Washington, DC: World Bank.

Mäler, K-G. (1991), 'National accounts and environmental resources', *Environmental and Resource Economics*, 1, 1–15.

Max-Neef, M. (1992), 'Development and human needs', in P. Ekins and M. Max-Neef (eds), *Real-life Economics: Understanding Wealth Creation*, London: Routledge.

Max-Neef, M. (1995), 'Economic growth, carrying capacity and the environment: a response', *Ecological Economics*, 15, 115–18.

Mitchell, R.C. and R.T. Carson (1989), *Using Surveys to Value Public Goods: the Contingent Valuation Method*, Washington, DC: Resources for the Future.

Nordhaus, W. and J. Tobin (1972), 'Is growth obsolete?', *Economic Growth*, National Bureau of Economic Research General Series 96E, New York: Columbia University Press.

Pearce, D. (1993), *Economic Values and the Natural World*, London: Earthscan.

van Dieren, W. (ed.) (1995), *Taking Nature into Account: Toward a Sustainable National Income*, New York: Springer-Verlag.

Weitzman, Martin (1976), 'Welfare significance of national product in a dynamic economy', *Quarterly Journal of Economics*, 90(1), 156–63.

Index